T0366105

Global E-Government:
Theory, Applications
and Benchmarking

Latif Al-Hakim
University of Southern Queensland, Australia

IDEA GROUP PUBLISHING
Hershey • London • Melbourne • Singapore

Acquisition Editor:	Michelle Potter
Senior Managing Editor:	Jennifer Neidig
Managing Editor:	Sara Reed
Development Editor:	Kristin Roth
Copy Editor:	Lanette Ehrhardt
Typesetter:	Jessie Weik
Cover Design:	Lisa Tosheff
Printed at:	Yurchak Printing Inc.

Published in the United States of America by
    Idea Group Publishing (an imprint of Idea Group Inc.)
    701 E. Chocolate Avenue
    Hershey PA 17033
    Tel: 717-533-8845
    Fax: 717-533-8661
    E-mail: cust@idea-group.com
    Web site: http://www.idea-group.com

and in the United Kingdom by
    Idea Group Publishing (an imprint of Idea Group Inc.)
    3 Henrietta Street
    Covent Garden
    London WC2E 8LU
    Tel: 44 20 7240 0856
    Fax: 44 20 7379 3313
    Web site: http://www.eurospan.co.uk

Product or company names used in this book are for identification purposes only. Inclusion of the names of the products or companies does not indicate a claim of ownership by IGI of the trademark or registered trademark.

Library of Congress Cataloging-in-Publication Data

Global e-government : theory, applications and benchmarking / Latif Al-Hakim, editor.
    p. cm.
  Summary: "Interest in e-government, both in industry and in academies, has grown rapidly over the past decade. This book provides helpful examples from practitioners and managers involving real-life applications; academics and researchers contribute theoretical insights"--Provided by publisher.
  ISBN 1-59904-027-1 (hardcover) -- ISBN 1-59904-028-X (softcover) -- ISBN 1-59904-029-8 (ebook)
 1. Internet in public administration. I. Al-Hakim, Latif, 1946-
 JF1525.A8G56 2006
 352.3'802854678--dc22
                        2006019121
British Cataloguing in Publication Data
A Cataloguing in Publication record for this book is available from the British Library.

Challenges of Managing Information Quality in Service Organizations is part of the Idea Group Publishing series named *Information Quality Management Series*.

All work contributed to this book is new, previously-unpublished material. The views expressed in this book are those of the authors, but not necessarily of the publisher.

Global E-Government:
Theory, Applications and Benchmarking

Table of Contents

Section II: E-Government Applications

Foreword

This book addresses three major issues relating to the use of information and communications technologies to transform government and bring government services closer to the public:

- By examining the practices of e-government in both developing and developed countries, this volume details the variations in e-government projects implementation and usage in different contexts and cultures.
- The theoretical frameworks and models resulting from a number of recent e-government researches in four continents present readers with state-of-art e-government concepts.
- The book provides a platform to benchmark the best practices in implementing e-government programs in the 21st century.

By so doing, the editor hopes this book will point readers in the proper direction, to not only understand the exact situation with e-government in the 21st century but also to manage e-government to their competitive advantage. With the phenomenon of e-government in its infancy, the authors have drawn from the experience of e-commerce in the private sector for intellectual contributions, in addition to findings from research work by both new and experienced academics in Europe, U.S., and Asia, to provide a broader framework for discussion.

E-government business model was born out of the private sector success in e-commerce over the last decade. E-government is beginning to deliver improvement in national productivity and professional support systems, assisting various government departments, and agencies, in processing information, solving service delivery problems, developing new services, and creating new knowledge. The need to exploit e-government capabilities to preserve and enhance organisational knowledge is clearly defined by this book.

This book is aimed at students in the final years of undergraduate business degrees, practicing managers taking part-time courses, and students on postgraduate courses doing business management, information systems management, government service administration, business policy, IT governance, strategic management, public office innovation, change management, decision making in government, organisation behavior, among others. The book also encompasses all the practical areas in which an IS strategist functions, and also those of IT services providers and business managers. The following criteria that are being used as the foundation for the best of textbooks on information systems are all explored in this book. They are e-business strategies and management concepts, the business and economics of e-government environment, opportunities and information about e-government, sociological aspects of e-government users behaviour, psychological aspects that influence consumption of e-government applications, strategic tools and tactics, market segmentation, e-government services product life cycles and categories, commercialisation, distribution, promotion, communications, organisation, analysis, application integration, future aspirations of e-government service providers, ethical issues, and much more.

The aim of this book is to disclose the motives and mechanisms of e-government services as it is developing and changing as the 21st century unfolds. E-government strategies cannot be described intelligently without exploring the fundamental features and problems faced by the public. This book appropriately demonstrates how governments from around the globe are approaching such issues with a significant degree of success.

Matthew W. Guah, PhD
London
March 2006

Preface

Abstract

This preface addresses the book Global E-Government: Theory, Applications and Benchmarking. *It points to four major interrelated trends in global markets over the last decade, which have brought the concept of e-government to the forefront of politics and top government officials. These trends are innovation, information society, globalisation, and democracy. The preface discusses the advantages and barriers of implementing e-government programs. The book covers various theoretical and applications aspects of e-government. It comprises 19 chapters organised into three sections: e-government theory and state-of-art, e-government applications, and benchmarking. The book provides insights and support for academic professionals as well as for practitioners concerned with the management of e-government programs.*

Introduction

Electronic government (e-government) is the use of information and communications technologies (ICT) to transform government by making it more accessible, effective, and accountable (InfoDev, 2002). This transformation should, according to the European Commission, be combined with organisational change and new skills to improve public services, increase democratic participation, and enhance public policy making (European Commission, 2005). E-government has the potential to change the relationship between government officials and the public (IPCS, 2003). The impact of e-government will depend not only on technology, but also on organisational resources and strategic vision.

There have been four major interrelated trends in global markets over the last decade, which have brought the concept of e-government to the forefront of politics and top government officials. These trends are as follows:

1. **Innovation:** The current era is associated with widespread and successive waves of technology-driven innovations in information and communication technologies. Technologies such as the Internet, network technologies, electronic commerce, World Wide Web (www), and mobile commerce bring with them ubiquitous connectivity, real-time access, low cost of information exchange, and overwhelming volumes of data and information. Organisations, individuals, and governments are increasingly using these innovative technologies for a large range of purposes.

2. **Information Society:** The world has experienced a transition from an industrial economy to an information economy. Data and information have become a strategic necessity for organisations (Eckerson, 2002). *Information Society* is a term for a society in which the creation, distribution, and manipulation of information has become the most significant economic and cultural activity (Whatis.Com, 2005). Some governments are making efforts to bring about social change in the move to the information economy (MobileMan, 2006). In June 2001, Lena-Hjelm Wallén, then Deputy Prime Minister of Sweden, said "In the modern information society knowledge is the driving force behind the development of whole nations (IDEA, 2005).

3. **Globalisation:** Changing conditions of competition have forced organisations to adopt an increasingly global strategy. Lambert and Copper (2000) point out that one of the most significant paradigm shifts of modern business management has been that individual businesses no longer compete as autonomous entities, but rather as supply chains. This requires business to deal with both local and international entities in their supply chain with minimal regard to the national boundaries. Dornier, Ernst, Fender, and Kpivelis (1998) provide significant statistics about the effect of globalisation on American industry. They indicate that about one fifth of the output of U.S. organisations is produced by foreign companies and one quarter of U.S. imports are between foreign affiliates and American parent companies. Free international trading, networking, and e-commerce facilitate globalisation. Even if companies do not participate in business overseas, the presence of foreign companies in local markets affects their competitive advantage. Governments can respond in various ways: for example, by liberalising trade and telecommunication policies and providing appropriate government regulations and legislation to help manage risk.

4. **Democracy:** A significant facet of modernisation is the recognition of the importance of interaction between governments and their citizens in decision making. Input from citizens in policy formulation and implementation are a crucial requirement for democracy. The European Commission considers wide participation in decision making the life blood of democracy (European Commission, 2005). ICT can reduce and overcome barriers between government and their citizens so long as citizens have sufficient access to ICT services.

The implementation of e-government is not limited to developed countries; rather e-government has now become a priority in an increasing number of developing countries. Evidence shows that "the most innovative uses of Internet in governance are appearing in the developing world" (InvoDev, 2002).

Advantage and Barriers

E-government offers impressive benefits and opportunities at a national level, including more efficient access to government services and officials, reduced government expenditures on administrative functions, increased public access to budget information, and increased access to government documentation and activities (IPCS, 2003). The World Bank emphasises that e-government promotes civic engagement by enabling citizens to interact with government official. In addition, e-government provides development opportunities for rural and communities with low service levels (InfoDev, 2002). From an economics viewpoint, e-government leads to lower information costs as well as lower transaction processing costs, thus saving human resources and providing more effective service levels which are available 24 hours a day, 7 days a week. This provides citizens with greater flexibility in processing transactions at a time of their convenience rather than only during working hours.

At an international level e-government serves as a worldwide showcase and permanent promoter of the country's political, cultural, and business aims (Kostopoulos, 2005). E-government may even considerably promote tourism. For example, the European Commission recommends that private sector and regional authorities of their member states work together to define and launch e-services to promote Europe and to offer user-friendly public information by 2005. The Commission is now developing a European Tourism Portal (eEurope, 2005). However, the effect on global economies is uncertain. The World Bank's Centre for Democracy and Technology considers that the global trend of increasing e-government may very well reduce income disparities between countries while increasing income inequalities within countries (InfoDev, 2002).

E-government requires careful study of the cultural, social, and economics environment. There are several issues requiring consideration:

1. **Process reengineering:** Neither advanced technology nor the automation of government procedures themselves can boost the effectiveness of e-government, enhance civic participation, or alter the attitude of bureaucrats towards citizens (IPCS, 2003). Rather, e-government introduces a new way of communication and relationship between the government-to-citizen (G2C) and government-to-business (G2B) and finally government-to-government (G2G) to manage a country's affairs. This requires redesigning the government processes to fit the new way of communications and interactions, that is, the application of Business Process Reengineering (BPR) to redesign government processes and functions. BPR can be defined as the fundamental rethinking and radical redesign of business processes to achieve dramatic improvements in critical, contemporary measures of performance such as cost, quality, service, and speed (Al-Mashari & Zairi, 1999).

2. **Physical boundaries:** E-government requires governments to reveal information and to form policies and design strategies in cyberspace where national boundaries are irrelevant while global forces and foreign legal systems are significantly relevant. This is completely different from traditional operations of governments.

3. **Improved responsiveness:** E-government is designed to promote better service levels and to create better relationships between citizens and government officials. This requires significant changes in the attitude of officials in considering citizens as

their customers, and also relies on citizens increasing their engagement and input in government processes and policy creation.

4. **Literacy:** It is readily apparent that the concept of e-participation requires not only the ability of a citizen to read and write but also a reasonable ICT knowledge. An e-government program should create opportunities to educate and train citizens in the use of ICT. E-literacy encompasses both ICT literacy and information literacy, and needs to be combined with other knowledge relevant to the particular education context (Institute of Education, 2004).

5. **Infrastructure:** Governments bear the main burden of providing adequate ICT infrastructure to their citizenry, and the success of e-government initiatives depends to a large extent on the quality of Internet access that governments make available to their users, particularly in the case of individual citizens.

6. **Skilled professionals:** Transformation to e-government requires specific human resources capable of operating, maintaining, and continuously and timely updating the government Web sites.

7. **Information sharing:** E-government necessitates timely information sharing electronically between various departments of the government and between government and citizens. Official bureaucratic attitudes, awareness of the importance of information sharing, the availability of suitable infrastructure, security of information, trust, lack of suitable legislation, and so forth, are factors which may affect the timely and transparent information sharing.

8. **Trust:** E-government requires a citizen to reveal personal information and communicate with officials in a very impersonal way compared with phone calls and face to face meetings. A high level of trust forms a critical factor for implementing a successful e-government program.

9. **Security and privacy controls:** As e-government services are introduced, so issues of security, privacy invasion and information integrity arise. Concerns related to online transaction security continue to be barrier for some. Confidence in information integrity and privacy depend on adequate data and network security as well as having controls in place to ensure that information can only be accessed or modified by those authorised to do so (Whatis.Com, 2005).

10. **Legislation and regularity compliance:** Legislation is another key challenge to successful e-government implementation. Without adequate legislation to guard against fraud, sabotage, and crimes associated with invasion of information systems and breaches of security and privacy, e-government cannot be trusted.

The Structure of the Book

Interest in e-government, both in industry and in academies, has grown rapidly over the past decade, and continues to grow. The book is written by experts from academia and industry with a threefold aim. One is to examine the practices of e-government in developing and developed countries; the second is to present recent theoretical research in e-government;

while the third section is to provide a platform to benchmark the best practices in implementing e-government programs. The book will be of interest to both:

- Practitioners and managers involved in e-government functions
- Academics and researchers in the field of information systems, in general, and in e-government, in particular

This book comprises 19 chapters organised into three sections: theory and state-of-art, applications, and benchmarking. The following is a brief description of each section of the book and the chapters included in them.

Section I: E-Government: Theory and State-of-Art

This section features eight chapters which deal with both theoretical aspects and state-of-art e-government concepts. The theoretical chapters are directly based on problems and challenges facing the implementation of e-government initiatives. The case study aspects provided in this section point directly to the applicability criterion.

The first chapter in this section, Chapter I, "Semantic Web Mining for Personalised Public E-Services" by Konstantinos Markellos, Penelope Markellou, Angeliki Panayiotaki, and Athanasios Tsakalidis, explores the way semantic Web mining technologies can be incorporated into the public e-services domain in order to better meet citizens' and authorities' requirements. It describes the various steps of the personalisation process and examines various support techniques in use today. A recommendation scenario for an e-city portal is provided. Finally the chapter illustrates current trends in the field suggesting directions that may lead to new scientific results in the area.

Chapter II is authored by Elena Mugellini, Maria Chiara Pettenati, and Omar Abou Khaled, academics from three European universities. Entitled "Requirements Analysis and General Functional Model of Seamless, Citizen-Oriented Service Delivery," the chapter outlines main requirements for the delivery of seamless services and presents a general functional model (e-government service marketplace) for the delivery of shared services to citizens at the transaction level (i.e., supporting a complete online handling of a service). The main functionalities of the e-government service marketplace are analysed in detail. Advantages, disadvantages, and the impact of this concept on the three fundamental axes — social, economic, and technical — are discussed as well. The chapter ends with some insights on future trends and open issues about seamless services delivery and enabling systems.

Chapter III, entitled "Automatic Governmental Cross-Agency Processes Using Web Service Orchestration: A Gap Analysis" by Jeffrey Gortmaker and Marijn Janssen, investigates the applicability of Web service orchestration for the automation of governmental cross-agency service delivery processes. Based on a case study using a specific computerised system known as BPEL4WS, the chapter shows a gap between the capabilities of Web service orchestration technology and the organisational arrangements needed for automating the processes. The chapter identifies three organisational issues that at least need to be addressed before governments can profit fully from the advantages of Web service orchestration technology:

(1) ensuring correct and in-time execution of business processes; (2) information sharing; and (3) responsibility and accountability.

Chapter IV features a state-of-art on the analysis of the role of government in e-business adoption with empirical evidence from Australia. The chapter, entitled "The Role of Government in E-Business Adoption" by Barbara Roberts and Mark Toleman, shows that government influence is multifaceted. Governments champion e-business adoption for national economic gain; they provide the physical network on which much of the e-business depends; and increasingly provide e-government services to improve regulation and compliance effectiveness. E-government in particular can act as a strong driver of organisational adoption for some types of e-business processes. The chapter discusses the external environmental factors implications and deals with perspectives of diffusion of innovation (DOI) theory and TAM related theories on the role of government in e-business adoption. The chapter hopes that further research by ICT professionals will guide future e-business project directions by improving the understanding of government's role in e-business adoption in practice.

In the Information Age, citizen-government interaction through information and communication technologies (ICTs) such as e-mail, digital policy forums, and real-time digital chat already, have happened. Digital deliberation is one example for such interaction. Chapter V, "Digital Public Sphere: Rhetoric or Reality?" by Seung-Yong Rho, argues that the policies should be made by the will of citizens in democratic governance but current practice of digital deliberation did not support this assertion. Citizens' unawareness of digital deliberation, citizens' lack of active participation, and public officials' less positive perspective on the digital deliberation make current digital deliberation unconstructive. The chapter concludes that citizens' strong will of active digital deliberation is a key to the success of digital deliberation in the democratic governance. In addition, public officials' positive view and strong support on the digital deliberation are important to make digital deliberation effective.

The central government in the United Kingdom is determined to employ new surveillance technology to combat the threat of terrorist activities. Chapter VI, entitled "Electronic Surveillance for the Public Good" by Liz Lee-Kelley and Ailsa Kolsaker, contributes to the current important debate on the relationship between citizens and the government, by discussing not whether electronic surveillance should be used, but rather, when it is acceptable to the populace. The chapter concludes that a reconciliation of state-interest and self-interest is critical for the success of e-governance; as such, electronic surveillance's mission has to be about serving the law-abiding majority and their needs, and its scope and benefits must be clearly understood by the visionaries, implementers, and the citizenry.

Chapter VII, entitled "A Community Facilitation Model for E-Government: A Case Study in Monitoring Water Quality" by Kyle Murray and Cory A. Habulin, introduces a community facilitation model for e-government. The central tenet of this approach is the empowerment of a segment of the population to act, by providing the tools and information necessary to tackle issues that have been difficult to address with traditional approaches to government. Under this model, government provides an initial spark and then plays a supporting role in the growth of the community. By doing so, the costs of the program are minimised while the impact of the program is maximised. The chapter examines the viability of the model by looking at a case study in water quality monitoring. The case illustrates the power of a government facilitated community of action to address an important problem, and it suggests that such a model can be applied globally and may be relevant to government initiatives beyond water monitoring.

Chapter VIII, entitled "Healthcare Network Centric Operations: The Confluence of E-Health and E-Government," is written by a consultant and an academic, Dag von Lubitz and Nilmini Wickramasinghe. The chapter proposes that in order for health care to reap the full benefits of the transition from the traditional pattern of operations to e-health, the implementation of the doctrine of health care network centric operations (HNCO) may become mandatory. Otherwise, millions if not billions of dollars will be spent on a futile chase of the definitions of how and when will the computer, health care provider, and health care administrator interact most efficiently and at the least expense. Drawing upon the strategies and techniques employed by the military to develop network centricity, the chapter outlines the essential components necessary for the establishment of the doctrine for HNCO, and highlights the integral role played by information, computer, and communication technologies (IC^{2}T). The chapter underscores the pivotal role of health care network centric operations (HNCO) for policy makers and governments and points at the important yet rarely acknowledged confluence of e-health and e-government.

Section II. E-Government Applications

This section presents nine chapters dealing with application challenges of e-government initiatives and programs. The first three chapters speak about the e-government applications in three developing countries: Nigeria, Egypt, and Sri Lanka. The next two chapters present e-government applications in two fast transition countries: Korea and China. The last four chapters present the application of e-government programs in developed countries, including the UK, Spain, Norway, and Japan.

Developing countries in Africa are making efforts to harness the new technology. Chapter IX, entitled "Moving Towards E-Government in a Developing Society: Glimpses of the Problems, Progress, and Perspective in Nigeria" by Princely Ifinedo, reviews the problems, progress, and prospects of e-government in Nigeria, a Sub-Saharan African (SSA) country. The chapter highlights the lessons from Nigeria for comparable nations in the SSA region as they prepare for e-government and concludes that governments in the developing countries of SSA can benefit from e-government initiatives, as do their counterparts in advanced nations, when the concept of e-governments is understood, and concerted efforts are committed towards institutionalising it in the region.

Chapter X, entitled "E-Government Emerging Trends: Organizational Changes" by Inas Ezz, demonstrates the importance and challenges considering technology adoption in general and e-government adoption in particular in the context of a key strategic process for the Egyptian government. The chapter deals with the foreign finance process and clarifies that the Egyptian Cabinet Information and Decision Support Center (IDSC) plays a key role in providing support for this process. The chapter comprises qualitative findings resulting from interviews with the CEO of IDSC, Ministry of Economy middle managers and executives, and academics from the Faculty of Economics and Policy in Cairo University and the American University in Cairo. The chapter deals with the organisational challenges affecting the foreign financing process and concludes that inter and intraorganisational integration technologies in the form of G2G or some of the new trends such as g-government can help in resolving some of those organisational challenges.

The level of preparedness to adopt e-government initiatives and activities is referred to as e-readiness. Chapter XI, "Towards Measuring True E-Readiness of a Third-World Country:

A Case Study on Sri Lanka" by Reggie Davidrajuh, talks about measuring true e-readiness of Sri Lanka. This chapter assesses e-readiness of Sri Lanka using a measuring tool that utilises 52 socioeconomic indicators. Based on the assessment, the chapter reveals that the measurement does not indicate true e-readiness of the country, as the tool does not model or incorporate parameters for measuring the domestic digital divide that exists between communities or groups within the country. The chapter proposes a method for incorporating the domestic digital divide measures in e-readiness calculations.

Chapter XII, "An Evaluation of Digital Deliberative Democracy in Local Government" by Seung-Yong Rho, evaluates the current status of digital deliberation in the local governments of Seoul Metropolitan area in Korea. The chapter reviews literature on digital democracy and develops a Web site evaluation framework of digital deliberative democracy of four stages: information acquisition, communication and consultation, citizen participation, and public deliberation. The chapter uses the framework to evaluate the current practices in digital deliberative democracy of 25 administrative districts in the city of Seoul. The results show that a few administrative districts have performed good practices in digital deliberative democracy. Though it could be said that many administrative districts have performed good practices of information acquisition (1st stage of digital deliberative democracy), communication and consultation (2nd stage), and citizen participation (3rd stage), public deliberation (4th stage) is not fully performed in the Web sites of the administrative districts. Based on the results, this research explores some policy recommendations to improve digital deliberative democracy.

Chapter XIII, entitled "The Development of Urban E-Government in China" by Zi Lu, Jing Zhang, Bing Han, Zhuopeng Deng, and Jie Lu, assesses and recognises the development of urban e-government in China from two main aspects: functionality and complexity. Nine Web sites of urban governments in China at three levels were selected for assessment of functionality. Data from these Web sites that was needed for the study was tracked and re-corded continuously for six weeks. The influence of e-government on urban modality and evolution are explored for complexity. The research shows that e-government has a leading role in the gathering and decentralisation of urban space, the organisation of material (people) flows, and the informal exchange in internal cities. The chapter states that the development of urban e-government in China is still at an early stage. It concludes that e-government enhances the control of urban material (people) flow.

Electronic delivery of government services (i.e., the National Health Service, Defence and Criminal Justice systems) becomes more commonplace in developing countries. Chapter XIV, entitled "Web Services in Government Policy: Case Study from UK National Health Service" by Mathew Guah, reports on a three years of research, which looks at the application of Web services into United Kingdom health care as a fulfillment of numerous semi and unsuccessful IT projects, that — fell short of delivering any tangible benefits. The chapter looks at the National Health Service's current IS strategy — fully dependent on Web services application — with the criteria of successful implementation, return on investment, increased productivity, innovation, and user benefits.

Chapter XV, "Empirical Study of the Municipalities' Motivations for Adopting Online Presence" by Susana de Juana-Espinosa, reveals the motivations for creating a Web page in local administrations, and thus determines the nature of those Web sites. A personal survey was addressed to the CIOs (chief information officers) of 65 city councils out of the 69 with Web sites in the province of Alicante (Spain), regarding their perceptions about the purpose of their Web pages. The results show that, although most councils confer a strategic orientation to their Web pages, communication goals are more popular than internal efficiency concerns. Consequently, a general lack of commitment is found with local e-government strategies. The chapter concludes that understanding the implications of this duality may help other public organisations develop their modernisation strategies.

User involvement in e-government is the subject of Chapter XVI. Entitled "User Involvement in E-Government Development Projects" by Asbjørn Følstad, John Krogstie, Lars Risan, and Ingunn Moser, the chapter introduces two Norwegian case studies that exemplify user involvement practices. User involvement methods and practices are in particular discussed with regard to the challenges of the wide range of users and stakeholders, legal limitations, and evolving goal hierarchies of e-government projects. The chapter identifies future trends and research opportunities within the field of user involvement in e-government development.

Chapter XVII, entitled "Local E-Governments in Japan: IT Utilization Status and Directions" by Sadaya Kubo and Tatsumi Shimada, explains the actual state of digital readiness of the local governments in Japan, and describes the stages of achievement in digitalisation and the direction that should be taken. The items being analysed are the digitalisation of governmental administration, services to residents, and information security. In order to clarify the direction of digitalisation, the chapter proposes stages of progress of the digitalisation of the local governments.

Section III. E-Government: Benchmarking

This section presents two chapters that deal with issues related to benchmarking: the performance of e-government implementation and applicability of a general framework for both developed and developing countries.

The first chapter of this section, Chapter XVIII, "E-Government, Democratic Governance, and Integrative Prospects for Developing Countries: The Case for a Globally Federated Architecture" by Jeffrey Roy, provides a conceptual framework for understanding e-government and considers the relevance and applicability of the framework for both developed and developing nations. The chapter explores the interface between domestic and transnational governance reforms in an increasingly digital era and stresses that the world in the twenty-first century needs a globally federated governance architecture, the design of which must include social, economic, political, and technological considerations. This strengthened focus on transnational governance systems must also be joined by the recognition of the dysfunctional nature of the present system of bilateral international assistance programs among countries. With improved governance conditions of transparency and trust transnationally — facilitated in part by a much more politically creative and aggressive use of new technologies — the resources allocated by each country across its various recipients would serve both developing nations and the world as a whole if they were pooled and coordinated through new transnational mechanisms.

Chapter XIX, entitled "E-Government Concepts, Measures, and Best Practices" by Shin Young-Jin and Kim Seang-Tae, explains how international agencies measure e-government according to standards and performance. The chapter explores e-government projects that have been accepted and performed as national policies in several developing and developed countries. It compares e-government readiness of 15 countries over the years 2002-2005. The chapter shows that the U.S. always has the highest readiness index. Denmark which ranked 9 in 2002 becomes the second ranked country in 2004 and 2005. The chapter also benchmarks the performance of top cities in digital governance in terms of privacy, usability, contents, service, and participation. The benchmark shows that Seoul ranks as the top city in digital performance followed by Hong Kong, with Singapore coming in third. New York is the fourth ranked city in digital performance despite the fact that the U.S. ranks first in e-government readiness.

References

Al-Mashari, M., & Zairi, M. (1999). BPR implementation process: An analysis of key success and failure factors. *Business Process Management Journal, 5*(1), 87-112.

Dornier, P., Ernst, R., Fender, & Kpivelis, P. (1998). *Global operations and logistics: Text and cases*. New York: John Wiley & Sons.

Eckerson, W. W. (2002). *Data quality and bottom line: Achieving business success through high quality data* (TDWI Report Series). Seattle: The Data Warehousing Institute.

eEurope. (2005). *E-government*. Retrieved May 13, 2006, from http://europa.eu.int/information_society/eeurope/2005/all_about/egovernment/index_en.htm

European Commission. (2005). *Transforming government*. Retrieved May 13, 2006, from http://europa.eu.int/information_society/doc/factsheets/010-egovernment.pdf

IDEA. (2005). *International IDEA democracy forum 2001: Democracy and the information revolution*. International Institute for Democracy and Electoral Assistance. Retrieved May 13, 2006, from http://www.idea.int/democracy/forum2001.cfm

InfoDev. (2002). *The e-government handbook for developing countries*. The Center for Democracy & Technology, Washington: The World Bank. Retrieved May 13, 2006, from http://www.cdt.org/egov/handbook/2002-11-14egovhandbook.pdf

Institue of Education. (2004). *Dictionary of confusing terms*. Retrieved May 13, 2006, from http://k1.ioe.ac.uk/schools/mst/LTU/staffsupport.definitions.htm

IPCS. (2003, June). *IPCS newsletter,* 191. Retrieved May 13, from http://www.icps.com.ua/doc/lg_es_eng_200301.pdf

Kostopoulos, G. K. (2003, July 4-6). E-government: The Dubai experience. In *Proceedings of the 2004 International Business Information Management (IBIM) Conference*, Amman, Jordan (pp. 13-15).

Lambert, D. M., & Cooper, M. C. (2000). Issues in supply chain management. *Industrial Marketing Management, 29*, 65-83.

MobileMan. (2006). *Information society*. Retrieved May 13, 2006, from http://mobileman.projects.supsi.ch/glossary.html

Whatis.Com. (2005). *Information society*. Retrieved May 13, 2006, from http://whatis.techtarget.com/definition/0,,sid9_gci213588,00.html

Acknowledgments

The editor is grateful to all those who have assisted him with the completion of this work. In particular, the editor would like to acknowledge his deepest appreciation to many reviewers for their time and effort. Amendments suggested by them were incorporated into the manuscripts during the development process and significantly enhanced the quality of the work.

Much credit should go to the editorial and production team at Idea Group Inc. The editor wants to thank Dr. Mehdi Khosrow-Pour, the executive director of Idea Group Inc., and Jan Travers, managing director, who provided needed support and coordination. Appreciation also goes to Kristin Roth, Michelle Potter, and Sharon Berger who gave their time willingly to describe many issues related to the preparation of this work and share their experiences with me. Additional acknowledgements are owed to Professor Chen Jin, of Zhejiang University (China), who provided assistance and help that allowed the editor to complete this project during his sabbatical leave at the University. A special thanks to the staff of the University of Southern Queensland for all of their assistance in seeing this work completed.

List of Reviewers

Susana de Juana-Espinosa	University of Alicante, Spain
Inas E. Ezz	Sadat Academy for Management Sciences , Egypt
Jeffrey Gortmaker	Delft University of Technology, The Netherlands
Matthew W. Guah	University of Warwick, UK
Princely Ifinedo	University of Jyväskylä, Finland
Marijn Janssen	Delft University of Technology, Netherlands
John Krogstie	SINTEF Research Institute, Norway
Zi Lu	Hebei Teacher's University, China
Jie Lu	University of Technology, Sydney (UTS), Australia
Heather Maguire	University of Southern Queensland, Australia
Konstantinos Markellos	University of Patras, Greece

Penelope Markellou	University of Patras, Greece
Elena Mugellini	University of Applied Sciences of Western Switzerland, Switzerland
Seung-Yong Rho	Seoul Women's University, Seoul, Korea
Barbara Roberts	University of Southern Queensland, Australia
Jeffrey Roy	Dalhousie University, Canada
Tatsumi Shimada	Setsunan University, Japan
Mark Tolman	University of Southern Queensland, Australia
Athanasios Tsakalidis	University of Patras, Greece
Shin Young-Jin	Ministry of Government Administration and Home Affairs, Korea
Nilmini Wickramasinghe	Illinois Institute of Technology, USA

Section I:
E-Government Theory
and State-of-Art

Chapter I

Semantic Web Mining for Personalized Public E-Services

Konstantinos Markellos, University of Patras, Greece, &
Research Academic Computer Technology Institute, Greece

Penelope Markellou, University of Patras, Greece, &
Research Academic Computer Technology Institute, Greece

Angeliki Panayiotaki, University of Patras, Greece

Athanasios Tsakalidis, University of Patras, Greece, &
Research Academic Computer Technology Institute, Greece

Abstract

As citizens are confronted with increasing volumes of information, boundless choices, and endless opportunities in the Web environment, the need for personalised public e-services is more compulsory than ever. This chapter explores the way Semantic Web mining technologies can be incorporated into public e-services domain in order to better meet citizens and authorities requirements. It describes the various steps of the personalisation process and examines techniques in use today to support it. In sequence, it introduces a recommendation scenario for an e-city portal. Finally, the chapter illustrates current trends in the field suggesting directions that may lead to new scientific results in the area.

Introduction

Over the last decade, we have witnessed the rapid evolution of the Web. This development allowed millions of people all over the world to access, share, interchange, and publish information. Moreover, public and private sector organisations are implementing highly functional and interactive Web-based applications that are accessible to any user with a computer, a Web browser, and a connection to the Internet. These potentials impact all dimensions of our daily life. Thousands of new Web sites are launched everyday providing e-services, accessible through Internet, suspending bureaucracy procedures, demanding personal contact of the users and loads of paper-based forms to be filled in. This "e-" prefix has been applied to a vast number of domains and applications such as e-commerce, e-business, e-learning, e-health, e-banking, e-marketing, and so forth, flavouring the respective domains with electronic services (e-services). This chapter focuses on e-government initiative, which relies on Web technologies in order to make the interactions between *government and citizens (G2C)* and also between *government and businesses (G2B)* easier, faster, and more efficient. It aims also at improving interdepartmental interactions on various levels of government for example *government-to-employees (G2E)* and *government-to-government (G2G)*, as well as the elimination of redundant services.

E-government is not only the vehicle of a public authority Web presence. Its aim is to transform the nature of a governmental authority into an interactive and integrated institution, thus providing added value to citizens. Moreover, a series of strategic, administrative, and operational benefits can be accomplished by this transition from traditional profile to electronic one including: best coverage of citizens' needs and consequently increase of their satisfaction, reduction of costs and response time, support of new and improved cooperations, automation of processes, upgrade of government's profile and flavour to a friendlier one for the citizens, access to more and reliable information, promotion of information and communication technologies (ICT) usage by both individuals and businesses, and so forth.

However, the aforementioned Web growth has created a crucial problem: information overload. As the Web is a large collection of semistructured and unstructured information sources, Web users often suffer from this information overload. To alleviate this problem, personalisation becomes a popular remedy to customise the Web environment for users. *Web personalisation* can be described, as any action that makes the Web experience of users personalised to their needs and wishes. Principal elements of Web personalisation include modelling of Web objects (pages) and subjects (users), categorisation and preprocessing of objects and subjects, matching between and across objects or subjects, and determination of the set of actions to be recommended for personalisation.

There is an essential difference between layout customisation and personalisation. In customisation, the Web site can be adjusted to each user's preferences regarding its structure and presentation. Every time a registered user logs in, the user's customised home page is loaded. This process is performed either manually or semiautomatically. In personalisation systems, modifications concerning the content or even the structure of a Web site are performed dynamically.

The most popular form of personalisation is *recommendations systems (RSs)* (Adomavicius & Tuzhilin, 2005). RSs have emerged in the middle of 1990s and from novelties used by a few Web sites have changed to significant tools incorporated to many Web-based applications (e.g., e-commerce, e-learning, etc.). Specifically, these systems take advantage of users' and communities' opinions in order to support individuals to identify the information or services most likely to be interesting to them or relevant to their needs and preferences. The recommendations may have various forms:

- Personalised offers, prices, products, or services
- Inserting or removing paragraphs, sections, or units
- Sorting, hiding, adding, removing, or highlighting links
- Explanations or detailed information, and so forth

At the same time, Web browsers provide easy access to myriad sources of text and multimedia data. Search engines index more than a billion pages and finding the desired information is not an easy task. This profusion of resources has prompted the need for developing automatic mining techniques on the Web, thereby giving rise to the term *Web mining* (Pal, Talwar, & Mitra, 2002). Web mining is the application of data mining techniques on the Web in order to discover useful patterns and can be divided into three basic categories: *Web content mining*, *Web structure mining*, and *Web usage mining* (Kosala & Blockeel, 2000). The first category includes techniques for assisting users in locating Web documents (i.e., pages) that meet certain criteria, while the second relates to discovering information based on the Web site structure data. The last category focuses on analysing Web access logs and other sources of information regarding user interactions within the Web site in order to capture, understand, and model their behavioural patterns and profiles and thereby improve their experience with the Web site.

The close relation between Web mining and Web personalisation has motivated much research work in the area. Web mining is a complete process and consists of specific primary data mining tasks, namely data collection, data reprocessing, pattern discovery, and knowledge postprocessing. The deployment of Web mining in the e-government domain relates to the analysis of citizen behaviour and the production of adequate adaptations. For example, given a specific citizen, the presentation of required information from an e-government portal can be tailored to meet individual needs and preferences by providing personal recommendations on topics relative to those already visited. This process is typically based on a solid user model, which holds up-to-date information on dynamically changing citizen behaviour. This enables on-the-fly portal content assembly, addressing exactly what the citizen needs to know without wasting time on topics the user is already proficient or not interested in.

Recently, *Semantic Web* is coming to add a layer of intelligence in Web-based applications. According to (Berners-Lee, Hendler, & Lassila, 2001), "the Semantic Web is an extension of the current Web in which information is given well-defined meaning, better enabling computers and people to work in cooperation." While a more formal definition by the W3C (http://www.w3.org/2001/sw) refers to "the Semantic Web [as] the representation of data on the World Wide Web. It is a collaborative effort led by W3C with participation from a large number of researchers and industrial partners. It is based on the resource description framework (RDF), which integrates a variety of applications using eXtensible Markup Language

(XML) for syntax and uniform resource identifiers (URIs) for naming." The capacity of the Semantic Web to add meaning to information, stored in such a way that it can be searched and processed provides greatly expanded opportunities for Web-based applications.

The combination of Web mining and Semantic Web has created a new and fast-emerging research area: *Semantic Web mining*. The idea behind the use of the Semantic Web to generate personalised Web experiences is to improve Web mining by exploiting the new semantic structures. With the integration of Semantic Web mining technologies, the provided Web applications will become smarter and more comprehensive (Markellou, Rigou, Sirmakessis, & Tsakalidis, 2004).

In this framework, *ontologies* that comprise the backbone of the Semantic Web appear as a promising technology for integrating with e-government applications, since they offer a way to cope with heterogeneous representations of Web resources. The reason that ontologies are becoming so popular is due to what they promise: "a shared and common understanding of a domain that can be communicated between people and application systems" (Davies, Fensel, & Van Harmelen, 2003, pp. 4-5).

In this framework, this chapter aims to investigate how Semantic Web mining technologies can be incorporated into e-government domain in order to create intelligent and personalised applications and produce useful recommendations for e-citizens through an e-city portal model. We describe the tasks that comprise the personalisation process, starting from the ontological schema, users' identification, modelling, classification, and analysis of their navigational behaviour, to the algorithm used for recommendations' production. Finally, we illustrate the challenges of the area and suggest directions that may trigger new scientific research.

Background

Web mining is the application of data mining techniques on the Web in order to discover useful patterns. Therefore, Web mining procedure can be viewed as consisted of four tasks (Etzioni, 1996):

- **Information retrieval (IR) (resource discovery):** it deals with automatic retrieval of all relevant documents, while at the same time ensuring that the nonrelevant ones are fetched as few as possible. The IR process mainly includes document representation, indexing, and searching for documents. The process of retrieving the data, either online or off-line, from the text sources available on the Web such as electronic newsletters, newsgroups, text contents of HTML documents obtained by removing HTML tags, and also the manual selection of Web resources. Here are also included text resources that originally were not accessible from the Web but are accessible now, such as online texts made for search purposes only, text databases, and so forth.

- **Information extraction (IE) (selection and preprocessing):** once the documents have been retrieved in the IR process, the challenge is to automatically extract knowledge and other required information without human interaction. IE is the task of identifying specific fragments of a single document that constitute its core semantic content and transform them into useful information. These transformations could be either a kind of preprocessing such as removing stop words, stemming, and so forth, or a preprocessing aimed at obtaining the desired representation such as finding phrases in the training corpus, transforming the presentation to relational or first-order logic form, and so forth.

- **Generalisation (pattern recognition and machine learning):** it discovers general patterns at individual Web sites or across multiple sites. Machine learning or data mining techniques are used for the generalisation. Most of the machine-learning systems, deployed on the Web, learn more about the user's interest than the Web itself.

- **Analysis (validation and interpretation):** it is a data driven problem, which presumes that sufficient data are available so potentially useful information can be extracted and analysed. Humans also play an important role in the information or knowledge discovery process on the Web, since the latter is an interactive medium. This is especially important for validation and interpretation but under Etzioni's view (1996) of Web mining, "manual" (interactive, query triggered) knowledge discovery is excluded and thus the focus is placed on automatic data-triggered knowledge discovery.

Web mining refers to the overall process of discovering potentially useful and previously unknown information or knowledge from Web data. In this sense, Web mining implicitly covers the standard process of *knowledge discovery in databases (KDD)* and can be viewed as an extension of KDD that is applied to data on the Web (Markellos, Markellou, Rigou, & Sirmakessis, 2004a).

Web mining can be categorised into three areas of interest based on which part of the Web is mined (Borges & Levene, 1999; Kosala & Blockeel, 2000; Madria, Bhowmick, Ng, & Lim, 1999), where the previously mentioned four steps can be applied:

- **Web content mining:** focuses on the discovery/retrieval of useful information from Web contents/data/documents. Web content data consist of unstructured data (free texts), semi-structured data (HTML documents), and more structured data (data in tables, database generated HTML pages).

- **Web structure mining:** focuses on the structure of the hyperlinks within the Web as a whole (interdocument) with the purpose of discovering its underlying link structure. Web structure data consist of the Web site structure itself.

- **Web usage mining:** mines the secondary data derived from Web surfers' sessions or behaviours and focuses on techniques that could predict user behaviour while the user interacts with the Web (Cooley, 2000). Web usage data can be server access logs, proxy server logs, browser logs, user profiles, registration data, user sessions or transactions, cookies, user queries, bookmark data, mouse clicks, and scrolls and any other data as the result of interactions.

More recently, Web usage mining (Srivastava, Cooley, Deshpande, & Tan, 2000) has been proposed as an underlying approach for Web personalisation (Mobasher, Cooley, & Srivastava,

Figure 1. Application of Web mining techniques in e-government

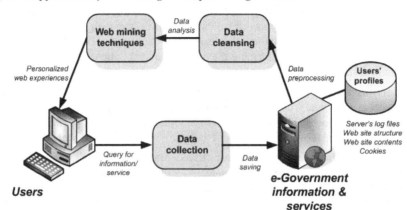

2000). The goal of Web usage mining is to capture and model the behavioural patterns and profiles of users interacting with a Web site. The discovered patterns are usually represented as collections of pages or items frequently accessed by groups of users with common needs or interests. Such patterns can be used to better understand behavioural characteristics of visitors or user segments, improve the organisation and structure of the site, and create a personalised experience for visitors by providing dynamic recommendations. In particular, Web usage mining techniques, such as clustering, association rule mining, and navigational pattern mining that rely on online pattern discovery from user transactions can be used to improve the scalability of collaborative filtering (CF) when dealing with click-stream and e-government data (Figure 1). E-government application constructs users' profiles integrating various sources of data, preprocesses the data and applies Web mining techniques to provide the users with personalised Web experiences.

There are many kinds of data involved in the Web usage mining process (Cooley, 2000):

- **Content:** the real data in the Web pages. This usually consists of, but not limited to, texts and graphics.
- **Structure:** data that describe the organisation of the content.
- **Usage:** data that describe the pattern of usage of Web pages, such as IP addresses, page references, and the date and time of accesses. Typically, the usage data comes from an Extended Common Log Format (ECLF) Server log.
- **User profile:** data that provides demographic information about users of the Web site. This includes registration data and customer profile information.

The deployment of Web mining in the e-government domain relates to the analysis of citizen behaviour and the production of adequate adaptations. For example, given a specific citizen, the presentation of required information from an e-government portal can be tailored to meet individual needs and preferences by providing personal recommendations on topics relative to those already visited. This process is typically based on a solid user model, which holds up-to-date information on dynamically changing citizen behaviour. This enables on-the-fly portal content assembly, addressing exactly what the citizen needs to know without wasting time on topics the user is already proficient or not interested in.

For the implementation and successful operation of e-government, the proper design, which will be the basis in order to receive a series of strategic, administrative, and operational benefits, is necessary. The application of e-government in the public domain can be gradually performed in 14 levels, easing the adjustment of the traditional governmental model to the electronic one. Depending on the maturity and the resources of each governmental authority, the authority is level-categorised and the bottom levels may gradually be applied. This allows the unobstructed flow of information from/to the public sector and gives the possibility not only to the citizens but also to the enterprises (private sector) to acquire better access in the services the state provides (Markellou, Panayiotaki, & Tsakalidis, 2003). An important level is the upgrade of portal with applications adjusted to every user, where Web mining techniques may be applied to improve access to information through the e-services provided (Markellou, Rigou, & Sirmakessis, 2005a, 2005b).

In order to personalise an e-government site, the system should be able to distinguish between different users or groups of users. This process is called *user profiling* and its objective is the creation of an information base that contains the preferences, characteristics, and activities of the users. In the Web domain, user profiling has been developed significantly since Internet technologies provide easier means of collecting information about the users of a Web site, which in the case of e-government sites are citizens that must be satisfied by the services provided. A user profile can be either static, when the information it contains is never or rarely altered (e.g., demographic information), or dynamic when the user profile's data change frequently. Such information is obtained either explicitly, using online registration forms and questionnaires resulting in static user profiles, or implicitly, by recording the navigational behaviour or the preferences of each user, resulting in dynamic user profiles (Eirinaki, & Vazirgiannis, 2003).

Another technique that can be used is the one of *clustering*. Page clustering identifies groups of pages that seem to be conceptually related according to the users' perception. User clustering results in groups of users that seem to behave similarly when navigating through a Web site. Such knowledge can be used in e-government in order to perform public services segmentation.

The classification technique can be applied after clustering in order to assign a new user to the defined groups. It uses features with high discriminative ability for defining the various profiles, for example, the profile of an active citizen may include the following values: Sex = male, $34 < = Age < = 40$, Job = worker, Education = basic, MaritalStatus = marital, NumberOfChildren = 4, and so forth. This knowledge can be used in applying personalisation to e-government services and better supporting the needs of the users providing the right information, to the right people, at the right time.

For discovering relations between different types of available information in an e-government environment, *association rules* can be applied. This technique may identify correlations between pages/users/services or other types of items, not directly connected and reveal previously unknown associations between groups of such items with specific similarities. The form of an association rule can be "65% of citizens that their MaritalStatus = marital search e-government portal for information about LifeEpisodes = having a baby" or "40% of the citizens who accessed help desk asked about online filling-in of tax returns and VAT." For example, the last rule may indicate that this information is not easily accessible or explanatory enough and requires redesign tasks from the portal technical group.

An extension of the previous technique comprises the *sequential pattern discovery* that can be used for revealing patterns of co-occurrence, which incorporates the notion of time. For example a pattern may be a Web page or a set of pages accessed immediately after another set of pages "55% of new businesses who apply for a certain certificate will use the certificate within 15 days" or "Given the transactions of a citizens who has not apply for any information/services during the last 3 months, find all citizens with a similar behavior."

Finally, as search engines often are met at e-government, personalised Web search systems may be used in order to enhance their functionality. In order to incorporate user preferences into search engines, three major approaches are proposed (Shahabi & Chen, 2003):

- **Personalised page importance:** modern search engines employ the importance scores of pages for ranking the search results, as well as traditional text matching techniques.
- **Query refinement:** a process composed of three steps: obtaining user profiles from user, query modification, and refinement.
- **Personalised metasearch systems:** metasearch systems could improve the retrieval rate by merging various ranked results from multiple search engines into one final ranked list.

E-City Model for Personalised Public E-Services

The scope of the proposed model is to provide useful insight into a local community and support its attempt to create the proper digital environment where the citizens will meet Information Society targets. The model focuses especially on the provision of personalised public e-services and incorporates techniques from Web usage mining and semantics. The first has been used effectively for producing personalisation and alleviates the problems and deficiencies associated with other traditional approaches such as collaborative and content-based filtering. However, it does not take into consideration the domain's semantic knowledge. Without this knowledge, the output of personalisation process ignores the underlying attributes and their properties. For these reasons the proposed model integrates these techniques, applies them into multiple sources of information and succeeds to provide users with better tailored experiences. In the next sections, we discuss the issues and the requirements of this integration.

E-City Portal's Model

The model that our approach is based on concerns an e-city portal (Markellou et al., 2003). This portal provides access to public information, services, and other resources. The following information/services are available for all citizens:

- Online city guide
- Guidelines for the citizens to perform certain governmental transactions
- Opportunities for financing for example call for proposals, contests, and so forth
- Laws, presidential enactments
- Announcements, news, press releases
- Links to other e-governmental portals/sites and sources of interesting information
- Information searching, help desk, FAQ, portal's map, and so forth

In order to access more advanced information/services and to assure portal's reliable and efficient operation, it is necessary to define the security policy (authentication, authorisation). According to this policy, the citizen uses a pair of login/password when entering the site in order to be recognised by the system until the citizen logs out. These services contain:

- Information publication and interconnection of various Internet sites
- Information search, retrieval, and data submission for further processing
- Send/receive e-mail to/from public authority, containing personal information
- Online filling-in of applications' forms, life episodes (having a baby, change of address, emigration, driving license acquisition), financial transactions, emergencies' confrontation, and so forth
- E-voting, e-learning, e-commerce, e-auctions, online libraries, and so forth
- Discussion forum with other citizens, complaints' submission

Additional functional characteristics relate to: multilingual support, statistical data, surveys, access for people with special needs, user's support, multiple communication channels (Web, e-mail, SMS, fax, etc.), portal's administration and content management tools, personalisation, availability (24/7), layered functionality, open-structure, and so forth (Tsoukalas & Anthopoulos, 2004).

The users of the portal are citizens and businesses and they can be classified according to their profiles (demographics, interests, field of experience, etc.) in order to match the e-city domain. The aim of the portal is to permit several users' classes to access information/services according to the privileges granted to them. So, each user class may address a subset of the domain or an intersection of more domains. User profiling is extremely useful to G2C and G2B services provided through public authorities with multiple fields of interest. In our example, the specific site adopts user profiling aspect to eliminate the provided information/

services only to the interesting, to the user, set of domains. Through this portal, the city's image provided to the public seems integrated and not a collection of various partial pieces. The users can be served by visiting a one-stop shop, while the integration of new portals (e.g., resources for tourists, immigrants, foreign students, etc.) is an easy task.

Ontological Schema

The efficient content management of the proposed e-city portal is a difficult and time-consuming task. The data originate from various sources and have heterogeneous formats (e.g., syntax, semantics, etc.). In order to solve this problem and support the personalisation process, the proposed model incorporates an ontological schema. This schema formulates a representation of the domain by capturing and specifying all of its available concepts, the relations between them, a hierarchy of terminology, other properties, regulations, conditions, axioms, and so forth. It can be depicted as a tree, where the root represents the most general class, the internal nodes all intermediate classes, and the leaves the specific items. Its role is important, especially in the knowledge discovery process, since it represents the domain's dependent knowledge and may affect the results.

The ontology allows the structured storage of the information, the semantic annotation, the performance of semantic querying and ontology-based browsing, and the personalised output presentation. It facilitates the users of the site to locate the desired information in a fast and easy way. Its "building" was a complex and time-consuming task and was based on our intuition in order to depict all domain notions, organise their taxonomic hierarchies, and represent their relationships. The development was akin to the definition of a set of data and their structure. In this way, the ontology can be considered as a knowledge base that is used further for extracting useful knowledge. Specifically, its role is to be used as an input for the mining phase in order to extract, combine, and transform the existing implicit and explicit knowledge (user class, history profile, portal content, and structure) into new forms. The output of this task is a list of possible recommendations. In particular, the ontology creates connections between entities according to different attributes that characterise them. Now using the specific user's history file, the user's preferences can be figured out.

The advantages of the semantic knowledge are significant since it facilitates the interpretation, analysis, and reasoning of the discovered usage patterns. Moreover, it enhances the recommendation phase since the user data are more systematically represented (Dai & Mobasher, 2005). Finally, it offers an accurate representation of the portal structure, which contributes in many tasks of the mining process; for example, it helps the cleaning task of the log files and the mapping of the usage data.

User's Identification and Modelling

The identification of the users who are accessing the portal and the gathering of all necessary information about them that will be further processed to analyse their behaviour comprise critical issues of our approach. The system should distinguish the first-time visitors from the returning ones and treat them differently. However, this task is not considered very easy or trivial, since privacy and anonymity risks in the online world limit the data availability (quantity and quality). In order to overcome this problem the site uses explicit user input through login/password procedures and registration forms that provide important demographic information and explicit user preferences.

The portal develops and maintains user models for capturing all appropriate information about users. These are internal representations that consist of the properties (attributes) of the users (identities), their interests, preferences, history, behaviour, and so forth. These models are based on the aforementioned registration and login tasks and also are dynamically inferred by tracking the users' interactions and navigations with the portal. The collection of user data is a continuous process and includes data from the server side (server logs, cookies, explicit input, etc.), from the client side (agents if the user allows their operation), and intermediary data (proxy servers, packet sniffers, etc.) (Pierrakos, Paliouras, Papatheodorou & Spyropoulos, 2003).

When the data are collected, preprocessing activities are performed in order to remove and filter redundant and irrelevant data, predict and complete missing values, transform and encode the data and resolve any inconsistencies. These tasks are of high importance since inaccurate data can mislead the pattern discovery process.

User's Classification

Then a classification step is performed. Its main objective is to assign users to a set of predefined classes based on specific attributes for example user ID, age, sex, nationality, occupation, and so forth. These classes represent different user models and features with high discriminative ability and are selected for their construction. This information can give useful insight and understanding of the existing data, as well as predict how new snapshots will behave. Classification requires a training dataset with preassigned class labels, since it is categorised as a supervised machine learning technique. Then the classifier (by observing the class assignment in the training set) learns to assign new data items in one of the classes. It is often the case that clustering is applied before classification to determine the set of classes.

We have based our categorisation model on a naïve Bayesian classifier, where each user X consists of a set of attributes $x_1, x_2, \ldots x_n$. We have defined m classes $C_1, C_2, \ldots C_m$. Given an unknown user X for which we do not know its class, the classifier predicts that X belongs to the class with the higher probability. The classifier assign X in class C_i if $P(C_i|X) > P(C_j|X)$ for $1 \leq j \leq m, j \neq i$. According to Bayesian theorem $P(C_i|X) = P(X|C_i)*P(C_i)/P(X)$. $P(X)$ is constant for all snapshots, so we need to maximise the expression $P(X|C_i)*P(C_i)$. For categorising X, we compute the probability $P(X|C_i)*P(C_i)$ for each class C_i. X will be assigned in class C_i if $P(X|C_i)*P(C_i) > P(X|C_j)*P(C_j)$ for $1 \leq j \leq m, j \neq i$. This means that X is assigned in the class with the maximum probability.

This classification model may be revised as time passes and updated based on collected users' transactions data. Users' assignment to classes might also be used for provoking interactions among users and enhancing collaboration and communication, as well as for allowing the portal to perceive useful insight of the "virtual communities."

Users' Navigational Behaviour Analysis

As we have already mentioned, the model also tracks all user interactions and activities in the portal as successive page requests. These requests are recorded in the server logs. Log files are then cleaned from all redundant information (such as secondary, automatically generated requests for page images, etc.). Combining the remaining requests with information about the way the portal's content is structured, the system distills user accesses to Web pages. The set of pages that have been accessed by a certain user during all past visits to the portal are stored in the user model. Then association rules' mining discovers relations between database items.

The aim is to find associations and correlations between different types of information without obvious semantic dependence. Moreover, correlations between pages not directly connected and previously unknown associations between groups of users with specific interests may be revealed.

An association rule example is {$page_i$, $page_j$} -> {$page_x$}, with support = 0.02 and confidence = 0.68. This rule conveys the relationship that users who accessed $page_i$ and $page_j$ also tend (with a confidence of 68%) to be interested in $page_x$. Support represents the fact that the set {$page_i$, $page_j$, $page_x$} is observed in 2% of the sets of movies accessed.

The discovered association rules may use as input, either the sets of pages accessed by all users or just the ones accessed by users that belong to the same class as the current one. Another option is to use both approaches and suggest the union of discovered topics. This scenario is very useful when association rules' mining inside classes fails to produce reliable recommendations due to lack of adequate input.

Recommendations' Production

The model (Figure 2) uses an algorithm for discovering interesting and unknown patterns from the preprocessed data (Markellou, Mousourouli, Sirmakessis, & Tsakalidis, 2005). Specifically, it filters the available pages that will be recommended to the user based on the class the user belongs to, the user's click-streams, the user's transaction history and ratings, and the portal's ontology metadata. The idea is to discard pages for which the predicted rate is below a predefined limit (α: threshold) and to recommend those with the higher predicted rate.

The procedure is the following:

- Find the status of the user (first-time visitor, returning visitor).

- If the user is first-time visitor, use the registration data in order to assign the user into a specific class. Then according to the user's class, find the most similar users to the current one. The similarity measure s used for this purpose computes the Euclidean distance between the vectors of users' models. In this way a first set of recommendations is produced.

Figure 2. Proposed recommendation model based on Web usage and ontological data

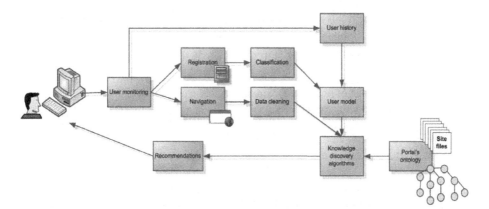

- If the user is returning visitor, use the user's history file and the pages that the user has already seen. Then according to the history file, find the most similar users to the current one analysing past transactions. The similarity measure s is also used for identifying the closest users. At the same time, the model uses the underneath ontological schema to discover other associations between the pages that the user has already seen. Consequently, a new list of recommendations is derived from the ontology and the user's history file.

- The model also uses the current session window of the user. This contains the pages the user has accessed in the current transaction. According to the user's current clickstream, extra recommendations can be produced by using association rules mining and the site ontology.

- Then for each user status produce the initial set of all possible recommendations that will be filtered by the algorithm and ordered in ascending form.

- Run the following algorithm:

  U: the set of all users.

  P: the set of all pages.

  R: the initial recommendations list.

  $r_{i,j}$: the rate that user i gives to page j.

  For each page P_j in the initial set of recommendations R:

   Check the history file.

   If the history file is empty then find from the U_i class the users U_s that have rated the page else find the users U_s that have similar behaviour (history) with U_i and also have seen the page.

For each user in U_s compute the rate $r_{i,j}$ that the U_i will set to the P_j taking into consideration their rates and their similarity with U_i.

If this rate is greater than a specified threshold α then add this recommendation to the final list.

End for

End for

Return the list of final recommendations to the user in ascending order (first the page with the biggest r).

Evaluation

To evaluate the proposed approach we measure the recommendation accuracy as a ratio of successful recommendations R_s among all recommendations. As R_s we consider those pages that the user actually clicks in his navigation. The preliminary evaluation experiments show that the whole process has been enhanced by the combination of site's ontology, user's history files, user's registration data, and association rules, which encompass all necessary knowledge about users' navigational attitudes. Currently we are working on collecting further data in order to extensively evaluate the approach using more metrics such as coverage that measures the ability of the system to produce all pages that are likely to be visited by users.

Challenges of the Area

On the road to enhance an e-city portal and treat each user individually, Web personalisation and techniques from the scientific areas of Web usage mining and Semantic Web can be applied. We strongly support the benefits for both public authorities and citizens are significant when the personalisation model really works. However, many issues still remain unclear and require further review and discussion.

First, determining and delivering personalisation is a data intensive task and requires numerous processing steps. This usually causes intolerably long response times, which in turn may lead to site abandonment. To avoid this constraint, parts of the process can be executed off-line or special algorithms and structures can be used to guarantee fast online operation.

Another problem relates to the data quantity and quality. Insufficient or limited data can significantly affect the results of the knowledge discovery process. Especially, the use of heuristics assumptions before the mining techniques' application will lead often to the production of unsuitable or incorrect patterns. Moreover, when a user has been lost in a Web site, the user's recorded clicks in the log file may lead to unsuccessful future recommendations. This problem of inaccurate data can become more problematic when the Web site structure is badly designed and implemented and the users visit "orphan" pages making them appear as popular.

When new pages and content are added in the portal because they have not been visited by users, the personalisation system does not recommend them even in the case they are relative. Besides, the more a page is suggested the more the users visit it, a fact that increases its probability as a candidate for future recommendations. On the other hand when we have new users in the portal we phase the "cold start" problem or else the "day one" problem because in the first day of site operation, it does not have available data in order to begin to produce recommendations. Particularly, the CF techniques have poor performance for the new items (users or pages). Moreover, as the number of users grows, the number of comparisons in many dimensions seriously influences the system scalability and performance.

Another challenge is to ensure personalisation accuracy. It is true that unsuccessful recommendations can slow down the process, confuse and disorientate users. It is preferable not to deliver any recommendations than deliver a set of useless or harmful ones. Apart from that, personalisation should be delivered in the appropriate way (avoiding user intrusion and loss of concentration) and not deprive user control over the whole process. Moreover, as e-government sites are dynamic environments, issues concerning the content or structure updating, for example, newly added topics, pages, services, and so forth, can be taken into consideration.

Last, privacy violation during the user modelling and profiling process should be encountered (Volokh, 2000). Many users are reluctant to give away personal information either implicitly as mentioned before, or explicitly, hesitant to visit Web sites that use cookies (if they are aware of their existence) or avoiding to disclose personal data in registration forms. In both cases, the user loses anonymity and is aware that all of the user's actions will be recorded and used, often without consent. Additionally, even if a user has agreed to supply personal information to a site, through cookie technology, such information can be exchanged between sites, resulting in its disclosure without permission. Although the new technologies and products for protecting user's privacy on computers and networks are becoming increasingly popular, none can guarantee absolute secure communications (Kobsa, 2001). Electronic privacy issues in the foreseeable future will become highly crucial and intense (Markellos, Markellou, Rigou, Sirmakessis, & Tsakalidis, 2004b).

Conclusion

Governments enhance their attempt to offer efficient, advanced, and modern services to their users (citizens and businesses) based on information and computer technologies and especially the Web. E-government "fashion" is radically expanding through the world and to several governmental sections (ministries, public authorities, departments, etc.). The remarkable acceptance of this powerful tool has changed the way of conducting various activities and offers citizens, businesses, and public authorities limitless options and opportunities. However, the emerging problem is not the provision of users with access to the e-governments' information and services, but the provision of users with the *right* information and service according to their specific needs and preferences. To this direction, Web personalisation and Web mining, especially Semantic Web mining, are used for supporting tailored Web experiences.

These techniques appear the most promising for the future, since they help to establish one-to-one relationships between users and governments, improve the performance of provided information and services, increase users' satisfaction, and promote their loyalty for the e-services provided. On the other hand, governments take advantage of them, as long as they save costs (e.g., transactions, communication, task management, etc.), improve response times, automate various processes, provide alternative channels of cooperation and communication, and upgrade and modernise their profile and image.

Many research and commercial approaches, initiatives, and tools are available, based on Web site structure and contents, user's navigation, behaviour and transaction history, server log files, and so forth. In order for the e-government to succeed, all techniques must take into consideration the problems that may encounter. In the case of personalisation, it will certainly benefit both providers (governmental authorities) and users (citizens, businesses, and other governmental authorities) to take into consideration the fact that personalisation requires rich and qualitative data in order to provide successful output. This is not always feasible, since many users are often negative towards the idea of being stereotyped. Additionally, personalisation requires a flexible Web structure, which will easily handle the Web site content update as well as the Web structure update.

Unfortunately, there is an extraneous factor that affects personalisation goal, which is the user itself. Many users are reluctant to give away personal information, are hesitant to visit Web sites that use cookies, or avoid disclosing personal data in registration forms. Users commonly consider their privacy in jeopardy since their personal data and the activities taken are all recorded in a Web site. They are skeptical whether e-government actually provides a strict and safe privacy and security policy for their data. In case e-government does provide a certain policy, users are sceptical whether the policy is undoubtedly safe and secure of any threats, hackers' attacks, and whether the information collected on them is not mishandled by certain unauthorised people (governmental employees or external users).

Summarising, governments should work hard in the direction of providing the legal framework to ensure the protection of users' privacy and to eliminate the possibility of misuse of their personal information. Moreover, governments should focus on dealing with data security issues, to avoid unwanted leaks of personal information. In this way, any extraneous factors will be eliminated and personalised public e-services will lead the future governmental model, suspending the existing bureaucratic model that "crucifies" not only citizens and businesses but also intergovernmental transactions.

References

Adomavicius, G., & Tuzhilin, A. (2005). Toward the next generation of recommender systems: A survey of the state-of-the-art and possible extensions. *IEEE Transactions on Knowledge Management and Data Engineering, 17*(6), 734-749.

Berners-Lee, T., Hendler, J., & Lassila, O. (2001). The Semantic Web. *Scientific American, 284*(5), 34-43.

Borges, J., & Levene, M. (1999, August 15). Data mining of user navigation patterns. In M. Spyliopoulou, J. Borges, & M. Levene (Eds.), *Web Usage Analysis and User*

Profiling: International WEBKDD'99 Workshop, San Diego, CA (pp. 31-36). Berlin; Heidelberg: Springer-Verlag.

Cooley, R. (2000). *Web usage mining: Discovery and application of interesting patterns from Web data.* PhD thesis, University of Minnesota, Department of Computer Science.

Dai, H., & Mobasher, B. (2005). Integrating semantic knowledge with Web usage mining for personalization. In A. Scime (Ed.), *Web mining: Applications and techniques* (pp. 276-306). Hershey, PA: Idea Group Publishing.

Davies, J., Fensel, D., & Van Harmelen, F. (2003). *Towards the Semantic Web, ontology-driven knowledge management* (pp. 1-9). Chichester; West Sussex, UK: John Wiley & Sons.

Eirinaki, M., & Vazirgiannis, M. (2003). Web mining for Web personalization. *ACM Transactions on Internet Technology (TOIT), 3*(1), 1-27.

Etzioni, O. (1996). The World Wide Web: Quagmire or gold mine. *Communications of ACM, 39*(11), 65-68.

Kobsa, A. (2001, July 13-17). Tailoring privacy to user's needs. Invited keynote. In M. Bauer, P. J. Gmytrasiewicz, & J. Vassileva (Eds.), *User Modeling 2001: 8th International Conference*, Sonthofen, Germany (LNCS/LNAI 2109, pp. 303-313). Berlin; Heidelberg: Springer-Verlag.

Kosala, R., & Blockeel, H. (2000). Web mining research: A survey. *SIGKDD Explorations: Newsletter of the Special Interest Group (SIG) on Knowledge Discovery & Data Mining, ACM, 2*(1), 1-15.

Madria, S. K., Bhowmick, S. S., Ng, W. K., & Lim, E. P. (1999, August 30-September 1). Research issues in Web data mining. In M. K. Mohania & A. M. Tjoa (Eds.), *Data Warehousing and Knowledge Discovery: First International Conference, DaWaK '99*, Florence, Italy (LNCS 1676, pp. 303-312). Berlin; Heidelberg: Springer-Verlag.

Markellos, K., Markellou, P., Rigou, M., & Sirmakessis, S. (2004a). Web mining: Past, present, and future. In S. Sirmakessis (Ed.), *Proceedings of the NEMIS Launch Conference 2003, International Workshop in Text Mining and Its Applications*, Patras, Greece (Series: Studies in fuzziness and soft computing, Vol. 138). Berlin; Heidelberg: Springer-Verlag.

Markellos, K., Markellou, P., Rigou, M., Sirmakessis, S., & Tsakalidis, A. (2004b, April 14-16). Web personalization and the privacy concern. In *Proceedings of the 7th ETHICOMP International Conference on the Social and Ethical Impacts of Information and Communication Technologies, Challenges for the Citizen of the Information Society*, Syros, Greece.

Markellou, P., Mousourouli, I, Sirmakessis, S., & Tsakalidis, A. (2005, October 18-20). Personalized e-commerce recommendations. In *Proceedings of the IEEE International Conference on E-Business Engineering (ICEBE 2005)*, Beijing, China (pp. 245-252).

Markellou, P., Panayiotaki, A., & Tsakalidis, A. (2003, June 3-6). E-government and applications levels: Technology at citizen service. In A. Palma dos Reis & P. Isaias (Eds.),

Proceedings of IADIS International Conference, E-Society 2003, Lisbon, Portugal (pp. 849-854). IADIS Press.

Markellou, P., Rigou, M., & Sirmakessis, S. (2005a). Mining for Web personalization. In A. Scime (Ed.), *Web mining: Applications and techniques* (pp. 27-48). Hershey, PA: Idea Group Publishing.

Markellou, P., Rigou, M., & Sirmakessis, S. (2005b). Web personalization for e-marketing intelligence. In S. Krishnamurthy (Ed.), *Contemporary research in e-marketing: Volume 1* (pp. 48-68). Hershey, PA: Idea Group Publishing.

Markellou, P., Rigou, M., Sirmakessis, S., & Tsakalidis, A. (2004). Personalization in the Semantic Web era: A glance ahead. In A. Zanasi, N. F. Ebecken, & C. A. Brebbia (Eds.), *Proceedings of the 5th International Conference on Data Mining, Text Mining and their Business Applications, Data Mining 2004* (pp. 3-11), Wessex Institute of Technology (UK), Malaga, Spain, Southampton. Boston: PWIT Press.

Mobasher, B., Cooley, R., & Srivastava, J. (2000). Automatic personalization based on Web usage mining. *Communications of the ACM, 43*(8), 142-151.

Pal, S. K., Talwar, V., & Mitra, P. (2002). Web mining in soft computing framework: Relevance, state of the art and future directions. *IEEE Transactions on Neural Networks, 13*(5), 1163-1177.

Pierrakos, D., Paliouras, G., Papatheodorou, C., & Spyropoulos, C. (2003). Web usage mining as a tool for personalization: A survey. *User Modelling and User-Adapted Interaction, 13*, 311-372.

Shahabi, C., & Chen, Y. S. (2003, September 22-24). Web information personalization: Challenges and approaches. In N. Bianchi-Berthouse (Ed.), *Databases in Networked Information Systems: Third International Workshop, DNIS 2003*, Aizu, Japan (LNCS 2822, pp. 5-15).

Srivastava, J., Cooley, R., Deshpande, M., & Tan, P. N. (2000). Web usage mining: Discovery and applications of usage patterns from Web data. *SIGKDD Explorations: Newsletter of the Special Interest Group (SIG) on Knowledge Discovery & Data Mining, ACM, 1*(2), 12-23.

Tsoukalas, A., & Anthopoulos, L. G. (2004). *Moving toward the e-city.* Retrieved July 3, 2006, from http://www.govtech.net/magazine/channel_story.php?channel= 17& id=92188

Volokh, E. (2000). Personalization and privacy. *Communications of the ACM, 43*(8), 84-88.

Key Terms

- **Click-stream:** It is a record of a user's activity on the Internet, including every Web site and every page of every Web site that the user visits, how long the user was on a page or site, in what order the pages were visited, any newsgroups that the user participates in, and even the e-mail addresses of mail that the user sends and receives. Both ISPs and individual Web sites are capable of tracking a user's click-stream.

- **Cookie:** The data sent by a Web server to a Web client, stored locally by the client and sent back to the server on subsequent requests. In other words, a cookie is simply an HTTP header that consists of a text-only string, which is inserted into the memory of a browser. It is used to uniquely identify a user during Web interactions within a site and contains data parameters that allow the remote HTML server to keep a record of the user identity, and what actions the user takes at the remote Web site.

- **Data mining:** The application of specific algorithms for extracting patterns (models) from data.

- **Extended common log format (ECLF):** An extended common log format file is a variant of the common log format file simply adding two additional fields to the end of the line, the referrer (the URL the client was on before requesting Web server URL) and the user agent (the software the client claims to be using) fields.

- **Government-to-business (G2B):** In the case of Government-to-Business, it refers to e-commerce in which government sells to businesses or provides them with services, as well as businesses selling products and services to government. The objective of G2B is to enable businesses to interact, transact, and communicate with government online, with greater speed and convenience.

- **Government-to-citizens (G2C):** Government-to-Citizens, according to experts, includes all the interactions between a government and its citizens that can take place electronically. The objective of G2C is to offer citizens faster, more responsive, more convenient, and less complicated means to public services.

- **Government-to-employees (G2E):** Government-to-Employees includes activities and services between government units and their employees. As the term implies, the objective of G2E is to develop and cultivate IT capabilities among government employees to deliver efficient and cost-effective services.

- **Government-to-government (G2G):** Interestingly, Government-to-Government seems to have dual significance. One, G2G is said to consist of activities between government and other ministries, departments, and agencies (MDAs) of the same government. The other meaning of G2G is a situation in which Governments have to deal with their other counterpart governments of different countries.

- **Knowledge discovery in databases (KDD):** The nontrivial process of identifying valid, novel, potentially useful, and ultimately understandable patterns in data.

- **Ontology:** It is a means for capturing the knowledge about a domain, in such a way that a shared understanding of it is created and can be used both by humans and computers. Ontology defines concepts that represent classes or sets of instances in the world, relationships, and other constraints among them. There are many ways of representing ontologies from lists of words, taxonomies, database schema, to frame languages and logics.

- **Recommendations systems (RSs):** They comprise the most popular forms of personalisation and are becoming significant business tools. RSs take advantage of users' and communities' opinions in order to support individuals to identify the information or products most likely to be interesting to them or relevant to their needs and preferences. The recommendations may have various forms, for example, personalised offers/prices/products/services, inserting or removing paragraphs/sections/units, sorting/hiding/adding/removing/highlighting links, explanations or detailed information, and so forth.

- **Semantic Web mining:** The idea of the Semantic Web mining is to improve the results of the Web mining by exploiting the new semantic structures of the Web, as well as to use Web mining to help build the Semantic Web. It is the combination of two complementary families of methods: Semantic Web methods and Web mining methods.

- **Semantic Web:** It is an extension of the current Web in which information is given well-defined meaning, better enabling computers and people to work in cooperation.

- **Server log:** Web servers maintain log files listing every request made to the server. With log file analysis tools, it is possible to get a good idea of where visitors come from, how often they return, and how they navigate through a site. Using cookies enables Web masters to log even more detailed information about how individual users are accessing a site.

- **Web mining:** The Web mining applies Data mining techniques on the Web. Three areas can be distinguished: Web usage mining analyses user behaviour, Web structure mining explores hyperlink structure, and Web content mining exploits the contents of the documents in the Web.

- **Web personalisation:** It is the process of customising a Web site to the needs of specific users, taking advantage of the knowledge acquired from the analysis of the user's navigational behaviour (usage data) in correlation with other information collected in the Web context, namely structure, content, and user profile data. Due to the explosive growth of the Web, the domain of Web personalisation has gained great momentum both in the research and the commercial area.

- **Web Usage mining:** The application of data mining techniques to Web click-stream data in order to extract usage patterns.

Chapter II

Requirements Analysis and General Functional Model of Seamless, Citizen-Oriented Service Delivery

Elena Mugellini, University of Applied Sciences of Western Switzerland, Switzerland

Maria Chiara Pettenati, University of Florence, Italy

Omar Abou Khaled, University of Applied Sciences of Western Switzerland, Switzerland

Abstract

Seamless services provide citizens with what they need to know in a particular topic without having to know which government level or agencies they must contact to get it. Seamless services meet efficiency targets, reduce costs, and respond to citizen demands for improved services; they help governments to be more citizen-centered, outcome-oriented, efficient, and accountable. This chapter outlines main requirements for the delivery of seamless services and presents a general functional model (e-government service marketplace) for the delivery of shared services to citizens at the transaction level (i.e., supporting a complete online handling of a service). The main functionalities of the e-government service marketplace are analyzed in detail. Advantages, disadvantages, and the impact of this concept on the three fundamental axes (social, economic, and technical) are discussed as well. The chapter ends with some insights on future trends and open issues about seamless services delivery and enabling systems.

Introduction

The rapid emergence and growth of information and communication technologies (ICTs) in everyday life of citizens has pushed government to transform itself into an electronic government (e-government) to serve citizens. The main limits in traditional public administration practices are mainly due to the bureaucracy complexity among the departments, excessive and time consuming duplication/multiplication of paperwork which lead to long waiting time both for citizens and for public administration officers.

Due to the complexity of administrative procedures (which is somehow necessary in order to protect and guarantee citizens' rights) the interaction with public administration can be perceived by citizens as a complex and time consuming experience. As a consequence, traditional services and service delivery processes would benefit from a redesign and reorganization according to a more *citizen-oriented approach*. Government needs to take advantage of information and communication technologies and new business models to improve efficiency and effectiveness of internal processes as well as change the nature and quality of government interaction with both citizens and businesses allowing *seamless service delivery*. Government could take advantage of ICTs not just putting existing paper-based processes into digital form but rather starting a profound transformation of the way it provides services as well as interacts with citizens. Thanks to seamless service e-government practices, government could become more efficient, transparent, and responsive by allowing citizens to have 24-hour, 7-day interactive access to all governmental services as well as perform online transactions with governmental agencies at a distance.

This chapter outlines the main requirements for the provision of such shared services and presents a general functional model (e-government service marketplace) for seamless service delivery. It discusses the advantages and disadvantages as well as the impact of e-government service marketplace concept according to the three fundamental e-government perspectives: social, economic, and technical. It provides a case study of e-government service marketplace concept application and eventually it provides some insights on future issues and emerging needs of seamless service delivery.

It is worth noting that privacy and security issues are beyond the scope of this chapter; as a consequence, they will not be analyzed in-depth.

Background

E-government refers to the use by government agencies of ICT to improve the way public administration interacts with citizens and businesses, and to improve the efficiency of the administrative process. Enhanced quality of service has been a major component of public administration reform over the past two decades, and the use of ICT in order to generate improvements in services has been a primary driver for e-government activity. In particular the use of the Internet has given a major boost to citizen-oriented, seamless services, and online services are increasingly seen as part of a broader strategy which aims to improve citizen satisfaction and interest in e-government. Online service targets have also been effective in motivating public administrations to examine the potential of the Internet and related technologies by applying them to existing services. One-stop offices, advice bureaus, information kiosks, and call centers have attempted to bring together information and services from different governmental agencies.

In order to evaluate e-government progress in some countries several stage models describing the evolution of public services have been developed (AOEMA, 2004; Persson & Goldkuhl, 2005; Suh, 2003). These models divide the development of e-government into several stages from simple information provision to more complex services (Table 1). All these models divide the development of e-government into several stages from simple information provision to more complex services. All of them start off with a stage of providing information to the public. Only the United Nations/American Society for Public Administration (UN/ASPA) model splits this stage into two distinct/separate levels: emerging and enhanced. After this, the models begin to differ from each other in a more substantial way. The Australian National Audit Office (ANAO), Swedish Agency for Administrative Development (SAFAD), and UN/ASPA continue with an interaction stage where there is increasing interaction between the agency Web site and the client.

Layne and Lee (2001) continue in their second stage, transaction, where internal systems of public administrations are integrated with the Web sites. This stage corresponds to the third stage in the ANAO and SAFAD models or the fourth stage in the UN/ASPA model. On the contrary the Capgemini model presents some differences as its fourth stage (transaction) corresponds to the third (partially) and fourth stage of ANAO or SAFAD models.

Table 1. E-government development stages

	E-Government Service Development Stage Models				
	ANAO (ANAO, 1999)	**SAFAD (Statskontoret, 2000)**	**Layne &Lee (Layne & Lee, 2001)**	**UN/ASPA (Ronaghan, 2001)**	**Capgemini (Capgemini, 2005)**
Service Stages	publishing information	information	catalogue	emerging	information
				enhanced	
	interactive information	interaction		interactive	one-way interaction
	transaction	transaction	transaction	transaction	two-way interaction
	data sharing	integration	vertical integration	fully integrated or seamless	transaction
			horizontal integration		

It clearly appears how differences between different models are usually minor differences and that there is a common trend to classify as the last level (i.e., the level that requires the highest level of technological sophistication, transformational effort, and economical investment) the one that requires a complete integration between several administrations in order to provide seamless (or integrated) transactional services. In other words despite different names of equivalent stages in different models, essentially the direction of e-government development always begins with only a presence and basic information where the technology is treated as simply another site on which to post information. Sites then move to a stage where interaction and communication between citizens, businesses, and governmental officials are developed and are the main focus. The next step is provision of real e-service delivery where the focus is on transactional service and citizens are able to accomplish complete routine tasks online. This stage requires an extensive use of technology that is not only a new way ("e-way") of doing traditional government but has the possibility of creating new and different ways for government to serve the citizens. For the sake of clarity in the rest of the chapter (when speaking about a stage model for service provision), we will refer to the four-stage Capgemini model (Figure 1).

As Figure 1 shows, while stages 1 and 2 provide a low level of service provision which requires a low level of technological sophistication, stages 3 and 4 require a high level of technological sophistication which allows for the delivery of high level services.

To date, e-government has enjoyed a level of political support in different countries, which have seen it as a tool to modernize public administration, as a symbol of modernity, as a way of promoting the development of ICT industry, and the move to an information society. The initial impressive results of e-government activities — the rapid appearance of several government Web sites and the development of portals — made information easy to find without requiring additional substantial funding. However after this initial enthusiastic phase, fewer efforts have been made to reach the next stages of e-service provision (stages 3 and 4 in Figure 1).

Figure 1. Capgemini four-stage model

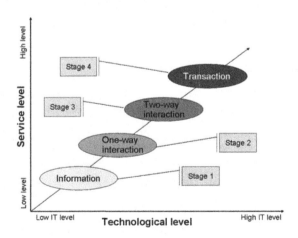

According to the Capgemini report (Capgemini, 2005) on online availability of public services (the survey covered 17 countries and examined 20 basic public services), the online sophistication of public service delivery in Europe is situated between one-way interaction (stage 2) and two-way interaction (stage 3) (measurement October 2004). Moreover when results are broken down into the target groups, citizens and businesses, it appears that online sophistication for governmental services are significantly higher for businesses than for citizens. The results of the survey also sketch out e-government progress: e-service improvements in the period 2001-2004 register an increase of six percentage points (Capgemini, 2005). This means that over the last three years, online development of public service has improved but much work still remains to reach the highest level of complete transactional public services (Halligan & Moore, 2004). There is more and more need for providing the glue interconnecting separate initiatives and efforts into a single and global approach (an integration model enabling the collaboration between participating governmental agencies and citizens).

The next stages of e-government will involve the development of hidden infrastructure, joined-up back-office systems, possible reengineering of administrative processes and more considerable funding with benefits which are likely to emerge slowly and be less evident. However this new phase is essential for seamless service delivery becoming a reality. The logic of customer-focus, seamless, and integrated e-government and the need to work in cooperation to ensure interoperability and reduce duplication applies as much as across jurisdictions as it does across agencies at the same level of government, and involves a number of issues, including:

- Ease-of-use and user-friendliness
- Personalized and accessible services
- Support of citizen migration across different countries
- Respect of public administration autonomy
- Integration of public administration legacy system
- Private and public service integration
- Continuous improvement and evolution of e-government solutions

In the following a detailed analysis of requirements for seamless service delivery from both citizen and public administration point of view is provided.

Requirements for Seamless Service Delivery

As services become more complex, efficiency considerations require greater cooperation between agencies in areas such as shared processing, data exchange, and authentication. The need of collaboration between agencies thus has both "front-office" (service to the customer) and "back-office" (efficiency in e-government) components (Mugellini, Abou Khaled, Pettanati, & Franco, 2005). The front-office refers to how public administration organization and efficiency is perceived from citizens; in this case the main requirements for a seamless service delivery concern user satisfaction about government services (user-friendliness, information accessibility, ease-of-use, etc.). On the other hand back-office refers to the internal operations of an organization that are not accessible or visible to the general public; in this case the main requirements for a seamless service delivery are about integration of heterogeneous information systems, interoperability between agencies, and so forth. Hence, the main requirements for a quality service delivery change align with the two different points of view: the citizen point of view and the public administration point of view.

From the citizen point of view the main requirements for seamless service delivery are about citizen-centered, effective, and efficient services; in particular the following needs can be outlined:

- **Focus on users' needs:** So far, services offered by public administrations were mainly focused on the expectations of the administrations themselves rather than on the real needs of the citizens. Public services should not be designed around public administration needs. Instead, they should be centered according to citizen needs (for instance either increasing the number of online services or decreasing administrative response time).

- **User-friendly services:** Provide citizen-oriented services hiding to the citizen the complexity and fragmentation of public administration performing the necessary operations for collecting the information to deliver government services instead of the citizen. Citizen comfort depends on the ergonomics of the services offered: the simplicity of the tasks to be carried out and the terminology used, but also the uniformity of presentation of services provided by different agencies. Moreover the move from one administration to another should not be troubling for the citizen: similar data should have similar names and similar actions have to be presented in the same way.

- **Personalized services:** Personalization of services over time by tailoring what the government provides to the individual citizen (Accenture, 2004). The development of e-government permits personalized processing, centered on the individual needs of each citizen; services can interpret available data within the context of a particular time, whereby services and information change as certain events occur.

- **Access and accessibility:** Provide 24/7 service availability (i.e., provide services to citizens every time they need them, wherever they are, increasing access possibilities while reducing delays). Services should be completely available to anyone with Internet access, or an opposite terminal should be provided, in order to save citizens from having to travel for simple matters (a better access to public services is important in peripheral or rural areas).

- **Transaction handling:** Allow service delivery at the transaction level (the highest interaction level between citizen and administration, supporting online handling of a complete service). Users can enter information and engage in electronic transaction with the administration. Seamless services at the transaction level require real-time responsiveness by government agencies to the service demand of citizens and the administration ability to share data with the other governmental agencies. This way, citizens can obtain high-level services without having to provide the same documentation or data time and time again and without having to move to several administrations.

- **Support migration across different countries:** Help citizens during their migration from one country to another. Since the integration of Europe into a single market, the citizens of the European Community member states should be able to migrate from one European country to another with as few problems as possible. Yet, mobile European citizens have to deal with time and money consuming administrative procedures. If the collecting of required documents costs a lot of time and money for citizens in their home country, for foreign citizens, the situation is even worse.

- **Quality of service:** Citizens should benefit from the information given, which must be up to date and offer relevant self-service options. Seamless services should improve citizen life providing simplified procedures and preventing them from wasting money and time. Moreover services should enable users to find out the status of their official papers or the progress of their requests and should reduce as much as possible the need for users to provide redundant information already held by the authorities.

From the administration point of view the main requirements of quality seamless service delivery include, among others, data reuse, services sharing as well as legacy system integration. Hence "interoperability" and "integration" are crucial issues for developing and implementing seamless services. It is worth noting that interoperability is not only a technical issue dealing with distributed computing, but it deals also with information sharing among different administrations and the redesign of administrative processes to support more effective delivery of e-government services. Three levels of interoperability are relevant to seamless service delivery: technical, semantic, and organizational (European Commission, 2003). The first one refers to technical issue of connecting computer systems, defining common communication protocols, and data formats. The second one concerns the exchange of information in an understandable way even between applications that were not initially developed for this purpose. The third one refers to enabling processes cooperation between agencies at the same level of government as well as across different jurisdictions. The main requirements for seamless service delivery according to the administration point of view are:

- **Flexibility:** Refers to efficient reuse of information while respecting technical and political capabilities of different administrations. *Reuse* refers to the possibility of reusing services and information instead of duplicated them at different agencies. *Efficiency* refers to the ability to quickly and easily create new services using a combination of new and already existing services. Finally "respect technical and political capabilities" means allowing each administration to provide services according to different interoperability levels that do not require the same level of technological sophistication.

- **Data storage:** Seamless services require the administrations to share information they hold. The qualitative and economic advantages of e-government are based on the possibility of sharing and exchanging data regarding the citizens. Therefore appropriate data storage and access mechanisms are required.

- **Integration of legacy systems:** Refers to promoting integration of legacy systems allowing a gradual transition from already existing information systems to the new ones. Different and heterogeneous applications should be able to exchange data and participate in a business process regardless of the implementation details (for instance, operating system or programming languages) underlying those applications, thus allowing technical interoperability.

- **Shared services:** Refer to the consolidation of administrative or support functions (human resources, information technologies, etc.) from several departments or agencies into a single organizational entity (Accenture, 2005); that is, services provided by different agencies are shared and composed in order to deliver more complex services to citizens, allowing organizational interoperability.

- **Interagency cooperation:** Public services are composed of several activities involving different agencies and frequently need to link and use data from multiple and diverse information resources. Therefore in order to deliver seamless services to citizens, it is necessary to enable a real interagency cooperation which allows services and information sharing, reducing the need for users to provide redundant information already held by the authorities. Interagency cooperation is about definition of sharing rules, cooperation policies as well as a common standard language thus allowing for organizational and semantic interoperability.

- **Horizontal and vertical integration:** Refers to promoting integration among agencies and departments within the same level of government (horizontal) and integration of central government services with state, local, or municipal services (vertical) (OECD, 2004). While horizontal integration has long been a goal of many countries and is still a challenge area, governments are now beginning to look beyond this to the next challenge: vertical integration. Vertical integration adds a layer of complexity to the e-government challenge but it is a fundamental challenge to integrate services for a seamless interaction for citizens.

- **Scalability and evolution over time:** Provide a flexible, scalable, and evolutionary solution in order to support changing and evolving needs of public administration. As public sector administrative organization, functional division, as well as legislative regulations evolve continuously, it is necessary to provide a technology-independent solution for seamless service delivery which facilitates system evolution over time. Finally, the use of standards and modeling techniques for formalizing system specification and conceptualization allow a better support of system evolution over time.

Table 2 summarizes the requirements elicited throughout the previous paragraphs for quality seamless service delivery.

Many interesting solutions have been developed so far, the majority of them based on providing an Internet site where citizens can find information about governmental agencies and providing limited interaction functionalities (Belgium Web site, n.d.; Austrian Web site, n.d.). While some portal provides information concerning service delivered by multiple administrations together with contact information, another portal goes one step further providing downloadable forms to request services. Very often, no support for complete online handling of the whole service is provided.

Table 2. Seamless service delivery requirements

Seamless service delivery requirements	
Citizen point of view	**Public administration point of view**
Focus on users' needs	Flexibility
User-friendly	Data storage
Personalized	Shared services
Access and accessibility	Integration of legacy system
Online handling of a complete service	Interagency cooperation
Practical value	Horizontal and vertical integration
Support migration	Scalability and evolution over time

More recently various middleware solutions are emerging as the dominant approach to technical integration in several countries, allowing a cooperative data exchange for the delivery of certain services (such as business services or taxation) or for providing increased quality services to citizens (services at stages 3 and 4) (Baldoni, Mecella, Contenti, & Termini, 2003; Pappa et al., 2003; Riedl, 2001). However a middleware oriented approach limits somehow the flexibility of the proposed solution in terms of both its integration with heterogeneous systems and its evolution over time. In order to design a flexible and interoperable system capable of easily evolving over the time a model-driven approach for system conceptualization and formalization is necessary. A model-driven system design, which is implementation and technology independent, allows overcoming limits of technology oriented systems in terms of reusability, interoperability, and transferability across different contexts. Moreover as front-office and back-office components are the two faces of the same coin, issues of both quality service provision and administration interoperability have to be fulfilled in order to provide seamless services. In order to address all these requirements it is necessary to provide an operating model of shared service, that is, a model of cooperative and open service sharing and information reuse between agencies. The concept of the e-government service marketplace aims at proposing a conceptual approach for defining an operating model of shared services which abstracts from implementation constraints and technological details hence easing flexibility, interoperability, and evolution over time.

The Concept of E-Government Service Marketplace

The e-government service marketplace (eGovSM) concept (Mugellini, Abou Khaled, Pettanati, & Kuonen, 2005) proposes a general functional model for shared, interoperable, and evolutionary services for citizens enabling and promoting horizontal and vertical integration of agencies within the public sector. According to the e-government service marketplace concept, agencies are provided with organizational and technical flexibility because their back-office structures are independent of marketplace front-line structures. The concept of

Figure 2. E-government service marketplace

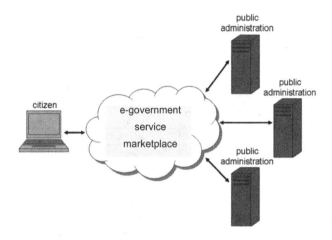

e-government service marketplace refers to an open and common virtual space for providing enhanced services to citizens which facilitates citizens' interaction with administrations hiding from citizens public administration complexity and fragmentation (Figure 2). Citizens gain value from increased access and reduced delays, improved service delivery, and less interaction with intermediaries, while administrations can flexibly share services and information as they are not required to meet the same level of technological sophistication.

The e-government service marketplace promotes the reuse of information as well as the sharing of services provided by different agencies. As it happens in a traditional marketplace (or "supermarket"), where a citizen can buy the products the citizen needs without caring about production and delivery process, the e-government marketplace aims at providing e-government services to citizens without requiring them to be aware of public administration complexity. For instance, for the delivery of a document, citizens will not be concerned with administration responsibility or geographical location of information. On the one hand, the e-government service marketplace can be considered an "interoperability intermediary" acting between agencies allowing the reuse and sharing of information at both horizontal and vertical levels (Figure 2). It allows interconnection and integration of multiple government agencies in order to deliver seamless services; services and information provided by multiple agencies are integrated and composed in order to support the online handling of a complete transaction (stages 3 and 4 of service provision). On the other hand, it can be considered a "communication intermediary" acting between the public administration and the citizen (Figure 2). It makes it easier for citizens to interact with public administrations, rebalancing relations between citizens and administrations and presenting e-government services in a citizen-oriented way. As stated before, the e-government service marketplace purpose is not only to use technologies to increase the efficiency of administrative process. It aims also to make it easier for citizens to interact with public administrations by presenting and structuring e-government services according to a citizen-oriented approach.

Figure 3. E-government service marketplace domain

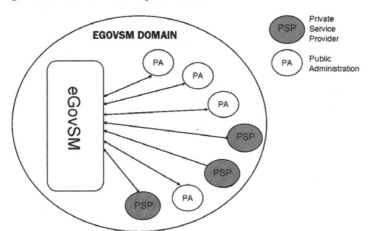

Moreover, as shown in Figure 3, the e-government service marketplace provides an open environment where commercial activities coexist with government services. While at its start-up eGovSM will start by integrating services of various public administrations (PA), then it will be open to, and it will promote as well, the participation of business company and private service providers (PSP). This way the marketplace will represent a common access point to "enriched governmental services." For instance if a citizen needs a driving license document the eGovSM will provide not only the "getting your driving license" service (public service) but also the service "driving school subscription" (private service). The e-government service marketplace domain is therefore defined as the ensemble of the e-government service marketplace and the administrations and private service providers connected to it (Figure 3). This domain represents somehow the "knowledge" of the e-government marketplace, that is, the service providers it knows about. All the administrations and private service providers that subscribe to the e-government service marketplace will be part of its domain.

As the e-government marketplace proposes an approach gradually integrating all the areas of public administration involved (state, regional agencies, administrations in the health and welfare sector), at the beginning not all the agencies will join the system sharing electronically their services and information. Moreover there will be agencies that will require a direct interaction with the citizen even if they participate in the marketplace — this is the case of a hospital where, for instance, an eyes check-up requires the citizen to physically move to the hospital.

Figure 4 shows the entities involved in the marketplace and possible interactions between them. The figure highlights three different types of public administrations (PAs). PAs of "type A" represent administrations subscribed to the eGovSM that automatically provide data to the marketplace without requiring the citizen to interact with them. PAs of "type B" represent administrations subscribed to the eGovSM that, even if they can automatically provide data to the marketplace, require a direct interaction with citizens (for example a

Figure 4. Gradual integration of public administrations

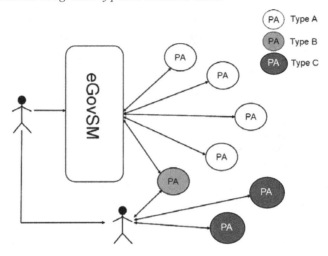

hospital in case of a medical check-up). Finally PAs of "type C" represent administrations that are not subscribed to the eGovSM and hence require a direct interaction with citizens to provide data. As Figure 4 shows, citizens interact directly with the eGovSM and agencies of types B and C.

The e-government service marketplace has to hide the regulatory, administrative, and procedural complexity to citizens presenting simple services which meet users' needs. The development of "global" services, defined on the basis of actions in the daily life of the citizen, regardless of how many administrations are involved (state, regional authorities, the health, the welfare sector, etc.), facilitates citizen interaction with the public sector. As the e-government service marketplace aims at facilitating citizen life not requiring users to provide information held by agencies time and time again, it has to provide a mechanism for identifying citizens which allows the automatic retrieving of this information. Often the delivery of a service is a complex process (consisting of multiple operations to perform) involving several agencies. The eGovSM has to guarantee an appropriate coordination as well as execution of all these operations. Finally it has to manage the interaction with administrations and private service providers. The main functions the e-government service marketplace ought to be able to perform are:

- Citizen interaction management
- Citizen identification
- Administrative process coordination
- Public administration interaction management

In the following paragraphs a more detailed description of these functions is provided.

Citizen Interaction Management

The eGovSM represents a common access point to public services presented and structured according to a citizen-oriented approach. By citizen-oriented service, we mean reorganizing the processes of services provision and delivery on the basis of citizens' needs rather than the internal needs of the government, as has been the practice so far. The problem lies in the fact that the existent organization of government is based on a division of work between several fields or competences (Vintar, Kunstelj, & Leben, 2002). Accordingly, administrative procedures and services are adapted and distributed over several public institutions. However, the problems of citizens do not usually apply merely to one single competence or one single public institution; instead they involve multiple institutions. Consequently these processes are complicated, time consuming, and expensive. The solution to these problems lies in the introduction of services designed around possible life events of the citizens. The life-event approach (Dipartimento per l'Innovazione e le Tecnologie, 2002; Life Event Portal, n.d.) considers government operations from the perspective of everyday life. Its main purpose is to overcome the existent structure and complexity of public institutions. One life event has to comprise all services as well as the corresponding processes needed to solve the customer's problem from the beginning to the end. In this way, all services needed to solve a particular problem or situation, are either linked or integrated into one single service. According to this model, citizens' life is described providing a list of events that (when occurring) result in a series of transactions between a citizen and different public sector organizations (Figure 5). Examples of life events could be "looking for a job," "moving home," "getting the driving license," "retiring," "having a baby," and so on.

The e-government service marketplace provides access to services aggregating them according to "life event metaphor" making the various public administrations involved in the delivery of such services transparent to citizens (Figure 5). The marketplace concept of

Figure 5. Seamless and citizen-oriented services in the e-government service marketplace

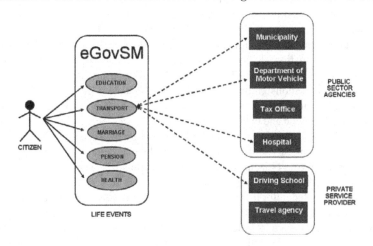

service consists in either the transmission or the reception of a document between offices. In the context of this chapter a document can be an official document (well-structured information) or "raw" information (not structured information).

The citizen interaction manager is also responsible for updating life events and services according to changes to the law or to the administrative process associated to the service. Moreover the e-government service marketplace will enable users to find out about the status of their official papers or the progress of their service requests. To conclude, the citizen interaction management can be defined as the following:

- The citizen interaction manager component is responsible for managing all the interactions between the citizen and the marketplace. Its main role is to organize, structure, and present governmental services according to citizens' needs (the life event metaphor). Moreover it has to manage and supervise citizen service request, for instance, informing the citizen about service request progress or possible alternatives in case the target administration is not yet electronically connected to eGovSM.

Citizen Identification

The delivery of seamless services requires an exchange of information between the e-government marketplace and the agencies that hold citizen data. Hence, the eGovSM needs a mechanism to find, according to the requested service, which administrations to contact in order to retrieve the necessary information (as previously defined, the delivery of a service corresponds to the transmission or reception of a document). In other words to deliver a service to the citizen, it is necessary to identify such a citizen. Such an identifier will contain information about the citizen that allows verifying if the citizen who is requesting the service meets the requirements for obtaining such service as well as identifying the agencies that hold the information necessary for delivering the service. Several identification options are possible (Ministère de la Fonction Publique, 2003): single significant identifier, single nonsignificant identifier, several nonsignificant identifiers, and single significant federated identifier. The single significant identifier, which can be general or sector-based, suggests somehow the identity of the citizen; hence it is not the best solution for protecting the privacy of citizens. On the contrary the nonsignificant single identifier does not contain citizen personal information; that is, it is not related to the identity of the citizen, but it has to be associated to sector identifiers. Then the problem arises from the necessity of a look-up table to match the single nonsignificant identifier with the sector identifier and, above all, the storage of this table. However this solution provides a greater protection of citizen freedom as it allows users to decide and manage which identifier accesses the different services. The same, in case of several nonsignificant identifiers allowing the access to different services, the problem of the look-up table and its storage still exists. Finally the single significant federated identifier allows citizens to use a single identifier to access all the services. This identifier contains citizen personal information, but as it is "federated" neither the government nor the identity federator itself are able to make the connection between the different identifiers (i.e., there is not a look-up table stored somewhere). According to the needs of the e-government service marketplace, the most suitable solution for the citizen identifier is the federated one. Each federated identifier will uniquely identify a citizen. This identifier will federate all the information about the citizen (such as name, birth date, birthplace, or sector-specific identifier) necessary to the e-government marketplace for identifying, every time, a service requested, the administration that holds a particular set of citizen data. It is worth noting that this identifier is not for privacy protection or security issues. Therefore other security mechanisms, for guaranteeing respect of privacy as well as positively identifying the citizen requesting the service, are required. The e-government service marketplace will manage this federated identifier but neither the marketplace itself nor any of the administrations will store the identifier; that is, there is not a centralized database of all the federated identifiers.

The management of the identifier will include the generation of the identifier and successive use. As the identifier federates specific information and country-specific sector identifiers, federated identifiers belonging to different countries will have a different structure (country-specific identifier structure). Hence, each e-government service marketplace will be able only to create and interpret identifiers belonging to its origin country. The creation of the identifier is done online by the e-government marketplace; a citizen wishing to obtain an identifier provides an ensemble of information the e-government marketplace uses, after a verification phase where the system checks the correctness and truthfulness of information provided by the citizen with the public administration, to create the identifier. The identifier is stored on an electronic card; thus only the citizen possesses it (in those countries where an electronic identity card has already been activated, it can be envisaged to stock the identifier on the identity card).

To conclude, the citizen identification functionality can be defined as the following:

- The citizen identifier is a federated identifier, containing citizen personal data, which allow the e-government service marketplace to find out the governmental agencies that hold citizen data. This identifier has a general structure which can be adapted according to country-specific needs. This identifier is not for security issues.

Administrative Process Coordination

As Figure 6 shows, life events are used to facilitate citizen navigation and search of services. However citizens do not consume a life event since this general structuring concept only represents the access interface to public services. Public services are the concrete products and services citizen are applying for. At the same time each public service consists of several processes — elementary operations to perform in order to deliver such a service. These elementary operations include among others prerequirements verification, constraints check, and information retrieval (see Figure 6).

Usually laws and administrative provisions fragment all the aspect of the life of a citizen according to multiple sectors (i.e., taxation, municipality, health, etc.). This fragmentation causes difficulties in delivering services to citizens, such as services composed of several activities involving different agencies and frequently need to link and use data from multiple and diverse information resources. Therefore in order to deliver seamless services to citizens it is necessary to coordinate the execution of all these activities and monitor the correct course of the whole process instead of the citizen. Citizens will not have to supply different

Figure 6. Life events to processes mapping

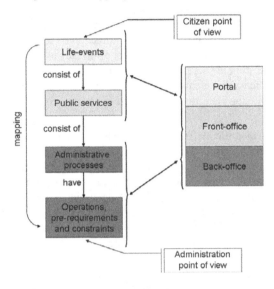

government agencies with the same information and documentation time and time again. Instead they will ask the government service marketplace for the service they need and the e-government marketplace will manage all the operations to obtain such a service (constraint verification, requirements check as well as information retrieve and exchange) on behalf of the citizen, thus reducing as much as possible the need for users to provide redundant information already held by the authorities. When a citizen requests a given service, as a service is usually composed by several activities involving different agencies, the market-place has to perform all these activities in order to correctly deliver the final service to the citizen. The marketplace translates the requested service (expressed according to life-event metaphor) into the corresponding administrative process and executes this process to deliver the document to the citizen. For each service provided by the marketplace a description of the process associated with such service is given as well. As administrative procedures and services are distributed over several public institutions, the e-government service market-place has to coordinate the execution of distributed tasks. Since service delivery is not only a mere retrieval of information but is subjected to the satisfaction of specific constraints, the e-government marketplace has also got to guarantee that all the constraints are satisfied before completing the delivery of a service.

The e-government service marketplace is responsible for verifying if the citizen requesting the service meets the requirements for obtaining the service and, if it is the case, coordinat-ing the operations for collecting the necessary information and creating the final document to be delivered.

It is worth noting that in order to respect public administration authority in delivering of-ficial documents, the marketplace will create, by default, only the "logic document" (i.e., an electronic document containing all the information required in the final document without formatting style and without the "status" of official certificate). This logic document will be sent to the administration responsible for delivering it to the citizen and the administration itself will create the physical official document. On the contrary if the administration delegates this function to the e-government service marketplace, the system will create the final document and deliver it to the citizen instead of the agency.

As stated, in order to provide seamless services to citizens, the e-government service marketplace has to exchange and retrieve a certain number of data regarding the user. Therefore citizen personal data has to be stored somewhere; several options are possible (Ministère de la Fonction publique, 2003): centralization, generalized exchange, or decentralization. The first option (centralization) requires centralizing all the data and administrative files of each user of the administration. This solution is not implemented in any country for evident reasons of privacy and individual freedom. The second option (generalized exchange) allows an indiscriminate exchange of data between administrative departments, which enables users to benefit from really simplified services as data held by one agency are accessible to any other; but on the other hand it does not offer a sufficient protection of citizen personal data. Finally the third option (decentralization) implies a decentralized storage of data with a controlled exchange between agencies. Data storage remains decentralized within each agency in respect of privacy and individual freedom issues. The e-government service marketplace implements a decentralized approach; it does not store a local copy of citizen data; data remains stored only within each agency as it has been the practice so far.

To conclude, the administrative process coordination can be defined as:

- The administrative process coordination is about the translation of a public service (expressed according to life-event metaphor) into the corresponding administrative process and the execution of all the operation associated to such a process (constraints verification, requirements check, etc.).

Public Administration Interaction Management

As elicited in the previous requirement analysis allowing public administration interoperability while integrating legacy systems is a key factor towards improving the quality of service delivery. Public administration interoperability has to be made possible respecting public administration autonomy and integrating legacy systems. For this reason eGovSM reach for interoperability by proposing a service-oriented approach, that is, distributed and independent administrations participate to the marketplace activity by exchanging services that provide a complete abstraction of the legacy systems explained later. Moreover each administration wanting to join the marketplace has to subscribe to it, declaring its availability to provide services and share data. In order to respect technical and political capabilities of public administrations, as well as providing a certain flexibility, as not all the agencies are at the same level of technological sophistication, eGovSM provides different subscription profiles, corresponding to different levels of interoperability both for providing as well as receiving data from the marketplace. Concerning the transmission of data from an agency to the eGovSM, four different subscription profiles are provided. In this way eGovSM allows

Table 3. Public administration types and subscription profiles

Subscription profiles Types of PA	Profile 0	Profile 1	Profile 2	Profile 3
Type A		X	X	X
Type B		X	X	X
Type C	X			

each administration to interact and cooperate with the marketplace according to its capability. The "Profile 0" refers to administrations that are not able to provide electronic data. The "Profile 1" refers to administrations that can provide elementary electronic functionalities (they are able to respond to yes/no questions). The "Profile 2" refers to administrations that are able to provide a richer set of functionalities (they can provide the marketplace with information or documents). The "Profile 3" refers to administrations that implement an instance of the eGovSM system. In the last case the administration information system is fully eGovSM compliant and it is able to provide the same functionalities of the eGovSM system. Concerning the communication of data from the eGovSM to the government agencies, each agency has two subscription possibilities: it can accept or not data from the marketplace. It is worth noting that considerations about public administration that have been done so far are valid for the private service provider as well.

Table 3 relates the four profiles with the three different types of public administrations previously introduced.

To conclude, public administration interaction management can be defined as the following:

•   Public administration management is about providing different levels of interoperability and legacy system integration in order to allow a gradual involvement of agencies with different levels of technological sophistication. The public administration manager is responsible for localizing and contacting agencies as well as integrating services and information of various administrations.

eGovSM Formalization:
The Model-Driven Approach

The concept of e-government service marketplace has been formalized using a model-driven approach which allows the development of a flexible, interoperable, and scalable environment. Using a system modeling approach makes it possible to define the system at business domain level and then translate it in a software system meeting the requirements of system generality, extensibility, and interoperability. In a continuously changing and evolving world as public sector (and also evolving technologies), it is very important to design a flexible system which is easy to maintain and reconfigure in order to meet changing and evolving needs of administrations. Moreover in a heterogeneous world as public sector, it becomes fundamental to provide different levels of abstractions in system representation and view in order to make possible and facilitate the communication between different actors involved (engineers, administrators, managers, etc.). A model-driven design allows specifying the concept without taking care of any implementation constraints or technological details. Model-driven approach refers to the use of models at different levels of abstraction in order to formally describe an information system. Separation and formalization, that is, modeling, are recognized as the best practices for system design and development. Modeling techniques allow the same model specifying system functionalities to be realized on multiple platforms. They allow different applications to be integrated by explicitly relating their models, enabling integration and interoperability and supporting system evolution as technologies change rapidly.

Arrangements and middleware solution for integrating back-office systems with customer-oriented interface may give the impression that collaboration and cooperation between agencies can be achieved primarily at the technical level. In practice this is unlikely to be the case. In effect collaboration for seamless service delivery is more than technical issues and it is likely to involve implementation of integration models, service delivery policies and standards, service quality, presentation of information and material, and a decision-making process. For these reasons a middleware-oriented approach, which concentrates and takes care only of technological constraints and implementation details, is not enough and a more conceptual (technology-independent) approach is required. This is why the concept of e-government service marketplace is first of all a conceptual model for a shared infrastructure enabling seamless service delivery, which can be afterwards converted into a physical and operational architecture (which will only correspond to one of the possible implementation solutions). Interoperability, integration, and evolution are crucial issues e-government has to deal with. As stated before, the main e-government objectives are to better deliver services to citizens, improve interactions with citizens, and provide more efficient government management. In order to achieve these goals a real collaboration between administrations and a fully integrated heterogeneous public administration information system is required (European Commission, 2003). Using modeling techniques to formalize an e-government system allows specifying system functionalities in a technology-independent way, thus enabling integration and interoperability and supporting system evolution. The e-government service marketplace has been formalized using a document based modeling approach (document engineering). Document engineering (Glushko, 2003) is evolving as a new scientific discipline for specifying, designing, and implementing systems belonging to very different business domains by using XML technology (World Wide Web Consortium, n.d.). The use of XML technology (Daum, 2003) allows the design and specification of a flexible, interoperable, and scalable system. It allows the description and formalization of the system in a technology-independent way, making it portable across different development environments, thus achieving maximum reusability and interoperability.

This allows us to provide a standard definition of the system which will be common for all implementation while guaranteeing a certain level of flexibility. According to the e-government service marketplace model, only basic functionalities and behaviors are defined, making possible to add and adapt this "basic" system specification to the specific needs of a particular context. This would eventually allow different administrations, even of different countries, to customize the system according to their needs while remaining fully compliant, thus interoperable, with other systems. The definition of the concept of e-government service marketplace transcends country-specific requirements and identifies elements that can be transferred across different contexts. Moreover the modeling of the eGovSM in a technology-independent way facilitates system evolution over time as public sector administrative organization, functional divisions as well as legislative regulations evolve continuously.

eGovSM Replication: The Concept of E-Goverment Service Marketplace Network

The concept of "network of e-government service marketplace" refers to an ensemble of interconnected e-government service marketplace domains, within a country or distributed over several countries. These multiple domains are able to work in a cooperative manner thus providing seamless services to a wider range of citizens. Interconnecting different e-government service marketplace domains allows sharing and integrating the knowledge of each of them, while respecting their autonomy and operational independence. The concept of network of e-government service marketplace represents an interesting solution to respond to the need of providing seamless services at the European level (pan-European services) while at the same time allowing each country to decide about implementation details of the eGovSM concept (for instance, which information the federated identifier should contain, life-events classification, and implementation and possible subscription profiles).

Figure 7. The concept of e-government service marketplace network

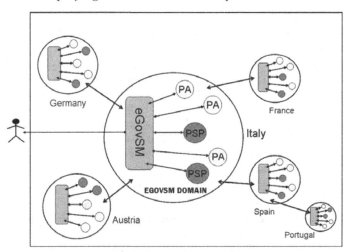

As Figure 7 shows, the network of eGovSMs will include all the known eGovSM domains. Each eGovSM has not to know about all the other domains, it is sufficient that each domain is known for at least another one. When an eGovSM is set up, it has to subscribe to (at least) another one in order to become part of the network.

This way each e-government service domain can be considered as a virtual organization in the grid (Foster, Kesselman, & Tuecke, 2001) domain. A Virtual Organization is defined as a dynamic set of individuals or institutions defined around a set of resource-sharing rules and conditions which share resources in a coordinated, secure, and flexible manner (Joseph & Fellenstein, 2004). Entities of an eGovSM domain (public administrations and private service providers) share information and services with the e-government service marketplace of that domain according to the sharing rules defined in such a domain (which can be different from domain to domain). The other domains have neither direct knowledge nor access to these resources and information. They only know about and can refer to the eGovSM of that domain. The concept of network of eGovSM seems to suitable represent an interagency cooperation at European level (see Figure 7), where each country has its own eGovSM platform which with the other service providers (governmental agencies and private businesses) forms the eGovSM domain of such a country. EGovSMs of different countries are part of the whole network and thus collaborate in order to provide pan-European seamless services. Citizens, by interacting only with one of the eGovSM of the network (see Figure 7), can access all the services offered by the whole network. This concept scales at a national level as well. For instance, different regions of the same country can implement their own eGovSM system. In this case each eGovSM domain contains agencies at local and regional levels, has its own, specific sharing rules, and collaborates with the other regional-level eGovSM domains in order to provide seamless services at the national level.

The Case of Provisional Driving License Delivery

To further illustrate the application of the developed framework, we used it to apply the concept of e-government service marketplace for the delivery of a Provisional Driving License in the Italian context. The case study is summarized to illustrate the main features of the framework and should not be considered a complete and exhaustive presentation of the e-government service marketplace functional model.

For any kind of government service there are a plethora of official forms that citizens are requested to fill in; moreover each form has its own prerequisites and routing cycle, each with its own fees. As a result, a simple service like the delivery of Provisional Driving License becomes a quite complicated and time-expensive task requiring citizens to move to several governmental agencies, providing the same information multiple times.

The Provisional Driving License (named "Foglio Rosa" in Italian) is a document issued by the Department of Motor Vehicle (responsible for delivering all services concerning driving licenses and vehicles) that allows a citizen to take driving lessons on the road for a six-month period. After the citizen has been issued the Provisional Driving License, the citizen has to pass the Final Driving Theory and Practical Driving Test to obtain the Full Driving License. The delivery of the Provisional Driving License has some conditions attached to it:

- The citizen must be 18 years old or over
- The citizen must exhibit an identity card or a passport
- The citizen must hold "moral requirements" (e.g., not to be a criminal, etc.)
- The citizen must provide a medical report (including an eyesight report)
- The citizen must pay the appropriate fees
- The citizen must provide two passport-type photographs

The traditional procedure for the delivery of such service requires the citizen to move to the postal office to pay the fees, to the hospital for medical check-up, the photos, and eventually to the Department of Motor Vehicle with all the previously collected documents and information and apply for obtaining a document ("Foglio Bianco") that allows the candidate to drive while waiting for the delivery of the Provisional Driving License. Once moral requirements are checked and confirmed the Provisional Driving License is issued and delivered to the citizen (which has to move to the Department of Motor Vehicle again). The eGovSM allows easing the whole procedure by reducing interaction between citizen and agencies and providing this service as a unique transaction to the citizen. Case handling, decision, and delivery of the requested service are completely treated by eGovSM via the Web by

Figure 8. Provisional driving licence delivery: Sequence diagram

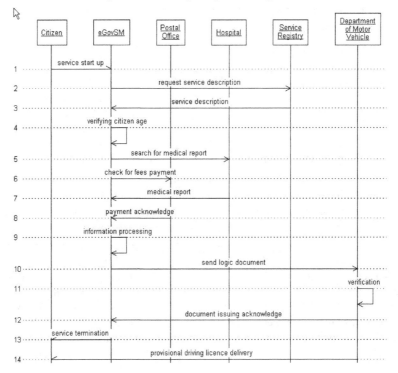

integrating participating agencies (hospital, postal office, department of motor vehicle, and so on). The citizen wishing to apply for a Provisional Driving License accesses the eGovSM via the portal and applies for the service (see Figure 8). The request is handled by the eGovSM that, as a first step, retrieves the document ("Process Descriptor") describing the entire process of Provisional Driving License from a dedicated registry. This document describes in a machine-readable way tasks and requirements that have to be executed and satisfied in order to deliver the service (for instance, verifying whether the applying citizen is 18 years old and over or holds moral requirements).

By following the instructions contained in the Process Descriptor, eGovSM checks whether the citizen is of age, whether the citizen has done the medical examination and payed the fees and, if this is not the case, eGovSM stops the process and informs the citizen about requirements that have not been satisfied or missing information.

Public administrations involved in the process of service delivery are located by processing the information contained in the citizen identifier (for instance, the "birthplace" information contained in the identifier tells the system the origin region of the citizen and allows focusing information search on specific governmental agencies). Once all requirements are satisfied and required tasks performed the eGovSM system provides the Department of Motor Vehicle with the logic document, that is, an electronic version of the final document to be delivered (meanwhile the citizen is informed by the eGovSM about the progress of the request). The Department of Motor Vehicle has to check the validity of the document, inform the eGovSM about it, and issue the final document to the citizen.

Analysis of Benefits of eGovSM Seamless Service Delivery

A shared and seamless service delivery has a major impact on e-government evolution process and several types of interconnected benefits can be identified. More specifically the impact of the concept of e-government service marketplace can be analyzed and evaluated according to three different perspectives:

- The social perspective
- The economical perspective
- The technical perspective

In fact, the use of information and communication technologies in public administration in order to improve service delivery process has tangible and intangible benefits from the social, economic, and technical points of view (Figure 9).

Figure 9. Impact of the e-government service marketplace

The Social Perspective

The social perspective refers to benefits which are perceived from citizens (i.e., customers of the service) or civil servants (i.e., the persons who are involved in or responsible for guaranteeing a quality service delivery to the customers). According to this point of view, an increased user's satisfaction is the main objective to reach. The user's satisfaction can be expressed in terms of:

- **Improved quality of information:** The user-friendliness and citizen-oriented approach for service delivery allow improving the way citizens interact with government agencies, making it easier for them to obtain the services they need without being concerned with "administrative" details which are not relevant for them.

- **Reduced administrative burdens:** The use of ICT in the provision of public services makes it possible to significantly reduce the administrative burdens for citizens that use these services. Citizens will have neither to move from an administration to another one wasting time and money, nor to provide the same information time and time again.

- **Improved access and accessibility:** Access and accessibility are two key issues enabling citizens to obtain online information. *Access* refers to the real possibility of consulting or acquiring government information electronically. *Accessibility* is the ease with which one can actually make use of the possibility of consulting government information electronically. Therefore accessibility emphasizes the perspective of end users of government information and their capacity to find, digest, and use relevant information. Improving the accessibility of online information can be achieved in terms of specific life events, that is, classifying and presenting services to citizens according to events that make sense in their lives.

- **Improved service level:** A major benefit of seamless service delivery is the improved service level. More precisely in terms of increased time availability and flexibility (24/7 availability, multichannel delivery) and transparency (availability of more detailed and complete information about the service). Using a Web-based system for service delivery allows citizens to access the services wherever they are and according to their device (PDA, PC, mobile phone, etc.). Improving service delivery is a means for decreasing time in completing transaction and reducing cost associated with citizen to government interactions. Moreover it allows improving civil servants work; it allows improving efficiency of civil servants by automating tedious and repetitive tasks and reducing cost of transactions for government processes. The rise in the use of online services will shorten queues at the counters, thus easing the work of the reception staff and enabling them to provide a better service.

- **Personalized service:** Increased capabilities for custom-made services (i.e., the possibility to customize electronic service delivery). Personalized services will inform citizens about the progress of their request or they will allow citizens to adapt to their needs the home page of the e-government service marketplace portal.

- **Multichannel service delivery:** The need to preserve choice is fundamental to any customer-focused strategy. Providing alternative delivery channels (for instance, phone and kiosk) and indeed choice of online access points improve chances of ensuring access and effectiveness. The e-government service marketplace mainly provides service via a Web-based interface (i.e., it requires an access via personal PC or dedicated kiosk), but it can be easily configured to provide information on other alternative channels thanks to the use of a model-driven specification approach.

- **Improved support to citizen mobility:** Since the integration of Europe into a single market, citizens of the European Community member states should be able to migrate from one European country to another with as few problems as possible. Yet, mobile European citizens have to deal with time and money consuming administrative procedures. If the collecting of required documents costs a lot of time and money for citizens in their home country, for foreign citizens, the situation is even worse. The concept of a network of e-government service marketplaces capable of cooperating across national borders can handle this problem and facilitate the migration of citizens.

The Economical Perspective

The economic perspective refers to economic benefits which can be obtained at the public administration. According to this point of view, the e-government service marketplace allows for:

- **Enriched public service:** The concept of e-government service marketplace provides an open environment where commercial activities can coexist with government services. This way the marketplace represents a common access point to "enriched governmental services." For instance if a citizen needs a driving license document, the eGovSM provides not only the "getting your driving license" service (public service) but also the service "driving school subscription" (private service).

- **Improved public-private partnership:** Public-private integration can improve e-government by direct provision to end users of government services. This integration can add value for both parties. Integration with nongovernment activity complements seamless government services. Public-private partnerships can help integrate and improve the delivery of government services both to benefit customers and to increase efficiency. So public-private partnerships can be, and have to be seen as, a means not only to share risk and investment, to bypass budgetary constraints, or to access specialized skills (for instance, for software development) but also to provide better services to citizens, thus maximizing benefits of e-government.

- **Reduced cost:** The automation of service delivery process and the use of electronic communication with citizens can lead to significant cost savings. The use of ICT enables the public sector to increase its services processing and delivery capabilities, while requiring less time and fewer personnel. This way a rebalancing from tedious and repetitive tasks towards more customer-oriented activities of civil servant work can be possible. Moreover according to the concept of e-government marketplace each agency is not obliged to implement an instance of the system with clear economic advantages and cost savings.

- **Decreased budgetary barriers:** Budgetary constraints can work against e-government seamless service delivery implementation especially for small agencies where the costs for a system development can be prohibitive. The concept of e-government service marketplace, as it does not require each administration to develop and implement an instance of the system architecture, represents a suitable solution for different-budget contexts.

- **Reduced process time:** The digitalization of public services can also significantly reduce the time it takes to process and deliver a service (process time), therefore saving precious time for public administration officials. Because data can be submitted electronically by customers and shared between different organizations, service information can be reviewed online in real time, allowing a greater responsiveness on the part of the administration.

- **Improved quality of information and information supply:** The direct input of data in electronic format by public service users reduces the number of errors, thus decreasing the number of citizen enquires or complaints, and makes it possible to build quality management information systems. Furthermore, the shared use of information and databases, made possible by electronic networks can also improve the quality of information and data supply.

- **Increased efficiency:** Improved information supply and service delivery contribute to increase the efficiency (i.e., the capability to convert resources and inputs into effects and impacts) of public service delivery. Tasks and costs can be more efficiently distributed, both within and between public sector agencies.

- **Increased economic competitiveness:** Seamless service delivery can provide a major contribution to increasing economic competitiveness at local, regional, national, or international levels. By streamlining bureaucratic procedures and increasing public sector efficiency, it plays a significant role in raising the productivity levels in the economy as a whole (IDABC eGovernment Observatory, 2005).

The Technical Perspective

The technical perspective refers to benefits the information and communication technologies bring to the public administration. The main advantages the concept of e-government service marketplace carries can be expressed in terms of:

- **Improved cooperation:** The concept of e-government service marketplace facilitates the cooperation at the technical level between agencies allowing seamless service delivery based on a shared service operating model. The e-government marketplace concept has the potential to improve collaboration across agencies and organizations but there are a number of regulatory barriers to pass beyond (for instance, accountability rules, designed to ensure responsible use of public resources by clearly identifying who does what, can impede collaboration as it may be unclear who is accountable for shared service delivery).

- **Shareable infrastructure:** A lack of compatible infrastructure between agencies can impede interagency collaboration, but the expense of implementing modern infrastructure can be a major barrier to the implementation of e-government initiatives. A shared infrastructure among agencies is one way of overcoming this problem.

- **Improved interoperability:** The concept of e-government service marketplace facilitates the interoperability between agencies according to two different aspects: integration of legacy systems and flexibility and independence from a specific technology.

- **Reuse of information:** Information is not duplicated multiple times and collected at different locations but it is reused when needed, thus avoiding useless replication of data and promoting decentralization of information.

- **Integration of legacy system:** The use of a service oriented paradigm allows integrating heterogeneous legacy systems. Distributed and independent administrations participate to the marketplace activity by exchanging services that provide a complete abstraction of the legacy systems.

- **Reduced process time:** The availability of electronic data makes it possible to automate and "e-enable" key steps of the decision-making and service delivery process.

- **Increased efficiency and flexibility:** On the one hand according to the marketplace concept each administration can participate and join the system according to different levels of integration and interoperability. This way allows creating a network of collaboration between different administrations while respecting their technical and political capabilities. Clearly the administration that evolves and improves its services has the ability to strengthen its participation to the e-government service marketplace by increasing its level of cooperation. On the other hand the concept of e-government service marketplace modeled in a technology independent way allows the development of different, yet interoperable, systems. Moreover its generality makes possible its development and utilization in different countries.

- **Evolution over time and scalability:** The concept of e-government marketplace allows a gradual participation and integration of each administration. The multiple subscription profiles it provides make possible for each administration to join the marketplace according to its technical and political capabilities.

Future Trends and Open Issues

As the field of seamless service delivery continues to grow and develop, much research should be done to fully take advantage of innovative approaches and technologies for e-service provision. Several pending or emerging issues that should be better investigated include the following:

- **Investigate emerging paradigm:** For distributed and shared collaboration. Given the high speed at which services are growing and changing continuously, shared and seamless service delivery is at the basis of grid service concept. According to the definition of grid, within a virtual organization it is possible to use in a flexible and shared manner distributed and heterogeneous resources all over the world in order to provide seamless, yet very complex, services. The concept of e-government service marketplace can be extended and enriched to make it more efficient in a distributed and heterogeneous world has the public sector is. The integration of grid concept can bring several advantages by making the discovery of services more dynamic, efficient, flexible, and distributed on a world-scale basis.

- **Measure performance:** Several performance measures should be used to evaluate efficacy and success of shared infrastructure for seamless e-service provision. For instance the amount of staff time to develop and set up such an infrastructure, the number of accesses on the site, the number of downloads, the number of problems resolved should be carefully measured and analyzed (Pavlichev & David Garson, 2004).

- **Provide legislative support for seamless service:** As previously stated collaboration between agencies for seamless service delivery is not only a technical issue; in order to promote and support interadministration data exchange, service sharing, and account-ability, an adequate and accurate legislative support is required. For instance digital signature mechanism for the future development of seamless service delivery needs to be adopted and integrated in present systems. The evolution of the law, in order to remove regulatory barriers to the development of seamless and shared services, is a fundamental component of the e-government development process. The development of seamless service delivery should be supported by a special legislation on shared and integrated services.

- **Measures improvement in citizen life:** It is crucial to research the effects of seam-less e-service delivery and what differences it is making in the citizens' lives. It is fundamental to understand whether citizens find it too difficult to use or whether they do not experience lower costs or more effective government. Improvement in citizen life could be measured in terms of increased level of citizen satisfaction with government and government services, increased level of citizen trust in government, or costs saved by seamless service provision (in terms of money and time).

- **Account for privacy issues:** Further efforts to continue to develop policies and techni-cal solutions around the key areas of security, authentication, and data storage in order to preserve and protect privacy of individual citizens' data are needed. In fact, if not handled correctly, this issue, more than any other, has the potential to undermine the support and development of e-government and seamless government initiatives.

Conclusion

Seamless delivery of public service is a fundamental challenge e-government has to deal with. As public services are very complex ones, in order to provide seamless service at the transaction level, different and multiple requirements, from both citizen and public administration point of view, have to be satisfied. The emerging concept of e-government service marketplace proposes a general functional model for shared and interoperable services enabling integration between agencies both at horizontal and vertical levels. This chapter has reviewed the requirements for seamless service delivery from both citizen and public administration points of view. It has presented a general functional model for seamless, citizen-oriented service delivery (eGovSM), and its main functionalities. The impact and advantages of this concept on the three main axes (social, economic, and technical) have been discussed as well. The chapter ends providing some insights on future trends and open issues about seamless services delivery and enabling systems.

References

Accenture. (2004). *eGovernment leadership: High performance, maximum value* (Technical report). Retrieved April 28, 2006, from http://www.accenture.com/xdoc/en/industries/government/gove_egov_value.pdf

Accenture. (2005). *Driving high performance in government: Maximizing the value of public-sector shared services* (Technical report). Retrieved April 28, 2006, from http://www.accenture.com/xd/xd.asp?it=enweb&xd=industries%5Cgovernment%5Cinsights%5Cmaximizing_value.xml

ANAO. (1999). *Electronic service delivery, including Internet use, by commonwealth government agencies* (Technical report). Retrieved April 28, 2006, from http://www.egov.vic.gov.au/pdfs/rpt18-00.pdf

AOEMA. (2004). *E-government from a user's perspective* (Technical report). Retrieved April 28, 2006, from http://www.apectel29.gov.hk/download/bfsg_14.pdf

Austrian Web site. (n.d.). Retrieved April 28, 2006, from http://www.help.gv.at/

Baldoni, R., Mecella, M., Contenti, M., & Termini, A. (2003). *Report on EU-PUBLI.com architecture prototype. Deliverable.* Retrieved April 28, 2006, from http://research.unisoft.gr/Eupublicomsite/workspace1/deliverables.htm

Belgium Web site. (n.d.). Retrieved April 28, 2006, from http://www.belgium.be

Capgemini. (2005). *Online availability of public services: How is Europe progressing?* Web based survey on electronic public service. Retrieved April 28, 2006, from http://europa. eu.int/information_society/eeurope/2005/doc/highlights/whats_new/capgemini4.pdf

Daum, B. (2003, March). *Modeling business objects with XML schema.* Morgan Kaufmann.

Dipartimento per l'Innovazione e le Tecnologie. (2002). *Front-office e servizi di e-government per cittadini ed imprese* (Technical report). Retrieved April 28, 2006, from http://www. innovazione.gov.it/ita/intervento/normativa/allegati/avviso_allegato1.pdf

European Commission. (2003). *Linking up Europe: The importance of interoperability for eGovernment services* (Technical report). Retrieved April 28, 2006, from http://www. csi.map.es/csi/pdf/interoperabilidad_1675.pdf

Foster, I., Kesselman, C., & Tuecke, S. (2001). The anatomy of the grid: Enabling scalable virtual organization. *International Journal of High Performance Computing Applications, 15*(3), 200-222.

Glushko, R. J. (2003, September 24-25). Document engineering. *Symposium on Coevolution of Technology Business Innovations*, San Jose, CA.

Halligan, J., & Moore, T. (2004). *E-government in Australia: The challenges of moving to integrated services* (Technical report). Retrieved April 28, 2006, from http://unpan1. un.org/intradoc/groups/public/documents/un/unpan019249.pdf

IDABC eGovernment Observatory. (2005). *The impact of e-government on competitiveness and jobs* (Technical report). Retrieved April 28, 2006, from http://europa.eu.int/id-abc/en/document/3851/254

Joseph, J., & Fellenstein, C. (2004). *Grid computing.* IBM Press.

Layne, K., & Lee, J. (2001). Developing fully functional e-government: A four stage model. *Government Information Quarterly, 18*(2), 122-136.

Life Event Portal. (n.d.). Retrieved April 28, 2006, from http://www.oasis.gov.ie/siteindex/ by_life_event.html

Ministère de la Fonction publique, de la Réforme de l'Etat et de l'Aménagement du territoire Secrétariat d'Etat à la Réforme de l'Etat. (2003). *Plan stratégique de l'administration électronique (PSAE) 2004-2007* (Technical report). Retrieved April 28, 2006, from http://www.adae.gouv.fr/article.php3?id_article=315

Mugellini, E., Abou Khaled, O., Pettenati, M. C., & Kuonen, P. (2005, March 29-April 1). eGovSM metadata model: Towards a flexible, interoperable and scalable eGovernment service marketplace. In *Proceedings of the IEEE Conference on E-Technology, E-Commerce and E-Service, EEE05*, Hong Kong, China (pp. 618-621).

Mugellini, E., Abou Khaled, O., Pettenati, M. C., & Franco, P. (2005, March 2-4). eGovernment service marketplace: Architecture and implementation. In *Proceedings of the TED Conference on eGovernment*, Bolzano, Italy (pp. 193-204).

OECD e-Government Studies. (2004). *The e-government imperative.* OECD Press.

Pappa, D., Kavadias, G., Spanos, E., Tambouris, E., Hoholis, D., Erkkilä, T., et al. (2003). *Platform integration and deployment report, description of the trials. Deliverable.* Retrieved April 28, 2006, from http://www.egov-project.org/gr/deliverables.htm

Pavlichev, A., & David Garson, G. (2004). *Digital government: Principles and best practices.* Hershey, PA: Idea Group Publishing.

Persson, A., & Goldkuhl, G. (2005, February 14-15). Stage-models of public e-services — Investigating conceptual foundations. In *Proceedings of the 2nd Scandinavian Workshop on e-Government*, Copenhagen, Denmark.

Riedl, R. (2001). *The conceptual system architecture of the FASME Project. Deliverable.* Retrieved April 28, 2006, from http://www.ifi.unizh.ch/egov/Deliverable_6.1.pdf

Ronaghan, S. A. (2001). *Benchmarking e-government: A global perspective* (Technical report). Retrieved April 28, 2006, from http://www.nettelafrica.org/docs/NetTel%20 Safari@the%20Equator%20(Uganda%202003)/Benchmarkingegovt.pdf

Statskontoret. (2000). *The 24/7 agency: Criteria for 24/7 agencies in the networked public administration* (Technical report). Retrieved April 28, 2006, from http://www.statsk-ontoret.se/upload/Publikationer/2000/200041.pdf

Suh, S. Y. (2003). *Promoting citizen participation in e-government* (Technical report). Retrieved April 28, 2006, from http://unpan1.un.org/intradoc/groups/public/docu-ments/UN/UNPAN020076.pdf

Vintar, M., Kunstelj, M., & Leben, A. (2002, April 25-27). Delivering better quality public services through life-event portals. In *Proceedings of the 10th NISPAcce Annual Conference*, Cracow, Poland.

World Wide Web Consortium. (n.d.). *XML schema part 0: Primer.* Retrieved April 28, 2006, from http://www.w3.org/TR/xmlschema-0/

Chapter III

Automating Governmental Cross-Agency Processes Using Web Service Orchestration:
A Gap Analysis

Jeffrey Gortmaker, Delft University of Technology, The Netherlands

Marijn Janssen, Delft University of Technology, The Netherlands

Abstract

In response to the demand for better service provisioning, governments from all over the world are looking for technologies to automate their cross-agency processes. This chapter investigates the applicability of Web service orchestration for the automation of governmental cross-agency service delivery processes by investigating a case study of a business counter. Our case study shows that Web service orchestration using BPEL4WS is a feasible technology for automating governmental cross-agency service-delivery processes, but also shows a gap between the capabilities of Web service orchestration technology and the organizational arrangements needed for automating the processes. We identified three organizational issues that at least need to be addressed before governments can profit fully from the advantages of Web service orchestration technology: (1) ensuring correct and in-time execution of business processes; (2) information sharing; and (3) responsibility and accountability.

Introduction

As an increasing number of governmental service-delivery processes involve multiple (semi-) autonomous agencies, a huge challenge for governments from all over the world is designing their cross-agency processes. This is caused by the inherent structure of public administration and by the need to become more customer-centric. First, the fragmented nature of governments (e.g., Wimmer, 2002) causes the activities that make up a single, atomic governmental service, for example, a liquor license, often involve several governmental agencies. Under the influence of governmental reforms, such as New Public Management (NPM) (e.g., Hood, 1991), governments became more decentralized, leading to more departments, agencies, or even external parties involved in service-delivery processes. An example is a liquor license, which includes tasks to be performed by several municipal departments, the fire department, the justice department, and the police.

The second main reason for cross-agency processes is the aim to reduce the administrative burdens, or "red tape," for citizens and businesses and to become more citizen centric (e.g., Cabinet Office, 2000; Dutch Government, 2003, 2004; Ongaro, 2004). The clients of the government, citizens, and businesses expect the public sector to increase their attention on customer service, just as businesses have done in response to the rise of Internet technologies (Donnelly, Wisniewski, Dalrymple, & Curry, 1995; McIvor, McHugh, & Cadden, 2002). This requires governments to rethink their service offerings, for example, start the joint offering of a permit to build a house and a permit to tear down the old building in place. Several (semi-) autonomous agencies working together to reach a common goal, here to deliver a service, is often called "joined-up government" (Ling, 2002; Pollitt, 2003).

Crucial to the improvement of governmental service delivery and the reduction of administrative burdens is the automation of cross-agency service-delivery processes. To offer seamlessly integrated services, the service-delivery processes of the different subservices should be coordinated. The cross-governmental collaboration in the delivery of services to its citizens is getting more and more attention and is one of the main issues in national e-government strategies (Accenture, 2005).

A promising technology that offers many advantages to the problem of automating cross-agency processes is Web service orchestration (Gortmaker, Janssen & Wagenaar, 2004). Web service technology is based upon the notion of a service-oriented architecture (SOA), an architectural paradigm according to which application functionality is not provided by large monolithic information systems, but is instead created by using relatively small-grained components which can be invoked as Web services. SOA provides the ability to register, discover, and use services, where the architecture is dynamic by nature. Web service orchestration coordinates Web services by means of a process flow in which the Web services are invoked according to a predefined sequence. Automating cross-agency business processes using Web service orchestration offers flexibility in business processes, so changes in law can be supported quickly. Moreover functionality encapsulated in components can be reused in various business processes and investments in legacy systems can be leveraged (Gortmaker et al., 2004).

The objective of this chapter is to investigate the feasibility of Web service orchestration technology for the automation of cross-agency processes, based on a case study of cross-governmental service-delivery processes at a business counter. First, we present an overview of Web service orchestration technology and introduce the business counter and its processes. Thereafter, we present a prototype to demonstrate the feasibility of Web service orchestration for the automation of cross-agency processes, and conclude that several important organizational-related issues need to be addressed when employing Web service orchestration for supporting cross-agency business processes.

Research Approach

In order to investigate the feasibility of Web service orchestration, both a literature review into Web services and Web service orchestration, and a case study were conducted.

The case study was conducted at the business counter for the hotel and catering industry at a medium-sized municipality in the Netherlands. This case was chosen because it is regarded as a best practice in the Netherlands as an account-manager-operated one-stop-shop. At the business counter, we analyzed five representative cross-agency service-delivery processes in detail: two processes that are needed for pouring liquor, a license to place gambling machines, an environmental permit, and a license for organizing special events. The processes were analyzed and a gap analysis was made by conducing semistructured interviews with policy makers, operational managers, back office employees, IT staff, customer representatives, and account managers from the business counter. Due to the explorative nature of this case study, interviews were conducted in a semistructured fashion, without a strict interview protocol, but with the use of some open questions to start and guide the interviews. A total of 12 people were interviewed between one and three times. Also, relevant memos, strategy statements, Web sites, and internal reports were studied.

Web Service Orchestration Technology

In this section we present a brief overview of Web service orchestration technology and related protocols. A more in-depth presentation of SOA, the Web service technology stack and Web service orchestration can be found in Gortmaker, Janssen, and Wagenaar (2005) and Janssen, Gortmaker, and Wagenaar (2006). Web service orchestration technology is based upon the notion of a *service-oriented architecture* (SOA). Due to its loosely-coupled nature, the SOA-paradigm is very suitable for orchestrating service-delivery processes that run across relatively autonomous agencies. Agencies can provide services to other agencies that can invoke them as subservices in their business processes. A SOA makes it possible to quickly assemble new compound services out of existing services.

Web services are an important technology for realizing SOA. Web services are a technology that enables the provisioning of functionality, on an application level, or on a business level, by means of a standardized interface in a way that they are easily invoked via Internet protocols. Web services are said to be modular, accessible, well-described, implementation-independent, and interoperable (Fremantle, Weerawarana, & Khalaf, 2002).

Web service technology consists of a collection of protocols needed to implement a SOA. This "Web service stack" first defines basic technologies, such as HTTP, XML, and XML schema for the creating of documents and communication between the different Web services. The basic functionality of a SOA is provided by the message and description layers. The interface of a Web service is defined by means of Web Service Definition Language (WSDL), and the messages by which the services can be invoked are defined using SOAP (simple object access protocol). To make it easier to discover existing Web services, a service provider can register its Web services in a Web service directory through UDDI (Universal Description, Discovery and Integration).

Higher on the Web services stack are the standards for service composition, combining two or more services together to obtain a new composite service. These are different ways to create composite services. One form of constrained aggregation is coordinating them by means of a process flow that invokes the different subservices. Service composition using process flows comes in two flavors: Web service orchestration and Web service choreography. The difference between these two forms is subtle, and they are therefore sometimes erroneously considered as synonyms. There is, however, a major distinction between the two. Web service choreography specifies only the possible sequences between the public message exchanges between different agencies. Web service orchestration requires that the whole process needed for offering the service is defined at one place. This is an executable process, defined from the perspective of one participant, and offers an overview of all internal and external Web services that need to be invoked in the process.

As choreography does not require the responsibility for the whole process to be located at one place, it is less suitable for the coordination of cross-agency service delivery processes. It can, however, be used for coordinating interactions between different agencies within the service-delivery process.

Wohed, Van der Aalst, Dumas, and Hofstede (2003) define an executable business process as specifying "the execution order between a number of constituent activities, the partners involved, the messages exchanged between these partners, and the fault and exception handling mechanisms." In Web service orchestration, these activities are typically performed by Web services that are invoked from a process by means of their standardized Web service interface.

Many competing proposals for process specification languages, including ebXML BPSS, WSCI, WSFL, XLANG, BPML, have been made, but the standard language for Web service orchestration is BPEL4WS, Business Process Execution Language for Web Services (Andrews et al., 2003), BPEL for short, a specification developed by IBM and Microsoft, based on their respective standards WSFL and XLANG. BPEL can be viewed as a layer on top of WSDL, as it uses the properties of Web services that are specified by means of WSDL.

A process that is specified in BPEL consists of two types of activities: basic activities that specify the tasks that are to be performed, such as *receive* an invocation, *reply* to the service requester, *wait* for a specified amount of time, and structured activities as *switch* for conditional branching, *while* for repeating parts of the business process, and *sequence* for performing tasks in parallel. The structured activities determine the structure, or the sequencing of the process, and the basic activities determine what happens in the process, for example, the invocation of a WS, receiving a message from a Web service, and so forth.

Business Counter

Although the business counter for the hotel and catering industry is viewed as a best practice as it consists of account managers functioning as one-stop shops and passing permit applications through to the back office, in the current situation, there is hardly any ICT support. A model describing the high-level interactions between the actors involved is depicted in Figure 1. For almost all permit applications, the applicant has to schedule an appointment with the business counter, after which the account manager coordinates the interactions with the back office and the other agencies. Many of the permit requests exceed the desired lead times.

The entrepreneurs, the customers of the business counter, are often bound to the opening hours of their own business and face difficulties having to meet the openings hours of the business counters. Moreover, they would like to have a faster response time and insight into the status of their requests, as this enables the further development of their business. The city council recognizes the entrepreneurs' needs and wants to know if Web service orchestration technology is suitable for improving the cross-agency processes.

Figure 1. Actors and interactions in liquor-licensing process

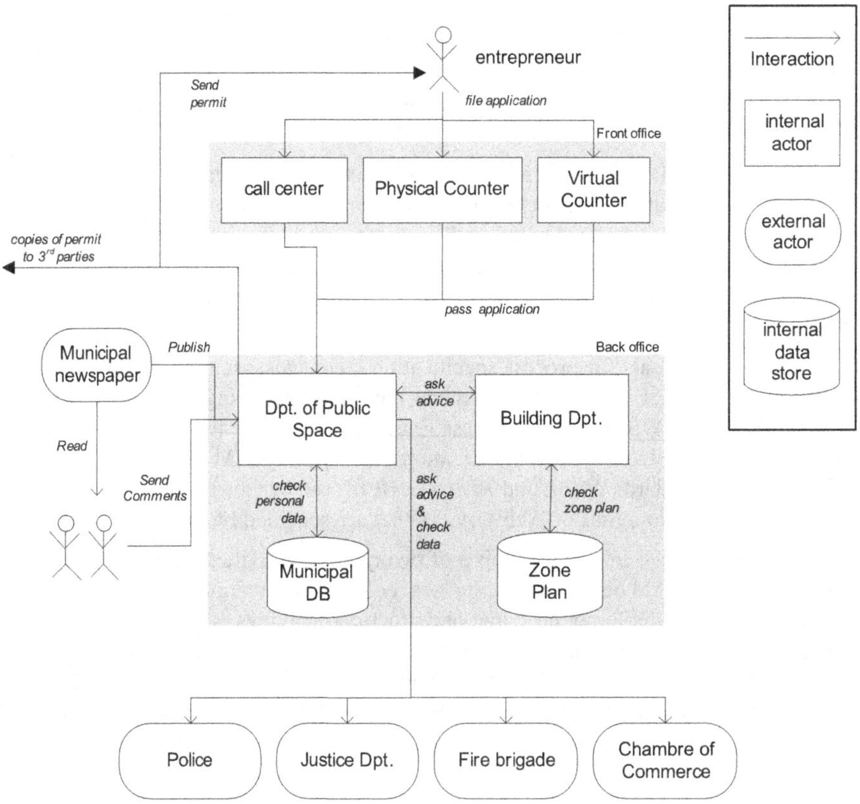

A liquor license[1] is one of the most important permits for the hotel and catering industry. Every restaurant or café that pours alcohol is obliged to apply for a license. For requesting a license, an entrepreneur can contact the business counter. After this first contact, an intake interview is planned, where civil servants of the business counter, the back office, and sometimes of other involved agencies are present. After this meeting, the entrepreneur has to fill in an application form and return it, together with the needed official documents, for example, a floor plan.

Hereafter, the name, address, and place of residence of the applicant are checked. If the applicant lives in the municipality, this activity is performed by the back office, otherwise a request has to be sent to another municipality. Next, the justice department is asked for advice; they check whether the applicant has a criminal record or not. The police are also asked for advice about the applicant, but look for "softer" evidence, for example, fines, crimes that were not proven, or for which someone has not been sentenced yet. Also the fire department is asked for advice concerning the construction and safety of the building. Finally, the building department has to check whether the building meets all legal requirements.

On the basis of these advices, the back office employee draws up a license, or a letter stating the reasons for refusing the license. Copies of the issues license are sent to third parties such as the police, the chamber of commerce, and the fire department.

Web Service Orchestration
at the Business Counter

To determine the feasibility of Web service orchestration for supporting cross-agency processes, a prototype of automating the liquor-licensing process using BPEL4WS was built. Figure 2 shows a graphical representation of a part of the cross-agency process implemented in BPEL. As real-life BPEL processes are usually very complex and consist of many elements, only part of the process could be shown. Also several process steps, mostly concerning the assigning of variables, were omitted from the picture. The figure contains a screenshot from Oracle JDeveloper BPEL Designer, the process designer belonging to their orchestration server, Oracle BPEL Process Manager (Oracle, 2004).

On the left of Figure 2 the file menu is shown, the BPEL process constructs are shown on the middle and right part of the figure. The process is started (see call out 2 in Figure 2) after the applicant initiates the BPEL process (1) by filling in an online application form on the client. First, an internal Web service (4) to check whether the form is correctly filled in, the "InputCheckService," is invoked (3). When not all fields are filled in correctly (5), an error-message is prompted back to the applicant (6). When the application is complete, two simultaneous subprocesses are started (7): the application is published in the municipal newspaper (8) (which was not implemented in this prototype) and a Web service at the police (10), "Advice_Police," is invoked (9) to get information about the criminal record of the applicant. Only a Web service providing access to the business processes of the police is shown in this picture, but every agency or organization, the justice department, the fire department, or the chamber of commerce that can offer Web service access to its business

Figure 2. Screenshot of BPEL-editor showing part of the liquor-licensing process

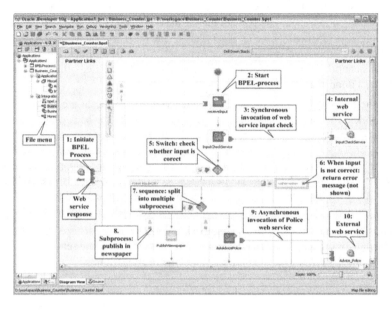

processes can be linked into a cross-agency process in similar fashion. The complex decision-making process on the license request is also not shown in the figure.

Gap Analysis

The prototype of the liquor-licensing process demonstrates that Web service orchestration using BPEL4WS is a feasible technology for automating the cross-agency processes at the business counter.

Although Web service orchestration is a suitable technology for automating governmental cross-agency processes, we found that several organizational-oriented issues need to be addressed when implementing Web services orchestration for automating cross-agency processes. We categorized the main issues into three categories: (1) ensuring the correct and in-time execution of subprocesses, (2) facilitating the sharing of information among the agencies, and (3) allocating responsibilities and ensuring accountability among agencies participating in the cross-agency processes. These three categories of issues will be discussed in more detail in the following subsections.

Correct and In-Time Execution of Business Processes

One of the main issues that should be dealt with when automating business processes is to ensure that every subservice in the cross-agency service-delivery process is fully completed in time. This aspect is further complicated by the fact that in cross-agency processes there is no hierarchical control of one agency over all the other agencies.

At the business counter, we found that guarding the lead times of the overall liquor-licensing process is a major problem, as some of the required subservices sometimes take a long time to complete, or are even not completed at all.

This problem was mentioned many times during the interviews, by employees of the business counter, employees of the governmental back offices, but also by the customers, who were frustrated that obtaining a permit could take so much time. One of the customers stated that it took so much time for a liquor license to be obtained. Although there were formal lead times that needed to be met by the municipality, there were no direct sanctions on those lead times, such as is the case with certain building permits, which are automatically granted if the lead times are exceeded. From the interviews with the employees at the municipality it turned out that it was relatively easy to extend a deadline. Deadline extension was possible by simply sending a letter to the requester. These employees indicated that other agencies involved in the licensing process not reacting in time were the major cause of these delays. One striking example is checking the address of applicants that live in another municipality, which has to be performed by the other municipality. This simple check can in practice take as long as three weeks or more, and can take as much as four requests before an answer can be expected. As there is no formal way of requesting the other municipalities to perform this task in time, controlling the lead times is difficult to accomplish.

A solution to this problem could be ensuring correct and in-time execution of every subservice by agreeing upon service levels between agencies, but simply agreeing beforehand upon service levels between the business counter and the different agencies is not sufficient. The service levels need to be constantly monitored, and mechanisms that respond when a service fails, when a service does not produce the required answer, or does not answer in time, should be put in place.

Information Sharing

Each actor has a registry storing different kinds of data. Data were sometimes found to be inconsistent between registries; that is, address data are updated by one agency but not by the others. Changes in data necessary for executing the activities of agencies should be immediately shared among these actors. The sharing of information between governmental agencies can also help to avoid opportunistic behavior of permit requesters. If one agency or department rejects a permit they might try to acquire the permit at another agency or department. Sharing of information should result in consistent decision making. Another advantage of information sharing is that entrepreneurs only have to fill in the personal data that has been changed in time or has to be added newly. When there are only two agencies involved, information sharing is still relatively straightforward. When multiple agencies that all use and update each others information, as is often the case with cross-agency service-delivery processes, are involved, this becomes more difficult.

In the case study at the business counter many issues related to inadequate information sharing were found. First, the customers complained about having to fill in the same information again every time applying for another license. Inconsistencies among different governmental databases were also found, as one customer stated that his business was registered under at least three different names in the databases of the tax office, the municipality, and the chamber of commerce. The employees at the business counter and the back office indicated that sometimes it was difficult to obtain a consistent view on the status of an application. When a customer was, for example, requested for additional information by the back office employee, the employee at the business counter would not always know this the next time he had a meeting with that customer. In other words, there was not something like an integral customer view. According to the employees at the municipality, that was also noticed by some "customers," as customers had the tendency to just ask another employee the same question when they got a negative answer from the first employee. Furthermore it was interesting to notice that the municipality did not have an overview of the licenses and permits granted in the past. If an overview was asked about, for example, the number of restaurants in the municipality, this was answered by asking the fire department, as they had their own database which apparently was more accurate. Even within the municipality, a different back office, such as the building department, had its own database. This database was also not linked to other databases within the municipality.

Currently, many of these problems were solved informally, by telephone, or by face-to-face communication. In case of the automation of these cross-agency processes, this ad-hoc way of solving problems is not possible anymore and a more robust information-sharing mechanism should be put in place. The issue of information sharing will become even more important when in 2007 a new law comes into effect. This law states that citizens cannot be asked to provide personal data already available somewhere else within the government (Dutch Government, 2003).

A major issue with information sharing is privacy (e.g., Ali Eldin & Wagenaar, 2004). Not all agencies need access to all collected personal data. A typical example is the data resulting from the check of the criminal record of the applicant. This data is privacy-sensitive and not relevant for other agencies. Therefore it should not be provided to other parties, such as the building department and the chamber of commerce.

Accountability and Responsibility

A major issue with orchestration is the allocation of responsibilities among the many actors. Who takes the overall responsibility for monitoring the progress and ensuring the quality of the individual performers and products/services provided? Who is accountable for failure when different services provided by external partners are orchestrated into the business processes? Clearly defined responsibilities and formal organizational procedures stating how to deal with these questions need to be agreed upon by all agencies involved in order to avoid surprises and ad-hoc actions when trying to deal with them.

Accountability is an important requirement for the whole public sector (Bovens, 1998). For governmental service-delivery processes, it is especially important that the processes are transparent, nondiscriminating, and consistent, and that the decisions made in the process are well motivated, and made by the right person. Citizens and businesses no longer accept a black-box view of the service delivery process, but want to know what steps are taken in a decision-making process.

Ensuring accountability for governmental service-delivery processes running across different organizations is especially difficult, as it has to cope with different (semi-) autonomous agencies that are involved in the process.

Problems with accountability of the cross-agency processes at the business counter were the inability to provide status information or to account for lead times by employees in the front office, as they did not have enough information for this. But also back office employees that often had difficulties explaining why lead times were exceeded, or what the status of an application was. The division of responsibilities was not always clear between the business counter and the back office. This was partly because before the business counter was put in place, the employee at the business counter used to work at the back office. Also employees at the business counter and back office stated they were each others stand in, even though they both had direct colleagues who would be more logical candidates for this from an organizational point of view. This makes it difficult and not transparent to answer questions of customers about why a certain decision was taken, or whether the correct procedures were followed.

Ensuring accountability of cross-agency service-delivery processes requires specialized coordination mechanisms that ensure that the outcome of every process step is recorded, and that the overall process has run the way it was supposed to. No one should be able to change the stored information, as the information might be used as evidence.

Future Trends in Web Service Orchestration

Business process automation was traditionally the field of workflow management (WfM) and business processes consisted mostly of human performed activities without using functionality offered by information systems. Nowadays, a shift from WfM towards BPM (Business Process Management) is occurring, where on top of the design, configuration, and enactment of business processes, also a module to analyze these processes is present (Van der Aalst, Hofstede, & Weske, 2003). Although Web service orchestration is a very promising technology, the developments in the orchestration market go rapidly. Orchestration servers are incorporating more and more levels of functionality. It is expected that future BPM products will be more and more capable to deal with invoking Web services and that BPEL implementations will offer more and more advanced workflow capabilities, or in other words that the paradigms behind Web service technology and business process management (BPM) will merge slowly (Zhao & Cheng, 2005).

We also observe that the Enterprise Application Integration market is converging with the Workflow/BPM market with as a provisional climax the acquiring of leading BPM-vendor Staffware by Enterprise Application Integrator Tibco (Tibco, 2004). Considering the current momentum behind BPEL, other BPM vendors are expected to support BPEL in the near future, all resulting in large BPM or business process integration suites with BPEL support that are capable of coupling applications, processes, and businesses.

Conclusion

The objective of this chapter is to investigate the feasibility of Web service orchestration technology for the automation of cross-agency processes. Based on a case study of cross-governmental service-delivery processes at a business counter and using a prototype we conclude that Web services and Web service orchestration in particular have huge potential for the automation of governmental cross agency service-delivery processes. We also conclude that the following three categories of organizational-oriented issues need to be addressed when implementing Web services orchestration for automating cross-agency processes to leverage the full potential of Web service orchestration technology: (1) ensuring the correct and in-time execution of subprocesses, (2) facilitating the sharing of information among the agencies, and (3) allocating responsibilities and ensuring accountability among agencies participating in the cross-agency processes. Further research focuses on supporting public managers in dealing with these issues when designing their automated cross-agency processes.

References

Accenture. (2005). *Leadership in customer service: New expectations, new experiences.* Retrieved June 23, 2006, from ftp://www.accenture.com/NR/rdonlyres/F4CE4C8-9330-4450-BB4A-AF4E265C88D4/0/leadership_cust.pdf

Ali Eldin, A., & Wagenaar, R. (2004). *Towards users driven privacy control.* Paper presented at the 2004 IEEE International Conference on Systems, Man and Cybernetics, The Hague.

Andrews, T., Curbera, F., Dholakia, H., Goland, Y., Klein, J., Leymann, F., et al. (2003). *Business process execution language for Web services version 1.1.* Retrieved June 23, 2006, from ftp://www6.software.ibm.com/software/developer/library/ws-bpel.pdf

Bovens, M. (1998). *The quest for responsibility: Accountability and citzenship in complex organisations.* Cambridge: Cambridge University Press.

Cabinet Office. (2000). *E.gov: Electronic government services for the 21st century.* Retrieved April 28, 2006, from http://www.number-10.gov.uk/su/delivery/foreward/frames.htm

Donnelly, M., Wisniewski, M., Dalrymple, J. F., & Curry, A. C. (1995). Measuring service quality in local government: The SERVQUAL approach. *International Journal of Public Sector Management, 8*(7), 15-20.

Dutch Government. (2003). *Actieprogramma Andere Overheid* (Action Program New Government). Retrieved December 10, 2005, from http://www.elo.nl/elo/Images/actieprog_elekt_overheid_12-98_tcm70-16092.pdf

Dutch Government. (2004). *Meer ruimte voor ondernemers door minder lasten — Van lastenproductie naar lastenreductie* (More room for entrepreneurs by decreasing the administrative burdens — from production to reduction of administrative burdens). Retrieved December 10, 2005, from http://www.minfin.nl/IPAL04-100.DOC

Fremantle, P., Weerawarana, S., & Khalaf, R. (2002). Enterprise services. *Communications of the ACM, 45*(10), 77-82.

Gortmaker, J., Janssen, M., & Wagenaar, R. W. (2004). *The advantages of Web service orchestration in perspective.* Paper presented at the 6th International Conference of Electronic Commerce, ICEC 2004, Delft, The Netherlands.

Gortmaker, J., Janssen, M., & Wagenaar, R. W. (2005). *Towards requirements for a reference model for process orchestration in e-government.* Paper presented at the TED Conference on E-Government, Bolzano-Bozen, Italy.

Hood, C. (1991). A public management for all seasons? *Public Administration, 69*, 3-19.

Janssen, M., Gortmaker, J., & Wagenaar, R. W. (2006). Web service orchestration in public administration: Challenges, roles, and growth stages. *Information Systems Management, 23*(2), 44-45.

Ling, T. (2002). Delivering joined-up government in the UK: Dimensions, issues and problems. *Public Administration, 80*(4), 615-642.

McIvor, R., McHugh, M., & Cadden, C. (2002). Internet technologies: Supporting transparency in the public sector. *International Journal of Public Sector Management, 15*(3), 170-187.

Ongaro, E. (2004). Process management in the public sector: The experience of one-stop shops in Italy. *International Journal of Public Sector Management, 17*(1), 81-107.

Oracle. (2004). *Oracle BPEL Process Manager.* Retrieved April 28, 2006, from http://otn.oracle.com/products/ias/bpel/index.html

Pollitt, C. (2003). Joined-up government: A survey. *Political Studies Review, 1*(1), 34-49.

Tibco. (2004). *TIBCO® Staffware Process Suite.* Retrieved April 28, 2006, from http://www.tibco.com/software/process_management/staffware_processsuite.jsp

Van der Aalst, W. M. P., Hofstede, A. H. M. t., & Weske, M. (2003). *Business process management: A survey.* Paper presented at the Business Process Management International Conference (BPM 2003), Eindhoven, The Netherlands.

Wimmer, M. A. (2002). A European perspective towards online one-stop government: The eGOV project. *Electronic Commerce Research and Applications, 1*(1), 92-103.

Wohed, P., Aalst, W. M. P. v. d., Dumas, M., & Hofstede, A. H. M. t. (2003). Analysis of Web services composition languages: The case of BPEL4WS. In *Proceedings of the Web Application Modeling and Development, Conceptual Modeling, ER 2003*, (LNCS 2813, pp. 200-215). Berlin-Heidelberg: Springer-Verlag.

Zhao, J. L., & Cheng, H. K. (2005). Web services and process management: A union of convenience or a new area of research? *Decision Support Systems, 40*(1), 1-8.

Endnote

[1]   A café needs two licenses to be allowed to pour alcohol: (1) a license to pour alcohol, and (2) a license to open a café. For the purpose of this chapter, we consider the integrated "liquor-licensing-process" which combines the two licenses.

Chapter IV

The Role of Government in E-Business Adoption

Barbara Roberts, The University of Southern Queensland, Australia

Mark Toleman, The University of Southern Queensland, Australia

Abstract

An analysis of the role of government in e-business adoption is provided in this chapter, with empirical evidence from Australia included. It is shown that government influence is multifaceted. Governments champion e-business adoption for national economic gain; they provide the physical network on which much of e-business depends and increasingly provide e-government services to improve regulation and compliance effectiveness. E-government in particular can act as a strong driver of organisational adoption for some types of e-business processes. Implications for theory from a DOI perspective are included. The authors hope that further research by IS professionals will guide future e-business project directions by improving the understanding of government's role in e-business adoption in practice, which in turn will improve theoretical understanding of how the benefits can best be maximized.

Introduction

Governments and big businesses are powerful stakeholders in driving and shaping econo-mies and the communities in which those economies operate. In particular, governments are able to maintain a dominant position at the top of the stakeholder pecking order due to their regulatory and fiscal power. This powerful position allows governments to exert influence on e-business adoption patterns in a variety of ways. The discussion ranges from indirect pressures resulting from governments' strong championship of e-business benefits through to direct influences arising from the legislative controls introduced for the digital economy, the provision of the physical network infrastructure as a critical enabling adoption factor, and the effects of e-government activity on e-business adoption in general. Both theoretical explanations and empirical evidence, based largely on an Australian perspective, are provided to support the discussion on the role governments play in e-business adoption.

Background

E-business is used for a wide range of purposes and types as the following definition illustrates: "the use of Internet technologies to link customers, suppliers, business partners, and employees using at least one of the following: (a) e-commerce Web sites that offer sales transactions, (b) customer-service Web sites, (c) intranets and enterprise information portals, (d) extranets and supply chains, and (e) IP electronic data interchange" (Wu, Mahajan, & Balasubramanian, 2003, p. 425). Also, it is often assumed that an explicit and close connection between e-business and competitive advantage exists, as the next definition illustrates: "As a way of doing business, e-business refers to the use of business processes that leverage technology — and especially the Internet and World Wide Web (the Web) — to maintain or create competitive advantage" (McKie, 2001, p. xvi). This automatic coupling of e-business with the delivery of some level of guaranteed benefit is one which appears regularly in the literature (Porter, 2001; Sawhney & Zabin, 2001). However the relationship between e-business and delivered benefit is unlikely to be consistent for all types of e-business processes, and does not necessarily exist for all stakeholders involved in its adoption and use. Despite this note of caution, many governments around the world are committed to providing e-government for their nation's citizens and organisations in the form of government information and services on the Web because of the expected benefits such as improved effectiveness and greater convenience of access (Gefen, Pavlou, Warkentin, & Rose, 2002; NOIE, 2003b; Turban, King, Lee, Warkentin, & Chung, 2002).

Internet-enabled e-business is credited with delivering a new type of Internet-based economy in which information flows are improved while associated costs are reduced (Dunt & Harper, 2002). Michael Porter's (2001) claim that "Internet technology provides better opportunities for companies to establish distinctive strategic positioning than did previous generations of information technology" (p. 65) supports the high confidence shown in e-business by government bodies and many business analysts (D. Anderson, 2000; NOIE, 2000; OIE, 2004a). Two major benefits of e-business adoption commonly identified are reduced costs and increased demand through increased services and new markets (Allen Consulting Group, 2002; OECD, 2002). These benefits directly flow from the Internet's intrinsic characteristics of providing low-cost and high-speed global communication, effectively reducing the limiting impact of geographic position and extending presence in the marketplace to 24 hours a day, 7 days a week.

Related benefits of e-business adoption promoted or marketed by Australia's National Office for the Information Economy (NOIE) include increased competitive advantage; provision of new ways of generating revenue; improved relationships with suppliers; improved services to clients; increased collaboration in the supply-chain; and improved business practices through the development of new business models built around the capability of networking (NOIE, 2002b). Thus e-business is closely associated with economic growth at both a national and organisational level in the minds of many, including economic and government analysts (Bakry & Bakry, 2001; Brown, 2002; Dunt & Harper, 2002; Porter, 2001). As a consequence, governments are not only keen to increase adoption rates by organisations, but are also keen to realize direct benefits by adopting e-business for the purpose of delivering government services more effectively, thus resulting in e-government.

Much of the empirical evidence and discussion included in this chapter are based on examples taken from Australia, and hence a brief background of the Australian government's efforts to promote and increase adoption within the Australian business community is examined next.

Government as Champion and Catalyst of E-Business Adoption: Australian Example

The Australian Government actively champions e-business adoption by Australian organisations in order to accelerate uptake and consequently improve the Australian economy. The Australian government's National Office for the Information Economy was restructured and renamed in April 2004, with the functions split between the new Australian Government Information Management Office (AGIMO), and the Office for the Information Economy (OIE). The research and strategic role setting function of NOIE has been taken on by OIE, with the government belief in e-business benefits clearly articulated: "Strengthening Australia's participation in the information economy will benefit all Australians by improving the efficiency of Australian firms, boosting the Australian economy and enhancing national wealth" (OIE, 2004a). The following statements of major objectives of OIE make their advocacy role clear: "identifying and promoting the business case for the adoption of e-business at the firm level, within supply chains and throughout industry sectors" and "to accelerate the uptake of electronic-business tools and practices that will lift the productivity and productive capacity of the Australian economy" (OIE, 2004a).

Thus, the Australian government explicitly promotes the adoption of e-business, particularly by small and medium sized enterprises (SMEs), because of the perceived benefit that e-business is expected to contribute to the future of the Australian economy (Brown, 2002). The case study methodology is frequently employed by government analysts, and case study reports are provided on government Web sites as examples of how organisations can derive benefit from adopting e-business practices (NOIE, 2001, 2002a, 2003a).

E-Government Adoption: Australian Example

The adoption of e-business technologies by governments for the purpose of providing better government services is a logical progression from simply acting as a champion for the technology. In 2003 NOIE produced a report, entitled "E-government Benefits Study" which detailed the Australian Government's aim to transform "traditional over-the-counter services to fully interactive online services" and that this transformation was driven by a "need to improve business processes, to engage citizens, and to provide services to yield better outcomes for government and citizens" (NOIE, 2003b). The report also claimed that increasingly it was Australians who were driving the demand for e-government in order to get easier access and save time (NOIE, 2003b). The push for increased e-government in Australia is mirrored in many other countries such as the U.S. (Cottrill, 2001; Gefen et al., 2002) and Singapore (Ke & Wei, 2004). Analysis of the successful e-government adoption in Singapore confirmed the finding that strong championship by government and clear articulation of the benefits to all stakeholders was an important factor in e-government success (Ke & Wei, 2004).

E-Business Adoption Factors: Government Factor in Context

A review of literature examining adoption of e-business identifies government-related behaviour as just one of the many influential factors that have been identified from a wide range of sources. In order to better appreciate the level of impact coming from government related activity, it is worth quickly reviewing the range of other influential factors so that the role of government with regard to e-business adoption can be placed in context.

Diffusion of Innovation Theory

A major theory, first published in 1962, on the adoption of innovations and the rate at which subsequent usage diffuses through the population of potential users — the diffusion of innovations (DOI) theory by Rogers (1995) — has general application to e-business and is now briefly examined. DOI theory posits that the factors influencing adoption rates by organisations are drawn from two major sources: (1) characteristics of the innovation itself and (2) characteristics of the adopting organisation (see Figure 1).

Five innovation characteristics are singled out in DOI as independent variables influencing adoption rates, and these relate to perceptions of (1) relative advantage over alternatives, involving a range of social, technical, and economic benefits; (2) compatibility with existing values, experiences, and needs; (3) complexity; (4) trialability; and (5) observability of the innovation. As might be expected, the degree of perceived relative advantage, encompassing the full range of possible benefits, is found to be one of the best predictors of an innovation's rate of adoption by diffusion scholars (Rogers, 1995, p. 216). Interestingly, with regard to the characteristics of the adopting organisation, while many characteristics of the adopting organisation have been identified and studied (shown in Figure 1), Rogers claims that the results from several hundred studies show only low correlations between the identified factors and organisation innovativeness, with size/resource capacity the most significant (Rogers, 1995, p. 381).

Figure 1. Independent variables related to innovation adoption by organisations from Rogers' DOI theory (1995)

Innovation Characteristics
1) perception of relative advantage over alternatives; (+)
2) perception of compatibility with existing values, experiences and needs; (+)
3) perception of complexity; (-)
4) the degree to which the innovation can be tried on a limited and experimental basis; (+)
5) the degree to which the results of the innovation can be observed. (+)

Organisation characteristics
1) Attitude towards change of individual leader (+)
2) Internal characteristics of organisation's structure
   Centralization (-)
   Interconnectedness (+)
   Complexity (+)
   Organisational slack (+)
   Formalization (-)
   Size (+)
3) System openness – the degree to which members of the system are linked to others external to the system (+)

In general, the degree of relative advantage an innovation delivers and the resource capacity/size of the adopting organisation emerge as the two most important of the identified factors (Rogers, 1995). The DOI theory also recognises that influence from managerial championship and opinion leaders acting as agents of change act as an accelerating force by affecting the potential adopters. Research by Fichman (2001) into the adoption of IT innovations specifically supports the DOI findings that the degree of perceived benefit and the size/resource capacity of the adopting organisation have significant explanatory power in understanding adoption and usage patterns.

TAM Related Theories

The technology acceptance model (TAM), a framework originally developed to explain the acceptance of information technology by individuals after the adoption and implementation stages have occurred (Davis, 1989) also identified perceived usefulness, which basically equates to perceived relative advantage or benefit, as the most significant construct in understanding acceptance and use of IT. Some variants of TAM have identified additional constructs which need to be taken into account in order to explain adoption of IT innovations by organisations. For example, work by Mathieson, Peacock, and Chin confirmed that the construct of perceived resources needed to be added to the simple TAM framework (Mathieson, Peacock, & Chin, 2001), while one of the latest variations to emerge, the unified theory of acceptance and use of technology (UTAUT), has also introduced additional broad brush constructs such as "social influence" to encompass managerial and opinion leader championship, and "facilitating conditions" to cover resource capacity and organisational conditions (Venkatesh, Morris, Davis, & Davis, 2003).

External Environment Factors

While external environment factors are not clearly identified in Rogers' DOI theory or the TAM variants discussed previously, the literature review confirmed the external environment to be an additional major source of influential factors on the adoption of complex information technologies such as e-business. This is particularly so for e-business due to high user interdependencies, potential to transform strategy and processes (Chau & Turner, 2001), and the potential to deliver organisation-wide business impact (Swanson, 1994). Environmental factors come from a wide range of sources and, for example, include characteristics related to industry, marketplace, culture, and government and industry regulatory conditions (Chengalur-Smith & Duchessi, 1999; Kwon & Zmud, 1987; Markus & Soh, 2002; Swanson, 1994; Yang, Yoo, Lyytinen, & Ahn, 2004). Factors related to national characteristics including culture, government policy initiatives, and legal regulations all appear to have strong explanatory power in improving understanding of e-business adoption and diffusion behaviours (Chen, 2003; Gibbs, Kraemer, & Dedrick, 2003; Palacios, 2003; Wong, 2003). Policy support and leadership from government are recognised as necessary and important enabling factors in providing an environment conducive for e-business adoption, while the provision of e-government services and online transaction options positively drive e-business adoption (Wong, 2003). Other critical enablers include pressure from multinational corporations; liberalisation of trade and telecommunications policies; improvement of telecommunications infrastructure; adequate legislation to manage risk; and the emergence of e-banking (Palacios, 2003).

For example, research into the initiation and adoption of client-server technology in organisations (Chengalur-Smith & Duchessi, 1999) identified three major sources of influence: (1) characteristics of the organisation itself, such as size, structure, and culture, including the selected migration strategy for the adoption of the technology; (2) characteristics of the technology itself, such as the complexity, scope, and cost of the system adopted; and (3) characteristics of the external environment, such as government regulation, the level of competition faced by the organisation, and the organisation's market position. Factors from all three areas were found to have a significant effect on the adoption process (Chengalur-Smith & Duchessi, 1999). As a second example, many factors from a range of sources were also identified as influencing diffusion of mobile broadband services in Korea (Yang et al., 2004). External environment features figure prominently, while software and telecommunication standards, the industry and government regulatory regime, marketplace forces, and internal skills and resources all contribute to usage levels. Complex relationships and interactions were found to occur between all influential factors, resulting in outcomes that are characterised by continual evolution and change (Yang et al., 2004).

Thus, it is reasonable to conclude that the factors influencing organisation adoption of e-business are many and drawn from numerous sources. In particular, an organisation's external environment is a rich potential source of influence on e-business behaviour at all levels: these include organisational, industrial, national, and global levels. It is clear from the previous discussion that government policy and activity does play a significant role in determining e-business adoption and usage by organisations, but it is not by any means the only key factor. To what extent government activity has the potential to influence e-business adoption, and the areas of e-business in which government influence is likely to have more impact than others is discussed in more detail after a brief discussion on implications related to the network externality characteristic of e-business.

Network Externality Influence on E-Business Adoption

The reliance of many e-business ventures on attaining sufficient critical mass with regard to adoption in order to be successful is due to the *network externality effect* (Katz, 1986). Network externalities apply to information technologies which rely on corresponding usage by others to be effective, or when "one person's utility for a good depends on the *number* of other people who consume this good" (Varian, 1999, p. 606). Network externalities apply to many e-business processes such as e-mail and use of Web sites because the benefit of these technologies does indeed depend on the number of users, with benefit rising as numbers rise. For example, e-mail is not effective if only a few intended recipients are using it to access their correspondence.

Government Power Influencing Adoption Numbers

Given that e-business technologies are sensitive to the network externality characteristic, it follows that the success of many e-business systems, including e-government services and online transaction systems, is dependent on the number of citizens and organisations who consume these products. If the number of adopters remains low, then the perceived benefits to the system owners, including government in this context, of improving effectiveness and efficiency as well as lowering costs will not be delivered. Thus the success of e-business and e-government relies on having sufficient adopters. As a result, it is in the best interests of powerful stakeholders to encourage and enable adoption rates to rise. To what extent governments are able to influence adoption rates will now be explored in more detail by looking at an empirical study from Australia which involved investigation of e-business adoption rates by wineries, with government influence an identified factor under investigation.

Empirical Study: E-Business Adoption by Australian Wineries

The study described here was carried out in 2003 and 2004 in order to better understand the nature and extent of Internet-enabled e-business adoption by Australian organisations, taking into account the different types of e-business practiced within organisations. The research consisted of two major phases: a qualitative, exploratory stage using interviews designed to identify key issues of relevance to wineries which allowed significant industry feedback to inform the final selection of factors and issues most relevant to e-business adoption by wineries, and a quantitative survey stage, using a self administered questionnaire, designed to collect both statistical and descriptive information in order to gain a clearer understanding of e-business activity and test propositions. The research was conducted for a master's thesis, and for those readers wishing to follow up on more details of the study, the thesis is available online at http://adt.usq.edu.au/adt-QUSQ/public/adt-QUSQ20050113.103311/index.html.

Selection of Wineries as Unit of Analysis

Australian wineries were selected as the unit of analysis for research into e-business adoption within Australia for a number of reasons. One reason is that wineries are a rich subject for research because they have a very diverse range of business processes that span the agricultural (primary), manufacturing (secondary), and marketing (tertiary) sectors. Wineries usually have a high level of involvement in all three areas (ACIL, 2002). Further, wineries also have to comply with a wide range of legislative requirements and are required to interact and transact with numerous government bodies as well as industry organisations. The wine industry is also increasingly important to the Australian economy as the industry continues to expand, largely due to exponential growth in export sales for the last 15 plus years (K. Anderson, 2000; Anderson, 2001). This ensured that both domestic and export markets were included, thus covering a wide range of market types.

Wineries also vary greatly in size and resource capacity, which contributes to their richness as a research subject. In 2003 there were more than 1,600 wineries in Australia. Of these wineries, almost one third of them are in the microsize category processing less than 20 tonnes of grapes each year. At the other end of the size spectrum the top 22 wine companies account for about 90% of the annual national crush and for 96% of all sales of branded wine (Winetitles, 2003). And finally, while some wineries are close to urban centres, many are located in regional areas with limited access to network infrastructure: this provided scope to collect useful information on the impact of network access issues.

Phase 1: Interview Methodology

Interviews, recommended as a suitable technique for exploring issues and gathering rich empirical data (Sekaran, 2003; Yin, 1994; Zikmund, 2000), were conducted with representatives from nine different wineries in mid-2003. All nine respondents were volunteered by their company as knowledgeable informants, and all were confident in their ability to portray the e-business activities of their own winery with a high degree of accuracy. The nine wineries represented a broad range of company structure, size, and position within the industry with some ranking in the top five wine companies in Australia in terms of production and sales. All nine wineries were engaged in export of wine, and all were using the Internet in some capacity in the running of their business. Employee numbers ranged from 12 to over 2,000, illustrating a huge variance in size and internal capacity.

The interviews were conducted in a semistructured way to make sure that each major e-business process domain was covered. General background questions were followed by more specific questions covering the winery's use of Internet technologies and related strategies. The extent of e-mail use was covered, as well as the range of Web sites, both external sites and sites belonging to the winery, that each winery used and for what purpose: in B2B — with suppliers, trading partners, and business customers such as distributors and retailers; in B2C — public Web sites and mailing lists; and in B2G — using government sites as an information source and for online compliance purposes. The respondents also provided information on the benefits and degree of relative advantage perceived to be delivered by the various e-business processes, and also on the factors that acted as facilitators or barriers to further adoption in each area. Cross-case analysis of the interview data helped to identify the major themes. Some themes appeared to be independent of the winery size, such as influence from e-government; while other themes appeared to be linked to size and market position.

Interview Finding: Government As E-Business Driver

While many factors of influence emerged during these interviews, this chapter focuses only on findings related to the perceived influence coming from government related activity. All interviewees identified the Australian government as one of the drivers of their winery's e-business behaviour. The types of e-business conducted with government ranged from e-mail to use of government Web sites for convenient access to government related information, and included several examples of online transaction processing and online submission of forms. Examples are now provided.

One winery respondent reported they use the Internet for access to government areas that are crucial in supporting their business processes:

We do actually do some compliance via the Internet such as Work Cover, and our tax. We do lodge our returns electronically, we do actually have occupation health and safety, and we have to keep abreast of the appropriate Australian standards on how things are done, and what plant materials you are supposed to use, so we do actually utilize that quite a bit to make sure we are meeting our requirements there so we do have people who are trained on the Internet constantly checking to see that what we are doing is correct.

Another respondent cited the following as an example of B2G communication within their business:

The EPA for example, or Environmental Protection Authority — legislation and reporting due to them is all electronic now. So that saves a lot of paperwork, postage and what not. You just update your records, your last results, and e-mail it, and the whole history is emailed together, and it is just a continuing spreadsheet type of format.

An example of online transaction processing is provided next. All wine exported from Australia must be approved as meeting a required level of quality before it is allowed to be exported. This quality control process is one example of the many legislative requirements facing Australian wineries, with compliance mandatory. Many wineries now process their Wine Export Approvals (WEAs) online. The option for gaining approvals using a Web-based process has been available for the last three to four years via the Australian Wine and Brandy Corporation Web site at http://www.awbc.com.au/.

The following comment from a small winery respondent illustrates the benefit of online WEAs and government sites in general:

wine export approvals — my brother now uses the Internet to do all that. There are all the application forms on the Internet, so he can do all of that via the net, so he doesn't have to talk to anybody and he gets the results back over the Internet or by email ... We are just about to put in some workplace agreements, so I have been to the Web-sites to check that out ... and we have to find the current wages for all the wages people, so we use those Web-sites to access that. We use the liquor licensing, we get all the permits and stuff for that ... that's really good — there are lots of government Web-sites that we use.

A second example of online transaction processing, one which applies to all Australian exporters and importers is examined next. At the time the interviews were conducted all Australian exporting companies were facing additional e-business process adoption for legislative compliance purposes due to the then impending roll out of the export component of a new system being developed by the Australian Customs Service (ACS). The Cargo Management Re-engineering project is Australia's largest ever public sector e-business project, and will consist of several subsystems to form the Integrated Cargo System (ICS). The ICS is designed to improve security and efficiency among other expected benefits. Visit http://www.customs.gov.au for details. The first system, the export component, went live in September 2004 after several delays from the initial scheduled cut-over period of late 2003. Use of the online interface to the ICS export system, while not actually mandatory, is strongly encouraged with a cost burden imposed for exporters choosing to use a manual process available through selected Australia Post Offices and customs offices.

Although the scheduled cut-over period to the new export component of the ICS was due soon after the time the interviews were conducted, awareness of the impending change to Customs' clearances among the interview respondents was variable, with only those from the larger companies raising it as an issue — respondents from the mid-size or small wineries seemed completely unaware of changes in this area. This indicates some flaws in communication by government in the initial stages of the project development.

The following excerpt from one respondent illustrates what, at the time of the interview, was thought to be the complete mandatory nature of the change:

Customs ... have brought in an edict that you will have to talk to them electronically by the end of September (2003) or you don't export ... To ship our goods overseas we have to talk to Customs, the Australian Customs Service electronically or we won't be able to ship. We have got to do that by the end of September.

Another respondent provided the following comment:

Australian Customs Service are putting in this new cargo tracking system which is why we have had to spend another $40,000 to work with this one, and we have to do it, it is compulsory, and we have to have it in by November this year. But part of this system is they have an online function of looking after a cargo status, so it is a cargo tracking system.

Yet another respondent's comment on the impending change in gaining Customs clearance follows:

We use a package called Trident — the Trident system interfaces directly with Customs in what is called an Exit One package. Now that's about to undergo a very, very significant change, and the actual way in which Customs handles the export of wines is about to undergo a fundamental change ... We came out of that with the instruction from Customs to apply for a digital certificate, so we need to get these processes in place.

Phase 2: Survey Methodology

A survey of all Australian wineries, excluding the microsize wineries processing less than 20 tons of grapes per year, was conducted in the latter part of 2004 using a self-administered questionnaire. The survey was designed to collect detailed information about the nature and extent of the wineries' e-business adoption, and among other things, to statistically test the proposition that some elements of e-business behaviour occur in response to government related activity on the Internet.

Responses were received from 198 of the 1,065 wineries, giving an overall response rate of 18.6%. The response rate varied by winery size, increasing significantly across the four size categories used in the analysis ($\chi^2(3) = 32.28$, $p < .001$). See Table 1 for winery size categories, population and response numbers. The survey collected basic background information on each winery, and included separate sections for each of the following types of e-business processes: e-mail; use of external Web sites; and three possible types of winery Web sites — public for B2C, extranet for B2B, and intranet for winery staff only. Feedback on the winery's overall use of e-business, along with identification of barriers to further (or any) adoption and general comments were also sought.

The survey included statements designed to test the proposition that government e-business activity was a factor of influence; respondents were provided with a 5-point Likert scale to show their level of agreement. The "Do not know" responses were treated as missing responses for the statistical calculations. The Likert scale, while strictly an ordinal scale,

Table 1. Winery size categories, population, and response numbers

Winery Size	Annual Tonnage Range	Population in 2003	Population %	Response		
				Number	% of Population	% of Total Response
Small	20-249	801	75.7%	120	15.0%	60.6%
Medium	250-999	150	14.2%	35	23.3%	17.7%
Large	1000-9999	88	8.3%	31	35.2%	15.7%
Very Large	10000 and over	26	2.5%	12	46.2%	6.1%

has been shown to have sufficient interval characteristics for the computation of means not to be invalid: "arithmetic means seem to closely reflect group attitudes towards the stimuli" (Hofacker, 1984). Therefore the response means illustrated differences in responses by winery size when the nonparametric tests for ordinal data showed a significant difference by size existed. Response differences by winery size for the factor statements were investigated using the Kruskal-Wallis K Independent Sample test. This test is appropriate for an ordinal scale and makes no assumptions about the underlying distribution of the data, which in this case was not normally distributed. Summary findings related to the role of government influence are now reported.

Survey Finding 1: Government Influences E-Mail and Use of Government Web Sites

The survey data analysis revealed that e-government activity influenced e-mail and external Web site use but had negligible direct impact on the operation or content of Web sites operated by the wineries. This is not particularly surprising when the purposes of the different e-business process types are considered, and is part of the wider finding that factors influencing e-business adoption do not impact in the same way across the various e-business process domains. Some specific government related results are detailed next.

With regard to e-mail use, three quarters of the wineries use e-mail to communicate with government agencies and departments, but small wineries, when compared with the larger wineries, find less convenience from using e-mail with government organisations. Turning to use of external Web sites, the most common type accessed by wineries are the specific wine industry Web sites, some of which are operated by Australian Government authorities (e.g., the Australian Wine and Brandy Corporation is the Australian government authority responsible for the promotion and regulation of Australian wine and brandy). Almost 90% of wineries, regardless of their size, use the Internet to access these sites. The next most common type of Web sites accessed by wineries is government sites connected with legislation and regulation compliance. In this case however, usage differs significantly by winery size: for example, 72% of small wineries compared with 100% of very large wineries ($\chi^2(3)$

= 11.88, $p < .01$, N = 155). For exporting wineries, usage of online compliance processes differed significantly by winery size. For example, approximately 45% of the small and medium wineries used the online compliance process for wine export approvals compared with approximately 75% of the large and very large wineries, a significant difference in usage level ($\chi^2(3)$ = 15.92, $p < .01$, N = 76). The same type of pattern was observed for wineries using the Web to process customs clearances, with only about 15% of small and medium wineries using this option, except that in this case the usage levels of very large wineries, at 64%, was markedly higher than that of the large wineries at 30%. The difference by winery size for online custom compliance is significant ($\chi^2(3)$ = 15.79, $p < .01$, N = 31). Note: the uptake of online compliance for export customs declarations has changed considerably since the export component of Australia's Integrated Cargo System went live in late 2004. Online transaction processing for export declarations is now close to 100%; see Table 2 for details.

Analysis of survey responses indicated B2G related e-business is increasing, with clear evidence that most respondents are finding compliance with government regulations easier due to the functionality and utility of e-government Web sites. Respondents also anticipated that their e-business activities in the next 12 to 18 months will be dominated by increasing use in the areas of B2B and B2G rather than the area of B2C. Overall there was a perception that the role of e-government on e-business adoption by wineries in general is significant, and is in fact a stronger and more influential factor than that of the direct relative advantage delivered by e-business to the wineries themselves.

Survey Finding 2: Network Infrastructure Limitations Acts as Major Barrier

Empirical evidence from the census survey revealed that the limitations of available network speeds and network connection costs are two common barriers to further e-business adoption by Australian wineries, with close to 50% of respondents citing these two issues as barriers. These barriers apply to wineries regardless of organisation size. Telstra is the only network carrier with physical lines into all regional and remote sites. The quality of the lines away from major cities and regional centres provides only limited support for e-business activity. For example, ADSL broadband connections are only available within approximately three and a half kilometres of an ADSL enabled exchange (Telstra, 2004), and many wineries are located outside this range. As one interview respondent made clear, inferior Internet access in regional areas is also accompanied by higher costs: regional businesses pay more to get less.

The following example illustrates the problem in terms of e-commerce costs. A very large, privately owned winery with offices in all Australian states uses online processes for compliance where possible. However, the main production centre is located near a major regional town situated further than three kilometres from the nearest Telstra exchange, with broadband access not available. The standard Internet connection at their regional production site has an annual cost of $11,000 and is 130 times slower than the speed of a similar Internet connection at their city office which has an annual cost of $2,000. The winery spends an additional $90,000 a year to upgrade their Internet connection speed at the regional winery location to acceptable speeds, and Telstra has required up-front contributions of approximately $100,000 for infrastructure upgrades. The winery has little choice other than to make these investments in order to get sufficient speed for transaction processing across the Web.

The winery research confirmed that improvements in network infrastructure quality and lowering associated e-commerce costs are needed in order to reduce the most common barriers facing Australian organisations in the adoption of e-business processes. The current limited penetration of broadband access in Australia acts as a serious inhibitor for growth of e-business adoption, particularly for SMEs and many regional organisations who find the cost burden of upgrading their own telecommunication infrastructure to ensure an acceptable Internet access speed is too high for the resulting level of benefit. The various levels of government recognise their responsibility for improvements in network infrastructure. For example, the Australian Federal Government has developed a national strategy for improving broadband access across the country in partnership with state and territory governments. Objectives include the development of a coordinated approach to future network development in order to reduce price and location barriers, and in particular to provide affordable broadband services in regional Australia (OIE, 2004b). The Victorian State Government has gone further, by agreeing to combine with Telstra to establish a high-speed fibre optic network across Victoria to connect all schools, police offices, and government offices at a total cost of over $120 million (Barker, 2005). Once implemented, this high speed Internet access will advantage e-business operations in Victoria in comparison with the other states.

Mandating Adoption Ensures E-Government Success

An interesting point to note from the interview comments provided previously is the awareness of the lack of choice with regard to compliance with the changes stemming from the government's power to regulate and to control the means by which compliance with regulation occurs. The wineries were not *choosing* to adopt online transactions for export clearance compliance — they simply had no choice in the matter. Nor were the respondents anticipating much in the way of direct benefit for themselves — instead they were acting in response to a directive they could not ignore because the directive came from a stakeholder with a much higher degree of power than themselves. It is reasonable to assume that all Australian exporting organisations, not just wineries, will have been conscious of their lack of choice in deciding whether or not to adopt the online process for ICS.

So how successful has the Australian Government been in forcing Australian exporters to process their export declarations via online transaction processing using digital signatures as evidence of identity? The answer is they have been extremely successful. In a correspondence from the Federal Minister for Justice and Customs (C. Ellison, personal communication, August 1, 2005), less than 1% of all export declarations have been lodged since ICS went live in September 2004 using the alternative manual paper system. The manual system is designed with disincentives: extra costs are attached and it is only available at a limited number of locations. The monthly breakdown of export declarations processed between

Table 2. Monthly export lodgment numbers by type for export component of ICS

Month	Lodgements of export declarations in Australia		Total	% Manual of Total
	Manual	Electronic		
Sep-04	250	8,961	9,211	2.71%
Oct-04	1,274	110,083	111,357	1.14%
Nov-04	827	111,486	112,313	0.74%
Dec-04	717	103,575	104,292	0.69%
Jan-05	600	85,558	86,158	0.70%
Feb-05	764	100,254	101,018	0.76%
Mar-05	677	110,308	110,985	0.61%
Apr-05	515	108,361	108,876	0.47%
May-05	502	111,894	112,396	0.45%
Jun-05	523	106,673	107,196	0.49%
Jul-05	331	78,458	78,789	0.42%
Totals	6,980	1,035,611	1,042,591	0.67%

September 2004 and July 2005 between the electronic and manual alternatives is shown in Table 1.

The Australian government has gone to great lengths to support exporting clients during the rollout of ICS by conducting training sessions in capital cities and large regional centres; providing online guides; and by providing an electronic simulation of ICS for new clients in order to build familiarity with the system. Broadband access is not required for the Web-based system to operate with full functionality, and clients in remote regions of Australia have successfully adopted the online system.

The example of successful ICS adoption by Australian organisations illustrates the point that organisations sometimes adopt e-business processes because of stakeholder pressure. It is not relative advantage or ease of use driving the adoption decision. The decision to adopt is forced because a more powerful member of the stakeholder group, one with sufficient power to mandate change, dictates how the process will be managed. The role of relationship management between stakeholders in the context of e-government projects and uneven stakeholder power is examined further in work by Chan, Pan, and Tan (2003).

The development and adoption of the ICS by the Australian government is an example of e-government designed for the benefit of government and the nations' citizens as a whole, with a particular focus on increasing security levels. The Australian government has chosen to introduce online compliance with online evidence of identity (EOI) via digital certificates and provision of online security via public key infrastructure (PKI) in order to reap benefits of better government rather than for benefit to the exporters and importers. The need for online EOI has forced all participating users of the online system to purchase digital certificates. In turn many organisations will, for the very first time, have overcome any hurdle which the lack of online evidence of identity had previously presented. It is possible that the introduction of the ICS within Australia may pave the way for increased adoption of other online transaction processes which require digital certificates for EOI purposes, although at this stage, this is merely speculation.

Figure 2. Modified set of influential factors for e-business adoption, based on DOI theory (Source: Rogers, 1995), with additions shown in italics

Innovation Characteristics
1) perception of relative advantage over alternatives; (+)
2) perception of compatibility with existing values, experiences and needs; (+)
3) perception of complexity; (-)
4) the degree to which the innovation can be tried on a limited and experimental basis; (+)
5) the degree to which the results of the innovation can be observed. (+)
6) the degree to which the number of adopters increases the benefit for at least one innovation adopter (+)

Organisation characteristics
1) Attitude towards change of individual leader (+)
2) Internal characteristics of organisation's structure
   Centralization (-)
   Interconnectedness (+)
   Complexity (+)
   Organisational slack (+)
   Formalization (-)
   Size (+)
3) System openness – the degree to which members of the system are linked to others external to the system (+)

External Environment Characteristics
1) Influence of supply chain stakeholders, can be either a positive or negative influence depending on market type and market position (+) or (-)
2) e-Government services and compliance processes (+) (optional and/or mandatory)

Future Research

There is much scope for future research in the role of governments with regard to e-business adoption and stakeholder relationships. The observations made in this chapter on the role of government in e-business adoption suggest that the theoretical framework from the DOI perspective needs modification when applied to e-business adoption. Figure 2 illustrates some suggested changes to the DOI theory by adding in an extra innovation characteristic related to the network externality effect when benefit depends on adopter numbers, while the stakeholder pressures from the external environment have also been included, with influence from e-government singled out because of its pivotal role in determining many e-business conditions and compliance processes within national boundaries.

E-government is still emerging and developing as a mechanism for reliable, secure, and effective government. As more e-government projects come online and experience grows, then analysis of the successes and failures will be vital to improving our understanding of how governments can best leverage benefit from e-business processes for their nation and citizens. Research by IS professionals will aid this analysis process and potentially guide future directions of both e-government projects and the provision of government controlled structuring conditions to allow e-business to flourish within the marketplace.

Conclusion

The role of government in e-business adoption has been shown to be multifaceted. First, governments play an important role as an e-business champion. The Australian government is committed to this role because of the strong belief that e-business will strengthen and improve the Australian economy. Second, governments are responsible for providing the physical network infrastructure that most of the nation's citizenry and organisations rely on for the conduct of their e-business practices. The quality, speed, and cost of this access are crucial elements in determining the effectiveness, depth, and extent of e-business adoption for many organisations. The example from Australia discussed earlier served to illustrate this point. Third, the development of e-government for the purpose of improving communication, flow of information, and online transaction processing to aid regulation awareness and compliance acts as a strong driver of e-business adoption in some, but not all, e-business process domains. There is evidence that governments can use their powerful stakeholder position to effectively force online adoption for compliance purposes when necessary, in order to maximise adopter numbers and thus increase the benefits for government and the nation to the level desired. A theoretical implication follows: all organisations with sufficient stakeholder power, whether private (big businesses) or government, have the potential to effectively mandate adoption of their own e-business processes which strongly depend on the number of adopters to achieve sufficient relative advantage.

References

ACIL. (2002). *Pathways to profitability for small and medium wineries.* ACIL Consulting. Retrieved from http://www.aciltasman.com.au/images/pdf/wine_report_v2.pdf

Allen Consulting Group. (2002). *Australia's information economy: The big picture.* Melbourne: NOIE.

Anderson, D. (2000). Creating and nurturing a premier e-business. *Journal of Interactive Marketing, 14*(3), 67-73.

Anderson, K. (2000). *Export-led growth.* Retrieved April 29, 2006, from http://www.rirdc. gov.au/reports/GLC/00-52.pdf

Anderson, K. (2001, May). Prospects ahead for the wine industry. *The Australian Grapegrower and Winemaker, 448,* 67-74.

Bakry, S. H., & Bakry, F. H. (2001). A strategic view for the development of e-business. *International Journal of Network Management, 11*(2), 103-112.

Barker, G. (2005, June 8). High-fibre diet for regions. *The Age.*

Brown, E. (2002). *Accelerating the up-take of e-commerce by small and medium enterprises* (Report and Action Plan). Small Enterprise Telecommunications Centre (SETEL). Retrieved from http://www.setel.com/au.smeforum2002

Chan, C. M. L., Pan, S.-L., & Tan, C.-W. (2003). *Managing stakeholder relationships in an e-government project.* Paper presented at the 9th Americas Conference on Information Systems, Tampa, Florida.

Chau, S. B., & Turner, P. (2001, December 5-7). *A four phase model of EC business transformation amongst small to medium sized enterprises: Preliminary findings from 34 Australian case studies.* Paper presented at the 12th Australasian Conference on Information Systems, Coffs Harbour, NSW, Australia.

Chen, T.-J. (2003). The diffusion and impacts of the Internet and e-commerce in Taiwan. *I-Ways, 26*(4), 185-193.

Chengalur-Smith, I., & Duchessi, P. (1999). The initiation and adoption of client-server technology in organizations. *Information & Management, 35*(2), 77-88.

Cottrill, K. (2001, March 5). E-government grows. *Traffic World, 265,* 19.

Davis, F. D. (1989). Perceived usefulness, perceived ease of use, and user acceptance of information technology. *MIS Quarterly, 13*(3), 318-340.

Dunt, E. S., & Harper, I. R. (2002). E-commerce and the Australian economy. *The Economic Record, 78*(242), 327-342.

Fichman, R. G. (2001). The role of aggregation in the measurement of IT-related organizational innovation. *MIS Quarterly, 25*(4), 427-455.

Gefen, D., Pavlou, P., Warkentin, M., & Rose, G. (2002). *EGovernment adoption.* Paper presented at the Eighth Americas Conference on Information Systems, Dallas, TX.

Gibbs, J., Kraemer, K. L., & Dedrick, J. (2003). Environment and policy factors shaping global e-commerce diffusion: A cross-country comparison. *Information Society, 19*(1), 5-18.

Hofacker, C. F. (1984). Categorical judgment scaling with ordinal assumptions. *Multivariate Behavioural Research, 19*(1), 91-106.

Katz, C. M. L. S. (1986). Technology adoption in the presence of network externalities. *Journal of Political Economy, 94*(4), 822-842.

Ke, W., & Wei, K. K. (2004). Successful e-government in Singapore. *Communications of the ACM, 47*(6), 95-99.

Kwon, T. H., & Zmud, R. W. (1987). Unifying the fragmented models of information systems implementation. In R. J. Boland & R. A. Hirschheim (Eds.), *Critical issues in information systems research* (pp. 227-251). New York: John Wiley & Sons.

Markus, M. L., & Soh, C. (2002). Structural influences on global e-commerce activity. *Journal of Global Information Management, 10*(1), 5-12.

Mathieson, K., Peacock, E., & Chin, W. W. (2001). Extending the technology acceptance model: The influence of perceived user resources. *The Database for Advances in Information Systems, 32*(3), 86-112.

McKie, S. (2001). *E-business best practices.* New York: John Wiley & Sons.

NOIE. (2000). *Taking the plunge 2000.* Canberra: National Office for the Information Economy.

NOIE. (2001). *Advancing with e-commerce: A summary of 34 case studies of small business e-commerce ventures.* Canberra: National Office for Information Economy.

NOIE. (2002a). *Advancing with e-business: Case studies.* Retrieved April 29, 2006, from http://www.dcita.gov.au/ie/publications/2002/november/advancing_with_e-business_case_studies

NOIE. (2002b). *The benefits of doing business electronically: E-business.* Retrieved April 29, 2006, from http://www.noie.gov.au/projects/ebusiness/Advancing/benefits/index.htm

NOIE. (2003a). *Advancing with e-business: Supply chain case studies.* Retrieved April 29, 2006, from http://www2.dcita.gov.au/ie/publications/2003/08/e-bus_supp_chain

NOIE. (2003b). *E-government benefits study.* Retrieved April 29, 2006, from http://www.noie.gov.au/publications/NOIE/egovt_benefits/index.htm

OECD. (2002). *Measuring the information economy 2002.* Retrieved April 29, 2006, from http://www.oecd.org/pdf/M00036000/M00036089.pdf

OIE. (2004a). *Information economy.* Retrieved April 29, 2006, from http://www.dcita.gov.au/ie

OIE. (2004b). *The national broadband strategy.* Retrieved April 29, 2006, from http://www2.dcita.gov.au/ie/framework/broadband

Palacios, J. J. (2003). Globalization and e-commerce: Diffusion and impacts in Mexico. *I-Ways, 26*(4), 195-205.

Porter, M. E. (2001). Strategy and the Internet. *Harvard Business Review, 79*(3), 63-78.

Rogers, E. M. (1995). *Diffusion of innovations* (4th ed.). New York: The Free Press.

Sawhney, M., & Zabin, J. (2001). *The seven steps to nirvana.* New York: McGraw-Hill.

Sekaran, U. (2003). *Research methods for business: A skill building approach* (4th ed.). New York: John Wiley & Sons.

Swanson, E. B. (1994). Information systems innovation among organizations. *Management Science, 40*(9), 1069-1092.

Telstra. (2004). *ADSL frequently asked questions.* Retrieved April 29, 2006, from http://www.telstra.com.au/demand/faq.htm

Turban, E., King, D., Lee, J., Warkentin, M., & Chung, H. M. (2002). *Electronic commerce 2002: A managerial perspective.* Upper Saddle River, NJ: Prentice Hall.

Varian, H. R. (1999). *Intermediate microeconomics.* New York: W.W. Norton & Company.

Venkatesh, V., Morris, M. G., Davis, G. B., & Davis, F. D. (2003). User acceptance of information technology: Toward a unified view. *MIS Quarterly, 27*(3), 425-478.

Winetitles. (2003). *Australian wine industry overview.* Retrieved April 29, 2006, from http://www.winetitles.com.au/awol/overview/wineries.asp

Wong, P.-K. (2003). Global and national factors affecting e-commerce diffusion in Singapore. *Information Society, 19*(1), 19-32.

Wu, F., Mahajan, V., & Balasubramanian, S. (2003). An analysis of e-business adoption and its impact on business performance. *Journal of the Academy of Marketing Science, 31*(4), 425-447.

Yang, H., Yoo, Y., Lyytinen, K., & Ahn, J.-H. (2004, February 25). *Diffusion of broadband mobile services in Korea: The role of standards and its impact on diffusion of complex technology system.* Paper presented at the e-Biz World Conference, Seoul, Korea.

Yin, R. K. (1994). *Case study research: Design and methods* (2nd ed.). Thousand Oaks: Sage Publications.

Zikmund, W. G. (2000). *Business research methods* (6th ed.). Orlando: The Dryden Press.

Chapter V

Digital Public Sphere:
Rhetoric or Reality

Seung-Yong Rho, Seoul Women's University, Korea

Abstract

In the Information Age, simultaneous citizen-government interaction through information and communication technologies (ICTs) such as e-mails, digital policy forums through bulletin boards, and real-time digital chat has already happened. Digital deliberation is one of examples for improving citizen-government interaction through ICTs. In this context, it is important to evaluate current practice of digital deliberation. That is, can we consider current practice of digital deliberation as authentic citizen participation in governance process? Based on the analysis of the current practice of digital deliberation through ICTs, unlike the expectation, this chapter argues that there was a lack of active participation by citizens as well as public servants. The policies should be made by the will of citizens in democratic governance but current practice of digital deliberation did not support this statement. Citizens' unawareness of digital deliberation, citizens' lack of active participation, and public officials' less positive perspective on the digital deliberation make current digital deliberation unconstructive. These practices have violated the principle of democracy, which is government by the people. The citizens' strong will of active digital deliberation is a key to the success of digital deliberation in the democratic governance. In addition, public officials' positive views and strong support on the digital deliberation are important to make digital deliberation effective.

Introduction

Citizen-government interaction is essential in a democratic society and for democratic governance. It, however, has not yet been well developed and structured in the literature. Some researchers in fields such as psychology, communication, political science, and public administration have provided grounds for developing a model of citizen-government interaction.

In the field of psychology, Riva, Giuseppe, and Galimberti (1997, pp. 141-158) identify two structural characteristics of interaction as the copresence of utterances and cognition. While the former occurs when one party communicates with the other party, the latter occurs through both parties' coordination of their action and their availability to one another. Communication is a cooperative action in which one party must receive a response from the other party in order to acquire what has been transmitted and understood. Then, they (Riva et al., 1997, pp. 147-148) suggest two models. One is the parcel-pose model in which one party passes information to the other party. In an information age, however, they argue that this model is replaced by the other model, the model of communicative interactionism, in which every communication is intended for both sender and receiver in a "double listening" process. The sender is continuously comparing what the sender has sent with the return communication.

Also, in the area of communication, much research has focused on the interaction among parties. That is, according to traditional communication theory research, there are two types of communication mechanisms: interpersonal and mass media mechanisms. While the interpersonal mechanism involves a face-to-face exchange between two or more individuals, mass media mechanisms transmitting messages, such as radio, television, and newspapers, enable one or a few individuals to reach an audience of many. In the digital age, however, research has paid attention to computer mediated communication, indicating the duality of interactivity and importance of the roles among parties, including sender and receiver (Rice, 1987, pp. 65-94). One of the important arguments in the field of computer mediated communication is that it involves the willing participation of parties, for instance, citizens and governments, in a communication process.

In contrast to research based on psychology and communication which have not incorporated the concepts of citizen, citizenship, government, and bureaucracy into their communication models, researchers in political science and public administration have considered the previous notions and the context of interactivity essential. In particular, in the fields of political science and public administration, citizen-government interaction has been mainly studied from the perspective of citizen participation.[1]

Scholars have pursued questions about citizen participation in groups, social activities, and political activities (Verba, Schlozman, & Brady, 1995). Many researchers in the area of political science and public administration have argued that citizen participation is essential in democratic governance since it helps build consensus in policies, enhances legitimacy in administrative decision making, and restores trust in government (Berman, 1997, pp. 105-112; Creighton, 1981; King & Stivers, 1998, pp. 3-18; Langton, 1978a, pp. 1-12; Sanoff, 2000). For example, social capital theorists consider citizen participation as the essence of the health of democracy. In addition, as O'Connell (1999) argues in *Civil Society: The Underpinnings of American Democracy*, effective citizenship makes government effective.

Citizen participation, therefore, is critical for the development of a democratic society and productive government.

Scholars in the field of public administration have discussed the relationship between citizens and governments. Some (Barrett & Greene, 1995; Gore, 1993) argue the customer model based on market-based and enterprise public administration theories, and Schachter (1997) suggests the owner model, viewing citizens as owners of government. Also, Smith and Huntsman (1997, pp. 309-318) propose the value-centered perspective exploring the notion of citizens as co-investors in the community. In addition, Luton (1993, pp. 114-134) proposes the grid of citizen-government connection based on the exploration of the motivations of citizens and public officials.

In the Information Age, simultaneous citizen-government interaction through information and communication technologies (ICTs) such as e-mails, digital policy forums through bulletin boards, and real-time digital chat has already happened. Digital deliberation is one of examples for improving citizen-government interaction through ICTs. For instance, Holzer, Melitski, Rho, and Schwester (2004) analyzed three cases of digital deliberation and argued that digital deliberation can play an important role to improve trust in government.

In this context, it is important to evaluate current practice of digital deliberation. That is, can we consider current practice of digital deliberation as authentic citizen participation in governance process? This study reviews current practice of digital deliberation both in Korean central government to figure out if it is authentic or not.

Information and Communication Technologies and Digital Deliberation

Deliberation has long been considered an essential component of genuine democracy. Deliberation[2] is careful thought and discussion about issues and decisions. Deliberation, therefore, is a process of consulting with others in a process of reaching a decision by appealing to reasons or common interests that everybody could accept (Bohman, 1996, pp. 4-9). Democratic discourse is at the center of what has become known in recent years as public realm theory. Political theorists such as Arendt (1958) and Habermas (1989) have devoted considerable attention to the importance of public discourse in modern democracies. In particular, the concept of the public sphere as discussed by Habermas (1984) and others includes several requirements for authenticity.

Generally, ICTs can create opportunities both for receiving important information and for participating in discussions. However, are ICTs conducive to deliberative governance? The issues raised by this question, however, are complex, abstract, and much more a question of judgment. There are two broad views of the impact of ICTs on deliberative governance. Whereas some (Blanchard & Horan, 1998, pp. 293-307; Klein, 1999, pp. 213-220) are optimistic, others (Kraut et al, 1998, pp. 1017-1031; Wilhelm, 1998, pp. 313-338) are not.

First, there are the technological optimists who see ICTs not only as easier and faster, but as qualitatively better — holding out new ways of existing, working, communicating, and participating in political life (Dutton, 1996, pp. 269-290; Negroponte, 1995; Ogden, 1994, pp. 713-729). In his book, *Democracy and Its Critics*, Dahl (1989, p. 339) argues that "tele-communications can give every citizen the opportunity to place questions of their own on the public agenda and participate in discussions with experts, policy-makers and fellow citizens." In addition, Grossman (1995, p. 15) offers that "big losers in the present-day reshuffling and resurgence of public influence are the traditional institutions that have served as the main intermediaries between government and its citizens: the political parties, labor unions, civic associations, even the commentators and correspondents in the mainstream press."

Cross (1998, pp. 139-143) discusses the relationship between ICTs and democracy, focusing on such democratic norms as (1) informing voters, (2) representativeness, and (3) participation. With respect to dissemination of information, ICTs play an important role as a mechanism for dissemination of government information to citizens (Korac-Kakabadse & Korac-Kakabadse, 1999, p. 216; Langelier, 1996, pp. 38-45; Lips, 1997). In addition, McConaghy (1996) argues that there would also be benefits to open government. By making more accessible the information which is used in the development of government policy, an information service would allow the citizen to be more fully involved in the democratic process. Also, in terms of representativeness, ICTs can enable policy makers to be aware of citizens' needs and opinions on policy issues. Finally, with respect to participation, McLean (1989, pp. 108-110) points out that ICTs potentially make direct participation possible because they overcome the problem of large, dispersed populations. Moreover, Arterton (1987, p. 189) argues that more citizens can participate because many of the burdens of participation are lowered, and this in turn will increase equity in public decision making (Arterton, 1987, pp. 50-51; Barber, 1984). Further, ICTs can facilitate better communication and information flows between citizens and policy makers and increase the number of voters who will participate in public decision making. This is closely related to the civil society model among four electronic democracy models suggested by Korac-Kakabadse and Korac-Kakabadse (1999, pp. 213-215).

The other view is less optimistic, maintaining that changing institutions and behavior patterns are a slow and problematic process. "It's so easy to imagine a scenario in which technology is used to get instant judgments from people. If it is used that way, we haven't seen anything yet when it comes to high-tech lynchings. ... Real democracy is slow and deliberative" (Conte, 1995). Electronic newsgroups, unless carefully moderated, can get out of hand. Unmoderated groups often get quite abusive and wander off topic. Politicians and other community leaders with whom citizens wish to interact become reluctant to engage, especially at the beginning of a dialogue, for they fear being "flamed" or losing their ability to lead from behind. Then, there is the problem of dealing with the overload of undifferentiated and uncategorized information and data. In addition, in spite of the increasing amounts of information now available, the increasingly wide distribution it receives, and especially the speed with which it is transferred, there is no evidence that the quality of decision making has improved or that decisions are more democratic.

*Figure 1. CitizenSpace, UK Online (Available at http://www.ukonline.gov.uk/CitizenSpace/
CitizenSpace/fs/en)*

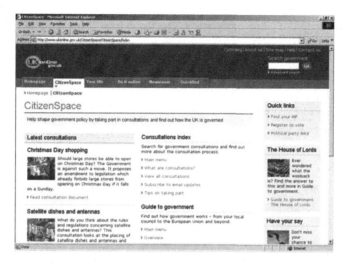

Digital Deliberation in Practice: CitizenSpace

An exemplary practice of digital deliberation in government is CitizenSpace in the United Kingdom (http://www.ukonline.gov.uk/CitizenSpace/CitizenSpace/fs/en). In this section, the practice of digital deliberation on the CitizenSpace in 2003 is briefly discussed.

UK online is a national drive to help citizens in the United Kingdom make the most of the Internet. UK online aims to give every citizen access to the Internet by 2005, with all government departments fully online. UK online Web sites are run by the Office of the e-Envoy. In UK online Web sites, CitizenSpace is a place to enable citizens to play a role in consultations and forums, as in Figure 1.

Citizens who register can receive e-mail updates for consultation. Consultation, simply, is public involvement in the governmental process. For effective consultation, information dissemination is necessary through e-mail as well as on the Web sites.

Since September 1, 2001, 619 topics had been consulted and were closed as of May 2, 2003. In addition, 174 topics remain open for consultation. Citizens can submit ideas or comments for consultation, related to a specific topic, by mail or through e-mail.

In terms of forums on CitizenSpace, five topics have been discussed. Table 1 summarizes citizen deliberation on the forum. As in Table 1, many citizens participated in a relatively short period. With regard to the forum on "Pensions Green Paper," the forum was grouped into 4 categories and a total of 187 comments were communicated during the forum period.

Table 1. Citizen deliberation on the forum of CitizenSpace

Title	Deliberation Period	Number of Comments
Pensions Green Paper: Better opportunities for older workers	March 6 - March 23, 2003	46
Pensions Green Paper: Building trust in the financial services industry	March 6 - March 23, 2003	34
Pensions Green Paper: Giving people the information they need to save for retirement	March 6 - March 23, 2003	41
Pensions Green Paper: Protection for members of company pension schemes	March 6 - March 23, 2003	65
E-democracy	July 16 - October 31, 2002	427

In the forum on e-democracy, 427 messages were exchanged among participants during about 100 plus days of the forum period. On average, interactivity occurred among about 5 or so participants a day.

Citizens raised specific issues for deliberation. For instance, 20 deliberation issues were raised in the forum of "Pensions Green Paper: Better opportunities for older workers," and 13 issues were raised for the discussion of "Pensions Green Paper: Building trust in the financial services industry."

Figure 2 illustrates citizen deliberation on a specific issue, "Keep it simple," in the forum on "e-democracy." Fifteen messages by 7 participants were posted from August 27 to October 30, 2002. Eight messages, however, were posted from August 27 to August 31 and 6 messages were posted from September 2 to September 9. Only 1 message was posted on October 30.

Digital Deliberation in Korea

In 1998, the Korean National Government developed a digital policy forum to ensure citizen participation online on the Korean Government's official Web portal as can be seen in Figure 3. On this Web portal, departments provide citizens with an opportunity to input their opinions on the policy issues. As of July 13, 2005, 411 policy issues have been discussed since September 18, 1998, about 60 policy issues a year. In this section, the practice of digital deliberation from 2001 to 2004 is analyzed.

In four years from 2001, 233 policy issues had been discussed online, about 60 issues a year. There, however, is a little difference among 4 years as can be seen in Figure 4. In 2001, only 28 policy issues had been discussed online, the lowest number of issues in 4 years, but in

Figure 2. Pattern of digital deliberation on "keep it simple"

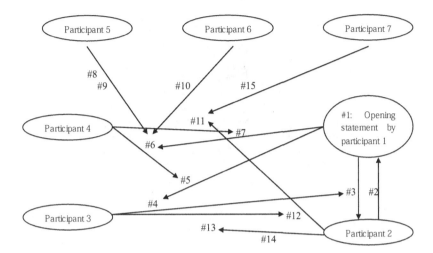

Figure 3. The R.O.K. Government's official Web portal (Available at https://www.egov. go.kr/default.html)

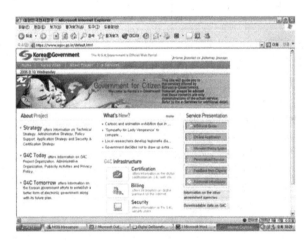

2002, 101 policy issues had been discussed online, the highest number of issues in 4 years. Also, 63 policy issues in 2003 and 41 policy issues in 2004 had been discussed.

As of 2005, the Korean central government consisted of 18 ministries, 4 agencies, and 16 administrations. All ministries, agencies, and administrations can provide citizens with an opportunity for participating in online discussion. As can be seen in Table 2, while 22 policy issues in 2001 and 28 policy issues in 2002 had been posted, only 2 in 2003 and 4 in 2004

Figure 5. The number of policy issues discussed online from 2001 to 2004

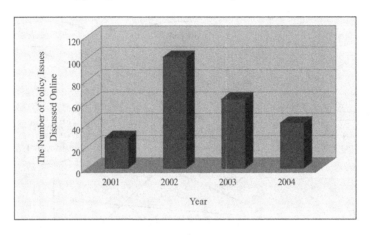

Table 2. The number of policy issues provided for discussion by 18 ministries

	2001	2002	2003	2004	Total
Ministry of Finance & Economy					0
Ministry of Education & Human Resources Development					0
Ministry of Unification					0
Ministry of Foreign Affairs & Trade	3	4			7
Ministry of Justice		12	2	1	15
Ministry of National Defense	10				10
Ministry of Government Administration & Home Affairs				3	3
Ministry of Science & Technology					0
Ministry of Culture & Tourism					0
Ministry of Agriculture & Forestry					0
Ministry of Commerce, Industry & Energy	9				9
Ministry of Information & Communication					0
Ministry of Health & Welfare					0
Ministry of Environment					0
Ministry of Labor					0
Ministry of Gender Equality & Family					0
Ministry of Construction & Transportation					0
Ministry of Maritime Affairs & Fisheries		12			12
Total	22	28	2	4	56

had been posted by ministries. Among 18 ministries, 6 ministries (Ministry of Foreign Affairs & Trade, Ministry of Justice, Ministry of National Defense, Ministry of Government Administration & Home Affairs, Ministry of Commerce, Industry & Energy, and Ministry of Maritime Affaires and Fisheries) had posed discussion issues in 4 years. None of these, however, had posted discussion issues every year. Only Ministry of Justice had posted discussion issues in three consecutive years from 2002, while Ministry of National Defense (2001), Ministry of Government Administration & Home Affairs (2004), Ministry of Commerce, Industry & Energy (2001), and Ministry of Maritime Affairs & Fisheries (2002) had an activity in only one year of those 4-year periods. Since not only this official Web portal but also each ministry Web site has provided citizens with policy discussion opportunities, every ministry has some difficulties to care for scattered Web sites for policy discussion. In addition, some policy issues have been discussed in the Web sites of Blue House. Integration of digital deliberation is needed.

In terms of the number of participants in policy discussion every year, while 251 participants in 2001 and 734 participants in 2002 had posted their opinions on the Web sites of digital policy forum, 605 in 2003 and 212 in 2004 had provided their opinions. Like the number of policy issues discussed on the Web sites, the number of participants every year had decreased.

With regard to the number of participant per discussion topic, about 9 citizens had participated in policy discussion of each topic in 2001 and about 7 participants a topic in 2002, as can be seen in Figure 6. Also, in 2003, there were about 10 opinions per topic, while about 5 opinions in 2004. Since only a few opinions about policy issues had been posted in 4-year period, the problem of representativeness exists.

As can be seen in Figure 7, there is a problem of digital divide. In 4-year period, the sum of opinions posted was 1,802. Of those, 42.39% was posted by participants in the age of 30s.

Figure 6. The number of participants per topic

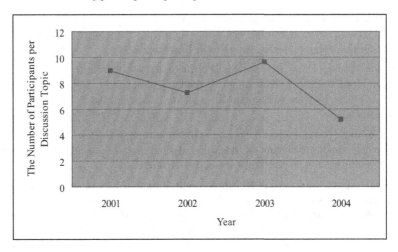

Figure 7. Percentage of participants per age group

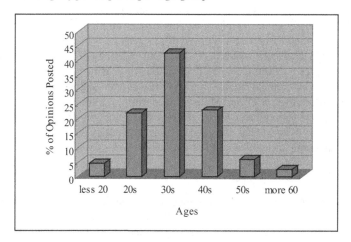

While 22.74% of opinions was posted by the age of 40s, 21.77% was posted by the age of 20s. Only 2.64% of opinions was posted by the age of more than 60. While the opinions of the age of 30s were overrepresented, the opinions of the age of more than 60 were less-represented.

In addition to the age group, with respect to gender, while 79.86% of opinions posted were by males, 20.14% were posted by females. While the opinions of males were overrepresented, the opinions of female were less-represented.

Implications and Policy Recommendations

There is a temptation to believe that ICTs are by its nature profoundly democratic. A number of powerful factors, however, militate in favor of significant changes in digital deliberative democracy. Of those factors, none is more basic than human.

In terms of technological barriers, such as (1) penetration of the Internet and other digital transmission technologies; (2) technological standardization; and (3) broadband capacity at reasonable prices, they are some relatively short-term barriers and the solution of these obstacles is in sight.

In addition to these technological barriers, the main barriers to the use of ICTs in digital deliberative democracy are human. Of those, digital divide such as generational factors and insufficient public interest in policy are obstacles to overcome.

One of social issues to be solved in contemporary information society is digital divide describing unequal access to ICTs based on such factors as race, ethnicity, income, education, and gender. Most research (U.S. Department of Commerce, 1995, 1998, 1999, 2000) has focused on access to ICTs for the study of digital divide. Mossberger, Tolbert, and Stansbury

(2003), however, categorize digital divide into four groups such as an access divide, a skills divide, an economic opportunity divide, and a democratic divide and show the current status of four types of digital divide based on empirical findings. Due to the digital divide, some groups in society, for instance, the elderly and the poor, have less voice in digital citizen participation. In digital citizen participation, as a result, the issue of representativeness should be seriously considered by public administrators.

In addition to digital divide, very few people wish to participate actively in government, preferring by and large to stay at home and enjoy the satisfactions of private life. The general lack of public awareness of the information available from a multitude of sources contributes to this state of affairs. As discussed earlier, less than 10 opinions per policy issue had been posted in digital deliberation on the Korean Governments' official Web portal.

In fact, ICTs play an important role to improve digital democracy. ICTs can facilitate direct communications between citizens and public managers. Thanks to ICTs, citizens can track and influence decision making at every step in the process from agenda setting to final vote.

ICTs, however, are not a panacea. Even though they have a great impact on digital democracy, ICTs also have some limitations to achieve the high level of fully developed digital democracy. The lessons from the analysis in this study as well as other research suggest the fundamentals or basics of the human nature. Without the changes of perceptions and behaviors of citizens and public servants, it is not easy to attain fully developed digital democracy only by information and communication technology. Active will of citizens and public servants is more fundamental than information and communication technologies. In addition, civic education is also important to improve digital democracy.

Conclusion

Contrary to the assumption of democratic theory, citizens are not well informed and aware of government policies, rules, and regulations. In addition, citizens are typically not particularly good at creating thoughtful opinions on them and taking serious consideration of opposing opinions. Through citizen-government interaction, citizens can be better informed and aware of government activities. Citizen-government interaction can be considered a learning process. In this sense, public deliberation in governance process is a key to improving authentic democracy.

In the information age, ICTs can facilitate public deliberation. Many countries around the world have developed digital deliberation system. For instance, CitizenSpace in the United Kingdom and Korean central government discussed earlier are exemplars.

As discussed above, however, current practice of digital deliberation through ICTs has some limitation. Unlike the expectation, there was a lack of active participation by citizens as well as public servants. The policies should be made by the will of citizens in democratic governance but current practice of digital deliberation did not support this statement. These practices have violated the principle of democracy, which is government by the people. The citizens' strong will of active digital deliberation is a key to the success of digital deliberation in the democratic governance.

Acknowledgments

The author would like to thank Bo-Eun Kim and Yun-Hee Do from Seoul Women's University for help in gathering the data on the activities of digital deliberation in Korea.

References

Arendt, H. (1958). *The human condition*. Chicago: University of Chicago Press.

Arterton, C. F. (1987). *Can technology protect democracy?* Newbury Park: Sage Publications.

Barber, B. (1984). *Strong democracy: Participatory politics for a new age*. Berkeley: University of California Press.

Barrett, K., & Greene, R. (1995, March 14). Capitol of bad management: Congress stacked the deck against D.C. then ignored its plight. Now it can share the blame. *Financial World,* pp. 50-71.

Berman, E. M. (1997). Dealing with cynical citizens. *Public Administration Review, 57*(2), 105-112.

Blanchard, A., & Horan, T. (1998). Virtual communities and social capital. *Social Science Computer Review,* 16, 293-307.

Bohman, J. (1996). *Public deliberation: Pluralism, complexity, and democracy*. Cambridge: The MIT Press.

Buber, M. (1970). *I and thou* (W. Kaufman, Trans.). New York: Charles Senbner's Sons.

Conte, C. R. (1995). Teledemocracy — For better or worse. *Governing, 8*(9), 33-37.

Creighton, J. L. (1981). *The public involvement manual*. Cambridge: Abt.

Cross, B. (1998). Teledemocracy: Canadian political parties listening to their constituents. In C. J. Alexander & L. A. Pal (Eds.), *Digital democracy: Policy and politics in the wired world* (pp. 132-148). Oxford: Oxford University Press.

Dahl, R. A. (1989). *Democracy and its critics*. New Haven: Yale University Press.

Dixon, N. M. (1996). *Perspective on dialogue: Making talk developmental for individuals and organizations*. Greensboro, NC: Center for Creative Leadership.

Dutton, W. H. (1996). Network rules of order: Regulating speech in public electronic forums. *Media, Culture and Society, 18*, 269-290.

Gore, A. (1993). *From red tape to results: Creating a government that works better and costs less*. Washington, DC: Government Printing Office.

Grossman, L. K. (1995). *The electronic republic: Reshaping democracy in the information age*. New York: Viking.

Habermas, J. (1984). *The theory of communicative action. Volume 1: Reason and the rationalization of society* (T. McCarthy, Trans.). Boston: Beacon Press.

Habermas, J. (1989). *The structural transformation of the public sphere* (T. Burger & F. Lawrence, Trans.). Cambridge: Harvard University Press.

Holzer, M., Melitski, J., Rho, S., & Schwester, R. (2004). *Restoring trust in government: The potential of digital citizen participation.* Washington, DC: IBM Center for the Business of Government.

King, C., & Stivers, C. (1998). Introduction: The anti-government era. In C. S. King & C. Stivers (Eds.), *Government is us: Public administration in an anti-government era* (pp. 3-18). Thousand Oaks: Sage.

Klein, H. K. (1999). Tocqueville in cyberspace: Using the Internet for citizen associations. *The Information Society, 15*, 213-220.

Korac-Kakabadse, A., & Korac-Kakabadse, N. (1999). Information technology's impact on the quality of democracy. In R. Heeks (Ed.), *Reinventing government in the information age: International practice in IT-enabled public sector reform* (pp. 211-228). London: Routledge.

Kraut, R., Patterson, M., Lundmark, V., Kiesler, S., Mukopadhyay, T., & Scherlis, W. (1998). Internet paradox: A social technology that reduces social involvement and psychological well-being. *American Psychologist, 53*, 1017-1031.

Langelier, P. (1996). Special series: Local government on the Internet. Part 3: Local government home pages. *Popular Government, 62*(3), 38-45.

Langton, S. (1978a). Citizen participation in America: Current reflections on the state of the art. In S. Langton (Ed.), *Citizen participation in America: Essays on the state of the art* (pp. 1-12). Lexington: Lexington Books.

Langton, S. (1978b). What is citizen participation? In S. Langton (Ed.), *Citizen participation in America: Essays on the state of the art* (pp. 13-24). Lexington: Lexington Books.

Lips, M. (1997, May 5-6). *Reinventing public service delivery through ICT: Lessons drawing from developments in the USA, UK, and the Netherlands.* Paper presented at the IFIP WG 8.5 Workshop, Empowering the Citizens Through IT, Stockholm, Sweden.

Luton, L. (1993). Citizen-administrator connections: Impacts on public facility-siting decision making. *Administration and Society, 25*(2), 114-134.

McConaghy, D. (1996). The electronic delivery of government services. *Comments on the UK Green Paper.* Unpublished government report.

McLean, I. (1989). *Democracy and the new technology.* Cambridge: Polity Press.

Mossberger, K., Tolbert, C. J., & Stansbury, M. (2003). *Virtual inequality: Beyond the digital divide.* Washington, DC: Georgetown University Press.

Negroponte, N. (1995). *Being digital.* New York: Knopf.

O'Connell, B. (1999). *Civil society: The underpinnings of American democracy.* Hanover, NH: Tufts University Press.

Ogden, M. R. (1994). Politics in a parallel universe. *Futures, 26*, 713-729.

Rice, R. E. (1987). Computer-mediated communication and organizational innovation. *Journal of Communication, 37*(4), 65-94.

Riva, G., & Galimberti, C. (1997). The psychology of cyberspace: A socio-cognitive framework to computer-mediated communication. *New Ideas in Psychology, 15*(2), 141-158.

Sanoff, H. (2000). *Community participation methods in design and planning.* New York: Wiley.

Schachter, H. L. (1997). *Reinventing government or reinventing ourselves: The role of citizen owners in making a better government.* Albany: State University of New York Press.

Smith, G. E., & Huntsman, C. A. (1997). Reframing the metaphor of the citizen-government relationship: A value-centered perspective. *Public Administration Review, 57*(4), 309-318.

U.S. Department of Commerce. (1995). *Falling through the net: A survey of the "have nots" in rural and urban America.* Retrieved April 29, 2006, from http://www.ntia.doc.gov/ntiahome/fallingthru.html

U.S. Department of Commerce. (1998). *Falling through the net II: New data on the digital divide.* Retrieved April 29, 2006, from http://www.ntia.doc.gov/ntiahome/net2/falling.html

U.S. Department of Commerce. (1999). *Falling through the net: Defining the digital divide.* Retrieved April 29, 2006, from http://www.ntia.doc.gov/ntiahome/fttn99/FTTN.pdf

U.S. Department of Commerce. (2000). *Falling through the net: Toward digital inclusion.* Retrieved April 29, 2006, from http://search.ntia.doc.gov/pdf/fttn00.pdf

Verba, S., Schlozman, K. L., & Brady, H. E. (1995). *Voice and equality.* Cambridge, MA: Harvard University Press.

Wilhelm, A. G. (1998). Virtual sounding boards: How deliberative is on-line political discussion. *Information, Communication & Society, 1,* 313-338.

Yankelovich, D. (1999). *The magic of dialogue: Turning conflict into cooperation.* New York: Simon and Schuster.

Endnotes

[1]   Citizen participation, according to Langton (1978b, pp. 13-24), refers to citizen involvement in administrative decision-making including service delivery and management decisions. Citizen-government interaction, therefore, is a broader notion than citizen participation since the former includes activities occurred in the transaction of public service which the latter rarely include.

[2]   To make the definition of deliberation clear, it is important to figure out the differences among other forms of communication such as dialogue, debate, and discussion. With regard to dialogue, Nancy Dixon (1996, p. 24) broadly refers dialogue as "special kind of talk." Also, suggesting an I-Thou relationship, Martin Buber (1970) develops the essence of dialogue. He argues that each group or person eventually reaches to say "you and me" instead of "you or me." According to Daniel Yankelovich (1999, p. 15),

therefore, it refers to "a process of successful relationship building." He (1999, pp. 41-46) suggests three central elements of dialogue such as equality without coercion, empathic listening, and probing of assumption. In terms of debate, it is a talk about win-lose in that each group or person defends its own and proves others wrong. In this sense, while dialogue emphasizes mutual understanding among participants, debate leads participants to a combative relationship. Also, Daniel Yankelovich (1999, p. 41) contrasts dialogue with discussion. According to him, while dialogue includes all three central elements discussed above, discussion lacks one or more of them, like debate. Regardless of the interchangeability, scholars such as Bohman (1996) make a distinction between deliberation and dialogue. According to him, while deliberation is "the process of forming a public reason — one that everyone in the deliberative process finds acceptable," (Bohman, 1996, p. 25), dialogue "opens up space for deliberation" (Bohman, 1996, p. 61). In this sense, according to him, deliberation is "dialogue with a particular goal" (Bohman, 1996, p. 57).

Chapter VI

Electronic Surveillance for the Public Good

Liz Lee-Kelley, University of Surrey, UK

Ailsa Kolsaker, University of Surrey, UK

Abstract

The central government in the UK is determined to employ new surveillance technology to combat the threat of terrorist activities. This chapter contributes to the important debate on the relationship between citizens and the government, by discussing not whether electronic surveillance should be used, but rather, when it is acceptable to the populace. From our analysis, we conclude that a reconciliation of state-interest and self-interest is critical for the success of e-governance; as such, electronic surveillance's mission has to be about serving the law-abiding majority and their needs, and its scope and benefits must be clearly understood by the visionaries, implementers, and the citizenry.

Introduction

Many contemporary social theorists argue that concerns that advances in electronic technologies would lead to panoptican societies have proved unfounded (see Bauman, 1998; Bogard, 1996; Boyne, 2000). The popular discourse of the Information Age embracing direct and indirect surveillance, supported by extensive systems of data capture and retention is overly technology-focused and insufficiently cognizant of cultural norms and impulses. The panoptican society implies a docile populace, an inactive community upon which Lyon's (2003) conception of profiling and surveillance of any number of individuals perceived as undesirable or dangerous are conducted. Yet, there is much to suggest that modern Western citizens are far from docile. According to Boyne (2000) and drawing on Mathieson's (1997) idea of the viewer society, Western reaction to the panoptical impulse renders it redundant by the propensity of normal, socialised subjects to engage actively in self-surveillance. This is illustrated by the ascendancy of the celebrity culture, the popularity of the "Big Brother," and similar reality television programmes, and the use of Web cams for "private" viewings. There is also a visible hunger for immediacy in knowledge and awareness of current events, and viewers' willingness to contribute to the dissemination process is redefining the role, content, and delivery of mass media. A recent example is the use of digital and mobile phone cameras in December 2005 to capture and provide evidence of the UK Buncefield oil depot fire (reputed to be the biggest industrial blaze in Europe), where the BBC news team actually used video images of the blaze relayed to them by nearby witnesses. The age of citizen journalism has arrived.

From a Foucauldian perspective the active engagement of citizens in these pursuits should come as no surprise. Foucault (1980) argues that participants in communities of practice not only internalise and accept behavioural norms, but also actively shape members' dispositions, and reinforce norms, controls, and exclusions. In the present context, far from being passive subjects of a regime, modern citizens must be viewed as active, willing contributors who not only accept, but sanction prevailing social practices. This is the synoptican society envisaged by Mathieson (1997) where surveillance has evolved from the few watching the many to the many watching the few. The individual as an active member of the media society has become habituated to being a watcher and is not overly concerned with being watched. Although Boyne (2000) has suggested ego investment in the continuation of this state of affairs, we would add that the thrill factor of being among the firsts to be at the scene of a dangerous or catastrophic event is also a strong motivator.

This is not to say, however, that the spectre of the panoptican society has disappeared completely. Current debates on the benefits and disbenefits of electronic technologies have begun to focus increasingly upon public surveillance. It might be argued that the voluntary participation of the citizenry actually increases the menace of the panoptican spectre, as those in power and with arguably a higher order agenda of monitoring and enforcing law and order could interpret the public's synoptic tendencies as evidence of tacit acceptance of all surveillance practices. The machinery of surveillance stands by and is ready to be employed — but by whom, for whom, in whose name, and in whose interest?

In this chapter we query whether a society that engages in apparently harmless (although some would argue, frivolous and mindless) voyeurism has now entered into what might be described as the panoptic-synoptican era where the watched are also watchers themselves. Rather than taking a populist view of the citizenry being reduced to what Lyon (2001, p. 41) has called a "digital person" quivering under an all-seeing, all-knowing Big Brother, this chapter examines the underlying logic for the growing tendency by the UK government towards electronic surveillance to instigate political and social changes for the public good. We consider public reaction not in isolation but as a general indicator of the power relationships between state and the citizenry, to provide an explanation of public distinction between acceptable and nonacceptable electronic governance.

Mechanisms of Surveillance

The UK has one of the most extensive and sophisticated surveillance systems in the world (FIPR, 2005). Indeed, the headlines and leading articles in the Independent newspaper (2004) claimed that around 20% of the world's closed-circuit television (CCTV) cameras could be found in the UK alone. Other recent press headlines also highlighted the extent to which new surveillance technology is being deployed — and welcomed — in a variety of contexts across the UK (Electronic Design, 2005; Liberty, 2005).

Border guards routinely employ thermal imaging devices in addition to the more mainstream CCTV cameras to monitor the citizenry and overseas visitors as they enter and exit UK airports, sea-ports, and the Channel Tunnel. Currently, a new generation of surveillance cameras are being trialled for UK airports. These Passive Millimetre Wave Radar cameras are supposed to be able to detect metallic objects concealed under our clothes. Although increasingly intrusive, citizen resistance to this kind of surveillance approach has been minimal, as it is widely recognised that technology can play a key role in locating explosive devices, illegal substances, contraband goods, illegal immigrants, and so on.

Surveillance technology is also used widely in other contexts. Military applications are finding their way into civilian crime detection and law enforcement. An example is the remote controlled airship which is rumoured to be under review by the London Metropolitan Police. In the central business district of London — the City — there are reported to be over 10,000 CCTV cameras (Electronic Design, 2005). A further 6,000 cameras are located throughout the London Underground (*The Guardian*, 2005). Station assistants are now trained to use the CCTV software to spot unattended baggage and to scan for untoward behaviour. These suspicious behaviour systems are new and untested in the judiciary system; significantly, the criteria for deciding suspicious behaviour are secret. Another little publicised example is the London Borough of Newham's supposed role as the beta-cite for the possible roll-out of Visionics' Mandrake facial recognition system across other London boroughs. This system has a database of faces and logs the times and dates of passersby at specified public areas. Amongst its many potential uses, it can be an effective tool for enforcing curfews and protecting private or "no-go" areas. Once again, the criteria for inclusion in the database and extent of public awareness or agreement are unknown.

The stated reasons for the increased use of surveillance technology vary. Before the London bombings on July 7, 2005, the emphasis was upon ensuring that those living in the UK have permission to be here, whilst post July 7 the main emphasis has been upon safeguarding the public against acts of terrorism. Since July 2005 government debate has moved on from whether as a society we ought to employ surveillance technology to where and how it ought to be deployed, despite protests from civil liberty groups such as Statewatch which have argued vociferously that there is no proven link between the presence of surveillance systems and crime prevention. Certainly, CCTVs do not seem to have a deterrent effect on brawls and drunkard behaviour common at weekends and after bars' closing hours in the larger cities, nor are they able to prevent more hideous crimes such as the recent alleged rape of a teenage girl in a pub toilet in Brighton, Sussex (*BBC News*, June 18, 2005).

In a densely populated but mobile world, one has to question whether any state can really hope to maintain a comprehensive overview of the activities of its population. For the UK with its mix of immigrant cultures, religions, and beliefs, it is unlikely that any surveillance short of that exercised in the old communist regimes would be sufficient to deter transgressors. Besides, new software techniques such as facial recognition, although promising, are costly and have yet to prove themselves. Despite these obvious hurdles, the UK government appears determined to invest in even greater deployment of surveillance technologies. For example, aside from an agenda to double the number of CCTV cameras on the London Underground by 2010, there is also a plan to introduce airline-style checks on the rail-link between Paddington station and Heathrow airport and at certain points on the London Underground.

Other imminent installations include the much criticised proposal to introduce biometric identity cards (ID) by 2007. The ID cards are intended to have two key benefits: first, to prevent terrorism and, second, to ensure that those entitled to use public services are able to do so. Total estimated cost ranges between £10.6 to £19.2 billion (LSE, 2005), with no figure given for ongoing updates as people are born, marry, change names, move house, and eventually die. The scheme has been much criticised for a number of naïve assumptions, such as that the cards will be impossible to forge; criminals and terrorists will be easily detected since they will not possess an ID card; ID cards will make crimes easier to solve, and it has been suggested by numerous groups that the ID card scheme is simply a smokescreen for establishing a national citizen database. The government's unwaivering belief in the scheme is taken as evidence (by protest groups and factions of the media) that amongst politicians the panoptican mentality is in the ascendancy once again. Yet, despite media interest and civil liberty groups' protestations, there has been little reaction from the public at large, either about ID cards or indeed concerning the increasing use of surveillance technology in general.

Public Perception of E-Government: A Paradox

Although authors such as Haggerty and Ericson (2001) may argue that the object of contemporary systems of surveillance is not punishment or control, we posit that e-governance in the Labour government context can be interpreted as the super-ability to observe, control, classify, and divide the population into categories of rich, poor, fraudster, bankrupt, crime risk, and so forth. That is, e-government or e-governance is a conduit with which our Labour government can deliver its Third Way ideology of state involvement and regulation. Public and private organisational policies of exclusion and inclusion may then be exercised based on the identified categorisations.

Possibilities for technology surveillance are numerous and extensive. Public intrusion into private lives is reinforced regularly by government broadcasts, such as a campaign by the DVLA advertising their ability to identify and fine late or overdue car-tax licences. Technology enabled eavesdropping or snooping of the unsuspecting populace includes police officers, M15 agents, and even private investigators working for government (and commercial) agencies. Indeed, the high penetration of mobile communication devices and mobile personal organisers (collectively known as MDs) in the UK makes phone-tapping easy, effective, and cost-efficient. As individuals carry their MDs with them, their location can be pinpointed and their conversation monitored — safely at a distance and without the need for excessive manpower. Defence electronic manufacturers such as TRW regularly sell specialised MDs to the security forces. Although most people are unaware of, or affected by, the surveillance on them, the discovery of being "spied on" can be a traumatic experience especially when there appears to be little recourse since the police are not obliged to confirm one's suspicion one way or the other. There is an independent watchdog — the Investigatory Powers Tribunal — but it would appear that neither it nor its predecessor have ever supported any complaint over phone tapping or electronic surveillance in the last 18 years (*BBC News*, November 12, 2003). In theory, any and every member of the population with a suitable mobile device is capable of being monitored; in practice, only a few are targeted — and even fewer will ever know that they are being watched. There is no way of confirming the extent of this kind of covert surveillance.

Despite the British public's tendency to have a fairly cynical view of politicians and their government agencies, individuals who have to endure any form of private surveillance are still surprised and hurt by the inability or unwillingness of public institutions and the legal system to protect them against this intrusion. If queried, it is likely that an individual will admit to some idea of the capability of technology for use in personal surveillance, but has somehow elected not to think about it or to continue in the belief that existing judicial and legal frameworks are sufficient to protect against such blatant violations of personal privacy. To do otherwise, would rock the very foundations of consensual democracy and accountability.

Whilst the Freedom of Information Act, which came into full force in January 2005, ameliorates the imbalance to some extent by allowing citizens to access categories of information previously held out with the public domain, unilateral exclusions and the need to pay for every request for disclosure diminishes its stated purpose of openness, transparency and ubiquitous access. The government's reply to the Science and Technology Select Committee's report on "the scientific responses to terrorism" (E-Envoy, 2003) provides a further hint of things to come and highlights the conflict between confidentiality and accountability. In the document the government reiterates its duty to ensure public safety and national security as well as its commitment to utilise "the best science and technology available" towards that goal. At the same time, the government considers it inappropriate and dangerous to release information that might be used by terrorists and the criminal fraternity. Resistance by those in public service to complete openness and free informational exchange highlights the difficult balance between respecting citizens' right to know and keeping secret information that they have deemed necessary to protect the law-abiding public from internal and external threats. Indeed, there are already some rumours of increased shredding of government documents.

Another case in point is a classified report by the National Criminal Intelligence Service (NCIS) agency proposing to require all communications service providers (CSPs) "to retain communications data originating or terminating in the UK, or routing through UK networks, including any such data that is stored offshore" for a period of seven years. The motive may be justified in terms of tackling cybercrime, but the wide-sweeping and indiscriminate retention methodology is open to question as it infringes the principles of the Data Protection Act (1998) and the Human Rights Act (1998).

Similarly, in the name of fighting money laundering and other financial crimes, the whole of the UK financial services industry is required to keep comprehensive records of their customers, which they, as effective owners of the data, could also use for their own marketing efforts. Blau's (1964) conception of human beings as value maximisers emerges here as those in official capacities or positions of trust are likely to desire some form of pay-off and as such, are inclined to selfish acts; the outcome of which could be the exploitation of the very public the surveillance mechanisms are allegedly designed to protect. Once again, it is unlikely that individuals would ever know how exactly and by whom the knowledge about their personal and financial data are being stored and used. It would seem that individuals are expected by the state and those in power to have faith and rely on the safety mechanisms of the larger "abstract systems" (Giddens, 1991). The question remains: who is watching the watchers? More to the point, what is the basis of our apparent lack of concern or apathy over the decisions and acts of others taken on our behalf? Of concern to the authors is the political reasoning that an apparently moral motive for public benefit is sufficient virtue in justifying such wide ranging power — to quote Martin Hollis (1998, p. 9), "it is not the sleep of reason which begets monsters."

Anxiety over being watched is very real as reflected in a U.S. Gallup Poll pre-September 11 which reported that people found the loss of privacy more disturbing than the prospect of nuclear war. Presumably the belief or paranoia — founded or otherwise — that the likelihood of government intrusion is much higher than nuclear conflict. Moreover, the tension between public access and protection of civil liberties in other areas of e-government is evident: public lethargy and marked reluctance to adopt government online services resulted in the discontinuation of the business section of the ukonline.gov.uk portal in April 2004. In the E-Envoy's fourth UK Online report, it had to acknowledge that although public awareness of online government services registered 96% of Britain's population, three quarters of them have never visited a government Web site. In a similar vein, public outcry against speed cameras has forced a review of the number and location of speed cameras across the UK.

The irony is that as society grows increasingly opaque, with individuals becoming more and more distant from their neighbours, more is known by the government about individuals. The long-term implications of a simultaneous erosion of societal closeness and increase in state knowledge about citizens are significant in terms of the tacit, consensual agreement between government and citizens. Once the state knows more about citizens than the citizens themselves, the ability of citizens to question and call to account the government for actions done in their name is diminished significantly. It could be argued that the populace is to be blamed for its own acquiescence and submission to increasing public profiling practices — perhaps the technology and media-led leisure pursuits in Western societies, as in the UK, have produced a generation that is largely ambivalent to the idea of being watched. That is, this apparent lack of public response is symptomatic of Foucault's constitution of participatory, self-regulating subjects and therefore a feature of Mathieson's synoptican society. But this explanation may be too superficial and the relatively subdued reaction to government surveillance practices, so far, may be attributable to good planning and communication (if one were generous) or simply, a fortuitous balance between peoples' expectations of their right to privacy and their right to personal safety. Alternatively, this may be the population's reaction to a perceived Orwellian approach to systematic governance and control manifested as a deliberate withdrawal and disengagement from the larger political and social domains.

Policy makers are reliant on their vision being implemented with competence, care, and good faith which, given the numerous failed citizens' charters and withdrawal of the recent UK Computer Within Reach programme (owing to poor distribution, faulty hardware, and exorbitant help-line costs) would suggest a disconnection between the visionaries and the administrators or implementers. The European Court of Human Rights' landmark judgement on the Geoff Peck case in 2003 highlights the problem of over-reliance on the "truth" of CCTV footage and the lack of a code of conduct or regulatory framework in the UK for government agencies and regulatory bodies such as the Broadcasting Standards Commission and Independent Television Commission, including the police. Mr. Peck, who was suffering from depression and attempting to commit suicide, was caught on camera with a knife. Without obtaining Mr. Peck's permission, the council had released the unpixelled video footage to first the local media, and even more inappropriately, to the BBC's special programme called "Crime Beat." Recent government's embarrassment and furore over a recent spate of whistle-blowing by civil servants (e.g., Katherine Gun from GCHQ) and accusations by a former cabinet minister of spying on Kofi Annan the UN Secretary General, are further indications of the rift between conflicting public policies and private beliefs. Other incidents include the PM Blair's office having to defend accusations of embellishing "evidence" to support the invasion of Iraq; Home Secretary Blunkett's resignation over the possible misuse of his position to fast-track a visa application; and the implied involvement of the PM himself in events leading to the death of senior government scientist David Kelly. How will the interest of each be reconciled with the interest of all? Who is to decide what public interest is and how can that be best protected without encroaching on individual rights?

Government decisions and actions may be explained as poor political judgement, inadequate systems, and procedures or mere error, but any indiscriminate or inappropriate use of power (whether perceived or real) is a regression away from the basic tenet of "government of the people by the people" envisioned by Abraham Lincoln in his Gettysburg address (1863). An ICM poll which revealed that people are three times more likely to trust the BBC than the government (Daily Telegraph, 2004) is a telling indictment of public disillusionment and growing cynicism of the benevolence of the government. On one level this relates to the growing unease about personal privacy, tracking, data storage, and sharing. On another such concerns reflect failing participation rates in civic society from a lack of respect for politicians, increasing suspicion of their motives, and growing distance between the government and its people; creating a situation of the more the government knows about the citizens, the less people would relate and trust the government to act in their interest.

We use a recent example to illustrate this point. Government concern for public safety resulted in a UK-wide ban on using a mobile phone while driving. However, a RAC study reported that 4 out of 10 drivers were still ignoring the mobile rules (*BBC News*, 2004); leading road safety campaigners to lobby for tougher penalties and for a total ban on *all* hands-free devices. This scenario offers an interesting insight into the kaleidoscope of modern UK society: in response to public opinion, health reports and in carrying out its role as state guardian, the government uses legislation to communicate the message that talking on the mobile phone while driving is dangerous to oneself and to others and must be stopped. Those affected are unconvinced and choose to show their distrust of this unwelcome interference through continuing use. Road safety campaigners (society's self-appointed watchers) react by calling for even greater sanctions and control measures.

The public may be forgiven if their perception is one of an increasingly integrated, comprehensive network of survey and control, in which those in power such as corporations, the government, and society's viewers or watchers appear to "cooperate" and "pool" their surveillance resources to produce a panoptic-synoptican form of totalitarianism beyond the hierarchical Orwellian Big Brother state. The difference between the muted response to growing and intrusive e-surveillance and the refusal to accept and participate in the more mundane services of online government and other e-government initiatives and legislatures is the basis of our thesis that the UK citizenry can and does distinguish between acceptable and unacceptable use of technology by the government, and that acceptability is anchored on a careful match between self interest and state interest. The government needs to understand this basic concept before assuming that in the panoptic-synoptican era, initiatives will automatically be accepted simply by claims that they provide for the greater good.

Power vs. Consensual Governance

Our discussion so far points to the rapid expansion of surveillance technology with only limited unease from the population to the increased monitoring of their daily lives. This lack of reaction may be desensitisation from the insidious synoptican society. Some authors have already surmised that this apparent citizen compliance is evidence of an increasingly authoritative state and an impotent public where rulers tend to put the pursuit and retention of power before all other scruples (e.g., Lyon, 2001) — and one which, in philosopher Plato's (427-347 BC) view, is a regrettable but natural outcome of democracy (see *The Republic*, Murphy, 1951; Kraut, 1997). He predicted that democracy would plunge into dissension and conflict with an indulgence of desire and permissiveness that erodes respect for political and moral authority, in which the young no longer fear and respect their teachers; they constantly challenge their elders and the latter ape the young. Plato opined that against this background would rise a "popular champion" who is tempted to "grasp the reins of the state." In Plato's analysis the "keeper" controls "the beast" by a study of its moods, wants, and habits. For the animal to be properly tamed it is important to know which of the creature's tastes and desires are admirable, or shameful, good or bad, right or wrong. It is possible that the UK Labour government views itself as that champion whose legitimacy and power is supported by its role as protector of the citizens, from external threats, and increasingly from their own actions, thus keeping in check democracy's tendency towards destructive chaos. Surveillance technology offers all this and more.

However, this perspective continues to propagate the idea of the top-down panoptic ability of a government with a reputation for limitless power and using the malevolent presence of widespread, 24/7 surveillance to intrude on society and individuals — for their own good, of course. We venture that, unlike the "old" panoptican era where there was no route by which those who were subjected to surveillance might redress the balance, new and more accessible technology has spearheaded a new synoptic movement in which the primary targets of surveillance (the citizens) are able to scrutinise their neighbours and critically, the keeper. This redresses the balance of power between groups in society and returns to the individual, the rights of control and self-determination, and the choice of the venue, manner, and extent of disclosure. We have entered the panoptic-synoptican era where technology has produced a media society of state and private watchers with complex motivations, and is legitimised through the generalised idiom of "public interest and right to know." In short, technology has created a new equality in terms of the ability to observe, record, and publish. This provides a powerful armoury against any perceived misuse of power by the government as evidenced by the recent spate of exposés on public and political figures.

We support John Mill's (1859) assertion that while individual liberty is paramount and "the only purpose for which power can rightfully be exercised over any member of a civilised community, against his will, is to prevent harm to others" (Mill, 1859-1869/1989, p. 68), growing infringements on individual liberty are to be expected as the state expands to cope with the pressures of the modern age. In 21st century society, governments such as the UK's have to grapple to control complex and interrelated international problems that have potentially devastating impact at the local level. If surveillance may be viewed as an attempt by the state to protect its citizenry from loss or harm, compliance could be interpreted as a pragmatic response to external threats. In pursuing this interpretation we also draw upon the work of Thomas Hobbes (1588-1679) which marks the emergence of the modern liberal and addresses the balance between the liberty of the individual and the power of the state. In *Leviathan* (1660), Hobbes investigated the circumstances under which inherently and profoundly self-interested human beings would put their rights of self-government to one side in the name of upholding peace, national security, and the long-term interests of the state. An external threat to national security creates precisely the conditions within which citizens are likely to acknowledge the need to balance individual liberty with state power in order to guarantee social and political order. We should not be surprised, therefore, by citizens' compliance with increased surveillance at border crossings and in other areas of possible harm from terrorist or criminal acts. Indeed we may even interpret their reaction as further evidence of the veracity of Hobbes' observation (which echoes Machiavelli's stance in *The Discourses*) that individuals act ultimately in their own self-interest. Despite privacy in the Western society being traditionally a valued human right, the basis of citizens' acceptance to intrusion is their recognition that the cost of personal safety is the sacrifice of a certain amount of privacy.

In Hobbes and Mills' analysis, when equality and security are in conflict, the former must give way to the latter. Although equality does not mean privacy, the conception of equality of power is underlined by the right to (of individuals) and the respect for privacy and confidentiality by the state. In our own analysis, the willingness to be subjected to any form of monitoring is context specific, and is given only when individuals perceive that the stated benefits of e-governance will satisfy their needs or protect them from external threats. In addition, individuals need to be confident that any information held on them by government authorities and agencies is within the legal bounds, that it is properly and securely stored with appropriate access authorisations and, when accessed, the information is treated with utmost sensitivity. While the government's vision of a "joined-up," fully integrated e-government has been communicated as desirable progress, the population appears less excited at the prospect of the crumpling of the "Chinese walls." Therein lies the basis of the acceptance paradox; whereas intrusion via e-surveillance is understood as protecting and preserving personal safety against some unwanted and unknown threats, information accumulated on individuals across government departments and agencies induces the Big Brother syndrome of unwarranted state interference. It also exposes the individual to threats of data loss, administrative errors, and, for some, the possibility of higher tax assessments and possible detection for any legal or moral transgressions. Besides, a single-platform e-government is vulnerable and subject to technical failure and deliberate or inadvertent malpractice, thus adding to the concern about the intentions of policy makers, the competency of those responsible for keeping citizens' data intact and safe. As a result, recent government's efforts to encourage citizens to interact with public sector agencies and to participate in policy-making "citizens councils" have produced minimal results. The dilemma between knowledge acquisition for benevolent governance and preservation of individual privacy grows increasingly more acute.

The government's ambition of using technology to access all the information about every citizen is legitimised through the emotive objective of public interest and safety. When supported by an equally ambitious legislative framework (e.g., the Regulation of Investigatory Powers Act) and backed by the EU's position on the retention of telecommunications data, it effectively drowns out individual cries against public snooping. It also ignores the public's ability to assess forms and reasons for intrusion. At stake here is not just a concern about individuals being reduced to electronic ciphers and losing their personal freedom, nor about an untrustworthy government; it is about the possibility of governance and protection being implemented under a flawed rationale, and one which is conducted with apparently little regard or awareness of the citizens' views and their evaluation of the impact on their lives. It is about the extent to which we can believe that our elected government and custodian of the nation truly have our interest at heart. In the UK, the use of cameras on London buses serves a dual purpose — they protect drivers from possible attack and dissuade rowdy behaviour by some passengers. Additionally, to keep bus lanes free from selfish and unthinking drivers, bus drivers are entrusted with the ability to photograph the culprits. In this example, there is convergence of state-interest and self-interest. The mutual advantage for those who have to police undesirable behaviour and those on the receiving end is clear, and when perceived as such, there is little negative reaction or protest. To be accepted, government surveillance policies and practices need to be appreciated as genuine efforts to provide and protect the citizenry.

Globalisation Effects of Technology on Governance

An important development is the emergence of a friction-free boundless global economy where the largest corporations operate and coordinate supply chains and distribution networks with precision and efficiency, and smaller organisations have had to revise their strategies likewise in order to survive. As global trade becomes the norm rather than that enjoyed by multinational organisations, governments are forced to review their stance on border control, trade levy, taxation, merger and acquisition regulation, and other trade-related policies. Further, increasing access by citizens of different nations to various levels of the media society also makes it impossible for individual governments to ignore the globalisation effects of technology and to continue to govern and legislate in isolation. There is no longer a terrorist problem in any specific country; terrorism is a global feature faced by a growing number of countries regardless of religion, colour, or creed. As demonstrated by the September 11, 2001 and July 7, 2005 incidents, individuals or groups with terrorist or criminal intent, as part of the panoptic-synoptican society, have been able to use technology to hatch their plots, survey the targets, and coordinate actual attacks. To protect their peoples, there is a need for greater coordination across nations. Aside from cultural and sovereign issues, there is the challenge of managing international relationships and providing governance on a vast scale.

We envisage that governments will have little choice but to continue investing in the latest technology for surveillance and control. A possible application is radio frequency identification (RFID), which can improve the government's ability to conduct surveillance activities en mass. It is possible to track individuals or groups of individuals using passive RFID tags. Small and portable, these tags are armed with a tiny antenna that does not require an internal energy source. When a surveilled target passes a reader (say an individual attempting to enter or leave a designated secure area), it will send a pulse of electromagnetic energy or radio wave that briefly activates the tag, which can be set to raise either a silent or audible alarm while relaying data on the individual to the relevant authorities. Commercial applications began by embedding a RFID tag in a product or a pet's collar for location purposes, although more innovative uses of the technology are emerging. Recent examples of RFID use include tagging deceased victims post Hurricane Katrina. The bodies are tagged and their medical records loaded on a RFID chip. Sister nightclubs in Barcelona, Spain, and Rotterdam, Holland apparently use temporary RFID implants as automated passes to their VIP lounges. Customers with the implants can order food and drinks with a wave of their arm. As an effective surveillance system, RFID can be deployed in almost any public or high-security area such as prison establishments, government buildings, military bases, airports, railway stations, and border controls.

Other digital advances include emerging ubiquitous technologies such as Digital Multimedia Broadcasting (DMB) and High Speed Downlink Packet Access (HSDPA) which underpin the development of 21st century mobile televisions (TVs). DMB service is already available in Korea, and its hardware market is expected to grow quickly. Other developments include Internet protocol TVs which have recently been launched in Hong Kong, Japan, and Italy. Wibro technology is another form of mobile Internet offering merged communication, broadcasting, and data services. These developments are amongst the most recent moves towards ubiquitous computing (ubi-comp). Ubi-comp can overcome traditional problems of citizen access and computer efficacy since the central precept of ubi-comp is that computer chips can be embedded into the structural fabric of our lives — whether at home, at the office, on lampposts, park benches, doorways, shopping malls, bank counters, and in cars or other forms of public transport. That is, mass broadcasting is not only possible, it can provide the government with the ability to reach and keep its citizens "informed" anytime and anyplace. In turn, individuals can interrogate the system for further information on anything of particular interest or concern. If installed with the latest microcamera technology, these ubi-comp systems will allow the government to watch its citizens in numbers and from across locations, something that is not feasible currently.

In e-governance terms, therefore, new and emergent technologies such as RFID and ubi-comp possess significant panoptic capabilities. They have the potential to curtail and reverse current synoptic practices of private viewers and society watchers, thus reverting to the few watching the many. For any government keen to use technology to perform its role as protector or to impose its political ideology and retain power over the people, these new advances offer almost limitless possibilities. And when conducted in partnership with large, global corporations, it can easily be interpreted as the rebirth of Orwellian draconism — the difference is that 21st century e-surveillance has the potential to be even more intrusive and extensive, operating as a global network. Imagine a world where unseen eyes are watching our every activity (or inactivity), and where the term "ubiquitous" refers to the possibility of entire populations being watched by the omnipresent few. This rather pessimistic projection does ignore parallel technological developments which individuals can use to preserve their synoptic abilities. Besides, raised on a diet of liberty and fair play, and having enjoyed the freedom of citizen broadcasting, it is unlikely that the UK public will want or allow the return of a purely panoptic society.

Conclusion

The UK government has put in place electronic systems which have the potential both to serve citizens and inhibit their freedoms. The government in reacting to recent terrorist events, has seen it necessary to forego the freedom of the masses in the pursuit of a small number of transgressors. For their part, citizens have demonstrated a high level of tolerance of potentially panoptic surveillance as they go about their daily business. That tolerance is based upon the consensual notion of state and citizens working as partners in our present panoptic-synoptican society. Technology has enabled the watched to turn their lens on the watchers, and increasing cooperation between the media and members of the public has given rise to a new generation of viewers, many of whom have taken upon themselves to act as self-appointed guardians of "truth," putting pressure on the accountability and transparency of government policies. There is little room for secrecy in our modern media-hungry society — the latest news, gossip, exposés, and public debate are instantaneously uploaded onto various media platforms for public consumption, making it difficult to distinguish what is in "the public interest" or who is protecting it and why. We caution that in the light of recent tendencies by certain disaffected factions towards anarchy and violence, failure by the government to understand the reasons behind public acceptance of some but not all of its e-governance efforts, and make explicit their objectives and scope of any new initiative, will only fuel any discord.

Regardless of the surveillant power of new technologies, the possession of power does not automatically legitimise it. Not all surveillance is considered unequivocally intrusive and we have demonstrated by our examples, when inappropriate assumptions of compliance have evoked vocal and active resistance. For Western democracies such as the UK, what is required is the employment of technology to enhance the credibility of the government as a "steward of society." The government should be careful not to use technology as a disciplinary instrument against the masses or to suppress dissenting views. From our discussion, it is clear that people are not overly disturbed by the type or even extent of surveillance, but they will not accept a government that is not open and convincing about the reasons and nature of surveillance. When the object for surveillance is transparent and evaluated as truly beneficial, then acceptance is likely. The central London congestion charge system is an apt example where all number plates are scanned and matched against a vehicle record and payment database. The logic for its implementation was made clear from its conception and as people begin to reap the benefits of a less congested London, it soon becomes another routine of daily life. We conclude that citizen compliance to e-surveillance is achieved only when there is a match between state and private interest.

References

Bauman, Z. (1998). *Globalization: The human consequences.* Cambridge: Polity.

BBC News. (2003, November 12). *Should we carry ID cards?* Retrieved April 29, 2006, from http://news.bbc.co.uk/1/hi/uk_politics/3264165.stm

BBC News. (2004, November 23). *Drivers ignoring "mobile rules."* Retrieved April 29, 2006, from http://news.bbc.co.uk/1/hi/uk/4034353.stm

BBC News. (2005, June 18). *Rape "filmed on mobile phone."* Retrieved April 29, 2006, from http://news.bbc.co.uk/1/hi/england/southern_counties/2998818.stm

Blau, P. (1964). *Exchange and power in social life.* New York: John Wiley & Sons.

Bogard, W. (1996). *The simulation of surveillance.* Cambridge: Cambridge University Press.

Boyne, R. (2000). Post-panopticism. *Economy and Society, 29*(2), 285-307.

Daily Telegraph. (2004, February 1). *This house seems to be full of bullies and wimps.* Retrieved April 29, 2006, from http://www.telegraph.co.uk/opinion/main.jhtml;sessio nid=HCXHDWLT2DDBDQFIQMGCM5OAVCBQUJVC?xml=/opinion/2004/02/01/do0104.xml&secureRefresh=true&_requestid=89500

E-Envoy. (2003, June). *www.ukonline.gov.uk and www.e-envoy.gov.uk Web site traffic figures.* Retrieved April 29, 2006, from http://e-envoy.gov.uk/MediaCentre/Current-PressReleaseArticle

Electronic Design. (2005, August 4). *Electronics can protect subways against terrorism.* Retrieved April 29, 2006, from http://www.elecdesign.com/Articles/ArticleID/10799/10799.html

European Court of Human Rights. (2003, January 28). *Chamber judgement in the case of Peck v. the United Kingdom.* Retrieved April 29, 2006, from http://www.echr.coe.int/Eng/Press/2003/jan/Peckjudeng.htm

Foucault, M. (1980). *Power/knowledge: Selected interviews and other writings 1972-1977.* Brighton: Harvester Press.

Foundation for Information Policy Research (FIPR). (2005, November). *Surveillance and security.* Retrieved April 29, 2006, from http://www.fipr.org/surveillance.html

Giddens, A. (1991). *Modernity and self identity.* Cambridge: Polity.

Guardian. (2005, August 11). *Eyes have it.* Retrieved April 29, 2006, from http://society.guardian.co.uk/e-public/story/0,,1546355.html

Haggerty, K., & Ericson, R. (2001). The surveillance assemblage. *British Journal of Sociology, 51*(4), 605-622.

Hobbes, T. (1660/1996). *Leviathan.* In J. C. A Gaskin (Ed.). Oxford: Oxford University Press.

Hollis, M. (1998). *Trust within reason.* Cambridge: Cambridge University Press.

Independent. (2004, January 12). *Big brother Britain.* Retrieved April 29, 2006, from http://news.independent.co.uk/uk/this_britain/article73167.ece

Independent. (2004, January 12). *How average Briton is caught on camera 300 times a day*. Retrieved April 29, 2006, from http://news.independent.co.uk/uk/this_britain/article73158.ece

Kraut, R. (Ed.). (1997). *Plato's republic: Critical essays*. Lanham, MD: Rowman & Littlefield.

Liberty. (2005). CCTV. Retrieved April 29, 2006, from http://www.liberty-human-rights.org.uk/privacy/cctv.shtml

Lincoln, A. (1863, November 19/1946). The Gettysburg Address. In R. P. Basler (Ed.), *The collected works of Abraham Lincoln*, Vol. II. Retrieved April 29, 2006, from http://showcase.netins.net/web/creative/lincoln/speeches/gettysburg.htm

London School of Economics. (2005, June 27). *The identity project: An assessment of the UK Identity Cards Bill and its implications*. Retrieved April 29, 2006, from http://www.lse.ac.uk/collections/pressAndInformationOffice/newsAndEvents/archives/2005/ID-Card_FinalReport.htm

Lyon, D. (2001). *Surveillance society: Monitoring everyday life*. Buckingham, Open University Press.

Lyon, D. (2003). *Surveillance after September 11*. Cambridge: Polity.

Machiavelli, N. (c. 1517/1950). *The prince and the discourses*. New York: Modern Library.

Mathieson, T. (1997). The viewer society: Michel Foucault's "Panopticon" revisited. *Theoretical Criminology, 1*(2), 215-234.

Mill, J. S. (1859-1869/1989). On liberty. In S. Collini (Ed.), *'On liberty' and other writings*. Cambridge: Cambridge University Press.

Murphy, N. R. (1951). *The interpretation of Plato's Republic*. Oxford: Clarendon.

Endnotes

[1]   School of Management, University of Surrey, Guildford , Surrey, UK (GU2 7XH), e-mail: l.lee-kelley@surrey.ac.uk

[2]   School of Management, University of Surrey, Guildford , Surrey, UK (GU2 7XH), e-mail: a.kolsaker-jacob@surrey.ac.uk

Chapter VII

A Community Facilitation Model for E-Government:
A Case Study in Monitoring Water Quality

Kyle B. Murray, University of Western Ontario, Canada

Cory A. Habulin, Government of Alberta, Canada

Abstract

This chapter introduces a community facilitation model for e-government. The central tenet of this approach is the empowerment of a segment of the population to act, by providing the tools and information necessary to tackle issues that have been difficult to address with traditional approaches to government. Under this model, government provides an initial spark and then plays a supporting role in the growth of the community. By doing so, the costs of the program are minimized while the impact of the program is maximized. We examine the viability of the model by looking at a case study in water quality monitoring. The case illustrates the power of a government facilitated community of action to address an important problem, and it suggests that such a model can be applied globally and may be relevant to government initiatives beyond water monitoring.

Introduction

Electronic government initiatives have become a key component of ambitious programs aimed at transforming the way that government operates, with a specific focus on becoming more citizen-centered, effective, and efficient (Grant & Chau, 2005). As such, electronically mediated government programs are an increasingly important part of the interaction between governments and their citizens. This is true in the largest and most well developed countries in North America and Western Europe as well as smaller nations such as Malta and Mauritius (Grant, 2005; UN World Public Sector Report, 2003). Whether the intended interactions are between any combination of individual citizens, not-for-profit organizations, businesses, or governments, the potential efficiency and cost-effectiveness of the electronic delivery of government services appears promising (Accenture, 2004). In addition, proponents of the expansion of e-government contend that it has a unique ability to empower citizens "by allowing them to contribute directly to the process of public government, as well as being a catalyst for economic and social development" (Grant, 2005, p. i).

In much the same way that corporations have increasingly adopted a market orientation rather than a product orientation — that is, a focus on their customers' needs and wants, and their relationships with their customers — governments are being encouraged to adopt a more citizen-centered view (OECD, 2003). Although not everyone agrees with this approach to government (Hutton, 2005), it is clear that there is a nearly universal desire for more efficient and effective government. It is also apparent that developing countries and developed countries will have to work together to deal with some of the most serious problems that governments face today — for example, terrorism, the drug trade, economic policy, healthcare and disease control, and environmental issues. For each of these concerns, managing critical information and gaining citizen support are prerequisites for effective government action. On both counts, the Internet, and electronically mediated communication more generally, offer a significant advantage over traditional approaches in the dissemination of information and the organization of disperse populations. However, to-date few useful models have been proposed that would allow governments to capitalize on these advantages, and even fewer of these models have real world examples of their application and their potential for success on a global scale (e.g., Grant & Chau, 2005).

In this chapter, we introduce a community facilitation model for e-government. The following sections describe the model and its theoretical underpinnings. In our model, government provides an initial spark and then plays a supporting role in the growth of the community. By doing so, the costs of the program are minimized while the impact of the program is maximized. In the following sections, we examine the viability of the model by looking at a case study in water quality monitoring. The case illustrates the power of a government-facilitated community of action to address an important problem, and it suggests that such a model can be applied globally and may be relevant to government initiatives beyond water monitoring.

Figure 1. Model for e-government facilitation of communities of action

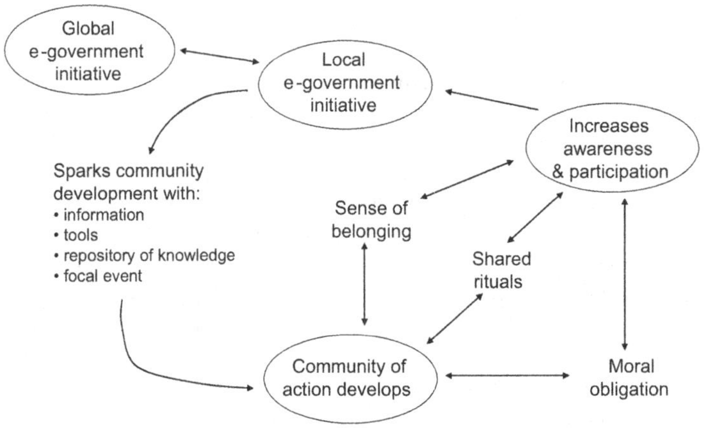

A Community Facilitation
Model for E-Government

We propose a general conceptual model (see Figure 1) that outlines an opportunity for governments to capitalize on the advantages of electronic communication over the Internet to facilitate the development of *communities of action*. The central tenet of this approach is the empowerment of a segment of the population to act, by providing the tools and information necessary to tackle issues that have been difficult to address with traditional approaches to government. Rather than command and control, within this framework government supports the development of a self-sustaining community by setting the wheels in motion for a low-cost citizen-driven initiative.

Our model is couched within the generic framework for e-government proposed by Grant and Chau (2005). In particular, our model is appropriate for both the short-term e-government goal of improving the delivery of services and the longer term goal of transforming government to be more effective and efficient citizen-centered organizations. In terms of service delivery, leveraging the capability of a Web site to collect and disseminate information within a targeted community of volunteers is a basic function for an e-government initiative that aims to facilitate community development. However, unlike information campaigns that focus on traditional advertising (television, radio, print, etc.) or direct mail (letters, brochures, flyers, leaflets, etc.), the Internet allows citizens to interact with the material, adapting the available tools and knowledge to their own uses. As a result, a Web site allows citizens to access information and connect with the government to the extent that they are comfortable and interested. Importantly, it also makes it easy to pass this information on and involve others in the program. Within the Grant and Chau (2005) framework, this level of functionality moves the initiative beyond the service delivery stage to citizen empowerment. Finally, as the community grows and evolves, the government and its citizens enter into a partnership wherein the problem/issue that the government originally defined is addressed through decentralized collaboration rather than centralized control.

Sparking Community Development

The process begins with a spark from the government. Having identified an issue (whether that identification is made by the government or its citizen) that can be addressed by citizen action, the government works to organize and allocate key resources to facilitate such action. For example, if the government is interested in expediting the process of taxation it can offer online resources for obtaining and filling out the forms, as well as submitting the completed forms and electronically transferring payments or refunds. To the extent that people adopt this method of submission, the government is saved the time, effort, and expense of transferring data from paper forms into digital formats for processing and storage. Another example is the ability of the government to collect data on environmental resources that are too numerous and dispersed to be addressed in a cost-effective manner without the support of citizen volunteers. This can be accomplished, as we will see in the case described below, by providing individuals with the tools and the knowledge they need to effectively collect data on the government's behalf. The general idea is that governments can put in place the resources required to facilitate the development of communities of action.

However, as was evident in the explosion of poorly planned commercial Web sites in the late 1990s, it is not enough to simply make the information (interactive or otherwise) available. It has to appeal to a specific segment of the market — in this case, a segment of the citizenry — and it has to be effectively promoted. This can be accomplished in a number of ways; however, in this chapter we will focus on one particularly effective technique that involves concentrating promotional efforts around a focal event that serves as an initial catalyst for a more comprehensive program. This technique has been used by charities (e.g., Terry Fox run for cancer, and the Live 8 concert for African poverty), special interest groups (e.g., gay pride parades, Earth Day, etc.), governments (e.g., Veteran's Day, national holidays, etc.), and others to draw attention and recognition. In facilitating a community of action this type of promotion is especially relevant as it provides a cost effective and efficient way to "get the message out" and motivate people to take action by suggesting a specific time and place to get involved. Having generated that initial interest and action, we propose that there are three components that are critical to successfully developing and sustaining an active community.

Three Critical Components

In our model, the community of action is created to increase awareness and participation in and around an important government issue. This can be on a local, regional, national, or international scale. In some instances, as in the case below, a program will be active at all levels of government within and between nations. The important point is that communities that contain these three components will have the potential to be sustainable and even grow in an organized and directed fashion with minimal government involvement. As a result, this model of community facilitation through e-government has the potential to address serious problems at a variety of geographic levels in a very efficient and cost-effective manner. The three components that we suggest are critically important to success in this regard are shared rituals and traditions (Douglas & Ishwerwood, 1979, Durkheim, 1965; Marshall, 1994), a sense of belonging (Gusfield, 1978; Weber, 1978), and a sense of moral obligation (Muniz & O'Guinn, 2001). We argue that these three components can effectively improve participation rates and contribute to an increase in awareness and visibility for a government initiative, above and beyond traditional approaches. As participation increases and citizens' hands-on involvement increases, their experiences further reinforce their preference for community membership and increase their commitment to the initiative (Hoch, 2002).

Shared rituals can take a number of different forms from prayer to the initiations of college fraternities and from riding a Harley Davidson to breastfeeding. In general, members of the community can identify themselves by some specific behaviors that they engage in. These rituals can create and help perpetuate the history and culture of the community, and they can help to define who the community is and what it does (Douglas & Isherwood, 1979). Moreover, rituals can transmit the norms and values of the community to its members as well as to outsiders (Marshall, 1994). In addition, from the perspective of e-government facilitated communities of action, shared behaviors of this sort can help to connect and sustain a community when many of its members are geographically dispersed and may never come into face-to-face contact with each other.

At the center of the notion of community is the members' sense that they are a part of something bigger than themselves. It is a feeling of connection to other people that are a part of the community, as well as a sense of being different from those who are not community members. It is not just about shared attitudes or superficial similarity (Muniz & O'Guinn, 2001), but a deeper "conscious of kind" (Gusfield, 1978). Finally, for our model to be effective, the members of the community need to feel an obligation to act in a manner that is consistent with the goals of the government, which in turn should be reflecting the goals of the citizenry at large. This sense of moral obligation to other members as well as to the community as a whole helps to motivate individuals to act and to act appropriately.

Global Diffusion of Regional Success

It is worth emphasizing that the type of community that we are describing differs from the notion of a community as an entity bounded by geography. That is, an e-government community is *not* defined by a particular geographic location the way a town is. In fact, one of the key advantages of the electronic facilitation of a community is that the community can be geographically diverse. This makes the global diffusion of a community based program, which was initially successful in one area, much more portable to new and different areas. In particular, the fact that the type of community that we are describing would generally be facilitated through an Internet Web site means that the information can be easily passed across regional boundaries and adopted or adapted by other governments facing similar issues. This allows communities in one region to learn from, and benchmark themselves against, groups that are pursuing similar goals through similar means in other parts of the world. The case study that follows examines one example of a project that began in one nation and has since received citizen participation in a wide variety of nations, both developed and developing. In particular we discuss a local adaptation of a global initiative, which illustrates the potential for a community facilitation approach to e-government.

A Case Study in Monitoring Water Quality

World Water Monitoring Day (WWMD) began as National Water Monitoring Day (NWMD) on October 18, 2002 to commemorate the 30th anniversary of the U.S. Clean Water Act. WWMD was created by America's Clean Water Foundation with two major purposes in mind. First, it was designed to serve as an educational platform to introduce people to the importance of water monitoring and connect them personally with efforts to protect and preserve their local watersheds. Second, it aimed to expand the base of information available about the health of each watershed over time. The success of the program lies in its ability to collect an unparalleled quantity of timely water quality data by coordinating people from geographically dispersed and, in some cases, isolated sites around the world. To pull it off in an efficient and cost-effective manner, WWMD has been a pioneer in the application of e-government principles to the facilitation of communities of action.

The program has a broad scope as it aims to reach participants from around the world. With the initial interactive Web site and program components designed and in place for the earlier, and less ambitious, NWMD project, the progression to the globally active WWMD was a natural one with little additional effort or expense. Since its inception as NWMD three years ago, WWMD has registered approximately 40,000 participants, about 5,000 of which are from outside the United States. This global community of volunteer water monitors has sampled at over 6,500 locations in 50 countries. In the following sections, we turn our attention to one specific instantiation of WWMD that was recently launched in the Canadian province of Alberta. In doing so, we illustrate the key components of the community facilitation model for e-government proposed in this chapter, and we discuss how such a model can be adapted and applied for this and other projects in both the developed and developing world.

Alberta Water Quality Awareness

Following the WWMD approach, the Alberta Water Quality Awareness (AWQA) Day program was designed as an education and awareness initiative aimed at increasing public consciousness surrounding the quality of freshwater systems throughout the province of Alberta. The program specifically targets watershed stewardship groups, school groups, and other community groups. However, it also encourages individual citizens to participate, by asking them to collect water samples, and aims to instill a personal connection between Albertans and their local waterbodies. By involving local citizens as equal partners and active leaders in water monitoring, this e-government initiative provides a spark for community development.

The Government of Alberta Departments of Environment and Agriculture, Food and Rural Development along with Agriculture and Agri-Food Canada and a number of non-profit partners have launched the first AWQA Day, to act as a pilot project and determine the success, feasibility, and community support for maintaining AWQA Day as an annual event. These programs fall among an extensive Web of volunteer citizen monitoring initiatives around the world such as bird counts, indicator species monitoring, and plant identification. What sets the more recent programs apart from their predecessors is the sophisticated use of, and level of integration with, the far-reaching and efficient forms of electronic communication.

The central activity supported by the AWQA Day program is the sampling and testing of local waterbodies for basic water quality indicators using a standardized test kit. Following the example set by WWMD, AWQA Day procured and distributed sampling kits that provided the supplies required to monitor the four basic water quality parameters: acidity (pH), temperature, dissolved oxygen content, and turbidity. These test parameters were chosen because they are easy to carry out in the field, and because they can reveal important changes and signal trouble spots in the overall health of the waterbody. Various aquatic organisms require differing ranges of these three characteristics within their habitat. Outside these ranges of acidity, temperature, turbidity, and available oxygen, certain reproductive and feeding processes are disrupted, which can result in species decline and elimination. Each test kit is able to test up to 50 water samples, which is important because it improves the efficiency and cost-effectiveness of the program by allowing volunteers to conduct tests at multiple locations or share the kits among members of a sampling group.

At the root of AWQA Day is the organization of funding, the production of promotional materials, the development of electronic communication tools, and the creation of an overall program design capable of sustaining AWQA Day as an ongoing event. These administrative functions are orchestrated by a central committee of interested and knowledgeable individuals from established government branches and non-profit organizations, along with the support of funding partners. WWMD served as a foundation for the Alberta initiative to capitalize on the knowledge and experience of an existing and successful program. As a result, the inaugural AWQA Day program was able to focus on building partnerships and promoting the education and awareness value of a volunteer monitoring program, while avoiding many of the pitfalls associated with the development of an entirely novel event.

Creating the Spark

The public presentation and promotion of the AWQA Day program was organized around four main areas: the Web site, promotional brochures and posters, incentive prizes for group participation, and field contacts. Program information, links, and resources on related topics and means of contacting others involved in water sampling are presented and accessed through the Web site, which is the critical touchpoint for AWQA Day. The subsequent core components of the AWQA Day design are developed to attract interested participants to the Web site and inform a broad audience of the existence of the program. The design of the program is relatively simple because it is primarily citizen-administered, through electronic access, with minimal support from the government and other coordinating agencies. This allows the program to emerge from the traditional top-down form of awareness building to a participant-owned, context-malleable education system.

In this way, participation in the AWQA Day program relies on the Internet for both participant registration and the ultimate reporting of water quality data. The Web site itself is a database supported interface that enables participants to access and modify their own personal profile within the database by logging on and receiving a unique user ID. Citizens of Alberta are able to register as individuals or as part of a group, locate the sites they will be monitoring, and enter their subsequent findings. Once the event has taken place, participants can access reporting information on all registered sampling sites on the basis of the four water quality indicators. This information is accessible online and retrievable in a number of ways. Results are plotted on a map of the Province of Alberta depicting locations of sampling sites and the range of values recorded for the four water quality indicators. The information is also reported by major watershed, by waterbody type, by municipality, or by participant affiliation.

However, the Web component of the program is not limited to the database of water sampling results. Similar to WWMD, the AWQA Day Web site supports numerous resources on water quality, volunteer monitoring, and other water related topics. Further, the interactive abilities of a Web-based program provide countless opportunities for personal interaction. For example, participants are able to access a calendar of community water sampling events, information on group participation and event-planning, links to other sites with local and international water monitoring initiatives and information on water system health. In addition, organizational functions such as built-in participant evaluations can ease the continuation of an up-to-date, efficient, and cost-effective program in subsequent years. These computer-mediated behaviors promote water stewardship and encourage the development of a water monitoring community.

Like WWMD the AWQA Day program is built around one central day, June 5. However, water sampling and program participation take place over a two-week period. During this time participants join events, festivals, and community programs where they become personally engaged with the health of watersheds in their area. The two week window of water sampling and data entry reveals a *snapshot* of water quality in the areas sampled, as multiple locations are tested within a short period of time with standardized equipment and techniques. Snapshot monitoring is a useful methodology for this type of volunteer program that is capable of increasing quality assurance in the results reported by reducing the seasonal and technical influences on water quality. Although, a single sample does not provide a comprehensive picture of water quality and many other extraneous influences are present, snapshot monitoring is an important indicator tool, especially as information on the health of our water resources is compiled over time.

Facilitating a Community of Action

Of course, WWMD and related programs, such as AWQA Day, are not the only means of water monitoring. Data is collected on the quality and health of waterbodies across the province and around the world by different government bodies and professional organizations. This type of monitoring builds scientific and quality assured data on waterbodies from various seasons and locations. However, it is clear that not all waterbodies can be effectively monitored in this way because of the tremendous expense and time commitment required. As a result, only a subset of the total water system has traditionally been monitored and those data are used as an indicator of the overall water system health in an area.

AWQA Day does not compete with ongoing practices but rather celebrates the various forms of monitoring by coming together at one focused and coordinated event. Volunteer monitoring provides an opportunity to expand on existing efforts and link participants with other like-minded citizens and their local watersheds, and at the same time build a repository of locally-generated water quality data. In this way, a large number of citizens are personally involved, and a wide span of watersheds, scattered throughout the province, are monitored. Participants are able to collect great quantities of data which fit with their own needs, wants, particular locales, and interests. Moreover, they are able to do so with an ease and efficiency that would be too expensive and too far-reaching a task for the limited number of professional field technicians and educational outreach specialists.

Shared Ritual, Moral Obligation, and a Sense of Belonging

Critical to the development and ongoing support of a community of action is the emergence or, in this case, intentional encouragement, of shared rituals, moral obligation, and a sense of belonging. Each of these elements is present in the AWQA Day community. At the heart of the program are the citizens who take an active role in using the test kits to collect data and play a part in the monitoring of provincial watersheds. By doing so, they all share in a *common ritual* at a specified time of year, organized through the AWQA Day Web site and facilitated by the government's supply of monitoring kits.

In fact, encouraging citizens to take part in assessing province-wide water quality is less about the collection and analysis of rigorous data than it is about increasing awareness of freshwater systems and water quality issues throughout the province. The AWQA Day program believes that the benefits and outcomes of this type of volunteer monitoring are strongly aligned with the goals of the program: to encourage protection of water resources, rekindle a sense of responsibility and stewardship towards local water systems, recognize potential sources of threat and harm to waterbodies, and rediscover the value of our water systems. In other words, even more important than the data collected is the *sense of moral obligation* that the volunteers feel towards their local water systems. The provision of a central and personal means of accessing the resources necessary to seek context-specific awareness is facilitated by electronic communication.

The thrust of citizen monitoring programs, such as WWMD and AWQA Day, is to develop the tools and resources necessary for citizen action and personal stewardship, which allows the program take on a life of its own and thrive within a framework of shared knowledge and common goals. Developing a *sense of belonging* to a community is integral to the success of the AWQA Day program. The program design supports a rudimentary collection of data and reporting of findings. However, the actual event of becoming involved, linking with other individuals and community members, and getting out there and participating, fosters a sense of belonging and a richer community experience (Selznick, 1996). The collaboration and coming together of interested citizens from across the focal area is essential to forming community ties which allow AWQA Day to develop a life of its own and to keep the associated administrative costs manageable. Sharing and community efforts are fundamental to this type of monitoring program. In this case, the community has the ability to build itself and use the Web site for purposes beyond the original intent.

Once in place, the AWQA Day Web site acts as a hub for water quality initiatives across the province, with numerous functions and abilities. As mentioned earlier, the Internet-based framework of these programs ensures flexibility in the capability, level, and growth of participant interaction. As the program matures, it becomes more and more an exercise in participant-owned information. The existing applications of the AWQA Day Web site, such as the event calendar, are important for the development of community involvement. Through event postings participants can link with ongoing local activities, existing knowledge and experience in their local areas, and get involved. Other facets of electronic communication may improve upon the initial community development through such outlets as online discussion forums and sharing boards, where the interpretation and extension of sampling results is in the hands of the participants. In this manner, the Web site acts as a spring board where the community of volunteer water monitors adapts the abilities of their new form of communication to keep stewardship and action at the forefront of their interest in water system health within their day-to-day lives.

This sense of belonging can be an especially important catalyst for action among community members that may otherwise feel isolated. In some cases, feelings of alienation surface with geographic isolation and are compounded by a history of government programs that have been imposed from a distance (Bell, 1998). Yet, isolated areas are often at the centre of the development and maintenance of environmentally favorable practices, especially with regard to natural resources. In many cases, these efforts rely on work within remote, rural, and impoverished areas. Individuals who carry the bulk of this responsibility tend to feel overwhelmed, unsupported, and unequipped to do the work required to change their practices to those of environmentally sustainable action. In Alberta, and elsewhere, rural areas are the most susceptible to this isolation (farms, ranches, etc.) and yet integral to bringing about action and practical change. The development of a community, with shared rituals, a sense of moral obligation, and a sense of belonging, can reduce the barriers of isolation (Wellman, 1999).

A Self-Sustaining Community

Our model of e-government community facilitation (Figure 1) depicts a self-reinforcing, and potentially self-sustaining, effect of community development. Specifically, we are suggesting that after a community develops to include the three critical components (i.e., a sense of belonging, shared rituals, and moral obligation), positive reinforcement helps to sustain and grow the community beyond the initial spark provided by the government. Each component can play an important role in increasing awareness and participation in the focal event. For example, the more you feel you belong to the community and have a moral obligation to the community, the more likely you are to participate (and entice others to participate) in the focal event. In turn, greater participation in the shared rituals has the potential to further increase the community members' sense of belonging and moral obligation. These processes then create a loop of feedback that, when positive, has the potential to strengthen the community and contribute to its ability to grow and evolve over time. The stronger and more successful the local community, and therefore the local government initiative, the greater the base from which the program can be adopted and adapted by other interested parties (e.g., other governments on a global scale).

Global Adoption and Adaptation

The community facilitation model should be of special interest to developing countries that lack the sufficient government resources or international support to tackle environmental (and other) issues directly, yet are faced with some of the most pressing problems on the planet. In many cases, developing countries deal with a global sense of isolation, impairing individuals' ability to take action in their daily lives to assess or at least discuss the quality of their local waters. The e-government model of community facilitation, as instantiated in the various volunteer monitoring programs, is applicable here as it supports and encourages citizen action in an efficient and cost-effective manner. World Water Monitoring Day is now active in 50 countries from the U.S. to Turkmenistan and from France to Pago Pago, and is monitoring over 6,500 sites (see Appendix A for more detail on WWMD and AWQA Day summary statistics). Central to each of these programs is the facilitation of a community of action, which is sparked by a government initiative, but relies on the energy of a community of volunteers to sustain and enhance it.

The Success of AWQA Day

AWQA Day's pilot year saw close to one third (substantially higher than the global average of one-fifth) of the 900 AWQA Day registrants reporting results from close to 1,000 sampling locations. This is interesting given that, in contrast to the user-pay structure of the WWMD program, AWQA Day provides the test kits free to registered participants. One might expect that when the kits can be obtained at no cost to the participant, the sense of obligation would be lessened. However, we find that a much higher percentage of Albertans who received kits reported results. The fact that the program registration is limited by the number of free kits available each year, may have had an impact here. With a smaller scope, AWQA Day was able to engage a more intimate community, yet still managed to span the barriers of geographical isolation within the province and provide monitoring data on areas that might otherwise have gone unexamined.

In general, the citizens of Alberta responded enthusiastically to initial AWQA Day promotions for a variety of reasons and with a broad scope of expectations. People expressed, through the overwhelming response to AWQA Day, a desire to act. They want to be a part of the process that increases awareness of, and collects important data on, the health of a resource that they rely on and share with so many others. However, the organization and community facilitation of the AWQA Day program provided the critical spark that encouraged such action and directed it in a meaningful way. In some cases, it was a need to become involved with monitoring the quality of their local water systems, because their livelihoods depend upon the sustainability of the resource. Others — for example, school classes, home-schooling groups, and other academic institutions — sought out AWQA Day as a means to connect students with a hands-on, practical experience of the freshwater systems studied within their curricula. The preservation of the integrity of natural ecological systems was the motivation for many more. AWQA Day provides a central focus and outlet for watershed stewardship and community groups to plan events, rally support, and encourage further action.

Conclusion

Electronically supported monitoring programs such as WWMD and AWQA Day, are still in the initial stages of development. Nevertheless, it is clear that communities can be built upon shared interests and a latent or unfocused desire for action by citizens. In addition, it seems that these types of programs are still evolving, adopting best practices from one region and disseminating them to others. As they continue to grow and adapt, and communication technologies continue to improve, this type of citizen centered initiative appears to have the potential to transform the way that government works (Grant, 2005). In the short-term, the potential for improving service delivery argues for the continued use of e-government systems where and when they can efficiently and effectively improve upon the more traditional bureaucratic infrastructure.

The case study described in this article illustrates one type of problem to which a community facilitation model of e-government can be applied. However, we believe that the general principles advocated here can be applied to a variety of problems that are beyond the scope of traditional centralized solutions. What the WWMD case study demonstrates is that having identified a problem, and a segment of the population interested in addressing that problem, governments can empower citizens to educate themselves and take action. Moreover, to the extent that the three critical components of a community are present, the community has the potential to be self-sustaining, able to grow and evolve with minimal ongoing government support.

The Internet is an especially useful and relevant technology in this regard, because it is a potent enabler of grassroots power (Urban, Sultan, & Qualls, 2000). Nevertheless, it requires that the technology is in place and accessible. In the developed world the Internet is becoming a pervasive part of everyday life. In the developing world it is far less prevalent, which may impede the ability of e-government initiatives in the places where they could have the greatest impact. Initiatives like MIT's Media Lab's $100 Laptop Project (HDLP) and the related One Laptop per Child vision (see http://laptop.media.mit.edu/), as well as programs like United Kingdom's Digital Links International (which collects and donates computers to developing countries; http://www.digital-links.org) are a step in the right direction. However, much more remains to be done to realize the global potential of e-government.

References

Accenture. (2004, May). eGovernment leadership: High performance, maximum value. *E-Government Executive Series*, 1-112.

Bell, M. M. (1998). *An invitation to environmental sociology*. Thousand Oaks, CA: Pine Forge Press.

Douglas, M., & Isherwood, B. (1979). *The world of goods*. New York: Basic.

Durkheim, E. (1965). *The elementary forms of the religious life*. New York: Free Press.

Grant, G. (2005). Realizing the promise of electronic government. *Journal of Global Information Management, 13*(1), i-iv.

Grant, G., & Chau, D. (2005). Developing a generic framework for e-government. *Journal of Global Information Management, 13*(1), 1-30.

Gusfield, J. (1978). *Community: A critical response.* New York: Harper & Row.

Hoch, S. J. (2002). Product experience is seductive. *Journal of Consumer Research, 29*(3), 448-454.

Hutton, J. G. (2005). *The feel good society: How the "customer" metaphor is undermining American education, religion, media and healthcare.* New Jersey: Pentagram Publishing.

Marshall, G. (1994). *The concise Oxford dictionary of sociology.* Oxford: Oxford University Press.

Muniz, A. M., Jr., & O'Guinn, T. C. (2001). Brand community. *Journal of Consumer Research, 27*(4), 412-432.

OECD. (2003). The case for e-government: Excerpts from the OECD Report "The e-government imperative." *OECD Journal on Budgeting, 3*(1), 62-96.

Selznick, P. (1996). In search of community. In W. Vitek & W. Jackson (Eds.), *Rooted in the land: Essays on community and place* (pp. 195-203). New Haven, CT: Yale University Press.

United Nations. (2003). *World public sector report 2003: E-government at the crossroads.* New York: United Nations Publications.

Urban, G. L., Sultan, F., & Qualls, W. J. (2000). Placing trust at the center of your Internet strategy. *MIT Sloan Management Review, 42*(1), 39-48.

Weber, M. (1978). *Economy and society.* Berkeley: University of California Press.

Wellman, B. (1999). *Networks in the global village: Life in contemporary communities.* Boulder, CO: Westview Press.

Appendix: WWMD Statistics and Sources

National Water Monitoring Day Summary Report. (2002). *World Water Monitoring Day.* Retrieved August 3, 2005, from http://www.worldwatermonitoringday.org/docs/2002sumrept.pdf

World Water Monitoring Day Summary Report. (2003). *World Water Monitoring Day.* August 3, 2005, from http://www.worldwatermonitoringday.org/docs/2003data/03sumrpt.pdf

WWMD Summary Report. (2004). *World Water Monitoring Day.* (2004). Retrieved August 3, 2005, from http://www.worldwatermonitoringday.org/docs/USAWWMD_summary.pdf

Real Time Results. (2005). Results page. *Alberta Water Quality Awareness Day.* Retrieved August 3, 2005, from http://www.awqa.ca/AWQA/mi_data/viewResults.asp

Chapter VIII

Healthcare Network Centric Operations:
The Confluence of E-Health and E-Government

Dag von Lubitz, MedSMART, Inc., USA, & Central Michigan University, USA

Nilmini Wickramasinghe, Illinois Institute of Technology, USA

Abstract

Healthcare has yet to realize the true potential afforded by e-health. To date, technology-based healthcare operations are conducted chaotically, at a wide variety of nonintegrated fronts, with little or no long-term strategy, and at a tremendous and ever increasing cost. This chapter proposes that in order for healthcare to ever reap the full benefits from e-health, it is imperative for the development of a doctrine of healthcare network centric operations. Otherwise, millions if not billions of dollars will be spent on a futile chase of the definitions of how and when the computer, healthcare provider, and healthcare administrator interact most efficiently and at least expense. The concept of a doctrine, "conceptual platform," that outlines the consequent, goal-oriented way forward, and integrates all constituent elements into a smoothly operating whole, is utilized to great effect in the military. Drawing upon the strategies and techniques employed by the military to develop a network centric doctrine, the chapter outlines the essential components necessary for the establishment of the doctrine for healthcare network centric operations (HNCO), and in so doing not only highlights the integral role played by information computer and communication technologies (IC²T) but also the pivotal role of policy makers and governments. In fact, HNCO underscores the important yet rarely acknowledged confluence of e-health and e-government.

Introduction

The rules of competition are changing as a result of the growth of global markets, the increased speed of business transactions, the technological revolution, and continued change in customer expectations. The growth, integration, and sophistication of information computer and communication technologies (IC²T) are changing our society and economy. Consumers and businesses have been particularly quick to recognize the potential and realize the benefits of the Internet and Internet-facilitated computer networks. The resultant "e-revolution" changed many aspects of the traditional "way of doing business," facilitated substantial changes in internal and external management styles, enabled increased efficacy of virtually all production stages and operations, and helped to extend the customer reach. As e-commerce or the application of IC²T to business matures, more attention is being placed on maximising its potential benefits to all areas of society. Two areas where much focus is now being placed regarding the use of IC²T to improve access to information and provide better access to services include public institutions and governments and healthcare.

E-government is defined as the use of IC²T to provide citizens and organizations with more convenient access to government services and embrace interactions within governments (government-to-government), between governments and citizens (government-to-citizen), and between governments and businesses (government-to-business) (Turban, King, Lee, & Viehland, 2004). An analogous definition holds for e-health, which involves the use of IC²T to provide all participants within the healthcare domain with better access to information and services (Wickramasinghe, Geisler, & Schaffer, 2005).

IC²T are without doubt the source and the platform of one of the greatest transformations of society since the invention of print and permit-free flow, access, and exchange of information, and the development of universal means of contact among humans. In practical terms, these technologies offer the possibilities for vast improvement of efficiency and cost reduction in business, provide a platform for dissemination of high quality education, facilitate healthcare delivery, and limit the potential for conflict. Already today, the impact of the increasingly more intensive IC²T use can be measured in the way local, national, and global political, economical, or social transactions are conducted. Yet, with the growing employment of IC²T in daily operations, it is also apparent that neither the optimal pattern of use has been developed (we need look no further, for example, than the productivity paradox (Haag, Cummings, & McCubbrey, 2004; Jessup & Valacich, 2005; Laudon & Laudon, 2004; O'Brien, 2005), nor a philosophy guiding such use has been contemplated despite the emerging chaos that threatens the future growth of the field. The impeding state of chaos is exemplified by the collapse of e-businesses in the 1990s (Affuah & Tucci, 2001; Kalakota & Robinson, 1999; Stiglitz, 2003; Wickramasinghe & Sharma, 2004). The need for optimization and doctrine development is most evident in the arena of healthcare that, at the moment, is the most costly budgetary item in the world's economy (McGown, Overhag, Barnes, & McDonald, 2004; Reinhardt, Hussey, & Anderson, 2002; Stats & Facts, 2002; von Lubitz & Wickramasinghe, 2005a; Wickramasinghe & Ginzberg, 2001; Wickramasinghe & Mills, 2002).

Irrespective of the particular healthcare system adopted by a country, governments will always be one of the major influencing forces and key actors of the healthcare stage. It should therefore be a logical extrapolation that e-government and e-health should share a significant overlap. One might even go to the extreme and suggest that e-health, especially for countries which only have a public healthcare system, is in fact a subset of e-government. And yet, the two are rarely if ever discussed together. This confluence between e-health and e-government is best highlighted in the doctrine of healthcare network centric operations (HNCO). We believe that by acknowledging this confluence, more effective policies and protocols can be developed which will facilitate the adoption and diffusion of HNCO and in turn will lead to more effective and efficient healthcare delivery.

In healthcare, despite their relatively late arrival, computer-based technologies will play the major role in management of services at all levels. Yet, while the concept of "e-health" brings the promise of improved economy, increased efficiency, greater equality, and wider range and availability of services, the increasingly diverging goals and philosophies, disparity in the emerging approaches, and frequent incompatibility or limited nature of the available or developed electronic platforms mitigate against such optimistic future. Moreover, the tendency to convert precise terms describing individual components of "e-operations" (operations or activities where IC^{2}T have been applied to make them electronic) into often meaningless "household" terminology adds superficial linguistic grandeur to quite nonglamorous and very common-sense notions, and transforms the latter into profoundly sounding expressions of a trivialized credo. The misconceptions serve to produce chaos that, in turn, diffuses the true value of the "electronic" in the context of healthcare, reduces its impact, and, consequently, delays its most significant contribution toward elimination of spatial and temporal barriers, and energized operational facilitation.

Presently, existing networks and e-health initiatives in healthcare represent distinctive and disconnected entities whose operation is, essentially, platform-centric, that is, concentrates on the operations of a single system (platform) without any regard for the operational inter-action among different systems (a "system of systems" or systems network, see von Lubitz & Wickramasinghe, 2005a, b, c, 2006). The consequent fragmentation and broad incompat-ibility of individual efforts has, in turn, a major influence on the access range to and sharing of high quality information existing among (or even within) the existing individual systems (ibid). For these reasons, despite providing very significant advantages to the local users (Wickramasinghe & Ginzberg, 2001; Wickramasinghe & Mills; 2002), the overall impact of the electronic information systems on either national or international healthcare operations continues to be relatively limited (von Lubitz & Wickramasinghe, 2005a) and nor does it provide the promised superior quality of care (Institute of Medicine, 2001).

Healthcare operations are conducted in a complex operational space. The limitations of a platform-centric approach in such environments are compounded by the fact that the limited (or inadequate) information extraction, gathering, and manipulation capabilities of individual systems are amplified by their frequent lack of interoperability (von Lubitz & Wickramasinghe, 2005a, b, c, 2006). Such limitations severely degrade the possibility of integrating inputs of complex, highly relevant data both from a wide variety of relevant (clinical data banks, for example) as well as seemingly nonessential sources (e.g., political, economical, geographical, ethnographic data pools) and has been the justification for taking a systems approach (Checkland & Scholes, 1990; Churchman, 1968). Environmental complexity of healthcare operations is often magnified by the presence of multiple actors (agencies, governmental bodies, global organizations, etc.) performing within the same space but using a wide variety of independent and non-intercommunicating platform-centric tools. As a consequence of the resulting chaos, the attainment (mission) of healthcare goals (objectives) is uncertainty, rather than information-driven (von Lubitz & Wickramasinghe, 2005c).

Healthcare Network Centric Operations (HNCO)

The *network-centric approach* stands in direct apposition to platform centricity (Alberts, Garstka, & Stein, 2000; Cebrowski & Garstka, 1998; von Lubitz & Wickramasinghe, 2005a, b, c, 2006). Its underlying conceptual framework is drawn from the pioneering work of Boyd (1987), who synthesized decision making, interaction with and control of a fast paced and unpredictably changing environment into a loop-like process (OODA Loop) (Figure 1) (Boyd, 1987; von Lubitz & Wickramasinghe, 2005b, c, d, 2006). Decision making in complex macroenvironments, particularly those characterized by a very rapid revolution cycle and a vast array of multispectral information inputs, is the primary beneficiary of the practical applications of Boyd's Loop. Application of Loop methodology allows for the interpretation of the environment of multidimensional action space (in this case, healthcare) as a set of simultaneous and intertwined events that characterize the space, and are both influencing and are influenced by the actor (e.g., a healthcare organization, clinician, or disease). Boyd's Loop-based thinking forces the actor into continuous extraction and synthesis of pertinent information and germane knowledge. Without such extraction / synthesis, information chaos and overload will rapidly ensue and force the operator into subjective selection of *seemingly* relevant inputs and disregard of other inputs *that appear, at the time of the analysis, to be inconsequential* (von Lubitz & Wickramasinghe, 2005c, 2006; von Lubitz et al., 2004). The ensuing responses to the objective pressures will thus derive from increasingly subjective data interpretation, leading to suboptimal decision making and the ultimate danger of catastrophic errors.

Application of Boyd's Loop and the associated continuous extraction and analysis of high quality information from the environment of the "operational space" provides yet another major advantage: the development of "information superiority" and the reduction of "information asymmetry" relative to the environment.

Each environment contains a complete set of data (information) that describe it. By extracting this information, the actor shifts the knowledge of the given environment from fully unknown (i.e., the environment containing all information that is hidden from the observer) to fully known (the observer uncovers the entire information content of the environment). In the process of uncovering the informational content of the environment, the actor shifts information asymmetry (from environment contained to actor extracted) in his favour and, at the same time, attains the state of "information superiority" (the actor knows progressively more about the faced environment, while the density of the unknown information

Figure 1. Boyd's (OODA) Loop depicting how the processes for making critical decisions can be framed in terms of the four key stages of orientation, observation, determination, and action.

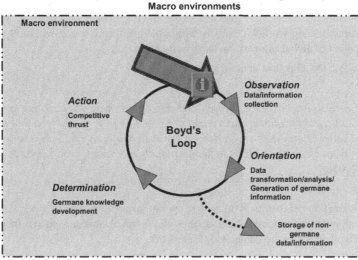

OODA Loop Activities That Support Decision Making on Complex Macro environments

Note: The loop revolves both in time and space, and that termination of each revolution (Action stage) modifies the environment with which the Observer interacts, and imposes a new set of "unfolding circumstances" that generate "outside information" and shape the subsequent "Orient" and "Decide" stages. (Adapted from von Lubitz & Wickramasinghe, 2005a, 2005b, 2005c)

contained within the environment diminishes during the extraction process). Hence, the highest possible rate of the shift of information asymmetry in favour of the actor and the maximum reduction of time needed for the attainment of valid information superiority are the principal goals of the actor acting in a complex, dynamically evolving environment. Both actor-biased information asymmetry and information superiority are also the principal countermeasure to the "information chaos" or information overload (Lehto, 1991; Prietula, Feltovich, & Marchak, 2000; Tole, Stephens, Harris, & Eprath, 1982) — elements that also characterize many aspects of today's healthcare (Arellano & Weber, 1998; d'Alessandro & Kreiter, 1999; Geiger, Merriles, Walo, Gordon, & Kunov, 1995).

In summary, information superiority provides asymmetric operational advantage not only assures complete control of the direction and tempo of all activities in a collaborative yet highly coordinated manner, but also facilitates attainment of the objective in the most effective and economical way possible.

The state of information superiority can be attained only through the effective use of IC^2T — a critical architectural element of doctrine of "network-centric warfare" created and currently implemented by the U.S. Department of Defense (Stein, 1998). The approach calls for the development of interconnected information grids creating a multilayered, robust network that facilitates information sharing among all participants within the operational space (Arellano & Weber, 1998; d'Alessandro et al., 1999). Drawing upon these ideas and the underlying logic of Boyd's OODA, a doctrine for healthcare network-centric operations has been proposed recently (von Lubitz & Wickramasinghe, 2005a), of which the principal element is the creation and employment of an effective integrated worldwide collection/dissemination/exchange IC²T grid that will allow free flow of standardized/structured data/information among worldwide actors within the healthcare space necessary to allow the development of global information superiority state.

The doctrine of HNCO is thus defined as:

unhindered networking operations within and among all three domains that govern all activities conducted in healthcare space and are based on free, multidirectional flow and exchange of information without regard to the involved platforms or platform-systems and utilizing all available means of ICTs to facilitate such operations. (von Lubitz & Wickramasinghe, 2005a)

The three distinct domains of networkcentric operations are very closely interrelated, and the space within which the domains overlap provides physical and conceptual infrastructure within which all activities are conducted (Figure 2a):

- **Physical domain:** the target that the healthcare intends to influence directly or indirectly. In addition to the most obvious goal of eliminating disease, other aspects of healthcare, for example, research and its policies, fiscal issues, political environment of healthcare, provider personnel, and patient education, belong to this domain. The data/information/knowledge within physical domain relate to its *present rather than future state* and are the easiest to collect. Cumulatively, the physical domain represents *the current state of healthcare reality.*

- **Information domain:** consists of all elements needed to generate, store, manipulate, disseminate/share/transform information, and disseminate/share the product of such transformation as knowledge in all its forms. All sensory inputs gathered are gathered within the information domain with the sensors representing a wide variety of entities (people and devices.) The output of the sensors may have a wide variety of forms/sensitivity (e.g., basic research data, diagnostic data from individual/multiple patient encounters, electronic health records, etc.) The information existing in this domain may not fully represent the current state of reality. However, all knowledge about that state emerges from and through the interaction with the information domain, and all communications about that occur through interactions within this domain. The information domain is particularly sensitive to incursions that may affect the quality of information contained within the domain. Hence, it must have appropriate security measures that prevent hostile intrusions in any form.

- **Cognitive domain:** constitutes all human factors that affect healthcare operations, such as education, training, experience, personal engagement (motivation), "open-mindedness," or even intuition of individuals involved in relevant activities. All these represent highly intangible quantities that are difficult to measure but form the basis for the selection of right timing, right place, and right effect of all actions undertaken within the healthcare. Even in the presence of well developed decision support systems provided by the information domain, deep situational awareness is created and decisions are made within the cognitive domain.

The technological backbone of network-centric healthcare is the World Healthcare Information Grid (WHIG) (von Lubitz & Wickramasinghe, 2005a, b, c, 2006) which utilizes Web and related Internet technologies, for example, HTML, TCP/IP, Web, JAVA, XTML, and so forth (Eysenbach, 2001; Eysenbach & Diepgen, 1998; Glaser, 2002; McGown et al., 2004; PricewaterhouseCoopers, 2003; Sharma & Wickramasinghe, 2004a; Sieving, 1999; Umhoff & Winn, 1999; Wickramasinghe & Ginzberg, 2001; Wickramasinghe & Mills, 2002). Figure 2a depicts the WHIG with its three distinct yet interconnected domains, each made up of interconnecting grids while Figure 2b identifies the key elements of the grid with its smart access portals, analytic nodes, and intelligent sensors (von Lubitz & Wickramasinghe, 2005b). Implementation of principles based on ASP (application software provider) philosophy and fusing them together with the concept of smart portals allows direct worldwide access to the WHIG that is essentially independent of the technology existing at the user site and that opens network-centric healthcare operations to practically all involved entities — whether individual healthcare providers or national/international bodies providing healthcare governance, monitoring, and policy development.

Figure 2. (a) The relationship among the operational domains in health care. Network-centric health care operations (NHCO) exist only in the territory where all three domains overlap; (b) The critical components of WHIG, including the smart portal, analytic nodes, and sensors (Adapted from von Lubitz & Wickramasinghe, 2005a, 2005b, 2005c, 2005d)

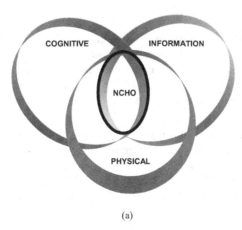

Three Domains Of Healthcare Operations

(a)

Figure 2. continued

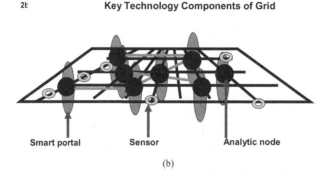

(b)

Future Trends: Implications
for Policy Makers and Governments

WHIG provides the technology backbone of HNCO; however, for WHIG to function as intended, providing pertinent information and germane knowledge in a seamless, effective, and efficient fashion to a decision maker anywhere anytime, various protocols and procedures must be developed at a global level. Without such standardization even the simplest of functions, such as the exchange of documents and other procurement information, connectivity, and e-commerce enabled benefits, become problematic while the critical goal of decreasing information asymmetry becomes unattainable. Unfortunately, standardization is woefully lacking in too many areas of healthcare let alone e-health. Given the global nature of WHIG, it is here that global bodies, such as the World Healthcare Organization (WHO) in conjunction with governments and policy makers, must develop policies, procedures, and standards that will enable the seamless functioning of WHIG. We identify four key areas that must be addressed:

1. **Information computer communication technology (IC²T) architecture/infrastructure:** The generic architecture for most e-health initiatives is similar to that required by WHIG. However this infrastructure that consists of phone lines, fiber trunks and submarine cables, T1, T3 and OC-xx, ISDN, DSL and other high-speed services used by businesses as well as satellites, earth stations and teleports must be available globally.

    A sound technical infrastructure is an essential ingredient to the undertaking of e-health initiatives by any nation. Such infrastructures should also include telecommunications, electricity, access to computers, number of Internet hosts, number of ISPs (Internet service providers) and available bandwidth and broadband access. To offer a good multimedia content and thus provide a rich e-health experience, one would require a high bandwidth. ICT considerations are undoubtedly one of the most fundamental infrastructure requirements.

Networks are now a critical component of the business strategies for organizations to compete globally. Having a fast microprocessor-based computer at home has no meaning unless you have high bandwidth based communication infrastructure available to connect computers with the ISP. With the explosion of the Internet and the advent of e-commerce, global networks need to be accessible, reliable, and fast to participate effectively in the global business environment. Telecommunications is a vital infrastructure for Internet access, hence also for e-commerce. One of the pioneering countries in establishing a complete and robust e-health infrastructure is Singapore which is in the process of wiring every home, office, and factory up to a broadband cable network which will cover 98% of Singaporean homes and offices (APEC, 2001; A report prepared for Asia Pacific Foundation, 2002a).

It is estimated that over 70% of world telephone lines are in countries with 15% of the world's population (Parker, 1998). The average number of telephone lines in industrialized countries is one for every two persons as compared to 13 lines per thousand people in emerging economies such as India and China (ibid). A sound technical infrastructure is a key ingredient to the future economic health of any given nation and should be a priority for all governments.

For example, in the Asia-Pacific region (APEC, 2001; Beal, 2000; Oxley & Yeung, 2001; A report prepared for Asia Pacific Foundation, 2002a; A study report on Thailand, 2001; Turpin, 2000), there are a number of "digital divides," not only between the richer and poorer countries, but divides between urban and rural populations and between more and less educated or affluent groups. Although the number of female Internet users in a number of countries in the region is catching up quickly with those of male users, women are less present when it comes to the actual use of the new technologies. Furthermore, in many of these countries, women make up the majority of the rural population, which is often marginalized in areas of telecommunication infrastructure, education, and training. Therefore, governments should formulate national IC²T and e-commerce strategies that help to ensure universal access for all socioeconomic groups. A number of prerequisites for access to IC²T include education and training, local content, sociocultural awareness, and a stable social, economic, and political environment. Appropriate technologies need to be developed to address the needs of disadvantaged communities.

2. **Building human capital/resources:** The disparity between educational standards of developed and developing nations in the world is significant (Roquilly, 2002; Sharma & Wickramasinghe, 2004a, b; UNCTAD, 2002). In order for healthcare network-centric operations to fully maximize the potential afforded by WHIG significant enhancement of human capital through education and training is required. Many of the developing nations through investment and foreign aid need to concentrate on developing human capacity, and increasing basic access to IC²T, as well as rapidly increasing the presence and access to the Internet. Moreover, the governments of disadvantaged countries must also exercise significant international pressure to lower costs of hardware and software while, at the same time, contemplating to form larger multinational user blocks capable of effective implementation of ASP principles. E-commerce adoption in

general requires improved e-commerce knowledge and skills, and improved language proficiency (especially in English as it is as the recognized principal technology / commerce language). For example, governments in many countries have started to introduce basic education in digital literacy in primary and secondary schools. Such training courses should be constantly updated as new innovations and practices emerge very rapidly in this field. Institutions responsible for human resource development of e-commerce personnel should provide appropriate incentives for e-commerce courses to be kept up-to-date. Increasing the number of programs or activities for human resource development for IC^2T and especially Internet use will only be effective if the education and training matches the changing needs of the industries concerned. It is important to note that only medical specialists require medical training but all people globally who need to interact with WHIG must have basic familiarity, training, and proficiency with use of IC^2T. Once again much of the onus falls on governments to set the agenda and priority for such an emphasis.

3.   **Fostering consumer trust:** Consumers are also concerned about a number of dimensions of trust; trust in the security of value passed during electronic transactions with organizations that are "virtual" in a disconcertingly ineffable way and trust in the privacy of personal data arising from electronic transactions (Fjetland, 2002; Ghosh & Swaminath, 2001; Panagariya, 2000; Roquilly, 2002). Other than in North America, Japan, and integrated Europe, the infrastructure for e-commerce is not in place for effective e-commerce transactions. The key reason for slow penetration has been the scale of investment in infrastructure, and the small volume of transactions over which to amortize (Dutta, 1999; A report prepared for the Asia Pacific Foundation, 2002b).

The security issue in particular is perceived as very important across the Asia-Pacific region, and the majority of SMEs, for instance, have a fear of electronics. This is primarily due to the low level of technology diffusion and awareness making it a psychological barrier for SMEs as confirmed in various reports (APEC, 2001; Beal, 2000; A report prepared for the Asia Pacific Foundation, 2002b). Many of these SMEs do not have technical expertise, and are not convinced that the technology standards, such as encryption, will protect them. Thus, SMEs are not willing to use electronic payment systems.

Given such a general lack of trust in developing nations with using e-commerce, it is likely that the trust issue will be a significant factor in e-health initiatives given the general sensitivity of healthcare information. Once again government and national bodies must make every attempt to foster trust. This will not be an easy task since in many developing countries people have a low level of trust for governments, corruption tends to be significant, and especially in rural areas, people tend to be very superstitious and leery of "modern methods." However, in many instances WHIG and healthcare network centric operations will offer these groups of people the best healthcare alternatives and thus significant effort must be made to build and foster trust.

Ethical concerns are inevitably related to healthcare operations based on network centricity. The notion of the governmental bodies having ready access to healthcare information of the citizens is among the major concerns in the U.S., and similar reservations are also voiced in Europe. The possibility of security breaches, similar to those that recently affected millions of credit card customers in the United States, demands a very stringent layer of protective layers that will assure prevention of commercial misuse of healthcare data. The seriousness of such intrusions is emphasized by the dynamic development of molecular biology and genetics that allow early determination of the likelihood to develop long-term debilitating diseases at the later stages of life. Misappropriation of such information may then affect the subsequent chances of employment, nature and availability of health insurance, and even acquisition of credit. While laws preventing such discrimination already exist in several Western countries, their enforcement is not simple and the fear of clandestine stratification into "health risk" classes whose quality and freedom of life is directly related to the long-term risk is a threat that needs to be addressed with utmost vigor now. At a less threatening, albeit far more practical level, the problems of the responsibility for the delivery of healthcare also need clarification.

Among the major obstacles to the development of an efficient national telemedicine network in the U.S. is the difficulty of assigning responsibility for treatment conducted across state borders. The dilemma becomes even more pertinent when healthcare expertise is projected across national borders. While there is no doubt that the rule of the "best medical practice" ought to be the prevailing one, the best practice has different definitions in different countries and what is considered the standard of care in one country may not be so in another. There is thus a clear need to develop generally accepted standards of delivery and the current acceptance of the concept of "evidence-based medicine" may offer the most useful foundation for further deliberations of such standards. These are but two of several problems that already either influence or are about to influence e-health in all its forms.

The magnitude of network centricity and its global nature will add even greater urgency to the need for their effective operational rather than merely political or legislative solution. At a purely technical level, while network centricity strengthens the efficacy and economy of global healthcare, it may also have an impact on access to it. Ideally, network-centric operations will support a continuously broadening access to high quality healthcare across the entire globe. In practice, however, there is a chance it may support improvements there where the level of the preexisting technology and sophistication in its use are already high while leaving those who lag behind, yet needing rapid improvement of even basic healthcare in the same position they are now — desperately struggling to satisfy the most elementary healthcare needs of the local population. It is thus evident that introduction of network centricity and the creation of WHIG require a fundamentally different approach to the one currently practiced: they can be made functional only when a state of intense, multilateral, and determinedly synergistic collaboration exists between corporate and governmental entities not only at the national but, even more importantly, at the international level. Ultimately, transparency, international synergism, and adherence to the highest ethical standards of operations will be among the most instrumental factors to convince the users (i.e., both deliverers and recipients of healthcare) that network centricity in healthcare offers tangible benefits that have been unattainable prior to the implementation of the concept.

4.   **Creating synergies between national and regional economic blocks:** For WHIG and HNCO to be fully functional, it is vital that synergies are created between national and economic blocks. For example, in similarity to the EU, all countries in the Asia-Pacific region should improve access to IC^2Ts, design the necessary legal and institutional frameworks to educate the governments, businesses, and civil society to more efficiently use IC^2Ts in their daily practices, and create an environment for further development of IC^2T use in general and in particular with a focus on healthcare. There is a tremendous need to support the integration and interoperability of regional e-commerce initiatives through various international and regional economic blocks such as the Asia-Pacific Economic Cooperation (APEC), North American Free Trade Agreement (NAFTA), and the European Union.

Another critical aspect that requires significant consideration to enable and facilitate the required synergies is that pertaining to legal and ethical issues. In general the Internet community has developed its own distinctive culture and a great part many of these behavioural norms function outside the realm of International Law given the current maturity of International Internet Law (Commission of the European Communities, 2003; De Ly, 1992, 2000; Nielson, 2000; Polanski, 2005; Polanski & Johnston, 2002). Given the sensitive nature of much of the information contained with healthcare interactions, this poses a significant problem and major stumbling block for the adoption of HNCO. This is clearly an area that requires significant discussion and will form the center of future research; we mention it here only in passing to note that it remains as yet a key area that needs to be addressed

Conclusion

It is beyond the scope of this chapter to discuss the details of the technology configuration of WHIG or provide guidelines for practioners. Interested readers can refer to other research (von Lubitz & Wickramasinghe, 2005a, 2005b, 2005c, 2005d; von Lubitz, Wickramasinghe, & Yanovsky, 2005) for details. The primary focus here is to highlight the key role for governments if we are to ever realize the full benefits of e-health.

The idea of WHIG and HNCO is to span many parties and geographic dimensions. To enable such a far reaching coverage, significant amounts of document exchange and information flows must be accommodated. Standardization is the key for this. Once a country decides to undertake e-health initiatives and become a "WHIG member," standardization policies, protocols, and procedures must be developed at the outset to ensure the full realization of the goals of e-health. The transformation to e-health by any country cannot be successfully attained without the deliberate establishment of standardization policies, protocols, and procedures which play a significant role in the adoption of e-health and the reduction of many structural impediments (Panagariya, 2000; Samiee, 1998). Fortunately, the main infrastructure of WHIG is the Internet which imposes the most widely and universally accepted standard protocols such as TCP/IP and http. It is the existence of these standard protocols that has led to the widespread adoption of the Internet for e-commerce applications.

Access to the technologies of e-commerce is defined by the WTO (World Trade Organization) as consisting of two critical components: (1) access to Internet services and (2) access to e-services (Health Insurance Portability and Accountability Act, 2001); the former deals with the user infrastructure, while the latter pertains to specific commitments to electronically accessible services. The user infrastructure includes number of Internet hosts and number of Web sites, Web users as a percent of the population as well as ISP availability and costs for consumers, PC penetration level, and so forth. Integral to user infrastructure is the diffusion rate of PCs and Internet usage. The United States and the United Kingdom have experienced the greatest penetration of home computers (Samiee, 1998). For developing countries, such as India and China, there is, however, a very low PC penetration and teledensity. In such a setting it is a considerable challenge then to offer e-health, since a large part of the population is not able to afford to join the e-commerce bandwagon. Countries, thus have to balance local call charges, rentals, subscription charges, and so forth, otherwise the majority of citizens will find these costs a disincentive. This is particularly significant for developing and emerging nations where access prices tend to be out of reach for most of the population. Upcoming new technologies hold the promise to increase the connectivity as well as affordability level and developing countries will need to seriously consider these technologies. In addition to access to PCs and the Internet, computer literacy is important and users must be familiar not only with the use of computers and pertinent software products but also the benefits and potential uses of the Internet and World Wide Web (ibid).

The key challenges regarding e-health use include (1) cost effectiveness that is less costly than traditional healthcare delivery; (2) functionality and ease of use: that is, they should enable and facilitate many uses for physicians and other healthcare users by combining various types and forms of data as well as be easy to use; and (3) they must be secure. One of the most significant legislative regulations in the U.S. is the Health Insurance Portability and Accountability Act (HIPAA) (2001).

Given the nature of healthcare and the sensitivity of healthcare data and information, it is incumbent on governments not only to mandate regulations that will facilitate the exchange of healthcare documents between the various healthcare stakeholders but also to provide protection of privacy and the rights of patients (Dyer, 2001). Some countries, such as China and Singapore, even control access to certain sites for moral, social, and political reasons while elsewhere transnational data flows are hindered by a plethora of regulations aimed at protecting domestic technology and related human resource markets (Ghosh & Swaminatha, 2001; Gupta, 1992; Samiee, 1998). Irrespective of the type of healthcare system; that is, whether 100% government driven, 100% private or a combination thereof, it is clear that some governmental role is required to facilitate successful e-health initiatives.

HNCO also serves to underscore the inextricable connection and intertwining of e-health and e-government which to date has rarely been researched let alone acknowledged. Moreover, for HCNO to become adopted successfully, it requires governments to develop policies and protocols which will in turn facilitate its usability. We identify four key areas that will have an important impact on the development of the necessary policies and protocols as IT education, morbidity, cultural/social dimensions, and world economic standing as elaborated upon below. It is interesting to note that these areas also impact the development of numerous e-government initiatives (Turban et al., 2004), once again highlighting the inextricable link between e-health and e-government.

- **IT education:** A sophisticated, well educated population boosts competition and hastens innovation. According to Michael Porter, one of the key factors to a country's strength in an industry is strong customer support (Porter, 1990). Thus, a strong domestic market leads to the growth of competition which leads to innovation and the adoption of technology enabled solutions to provide more effective and efficient services such as e-health and telemedicine. As identified earlier, the health consumer is the key driving force in pushing e-health initiatives. We conjecture that a more IT educated healthcare consumer would then provide stronger impetus for e-health adoption.

- **Morbidity rate:** There is a direct relationship between health education and awareness and the overall health standing of a country. Therefore, a more health conscious society, which tends to coincide with a society that has a lower morbidity rate, is more likely to embrace e-health initiatives. Furthermore, higher morbidity rates tend to indicate the existence of more basic health needs (World Health Organization, 2003) and hence treatment is more urgent than the practice of preventative medicine and thus e-health could be considered an unrealistic luxury and, in some instances, such as when a significant percentage of a population is suffering from malnutrition related diseases, is even likely to be irrelevant, at least in the short term. Thus, we conjecture that the modifying impact of morbidity rate is to prioritize the level of spending on e-health vs. other basic healthcare needs.

- **Cultural/social dimensions:** Healthcare has been shaped by each nation's own set of cultures, traditions, payment mechanisms, and patient expectations. While the adoption of e-health, to a great extent, dilutes this cultural impact, social and cultural dimensions will still be a moderating influence on any countries e-health initiatives. Another aspect of the cultural/social dimension relates to the presentation language of the content of the e-health repositories. The entire world does not speak English, so the e-health solutions have to be offered in many other languages. The e-health supporting content in Web servers/sites must be offered in local languages, supported by pictures and universal icons. This becomes a particularly important consideration when we look at the adoption and diffusion of evidence-based medicine as it will mean that much of the available evidence and case study data will not be easily accessible globally due to language barriers.

Therefore, for successful e-health initiatives it is important to consider cultural dimensions. For instance, an international e-commerce study by International Data Corp. indicates that Web surfing and buying habits differ substantially from country to country (Wilson, 1999) and this would then have a direct impact on their comfort to use e-commerce generally and e-health in particular, especially as e-health addresses a more fundamental need. Hence, the adoption of e-health is directly related to ones comfort with using the technology and this in turn is influenced in a major way by cultural dimensions. Also connected with cultural aspects is the relative entrepreneurial spirit of a country. For example, a study (Hofstede, 1984) indicates that in a cultural context, Indians score high on "uncertainty avoidance" criteria when compared to their Western counterparts. As a result, for example, Indians do not accept change very easily and are hostile towards innovation. This then would potentially pose a challenge to the starting up of e-health initiatives whose success depends on widespread adoption for their technological innovations. Thus, we conjecture that fear of risk and absence of an entrepreneurial mindset as well as other cultural/social dimensions can also impact the success of e-health initiatives in a given country.

- **World economic standing:** Economies of the future will be built around the Internet. All governments are very aware of the importance and critical role that the Internet will play on a country's economy. This makes it critical that appropriate funding levels and budgetary allocations become a key component of governmental fiscal policies so that such initiatives will form the bridge between a traditional healthcare present and a promising e-health future. Thus, the result of which would determine success of effective e-health implementations and consequently have the potential to enhance a country's economy and future growth.

A healthy society is in the interests of all governments. As labor costs increase and productivity is critical to economic development, a healthy population is naturally able to contribute more significantly to increasing GDP. Coupled with the fact that healthcare remains the most expensive item for any government, it behooves governments to make healthcare a top priority on their agenda. The doctrine of HNCO serves to outline a coherent and systematic approach for harnessing the full potential of IC^2T for healthcare and the ability to realize the promises of e-health. However, if this is to occur, e-health must become a top priority on all government agendas. Moreover, governments must go further than just acknowledge the importance of e-health to focusing their energies and efforts to address the key impediments we have identified and that currently preclude the ubiquitous adoption of HNCO.

The World Economic Forum's Global competitiveness ranking measures the relative global competitiveness of a country. This ranking takes into account factors such as physical infrastructure, bureaucracy, and corruption. It is a simple extrapolation of the combination of these factors to postulate that the combination of a weak physical infrastructure with high levels of bureaucracy and corruption will constitute a significant impediment to the establishment of successful e-health initiatives. Surely, network-centric healthcare operations will not change these realities. On the other hand, the possibility for a rural healthcare provider working in an even most oppressive political and economical environment to enter WHIG and benefit from the combined global healthcare expertise will be without doubt a step in the right direction. And many steps in the right direction will ultimately help to redress the level of current inequalities in access to the most fundamental right of all humans across the globe — health.

References

Affuah, A., & Tucci, C. (2001). *Internet business models and strategies*. Boston: McGraw-Hill Irwin.

Alberts, D. S., Garstka, J. J., & Stein, F. P. (2000). *Network centric warfare: Developing and leveraging information superiority* (CCRP Publication Series, pp. 1-284). Washington, DC: Department of Defense. Retrieved May 5, 2006, from http://www.dodccrp.org/publications/pdf/Alberts_NCW.pdf

APEC. (2001). *The new economy and APEC.* Report to the Economic Committee of APEC. Retrieved May 5, 2006, from http://www.diw.de/deutsch/produkte/veranstaltungen/docs/apec-report.html

Arellano, M. G., & Weber, G. I. (1998). Issues in identification and linkage of patient records across an integrated delivery system. *Journal of Healthcare Information Management, 12*, 43-52

Beal, T. (2000). *SMEs and the World Wide Web: Opportunities and prospects.* In A. M. Asri (Ed.), *Small and medium enterprises in Asia Pacific* (Vol. III Development Prospects, pp. 102-134). Commack, NY: Nova Science Publishers.

Boyd, J. R. (1987). *COL USAF, in "Patterns of Conflict", unpublished briefing.* Retrieved from "Essence of Winning and Losing", http://www.d-n-i.net

Cebrowski, A. K, & Garstka, J. J. (1998). Network-centric warfare: Its origin and future. *US Nav. Inst. Proc., 1*, 28-35

Checkland, P., & Scholes, J. (1990). *Soft systems methodology in action.* New York: Wiley.

Churchman, C. (1968). *The systems approach.* New York: Del Publishing.

Commission of the European Communities (2003). *First report on the application of Directive 2003/31/EC of the European Parliament and of the Council of 8 June 2000 on certain legal aspects of information society services, in particular, electronic commerce, in the Internal Market (Directive on electronic commerce)* (pp. 1-25). Brussels.

d'Alessandro, D. M., & Kreiter, C. D. (1999). Improving usage of pediatric information on the Internet: The Virtual Children's Hospital. *Pediatrics, 104*, e55.

De Ly, F. (1992). *International business law and Lex Mercatoria.* Amsterdam, London, New York, Tokyo: T. M. C. Asser Instituut — The Hague.

De Ly, F. (2000). Emerging new perspectives regarding Lex Mercatoria in an era of increasing globalization. In *Festschrift für Otto Sandrock* (pp. 179-204). Heidelberg: Verlag Recht und Wirtschaft.

Dutta, A. (1999). The physical infrastructure for electronic commerce in developing nations: Historic trends and the impacts of privatization. *International Journal of Electronic Commerce, 2*(1), 63-82.

Dyer, K. A. (2001). Ethical challenges of medicine and health on the internet: A review. *JMIR, 3*(2). Retrieved from http://www.jmir.org/2001/2/e23

E-Health and the Practicing Physician. (n.d.). Retrieved May 5, 2006, from http://www.medscape.com

E-Health in the Medical Field. (n.d.). Retrieved May 5, 2006, from http://www.american-telemed.org/ehealth/ehealthH.htm

Eysenbach, G. (2001). Journal of Medical Internet Research is now indexed in Medline. *Journal of Medical Internet Research, 3*(3), e25.

Eysenbach, G., & Diepgen, T. L. (1998). Towards quality management of medical information on the Internet: Evaluation, labeling, and filtering of information. *BMJ, 317*, 1496-1500.

Fjetland, M. (2002). Global commerce and the privacy clash. *Information Management Journal, 36*(1), 54-58.

Geiger, G., Merriles, K., Walo, R., Gordon, D., & Kunov, H. (1995). An analysis of the paper-based health record: Information content and its implications for electronic patient records. *Medinfo, 8*(1), 295.

Ghosh, A. K., & Swaminatha, T. M. (2001, February). Software security and privacy risks in mobile e-commerce. *Communications of the ACM, 44*(2), 51-58.

Glaser, J. (2002). *The strategic application of information technology in health care organizations* (2nd ed.). San Francisco: Jossey Bass.

Gupta, U. (1992). Global networks: Promises and challenges. *Information Systems Management, 9*, 28-32.

Haag, S., Cummings, M., & McCubbrey, D. (2004). *Management information systems for the Information Age* (4th ed.). Boston: McGraw-Hill Irwin.

Health Insurance Portability and Accountability Act (HIPPA). (2001). *Privacy compliance executive summary.* Washington, DC: Protegrity Inc.

Health Technology Center. (2000). *A survey conducted for the Health Technology Center (HealthTech) by Harris Interactive in cooperation with Pricewaterhouse Coopers and the Institute for the Future (IFTF)*. Retrieved May 5, 2006, from http://www.ncddr. org/cgi-bin/good-bye.cgi?url=http://www.healthtechcenter.org

Hofstede, G. (1984). *Culture's consequences, international work related values.* Beverly Hills: Sage.

Institute of Medicine. (2001). *Crossing the quality chasm: A new health system for the 21st Century Committee on Quality of Health Care in America Institute of Medicine.* Washington, DC: National Academy Press.

Jessup, L., & Valacich, J. (2005). *Information systems today* (2nd ed.). Upper Saddle River, NJ: Prentice Hall.

Kalakota, R., & Robinson, M. (1999). *E-business roadmap for success.* Reading, MA: Addison-Wesley.

Laudon, K., & Laudon, J. (2004). *Management information systems* (7th ed.). Upper Saddle River, NJ: Prentice Hall.

Lehto, M. R. (1991). A proposed conceptual model of human behaviour and its implications for design of warning. *Percept. Mot. Skills, 73*, 595-611.

McGowan, J. J., Overhag, J. M., Barnes, M., & McDonald, C. J. (2004). Indianapolis I3: The third generation integrated advanced information management systems. *J Med Libr Assoc, 92*, 179-187.

Nielsen, J. (2000). *Designing Web usability: The practice of simplicity.* Indianapolis, IN: New Riders Publishing.

O'Brien, J. (2005). *Management information system* (6th ed.). Boston: Irwin McGraw-Hill.

Odyssey Research. (n.d.). Retrieved May 5, 2006, from http://www.odysseyresearch.org

Oxley, J. E., & Yeung, B. (2001). E-commerce readiness: Institutional environment and international competitiveness. *Journal of International Business Studies, 32*(4), 705-723.

Panagariya, A. (2000). E-commerce, WTO and developing countries. *The World Economy, 23*(8), 959-978.

Parker, B. (1998). *Globalization and business practices.* Beverley Hills: Sage.

Polanski, P. (2005, June 17-19). Common practices in the electronic commerce and their legal significance. In *Proceedings of the 18th Bled E-Commerce Conference*, Bled, Slovenia (pp. 170-189).

Polanski, P. P., & Johnston, R. B. (2002, January 5-8). International custom as a source of law in global electronic commerce. In *Proceedings of the 35th Hawaii International Conference on System Sciences* (CD-ROM), Big Island, HI.

Porter, M. (1990). *The competitive advantage of nations.* New York: Free Press.

PricewaterhouseCoopers Healthcare Practice. (2003). Retrieved May 5, 2006, from http://www.pwchealth.com

Prietula, M. J., Feltovich, P. J., & Marchak, F. (2000). Factors influencing analysis of complex cognitive tasks: A framework and example from industrial process control. *Human Factors, 42*, 56-74.

Reinhardt, U. E., Hussey, P. S., & Anderson, G. F. (2002). Cross-national comparisons of health systems using OECD data. *Health Affairs, 3*, 169-181.

Report prepared for Asia Pacific Foundation. (2002a). *Asia-Pacific E-Commerce: B2B & B2C.* Retrieved May 5, 2006, from http://www.gii.co.jp/english/em11033_asia_ec_toc.html

Report prepared for Asia Pacific Foundation. (2002b). *E-commerce and Asia Pacific, Castle Asia Pacific.* Retrieved May 5, 2006, from http://www.gii.co.jp/english/em11033_asia_ec_toc.html

Roquilly, C. (2002). Closed distribution networks and e-commerce: Antitrust issues. *International Review of Law, Computers & Technology, 16*(1), 81-93.

Samiee, S. (1998). The Internet and international marketing: Is there a fit? *Journal of Interactive Marketing, 12*(4), 5-20.

Sharma, S., & Wickramasinghe, N. (2004a). E-health with knowledge management: Areas for tomorrow. In N. Wickramasinghe, J. Gupta, & S. Sharma (Eds.), *Creating knowledge-based healthcare organizations* (pp. 110-124). Hershey, PA: Idea Group Publishers.

Sharma, S., & Wickramasinghe, N. (2004b). Obstacles to SMEs for e-adoption in the Asia Pacific region in ebusiness, egovernment & small and medium enterprises: Opportunities and challenges. In Al-Qirim et al. (Eds.), *E-business, E-government & Small and Medium Enterprises: Opportunities and Challenges* (pp. 112-133). Hershey, PA: Idea Group Publishing.

Sieving, P. C. (1999). Factors driving the increase in medical information on the Web: One American perspective. *Journal of Medical Internet Research*, 1. Retrieved May 5, 2006, from http://www.jmir.org/1999/1/e3

Stats and facts. (2002). Global health cost and care comparisons. *Manage Care Interface, 15*, 66-77.

Stein, P. (1998). *Observations on the emergence of network centric warfare.* Retrieved May 5, 2006, from http://www.dodccrp.org/research/ncw/stein/_observations/steincw.htm

Stiglitz, J. E. (2003). *The roaring nineties.* New York: Norton & Co.

Study report on Thailand. (2001). *SMEs and e-commerce*, Asia Pacific Foundation.

The higher the connection speed, the higher the value: Broadband use as an indication of value amongst e-health users. (2001). *Cyber Dialogue Cybercitizen Health Trend Report 2001*, No. 49.

Tole, J. R., Stephens, A. T., Harris, R. L., Sr., & Eprath, A. R. (1982). Visual scanning behavior and mental worlkload of aircraft pilots. *Aviat. Space Environ. Med., 53*, 54-61.

Turban, E., King, D., Lee, J., & Viehland, D. (2004). *Electronic commerce.* Upper Saddle River, NJ: Prentice Hall.

Turpin, T. (2000). SMEs and technology diffusion in Asia Pacific-Pacific economies: Indonesia a case-study. In *Proceedings of the Annual Conference of the Academy of International Business Southeast Asia Pacific Region, International Business Research Institute,* University of Wollongong, Australia (CD-ROM).

Umhoff, B., & Winn, J. (1999, May 1). The healthcare profit pool: Who stands to gain and lose in the digital economy. *Health Forum Journal.*

von Lubitz, D., & Wickramasinghe, N. (2005a). Healthcare and technology: The doctrine of networkcentric healthcare. *International Journal Healthcare Technology Management, 4*, 322-343.

von Lubitz, D., & Wickramasinghe, N. (2005b). Networkcentric healthcare: Outline of the entry portal concept. *International Journal of Electronic Business, 1*, 16-28.

von Lubitz, D., & Wickramasinghe, N. (2005c). Networkcentric healthcare and bioinformatics. *International Journal on Expert Systems.*

von Lubitz, D., & Wickramasinghe, N. (2005d). Creating germane knowledge in dynamic environments. *International Journal of Innovation Learning.*

von Lubitz, D., & Wickramasinghe, N. (2006, January). Networkcentric healthcare: Strategies, structures and technologies for managing knowledge. In *Proceedings of the IRMA Conference*, Washington, DC.

von Lubitz, D., Wickramasinghe, N., & Yanovsky, G. (2005). Networkcentric healthcare operations: The telecommunications structure. *International Journal on Global Technology.*

von Lubitz, D., et al. (2004). Medical readiness in the context of operations other than war: Development of first responder readiness using OODA. In *Proceedings of the Loop Thinking and Advanced Distributed Interactive Simulation Technology Symposium,* Istanbul, Turkey. Retrieved May 5, 2006, from the Defence and National Intelligence Network, http://www.d-n-i.net/fcs/pdf/von_lubitz_1rp_ooda.pdf

Web Based Second Opinion. (n.d.). Retrieved May 5, 2006, from http://www.eclevelandclinic.org

Wickramasinghe, N., Fadlalla, A., Geisler, E., & Schaffer, J. (2004). A framework for assessing e-health preparedness. *International Journal on Electronic Healthcare (IJEH)1*(3), 316-334.

Wickramasinghe, N., Geisler, E., & Schaffer, J. (2005). Assessing e-health. In Spiel & Schuring (Eds.), *E-health systems diffusion and use: The innovation, the user and the use it model* (pp. 294-323). Hershey, PA: Idea Group.

Wickramasinghe, N., & Ginzberg, M. (2001). Integrating knowledge workers and the organization: The role of IT. *International Journal Healthcare Quality Assurance, 14*(6-7), 245-253.

Wickramasinghe, N., & Mills, G. (2002). Integrating e-commerce and knowledge management: What does the Kaiser experience really tell us? *International Journal of Accounting Information Systems, 3*(2), 83-98.

Wickramasinghe, N., & Sharma, S. (2004). Key factors that hinder SMEs in succeeding in today's knowledge based economy. *International Journal of Management and Enterprise Development, 2*(2), 141-158.

Wilson, T. (1999). Not a global village after all? Consumer behavior varies widely by country. *Internetweek, 792*(13), 792.

World Health Organization (WHO). (2003). Retrieved May 5, 2006, from http://www.emro. who.int/ehealth/

Section II:
E-Government Applications

Chapter IX

Moving Towards E-Government in a Developing Society:
Glimpses of the Problems, Progress, and Prospects in Nigeria

Princely Ifinedo, University of Jyväskylä, Finland

Abstract

The use of information communication technologies (ICT) in governance is growing rapidly in many parts of the world. Developing countries in Africa are also making efforts to harness the new technology. In this chapter, we review the problems, progress, and prospects of e-government in Nigeria, a sub-Saharan African (SSA) country. Governments in the developing countries of SSA can benefit from e-government initiatives, as do their counterparts in advanced nations, when the concept of e-governments in SSA is understood, and concerted efforts are committed towards institutionalizing it in the region. This chapter provided useful insights in this regard. We discussed the contribution of the chapter to information systems (IS) research, and we highlighted the lessons from Nigeria for comparable nations in the SSA region as they prepare for e-government.

Introduction

E-government, as described by the World Bank, is the use of ICT to transform government by making it more accessible, effective, and accountable to its citizenry (*Info*Dev, 2004). E-government involves the utilization of technologies such as the Internet to improve the services, functions, and processes of governance (Cottrill, 2001; Heeks, 1999, 2001; Moon, 2002; Watson & Mundy, 2001). It involves more than establishing a Web server and hosting government sites (Sanchez, Koh, Kappelman, & Prybutok, 2003). However, the Internet plays a vital role in establishing e-government initiatives (Golden, Hughes, & Scott, 2003; Sharma & Gupta, 2003). The World Bank (*Info*Dev, 2004) provides a guideline for developing countries regarding e-government initiatives. The body asserts that e-government initiatives should target the following:

- Promote civic engagement by enabling the public to interact with government officials and vice versa

- Promote accountable and transparent governments in which the opportunities for corruption are reduced

- Provide a greater access to government information and activities

- Provide development opportunities, especially the sorts that benefit rural and traditionally underserved communities

Likewise, the United Nations Division for Public Economics and Public Administration and the American Society for Public Administration (UNDPEPA/ASPA, 2003, p. 6) state:

E-government is about opportunity ... to provide cost effective services to the private sector ... to enhance governance through improved access to accurate information and transparent, responsive, and democratic institutions.

Furthermore, e-government can be an emerging model involving both the citizenry and the state, where the importance of citizen input in policy formulation and implementation are recognized and valued (Navarra & Cornford, 2003). Wimmer and Traunmuller (2001) contend that the main objectives of e-government should include the following: (1) restructuring administrative functions and processes; (2) reducing and overcoming barriers to coordination and cooperation within the public administration; and (3) the monitoring of government performance. Others view e-government as a sort of public service that operates in a "one-stop, non-stop" manner (Lawson, 1998). Heeks (2001) describes e-government as i-governance or integrated governance, which enables the integration of both the processing of information by people and the use of communication technologies in achieving the objectives of governance.

It is important to note that e-government does not create good governance, but that good governments use it to better their governance. E-government has the potential of transforming public services, as well as reengineering the fundamental relationship between government and citizen (Heeks, 1999; Moon, 2002; Watson & Mundy, 2001). Increasingly, advances in ICT have accelerated the growth of e-government in both the developed and developing countries around the world (Accenture, 2004; Kaaya, 2003). Countries such as the United States, Canada, and Australia lead in the deployment of e-government (Accenture, 2004; Huang, Ambra, & Bhalla, 2002; UNPAN, 2005), and many other governments around the world are making serious efforts to join them (see UNPAN, 2005). More importantly, reports have shown that "the most innovative uses of the Internet in governance are appearing in the developing world" (InfoDev, 2004, p. 8). However, many countries in developing regions continue to struggle in their attempt to improve government services using ICT facilities because of the lack of infrastructural support (Accenture, 2004; UNDPEPA/ASPA, 2003; UNPAN, 2005).

The benefits of e-government come in different forms. Some relate to the provision of fast, inexpensive services to the population (Heeks, 2001) and for socioeconomic development and political reformations for developing countries (Breen, 2000; Cottrill, 2001; Kaaya, 2003; Ifinedo, 2004; Ifinedo & Uwadia, 2005; *Info*Dev, 2004). E-government enables the citizenry to participate in the governance of their country (Cottrill, 2001; Heeks, 2001; Moon, 2002). Nowhere is this benefit more relevant than in the developing countries, where governance excludes a majority of their populations by either commission or omission. Similarly, corrupt practices that are rampant in many developing countries, including SSA, could benefit from a purposeful e-government initiative (Ifinedo & Uwadia, 2005; *Info*Dev, 2004). Unfortunately, several barriers confront developing countries that result in the slow diffusion of e-government initiatives. Some of the barriers or problems have their roots in cultural orientations of the region, to include poor infrastructural, organizational, political, economical, and social factors (Ajayi, 2003a; Heeks, 1999; Ifinedo, 2005; Mbarika, Musa, Byrd, & McMullen, 2002; Moulder, 2001; Odedra, Lawrie, Bennett, & Goodman, 1993; Oyebisi & Agboola, 2003; Straub, Loch, & Hill, 2001; Wade, 2001). These problems are discussed in-depth in latter sections of this chapter.

We will next discuss the history of computers and the development of ICT polices in Nigeria, followed by a summary of its sociopolitical and economic environment. We will also discuss the constraints or problems facing the emergence of e-government initiatives in Nigeria, followed by discussions of the progress on the ICT and e-government fronts in the country. Finally, we will make concluding remarks.

History and Use of Computers and ICT Policy Growth in Nigeria

Records from the Nigerian Federal Office of Statistics (FOS) show the first computer sold in Nigeria was to the Nigerian Ports Authority (NPA) by ICL in 1948 (UNU, 2004) during the British colonial administration in Nigeria. However, the first digital computer appeared in Nigeria in 1962 (UNU, 2004). The diffusion and use of ICT products in the country seem to have an elitist dimension (Anandarajan, Igbaria, & Anakwe, 2002; Tiamiyu, 2000), because people working for large multinationals, local banks, and government agencies appear to use ICT products more than do other members of the population (Anakwe, Anandarajan,

& Igbaria, 1999; Anakwe, Simmers, & Anandarajan, 2002; Ehikhamenor, 2003; Tiamiyu, 2000). Nationwide, the use, adoption, accessibility, and availability of ICT products and infrastructure in Nigeria is very poor (Anakwe et al., 1999; Anakwe et al., 2002; Anandarajan et al., 2002; Darley, 2003; Dutta, Lanvin, & Paua, 2003; Odedra et al., 1993; Tiamiyu, 2000), despite the early starting date.

During the late 1970s, the Nigerian government promulgated an indigenization decree that set apart business categories for Nigerians only. The computer business was one such area. IBM, one of the three main computer vendors in Nigeria during this period, elected to leave the country. The indigenization decree stimulated an influx of several indigenous firms into the computer business. This was good for the country because of the increased computer purchases during that period. From 1975 to 1977, the country recorded 39 computer (mini-computer and mainframe) installations compared to 197 installations from 1978 to 1980, the period following the promulgated decree (UNU, 2004). By 1988, the number of computer installations in Nigeria had reached 754 (UNU, 2004).

Additionally, by the late 1970s the Nigerian government established the Central Computer Committee (CCC), whose mandate was to create standards for users and vendors of computers in Nigeria and develop inputs for the national policy on computing (UNU, 2004). Unfortunately, the incoming government dismantled this body. Consequently, the country was without any national ICT policy for many years (Ifinedo, 2004). It was not until the year 2000 that the country began to clamor for a new national ICT policy that resulted in the birth of the Nigerian telecommunication policy. The country again witnessed an expansion in ICT products diffusion and use. In addition, a governmental agency called the Nigerian Communication Commission (NCC) that was formed in 1992 was reactivated in 2000 (Anakwe et al., 1999, 2002; Ifinedo, 2004). The Nigerian national ICT policy became more effective when the new civilian government created the Nigerian IT Development Agency (NITDA), whose mandate was to administer the ICT policy for the country (NITDA, 2001). NITDA's strategies include the establishment of an e-government model for Nigeria in specific areas such as e-administration, e-judiciary, e-healthcare, e-taxation, e-education, and so forth (Ajayi, 2003b).

Further, evidence suggests that the use of ICT products by the ordinary Nigerian citizen and government officials is growing remarkably (Ajakaye & Kanu, 2004; Ajayi, 2003a, b; Hamilton, Jensen & Southwood, 2004). Nigeria seems to be moving in the right direction with the formulation of its new national ICT policy, which appears to promote e-government initiatives. However, the main problem for the country continues to be the unavailability or poor condition of the enabling infrastructure for e-government, such as telecommunication facilities. Nigeria has unfavorable statistics on its ICT infrastructure (Dutta et al., 2003). For example, basic telecommunication services such as telephone lines, Internet access, and so forth, required for e-government are inadequate in the SSA region, including Nigeria (Ifinedo, 2005; Mbarika et al., 2002). The teledensity (number of telephones lines per 100 inhabitants) in Nigeria in 1999 was 0.5, but rose to 2.0 in 2002 only after the Nigerian government liberalized the ICT sector (Ajayi, 2003a, b). Similarly, Nigeria's Internet usage is poor (ITU, 2005). In 2002, there were 100,000 Internet users in Nigeria (CIA: World Factbook, 2004). However, the current estimate of Internet users in Nigeria is around 3 million people (Ifinedo, 2004; Nigerianetguru, 2004). This is at about 1% of the population, which is not encouraging.

Socio-Political and Economic Environment in Nigeria

Nigeria is the most populous country in Africa with a population of about 140 million people. It gained independence in 1960. The country has a long history of military coups — six were successful and many others unsuccessful (CIA: World Factbook, 2004; Idowu, 1999). The country became a democracy again in 1998. The Nigerian economy depends on crude oil exports. Political instability, corruption, and poor macroeconomic management are some of the major challenges facing the Nigerian state (Idowu, 1999; Ifeka, 2000; Ifidon, 1996). Nigeria's former military rulers failed to diversify the economy, making it overly dependent on the oil sector, which provides 20% of GDP, 95% of foreign exchange earnings, and about 65% of budgetary revenues (CIA: World Factbook, 2004). These military leaders were also corrupt (Idowu, 1999; Ifeka, 2000; Ifidon, 1996). With such bad examples in leadership, corruption and inefficiency in governance became almost a way of life (Obasanjo, 2004). Over the years, Nigeria has been one of the most corrupt nations in the world (TICP, 2003). Obtaining government services in Nigeria can be a difficult exercise (Ifinedo, 2004; Ifinedo & Uwadia, 2005).

Despite the abundance of crude oil in Nigeria, the country ranks as one of the poorest nations in the world (CIA: World Factbook, 2004). Table 1 summarizes some economic indicators for Nigeria. A Global Technology Report (Dutta et al., 2003), using data from the International Telecommunications Union and the World Bank, compared the readiness of 82 countries for an increasingly networked world. Nigeria fared woefully in almost all indicators. For example, Nigeria ranked 55th for buyers' level of sophistication of products and services; 78th for the availability of mobile Internet users; 81st for the availability of public access to the Internet; 77th for adult literacy; 80th for secondary school enrollment; and 82nd for the cost of local calls and the cost of residential phone subscription. The list included most of the OECD countries and other developing countries such as Namibia, Mauritius, Latvia, Tunisia, and Jordan.

The socioeconomic and political environments in Nigeria are unfavorable. It may be argued that such dire conditions might not be conducive for the emergence of e-government. However, the World Bank's guidelines (*Info*Dev, 2004) suggest that e-government initiatives can help reduce these shortcomings. Policy makers in Nigeria have started clamoring for the adoption of e-government as a tool that could help the nation overcome some of its ills (Ajakaye, 2004). For example, the current President of Nigeria delivered a speech at the First Stakeholders Conference on National e-Government Strategies and implementation for Nigeria. Excerpts from the speech as follows support our statement:

Table 1. Socioeconomic indicators of Nigeria (Source: CIA: World Factbook, 2004)

Country	Literacy % of Population, 2003	Life Expectancy (years), 2003	GDP per Capita (USD), 2002	Internet Users, (2000)	Electric Production billion (kWh)
Nigeria	68%	51.01	$900	100,000	14.55 (2001)

*The emphasis, style and programmes of this administration have always centred on reorienta-
tion of civil servants and public officers towards a change in the ways of doing government
business in a transparent, efficient and effective manner.*

*We have taken major steps, namely, privatisation, deregulation and monetisation towards
accomplishing the goal of a compact, accountable and productive government. There is no
going back to the old ways. However, the backroom engine, which will run good governance through due diligence, due process and transparency, actually needs to be formally
strengthened and institutionalised for widespread effectiveness through computer assisted
modern processes now commonly known as e-government.* (Obasanjo, 2004)

We can therefore say that the Nigerian political leadership has realized the need for change
in the governance of the nation and believes that e-government can help bring about such a
change. Let us now turn our attention to the constraints or problems facing the emergence
of e-government initiative in Nigeria.

Problems Facing E-Government
Initiatives in Nigeria

Organizational Problems

Effective communication and organizational skills are needed to maintain the vision, values,
and aspirations of all stakeholders in an e-government (Garnett, 1992; Sharma & Gupta,
2003). This calls the role of government functionaries in Nigeria into question. Would they
be sincere in implementing and managing e-government properly? Do they understand the
prerequisites for e-government? The reality is that government agencies and officials in
developing countries might perceive e-government as a potential threat to their power and
viability, and as such, may show reluctance in promoting the objectives of e-government
(Kaaya, 2003; Sanchez et al., 2003). Heeks (2002) recounts examples where e-government
efforts in Africa totally or partially failed due to "people" factors. The failures of previously discussed committees in Nigeria mandated with ICT issues were attributed to a lack
of organizational skills or commitment (see, Ifinedo, 2004). As was discussed, one body is
formed and then disbanded for another. For example, prior to NITDA, the NCC was created
to lead the nation towards the Information Age, and CCC before it. Even after the formation
of NITDA in 2001, the Director General of the body openly expressed disappointment in
2003, asking why the national ICT Bill had not been passed into law (Ajayi, 2003b). In many
respects, this highlights the lack of organizational vision or commitment from the top.

Social and Cultural Problems

Nigeria is a large country, with approximately 60% of the populace living in rural areas
(CIA: World Factbook, 2004). Illiteracy is rife — at about 40% of the population (CIA:

World Factbook, 2004; Dutta et al., 2003; Ifinedo, 2005; Oyebisi & Agboola, 2003), and secondary education enrollment is low (Dutta et al., 2003; Ifinedo, 2005). Regarding the cultural orientations of Nigerians, Ojo (1996) asserts that ICT and other technology-based disciplines will thrive better in cultures that have a mechanistic view of the world, unlike Africa where informality thrives. The impact of culture on ICT adoption in the developing countries has been a topic of interest in IT / IS literature (e.g., Anakwe et al., 1999, 2002; Straub et al., 2001). Findings from Straub et al.'s study indicate that sociocultural factors are vitally important in ICT-related issues for developing societies (Anakwe et al., 1999, 2002; Anandarajan et al., 2002).

The attitude or culture of self-motivation among government functionaries is rife in Nigeria (Ojo, 1996). This includes a tendency to overpoliticize decision making, indulge in shoddy practices, and institute complex bureaucratic procedures to gain personal advantages. Some of these shortcomings were cited as reasons why poor governance prevails in the SSA region (Heeks, 2002; Ifinedo 2005; Ojo, 1996; Sachs & Warner, 1997). We can therefore imply that those with power or interests to protect in the SSA region, including Nigeria, might not see any benefits to e-government or might want to sabotage it. West (2004) argues that the cultural norms and patterns of individual behavior affect the manner in which technology is used by citizens and policy makers of a country.

Economic Constraints

The economic situation is dire for both the country and its population. Nigeria is poor and indebted (World Bank Group, 2004). The cost of a PC in Nigeria is six times the monthly wage of an average worker. The cost of subscribing to a telephone line or owning one is beyond the reach of an average citizen. The same is true with procuring Internet access in Nigeria. Ordinary citizens cannot afford such services (Ajakaye & Kanu, 2004; Dutta et al., 2003). Computers and Internet access are two vital facilities required for any e-government engagements, but when such facilities are lacking, as is the case with Nigeria, it remains to be seen how e-government can be adopted by the people who need it. The Nigerian government might not have the resources to implement e-government services because many of the resources have been diverted to issues such as reducing poverty and the servicing of foreign loans (Ogwumike, 2002).

Infrastructural and Technical Constraints

As with the rest of SSA, Nigeria's Internet access is poor (Internet World Stats, 2004; ITU, 2005). There are about 3 million Internet users in a country of 140 million inhabitants — this is less than 1% of the population! Access to the Internet is crucial for e-government services, but is of little help with insufficient bandwidth. Only recently did a few countries in Africa procure bandwidths greater than 10 million bps (The African Internet, 2002). Previously, many in Africa had bandwidths between 64,000 bps and 256,000 bps due to high international tariffs and lack of circuit capacity in the region (The African Internet, 2002; Internet World Stats, 2004). The investments — local and foreign — in such facilities are low on the African continent (The African Internet, 2002; Ifinedo, 2005; ITU, 2005).

Under the military dictatorships in Nigeria, the country witnessed poor inflow of investments. The telecoms sector was adversely affected by that situation (Ndukwe, 2005), and was worsened because many states in Africa, including Nigeria, often provide telephone services to their citizens. Therefore, inefficiency and poor quality were often associated with such services. Another major infrastructural constraint in Nigeria is inadequate power generation (Table 1). However, government functionaries in the country now realize that any successful e-government initiative depends on a steady supply of electric power (Musari, 2004).

In addition to inadequate infrastructure, Nigeria also lacks qualified IT professionals (Dutta et al., 2003; Odedra et al., 1993; Ojo, 1996; Oyebisi & Agboola, 2003). This might hamper e-government efforts, as skilled hands needed to develop such services are not readily available. Nigerian universities do not graduate enough skilled IT professionals to match its current ICT needs (Ifinedo, 2005; Oyebisi & Agboola, 2003). Oyebisi and Agboola (2003) assert that the highest enrollment in the University for Science and Technology in Nigeria between 1991 and 1998 per 1,000 inhabitants was 0.31, with only 0.05 per 1,000 students earning a postgraduate degree during the same period.

Progressive Initiatives on the ICT and E-Government Fronts in Nigeria

Clearly, the ICT problems facing Nigeria can be classified under three broad categories: institutional, infrastructural, and human resources. International bodies, such as the UN ICT TASK Force (2004) and UNPAN (2005), use these categories when highlighting ICT issues in developing countries. We will also use these categories to discuss the progressive initiatives on the ICT and e-government fronts in Nigeria.

Institutional and Organizational Initiatives

The current Nigerian government has shown commitment towards promoting ICT and e-culture (Ajayi, 2003b; NITDA, 2001; Obasanjo, 2004). For example, a conference called eNigeria (http://www.enigeria.org) convenes annually to promote e-society awareness in the country. The forum brings together local academics, businesses, software multinationals, and IT professionals and their colleagues from the Diaspora. Policy issues relating to e-government are now entertained. Further, Nigeria has also sent top government delegations overseas to acquire specific e-government skills. For example, a fact-finding mission visited India to learn how the e-voting systems work there.

The President of Nigeria is the vanguard for the spread of e-society/e-government in Nigeria (Obasanjo, 2003, 2004). Today, Nigeria has a well-focused national ICT policy managed by technocrats (Ajayi, 2003a, 2003b; NITDA, 2001). Based upon the country's leadership, Nigeria now strives to implement directives from the World Summit on the Information Society and e-Africa Commission (Ajayi, 2003a; Obasanjo, 2004). Both bodies have guidelines to help developing countries in Africa and elsewhere achieve sustainable development through ICT.

In particular, the new Nigerian national ICT policy pays attention to e-government aspects of those directives (Ajayi, 2003a, 2003b; NITDA, 2001; Obasanjo, 2004).

NITDA has programs that provides IT education and awareness to top government functionaries, lawmakers, and other administrators. For example, NITDA has developed partnerships with private organizations like CISCO to train Nigerians in relevant IT areas (Ajayi, 2003b). The Enterprise Technology Centre (ETC) is a partnership between NITDA and two private companies to provide IT training for Nigerian civil servants. The head of the Nigerian civil service recently led all the Permanent Secretaries (Divisional Heads of Service) for a two-week IT training course. E-government basics were among the skills learned at these seminars (Ajayi, 2003a, 2003b). These initiatives are vital because exposing top government functionaries to the workings of ICT products in governance (or e-government in general) might lower their resistance. With support from these officials, e-government endeavors may be successful for a variety of reasons, including ownership of the process for government officials (Heeks, 1999, 2002). Additionally, the Nigerian government is strengthening its legal and regulatory framework related to ICT, including the Internet use (Ajakaye, 2005). This might give confidence to prospective users of any emerging e-government initiative in the country.

The federal government of Nigeria now has a Web portal (http://www.nigeria.gov.ng/). Some state governments (there are 36 states in Nigeria) operate their Web portals as well (Ifinedo, 2004). These Web sites provide the public with government information and have some downloadable forms. Overall, the level of services provided by Nigerian e-government portals only facilitate "one-way service delivery," which is the second stage of a four-stage model developed by Layne and Lee (2001). See the illustrations in Table 2. The original

Table 2. The four stages of e-government development in Nigeria (Adapted from Layne & Lee, 2001)

Phase	Description	Practice	Function
Stage 1	Government information delivery	Creating a Web site; putting the government information on the Web	Providing information services for the public
Stage 2	One-way service delivery	Transforming some services to the Web sites; providing service passively, not exchanging information between governments and the public actively	Providing downloadable forms; providing some operational services for the public
Stage 3	Two-way service delivery	Transforming more services on Web sites; supporting information exchanging between governments and the public	Services and forms on-line; simple interactivity between government and the public; changing to customer-focus service gradually
Stage 4	Complete e-government	Federal government, state governments, and local government sharing information via networks; and the provision of complex service to the public	Services and forms on-line; customer-focus service; integrating different functions; providing full functions for public interactivity; total and complete engagement

model represents the "stages of growth" model based on the experience of e-government practices. Likewise, other e-government models identify Nigeria's e-government services as only informational (UNPAN, 2005). Advanced stages of e-government include "two-way service delivery." However, it must be stressed that the transition to the advanced stages of e-government has begun in Nigeria (Ajayi, 2003a; Ujah, 2003). The vice president of Nigeria recently revealed plans to incorporate other advanced services into the Nigerian e-government effort by the year 2008 (Ujah, 2003).

In an effort to enhance e-government in Nigeria, the National e-Government Strategies Ltd (NeGSt), http://www.negst.com/, has been formed to oversee the national e-government project. It is a partnership between NITDA and the private sector, whose goal is to implement the backbone of the Nigerian e-government infrastructure. The private participants are in fact shareholders in the project. Essentially, the goal is to improve organizational performance, service delivery, and the participation of ordinary citizens in governance through ICT, and the shareholders provide the resources for the project. Zinox, a local IT organization, and multinational IT companies, including Microsoft, Oracle, and Accenture, provide technical expertise and infrastructure. Local banks, including The First Bank of Nigeria, provide funding for the project (Ikhemuemhe, 2004a).

Human Capacity Initiatives

Given the dire economic climate in SSA, including Nigeria, improving the situation is a challenge for both the government and the wider international community. The recent debt relief extended to Nigeria is helpful (*BBC News*, 2005). One might argue that as resources are no longer needed to service foreign debts, other pressing activities, such as the promotion of e-government (or the use of ICT in governance) might benefit. In essence, e-government has successfully emerged in societies where the population has the resources to buy ICT facilities and possesses the relevant skills and knowledge to appreciate IT-related innovations (Accenture, 2004; UNPAN, 2005). Poverty and lack of skills are major inhibitors of e-government in Nigeria. The Nigerian government has commenced projects to ameliorate these challenges.

In addition to finding ways to alleviate poverty in the country (Ogwumike, 2002), the Nigerian government is also preparing its future generations for the reality of the modern world. The Nigerian government aims to bring down IT illiteracy rates in the country as it develops, implements, and supports several programs. One example is the SchoolNet Nigeria DigiNet project (DigiNet, 2005), which addresses the low IT literacy among Nigerian secondary school students and their teachers. The DigiNet project will be implemented in 185 schools nationwide during the first phase, with plans to extend the project to about 1,000 schools nationwide. So far, 35 schools have benefited from the program. Similarly, another project is the Nigerian University Network (NUNet) that focuses on the development of human capacity within academia in Nigeria. Designed to train the staff of 46 federal universities in relevant IT areas, these and similar projects will improve the level of human capacity regarding IT use in the country. We previously discussed how NITDA is forming partnerships with IT companies to train Nigerian civil servants.

Nigeria was selected as one of World Bank's Education for All (EFA) "fast track" countries. It is hoped that Nigeria will be able to reduce its adult illiteracy as assistance from bodies such as the World Bank bring education to the disadvantaged sector of Nigeria (Patel, n.d.).

Infrastructural Support Initiatives

The telecommunication sector in Nigeria has been deregulated and liberalized (Ndukwe, 2004; Obasanjo, 2004). Nigeria now has 4 licensed mobile operators, 35 Internet service providers, and 5 million mobile lines. Overall, Internet access in the country is improving (Ajakaye & Kanu, 2004; Hamilton et al., 2004; ITU, 2005; Ndukwe, 2005). There were only 100,000 Internet users in Nigeria in 2002, but the situation is now much better (ITU, 2005). Nigeria is improving its ICT sector with several new initiatives. For example, in 2003 the country launched its first data satellite, NigeriaSat-1 (*BBC News*, 2003), and contracts have been signed for the launching of another telecommunication satellite (Ajakaye, 2005; Ndukwe, 2005). Further, NITEL (Nigerian Telecommunication Ltd.) has started installing optical fiber network links to major cities in the country. This initiative benefits from the US$637 million optic fiber network (SAT-3/WASC/SAFE) along the coast of Africa (Ajayi, 2003a). With this progress, Nigeria is emerging as one of the best performing nations in terms of ICT products use and diffusion in SSA (Ajayi, 2003a, 2003b; Hamilton et al., 2004; ITU, 2005). Apparently, the investment climate of the telecom sector is vibrant. The liberalized and deregulated policies have permitted foreign entities to participate in the sector. According to the President of Nigeria, the telecommunication sector received foreign direct investments (FDI) of US$4 billion in 2003 (Ndukwe, 2004, 2005; Obasanjo, 2003, 2004).

Nigeria has recently seen the emergence of homemade computers (Ajayi, 2003b; Ifinedo, 2004). Previously, all computers used in the country were imported. The chief executive officer of Zinox, a local computer manufacturer, estimated the market in Nigeria to be around 100,000 computer sales per year. He notes that "Zinox's share is 25%, Omatech (another local manufacturer) is 5-7%, and Hewlett-Packard leads with 30% of the market share" (Odwumfo, 2004). These revelations are encouraging, and the spread of computers in the country, particularly the availability of homemade computers sold at about half the price of imports, will help improve the availability of this primary facility for e-government. Also, the country seems to be addressing its poor electric power generation capacity. The President of Nigeria suggested that within the first four years of his administration, electric power generation has gone up 250%, from 1400 mw to 4800 mw (Obasanjo, 2004).

Furthermore, some specific e-government projects were commissioned in the country. The Nigerian federal government and some state governments have committed resources to improving government-to-government services. For example, the Public Service Network (PSNet) is a project that hopes to provide broadband Internet access to the State Secretariat and the agencies of state ministries in order to facilitate fast and efficient governance through ICT (Ajayi, 2003b; Ikhemuemhe, 2004b).

Similarly, the federal government has created public awareness for e-government with its mobile Internet units (MIU). These are locally manufactured buses equipped with communication infrastructure such VSAT, computer terminals, printers, and so forth. They travel from town-to-town disseminating e-government information to Nigerians (Figures 1 and

Figure 1. Mobile Internet unit (MIU)

Figure 2. Inside the mobile Internet unit (MIU)

2). The MIUs serve as an awareness campaign and utility tools. Additionally, NITDA has been involved with the development of the Nigerian Keyboard. This is an adaptation of technology for local use, which is vital in the success of e-government initiatives (*Info*Dev, 2004). Illiteracy is reported to be high in Nigeria (CIA: World Factbook, 2004; Patel, n.d.), but a closer look of the phenomenon presents a different perspective. Many of these "illiterates" (in English) are literate in their native tongue, and, in some cases (for those attending Koranic schools), read Arabic as well. The adapted keyboard provides an opportunity for many to participate in any emerging e-government. The Nigerian Keyboard project could ensure that all citizens become active in the mobilization of critical mass for e-government in Nigeria.

The Prospects and Benefits of E-Government for Nigeria

Some have suggested that IT-related projects, including e-government initiatives, may not be suitable for societies in SSA where informality thrives (Ojo, 1996). However, e-government is gaining prominence across Africa (see Heeks, 2002; Kaaya, 2003; UNPAN, 2005). As was discussed, e-government is about seizing the opportunity to enhance governance through improved access to government information using ICT. Nigeria might benefit from e-government initiatives (in its advanced forms) in many ways. The climate of political instability that has bedeviled the country could be checked through e-government endeavors. How? Inefficiency, poor accountability, and a lack of transparency are among the reasons why undemocratic leaders in SSA survive (e.g., Idowu, 1999; Ifeka, 2000; Ifidon, 1996). Properly implemented e-government initiatives could help improve the culture, lack of transparency, and accountability seen in Nigeria. For example, e-government initiatives were used in India to fight corruption (*Info*Dev, 2004).

When government data resources are visible to several stakeholders in digital formats, the manipulation of these resources by unscrupulous functionaries may become less attractive. Furthermore, Wimmer and Traunmuller (2001) contend that the main objectives of e-government include restructuring administrative functions and processes as well as the monitoring of government performance. The leadership in Nigeria hopes that e-government initiatives might help it improve its governance (see excerpts of the President's speech). In Nigeria, anecdotal evidence suggests that poor monitoring by government officials can lead to inconveniences such as a service administered to several parties simultaneously. For instance, a minister in Nigeria has publicly acknowledged that e-government would help check problems of multiple land allocation in the capital city of Nigeria (IFG.CC, 2005). In the same vein, others have suggested that e-government can help solve the problems with revenue collection in Nigeria (Ifinedo, 2004). Some multinationals and their conniving government officials are exploiting inefficiency in government services to defraud the nation of valuable revenues (Igbikiowubo, 2005). An improved service, supported by digital facilities, could be helpful to government and business. For instance, Mauritius has reported a huge success through its online taxation systems (*Info*Dev, 2004).

E-government can reduce or overcome barriers of coordination and cooperation within the Nigerian public administration. Centralized databases and standards could become available to several government agencies. Interoperability between government agencies increase and duplication of services may decrease. A poor country like Nigeria could benefit from such cost effectiveness in governance when common standards and timely data resources are shared. The improved services may enhance decision making in governance. The ongoing PSNet project in Nigeria is clearly a step in the right direction.

E-government may also spawn other opportunities for the nation. For example, the Nigerian society will be transformed when information technology and knowledge become widespread. It is important that Nigeria integrate into the changing world where information and knowledge increasingly become the differentiating criteria (Ifinedo, 2005). Thus, new skills will be learned from the emergence of ICT use in governance that might better prepare the country for the changing world, or help improve Nigeria's position in the globally networked world, which at the present leaves much to be desired (Ifinedo, 2005). E-government and related projects in many countries around the world are known to be contributing, either directly or indirectly, towards the total transformation of those societies (Accenture, 2004; UNPAN, 2005; Watson & Mundy, 2001). Importantly, the Nigerian economy benefited immensely through the creation of new jobs following the introduction of mobile telephony in the country (Ifinedo, 2004; ITU, 2004). It is possible that similar benefits could emerge from e-government initiatives, going by the trend of Cybercafés diffusion in Nigeria (Ajakaye & Kanu, 2004).

Conclusion

In this chapter, we chose Nigeria to discuss some of the problems inhibiting the emergence of e-government in the SSA region. The main problems facing the emergence of e-government in Nigeria have their roots in socioeconomic inadequacies that were known to plague several countries in the SSA region. Some of the problems discussed include poor organizational skills, inadequate infrastructural support, and poor or unavailable human capital resources.

Further, we highlighted some of the progressive initiatives undertaken in Nigeria aimed at providing an enabling environment for the emergence of e-government. This discourse noted plans and projects in Nigeria such as the development of a national IT policy, liberalizing the telecommunication sector, and IT awareness campaigns with innovations such as mobile Internet units (MIU) and the Public Service Network (PSNet). Despite these efforts, we indicated that e-government practices in Nigeria are infantile — government Web services currently provide one-way service delivery. However, efforts are underway to improve e-government services in the country. To that end, a partnership between the government and private stakeholders was formed. Importantly, we noticed that the leadership in Nigeria believes that e-government could become a useful tool to provide efficient and effective services. The Nigerian policy makers appear to believe accountability and transparency in governance can be enhanced through e-government. The chapter discussed the prospects and benefits of e-government to the Nigerian society. We suggested ways in which e-government can transform public services by reengineering the fundamental relationship between the Nigerian government and its citizens.

This chapter provides lessons for other developing countries in the SSA region. First, we noticed that the political will of the Nigerian leadership was vital in the creation of an enabling environment such as favorable national ICT policies and the emergence of e-government initiatives. Second, the Nigerian government promoted a series of plans and initiatives aimed at preparing the citizenry for the change that e-government might bring. These positive steps taken by the government are encouraging and may help to reduce future resistance, while simultaneously generating critical mass for e-government. Third, the Nigerian government followed the directives of various international bodies and formed necessary partnerships with other entities (UN ICT TASK Force, 2004). The Nigerian government sought funding for its e-government project from local financial institutions and technical expertise from IT multinationals. Fourth, the Nigerian government adopted favorable reforms and economic policies such as the deregulation and liberalization of the telecommunication sector. As other nations in the region prepare for the emergence of e-government, they might consider some of the efforts undertaken in Nigeria.

Finally, the revelations from Nigeria regarding e-government and ICT policy confirm that some cultures tend to follow or take initiatives from those who have power or leadership roles (Anakwe et al., 1999, 2002; Anandarajan et al., 2002; Hofstede, 2001). As was discussed here, progress occurred on the ICT and e-government fronts in Nigeria only when the President of Nigeria supported such causes. Other factors, including external influences, could also account for the changes in the country pertaining to these issues. Nonetheless, we would like to propose that e-government and other IT-related endeavors spread more favorably in the SSA when the region's leadership accepts that their citizens expect them to take bold steps in these areas. In Nigeria, the current president championed the cause of new ICT policy changes and e-government. This is worthy of emulation in comparable nations in the region. Future study on e-government in Nigeria may add to this present discussion by investigating how commitments from state leadership can enhance e-government efforts. Particularly, research could investigate how the interests of the various stakeholders in Nigerian e-government project are managed. Research efforts can be directed towards examining the perceptions of Nigerians regarding e-government plans and projects such as the PSNet and MIU.

References

Accenture. (2004). *High performance government*. Retrieved May 6, 2006, from http://www. accenture.com

African Internet, The. (2002). *A status report*. Retrieved May 6, 2006, from http://www3. sn.apc.org/africa/afstat.htm

Ajakaye, T. (2004). *E-government will be like hurricane*. Retrieved May 6, 2006, from http://www.thisdayonline.com/archive/2004/03/18/20040318e-b08.html

Ajakaye, T. (2005). *Data protection, storage, e-government and Nigerians*. Retrieved May 6, 2006, from http://www.e-lo-go.de/html/modules.php

Ajakaye, T., & Kanu, O. (2004). *Cybercafé, cybercafé everywhere*. Retrieved May 6, 2006, from http://www.thisdayonline.com

Ajayi, G. O. (2003a). Role of government in IT development: Status report e-Nigeria. In *Proceedings of e-Nigeria 2003*, Abuja, Nigeria. Retrieved May 6, 2006, from http://enigeria.org/2003/10029003/index.html

Ajayi, G. O. (2003b). *E-government in Nigeria's e-strategy*. Paper presented at the 5th Annual African Computing and Telecommunications Summit, 2003, Abuja, Nigeria.

Anakwe, U., Simmers, C., & Anandarajan, M. (2002). *Internet usage in an emerging economy: The role of skills, support and attitudes* (Working Paper No. 205). New York: Pace University.

Anakwe, U. P., Anandarajan, M., & Igbaria, M. (1999). Information technology usage dynamics in Nigeria: An empirical study. *Journal of Global Information Management, 7*(2), 13-21.

Anandarajan, M., Igbaria, M., & Anakwe, U. (2002). IT acceptance in a less-developed country: A motivational factor perspective. *International Journal of Information Management, 22*, 47-65.

BBC News. (2003). *Nigeria enters space age*. Retrieved July 28, 2005, from http://news. bbc.co.uk/1/hi/world/africa/3141690

BBC News. (2005). *Nigeria to get $18bn debt relief*. Retrieved May 6, 2006, from http://news.bbc.co.uk/2/hi/business/4637395.stm

Breen, J. (2000). At the dawn of e-government: the citizen as customer. *Government Finance Review, 16*(5), 15-20.

CIA: World Factbook. (2004). *Country report: Nigeria*. Retrieved May 6, 2006, from http://www.cia.gov

Cottrill, K. (2001). E-government grows. *Traffic World, 265*(10), 19.

Darley, W. K. (2003). Public policy challenges and implications of Internet and the emerging e-commerce for sub-Saharan Africa: A business perspective. *Information Technology for Development, 10*, 1-12.

DigiNet. (2005). *SchoolNet Nigeria DigiNet*. Retrieved May 6, 2006, from http://www.snng.org/home.htm

Dutta, S., Lanvin, B., & Paua, F. (2003). *Global information technology report 2002-2003*. New York: Oxford University Press.

Ehikhamenor, F. A. (2003). Information technology in Nigerian banks: The limits of expectations. *Information Technology for Development, 10*, 13-24.

Garnett, J. L. (1992). *Communicating for results in governments*. San Francisco: Jossey-Bass Publishers.

Golden, W., Hughes, M., & Scott, M. (2003). Implementing e-government in Ireland: A roadmap for success. *Journal of Electronic Commerce in Organizations, 1*(4), 17-33.

Hamilton, P., Jensen, M., & Southwood, R. (2004). *African Internet country market profiles*. Retrieved May 6, 2006, from http://www.balancingact-africa.com/profile1.html

Heeks, R. (1999). *Reinventing government in the Information Age: International practice in IT-enabled public sector reform*. New York: Routledge.

Heeks, R. (2001). *Understanding e-governance for development* (iGovernment Working Paper Series, (Paper No. 11). University of Manchester, Institute of Development Policy and Management.

Heeks, R. (2002). *E-government in Africa: Promise and practice* (Paper No. 13). University of Manchester, Institute for Development Policy and Management.

Hofstede, G. (2001). *Culture's consequences: Comparing values, behaviours, institutions, and organizations across nations*. New York: Sage Publications.

Huang, W. D., Ambra, J., & Bhalla, V. (2002, August 9-11). Key factors influencing the adoption of e-government in Australian public sectors. In *Proceedings of the 8th Americas Conference on Information Systems*, Dallas, TX (pp. 577-579).

Idowu, O. O. W. (1999). Citizenship status, statehood problems and political conflict: The case of Nigeria. *Nordic Journal of African Studies, 8*(2), 73-88.

Ifeka, C. (2000). Conflict, complicity and confusion: Unravelling empowerment struggles in Nigeria after the return to democracy. *Review of African Political Economy, 27*(83), 115-123.

IFG.CC. (2005). *Theme: Nigeria*. Retrieved May 6, 2006, from http://www.e-lo-go.de/html/modu

Ifidon, A. F. (1996). Citizenship, statehood and the problem of democratisation in Nigeria. *Africa Development, 4*(21), 93-107.

Ifinedo, P. E. (2004, July 4-6). E-government — precursors, problems, practices and prospects: A case of Nigeria. In K. S. Soliman (Ed.), *Proceedings of the 2004 International Business Information Management (IBIM) Conference 2004*, Amman, Jordan (pp. 1-10).

Ifinedo, P. (2005). Measuring Africa's e-readiness in the global networked economy: A nine-country data analysis. *International Journal of Education and Development using ICT, 1*(1), 53-71.

Ifinedo, P., & Uwadia, C. (2005, May 25-28). Towards e-government in Nigeria: Short-comings, successes, swish or sink. In *Proceedings of the International Federation of Information Processing (IFIP) WG 9.4 Conference*, Abuja, Nigeria (pp. 75-86).

Igbikiowubo, H. (2005). *Chevron in $10.8bn tax evasion mess*. Retrieved May 6, 2006, from http://allafrica.com/stories/200507250102.html

Ikhemuemhe, G. (2004a). *Government/private sector partner to deliver e-government*. Retrieved May 6, 2006, from http://www.e-lo-go.de/html/modules.php

Ikhemuemhe, G. (2004b). *Ogun State warms up for e-government*. Retrieved May 6, 2006, from http://www.e-lo-go.de/html/modules.php

*Info*Dev (Information for Development Programme). (2004). *E-government handbook for developing countries*. Retrieved May 6, 2006, from http://www.infodev.org

Internet World Stats. (2004). *African countries reports*. Retrieved May 6, 2006, from http://www.internetworldstats.com/africa.htm

ITU (International Telecommunications Union). (2004). *Nigeria's GSM Umbrella people*. Retrieved May 6, 2006, from http://www.itu.int

ITU (International Telecommunications Union). (2005). *Country statistics*. Retrieved May 6, 2006, from http://www.itu.int

Kaaya, J. (2003). Implementing e-government services in East Africa: Assessing status through content analysis of government Websites. *Electronic Journal of e-Government, 2*(1), 39-54.

Lawson, G. (1998). *Netstate-creating electronic government*. London: Demos.

Layne, K., & Lee, J. (2001). Developing fully functional e-government: A four stage model. *Government Information Quarterly, 18*(2), 122-136.

Mbarika, V. W., Musa, P. F., Byrd, T. A., & McMullen, P. (2002). Teledensity growth constraints and strategies for Africa's LDeveloping countries: Viagra prescriptions or sustainable development strategy? *Journal of Global Information Technology Management, 5*(1), 25-42.

Moon, J. M. (2002). The evolution of e-government among municipalities: Rhetoric or reality? *Public Administration Review, 62*(4), 424-433.

Moulder, E. (2001). E-government ... If you build it, will they come? *Public Management, 83*, 10-14.

Musari, M. (2004). *Successful e-government depends solely on steady power supply*. Retrieved May 6, 2006, from http://www.egov.vic.gov.au/International/Africa/africaindex.htm

Navarra, D. D., & Cornford, T. (2003, August 4-6). A policy making view of e-government innovations in public governance. In *Proceedings of the 9th Americas Conference on Information Systems*, Tampa, FL (pp. 827-834).

Ndukwe, E. (2004). *Use of wireless infrastructure for accelerating universal service provision in Nigeria*. Retrieved May 6, 2006, from http://www.itu.int/digitalbridges/docs/presentations/20-Ndukwe.pdf

Ndukwe, E. (2005). *Nigeria, gateway to West African market.* Retrieved May 6, 2006, from http://www.techtimesnews.net/industry.asp?id=446

Nigerianetguru. (2004). *Nigerian Internet guru.* Retrieved May 6, 2006, from http://www. nigerianetguru.com/

NITDA. (2001). *NITDA begins strategic action plan for the implementation of Nigeria IT policy.* Retrieved May 6, 2006, from http://www.nitda.gov.ng

Obasanjo, O. (2003). *The president of Nigeria's speech delivered at the World Summit on the Information Society (WSIS) Geneva, Switzerland.* Retrieved June 8, 2005, from http://www.nigeriafirst.org/objspeeches/2003/geneva2003.htm

Obasanjo, O. (2004). *Speech by His Excellency President Olusegun Obasanjo at the Stakeholders Conference on National eGovernment Strategies and Implementation for Nigeria.* Retrieved May 6, 2006, from http://www.nigeriafirst.org/objspeeches/2004/stakeholders_conf.html

Odedra, M., Lawrie, M., Bennett, M., & Goodman, S. (1993). Sub-Saharan Africa: A technological desert. *Communication of the ACM, 36*(2), 25-29.

Odwumfo, M. (2004). *Zinox Technologies' CEO Emelonye: Nigerian PC market is only 100,000 sales a year but growing.* Retrieved May 6, 2006, from http://listserv.media. mit.edu/pipermail/odwumfo/2004-May/000367.html

Ogwumike, O. F. (2002). An appraisal of poverty reduction strategies in Nigeria. *CBN Economic and Financial Review, 39*(4), 1-17.

Ojo, S. O. (1996). Socio-cultural and organizational issues in IT application in Nigeria. In M. Odedra-Straub (Ed.), *Global information technology and socio-economic development* (pp. 99-109). New Hampshire, PA: Ivy League Publishing.

Oyebisi, T. O., & Agboola, A. A. (2003). The impact of the environment on the growth of the Nigerian IT industry. *International Journal of Information Management, 23,* 313-321.

Patel, I. (n.d.). *Emerging tends in adult literacy policies and practice in Africa and Asia.* Retrieved July 11, 2005, http://www.unesco.org/education/partners/cco/English/

Sachs, J. D., & Warner, A. M. (1997). Sources of slow growth in African economies. *Journal of African Economies, 6*(3), 335-376.

Sanchez, A. D., Koh, C. E., Kappelman, L. A., & Prybutok, V. R. (2003, August 4-6). The relationship between IT for communication and e-government barriers. In *Proceedings of the 9th Americas Conference on Information Systems,* Tampa, FL (pp. 835-844).

Sharma, S. K., & Gupta, J. D. N. (2003). Building blocks of an e-government: A framework. *Journal of Electronic Commerce in Organizations, 1*(4), 1-15.

Straub, D. W., Loch, K. D., & Hill, C. E. (2001). Transfer of information technology to developing countries: A test of cultural influence modeling in the Arab world. *Journal of Global Information Management, 9*(4), 6-28.

Tiamiyu, M. A. (2000). Availability, accessibility and the use of information technologies in Nigerian federal agencies: A preliminary survey. *Information Technology for Development, 9,* 91-104.

TICP (Transparency International Corruption Perceptions Index). (2003). *Rankings for 2003*. Retrieved May 6, 2006, from http://www.transparency.org/cpi/2003/cpi2003.en.html

Ujah, E. (2003). *Government to begin e-governance in 2008*. Retrieved May 6, 2006, from http://www.e-lo-go.de/html/modules.php

UN ICT TASK Force. (2004). Retrieved May 6, 2006, from http://www.unicttaskforce.org/index.html

UNDPEPA/ASPA. (2003). *Benchmarking e-government: A global perspective*. Retrieved May 6, 2006, from http://www.unpan.org/egovernment.asp

UNPAN. (2005). *UN global e-government readiness report 2004*. Retrieved May 6, 2006, from http://www.unpan.org/egovernment4.asp

UNU (United Nation University). (2004). *Growth of information technology — Nigeria*. Retrieved May 6, 2006, from http://www.unu.edu/unupress/unupbooks/uu19ie/uu19ie0e.htm

Wade, R. (2001, March 5-6). *Speeches/Commentaries by Prof. Robert Hunter Wade*. Presented at the OECD/UNDP Conference on the Knowledge Economy, Paris, France.

Watson, R. T., & Mundy, B. (2001). A strategic perspective of electronic democracy. *Communications of the ACM, 44*(1), 27.

West, D. M. (2004). E-government and the transformation of service delivery and citizen attitudes. *Public Administration Review, 64*(1), 15-27.

Wimmer, M., & Traunmuller, R. (2001, September 6-8). Trends in electronic government: Managing distributed knowledge. In *Proceedings of the 11th International Workshop on Database Expert Systems Applications*, Greenwich, London, UK (p. 340). New York: Springer.

World Bank Group. (2004). *Report on Nigeria*. Retrieved May 6, 2006, from http:// www.worldbank.org/

Chapter X

E-Government Emerging Trends:
Organizational Challenges

Inas E. Ezz, Sadat Academy for Management Sciences, Egypt, &
Brunel University, UK

Abstract

This chapter demonstrates the importance and challenges considering technology adoption in general and e-government adoption in particular in the context of a key strategic process for the Egyptian Government. Thus our empirical findings are based on the foreign financing decision-making process of Egypt extending previous work on e-business technologies and e-government adoption in general and government-to-government (G2G) in particular. Although new trends in government support appear, such as u-government, g-government, and Me-government, none of the leading countries have reached full integration. Among some of the possible reasons is that technology adoption relies not only on the factors presented in the TAM model, but also on solving one of the most important challenges from our point of view, namely, organizational problems, which will be highlighted through our case studies. Our discussion includes identifying and documenting the decision-making processes crossing different ministries, which is a challenging task by itself. Although adopting technologies needs infrastructure, such as the IT-ready process, inter and intraorganizational integration technologies in the form of G2G or some of the new trends such as g-government, can help in resolving some of those organizational challenges existing at those strategic processes.

Introduction

Although several information systems (e.g., decision support systems, executive information systems) might be regarded as new trends or enhancements of technology and as isolated topics, we do believe that the advances of information systems have to be considered as broadening the scope of information systems. This idea is supported by Laudon and Laudon (2003); as they present, the scope of information systems has been widening from technical changes in the 1950s, managerial control in the 1960-1970s, institutional core activities in the 1980-1990s, to vendors and customers beyond the enterprise in 2000-2005. Widening the scope of information systems crossing organization boundaries has been possible through the networking and Internet revolution (O'Brien, 2003). Consequently, some trends have evolved, such as e-business, e-commerce, and e-government. Those issues do not neglect the existence of other information systems types, which are mainly used to integrate the organization, such as enterprise systems and supply chain management systems (O'Brien, 2003). Thus, the issue of e-business implies integrated systems within and outside the organizational boundaries, from our perspective.

The issue of e-government, which is the main focus of this chapter, is far more complex than the e-business, as the governmental decision-making processes at the strategic level might not be implemented in the same organization. Further, one process phase might be performed in different organizations that are not located at the same place. Thus although virtual organizations / e-business might be a solution to integrate those decision-making process, the complex decision making environment at that strategic level of a country is a barrier by itself.

Similar to the domain of e-business at the government level, as Bonham, Seifert, and Thorson (2003) present e-government (introduced in the next section), might be viewed in the context of three sectors: government-to-business (G2B), government-to-government (G2G), and government-to-citizen (G2C). In order to explore the importance and challenges of integrated e-government adoption (especially G2G) in practice, this chapter presents empirical findings from a study of the Debt Management and Foreign Financing Project in Egypt, managed by the country's Cabinet Information and Decision Support Center (IDSC).

With the arrival of new trends of e-government, organizational challenges remain vital, and are increasingly complex. Thus, the results of our case studies are going to be linked with some of the challenges of emerging technologies to investigate whether some patterns can be related to our results. Thus, in the next of this chapter, we introduce the term *e-government* and the technology adoption model (TAM) and end by introducing some e-government trends. The third section provides an overview of the IDSC and the importance of the foreign financing process for Egypt. The fourth section presents the methodological approach adopted in the research. The fifth section provides an understanding of the foreign financing process, while the sixth section presents some of the organizational issues preventing successful G2G adoption now. The seventh section highlights the implications of the case study on e-government adoption, while the eighth section summarizes e-government trends and challenges. The chapter concludes with the implications of our research for the IDSC and a more general set of conclusions that we envisage will influence future research in e-government, with a reference to patterns related to new trends challenges.

Background

Similar to e-business, the term e-government has been defined from different perspectives. These definitions range from making services available online: "Any usage of government online at all levels (federal, state, local)" (Sakowicz, n.d., p. 1) to general definitions describing e-government as another definition provided by Sakowicz (n.d., p. 1): "the use of information and communication technologies (ICT) to transform government by making it more accessible, effective and accountable." This idea of inconsistency of e-government definitions is supported by Bonham et al. (2003) as they believe that e-government means different things to different people. As they clarify, some observers define e-government in terms of specific actions: using a government kiosk to receive job information, applying for benefits through a Web site, or creating shared databases for multiple agencies. Other observers define e-government more generally as automating the delivery of government services. While perceptions of e-government vary widely, some common themes can be identified that capture its evolutionary nature.

The previously mentioned definitions of e-government describe e-government from different perspectives and may complement the global picture of what an e-government is. Nevertheless, they are not comprehensive from our point of view, as they do not include the three major sectors of e-government mentioned by Bonham et al. (2003) and also by the World Bank Group (n.d.): G2G, involving both intra and interagency exchanges at the national level, as well as exchanges between the national, provincial, and local levels (Atkinson & Ulevich, 2000); G2B (Gilbert, 2001); and G2C (Hasson, 2001). Some observers also identify a fourth sector, government-to-employee (G2E). Since G2E operations tend to focus on internal administrative activities, they can be considered a subset of the G2G sector.

We adopt a more comprehensive e-government definition, as it refers to G2G, G2B, G2C, and G2E, as well as the technology infrastructure: E-government can be regarded as an "information system aided handling of public administration processes using information and communications technology and is believed to lead to better delivery of government services, improved interaction with business and industry, citizen empowerment through access to information, or more efficient government management (Rötter, 2003). The resulting benefits include increased accountability and transparency, less corruption, greater convenience, increased citizen involvement, greater efficiency, and cost reductions for the government and the adopter of e-government services. E-government also facilitates the provision of new and enhanced services and encourages citizen participation in political processes (Gupta & Jana, 2003; Jaeger, 2003; Relyea, 2002; World Bank Group, n.d.).

There are several studies that measured the governments employing e-government, such as the United Nations, World Public Sector Report (2003) presenting a "Web Measure Index" to evaluate the aptitude of 191 governments to employ e-government as a tool to inform, interact, transact, and network. These studies conclude that the provision of e-Government services is still far from reaching full effectiveness. Moreover, some studies found that the growth of e-government service provision has rather slowed down in the past year, indicating that e-government service efforts may plateau on a suboptimal level. The reasons for the comparably slow spread of e-government services has been discussed in a number of studies (Jaeger, 2003; Moon, 2002; Reddick, 2004; Wescott, 2002). They include inertia, security and confidentiality, lack of computer skills, difficulties in carrying out organizational change, and the nature of public sector financing and procurement practices. In addition, the technology acceptance model (TAM) has been widely adopted in this context. According to TAM, adoption behavior is determined by the intention to use a particular system, which in turn is determined by perceived usefulness and perceived ease of use of that system. Although information systems researchers have investigated and replicated the TAM, and agreed that it is valid in predicting the individual's acceptance of various corporate IT, TAM's fundamental constructs do not fully reflect the specific influences of technological and usage-context factors that may alter the acceptance of the users (Moon & Kim, 2001). Wang (2003) says that some researchers discussed this model from different perspectives and that future technology acceptance research needs to address how other variables affect usefulness, ease of use, and user acceptance. However, factors affecting the acceptance of a new IT are likely to vary with the technology, target users, and the context. Recent research has indicated that "trust" has a striking influence on user willingness to engage in online exchanges of money and personally sensitive information (Hoffman, Novak, & Peralta, 1999).

To complement these studies, this chapter highlights some additional barriers that future quantitative research could take into consideration as constructs under investigation to extend TAM. This is highly important because although none of the countries have yet reached full e-government adoption, some new trends have evolved in the domain, with more emphasis on inter and intraorganizational integration requested for their infrastructure. Thus, before introducing our case study, we will briefly discuss some of the new trends necessitating further research efforts towards integration technology adoption challenges as a step to introducing a more comprehensive framework for assisting in the discussion of such electronic trends.

Some of these trends have been presented by Burgelman, Centeno, and Bogdanowicz (2004) in a report investigating the key policy and research challenges of e-government in EU in 2010. These include mass customized Me-government supported by multiplatform, multi-media, multichannel approaches, starting in 2005. In addition the European Union has set year 2010 as the time where this continent shall emerge as "The world's most competitive and dynamic knowledge-based economy", simply called EU 2010 vision. It came along with the objective to shape "Knowledge Based European Society", through 4 (four) frameworks: European Research Area, Enlargement, eEurope action plans and other supporting policies (Filos & Zobel, 2004). Other trends include u-government extending m-government, and g-government in the form of geo-portals. U-government refers to ubiquitous government, established in 2003 (silicon trust, n.d.). *Ubiquitous* is one of the popular terms used these days originating from American researcher Weiser (1992). The key issue here is that in-teractions and transactions between governments and their citizens are now possible any-where, anytime, unconstrained by power lines and telephone wires. It has been argued that u-government will provide new opportunities to build relationships between governments and their customers. For example, a variety of devices, from PDAs to embedded chips, will push Internet access into the most remote corners of any nation. From our perspective, that integration between involved organizations might be at a larger scale, which adds to the complexity of integration. As Lallana (2004) argues, u-government is, at most, five years away from full realization.

The term *g-government* refers to using the Internet and geographical information systems (GIS) to create more effective government. The combination of readily available Internet access and maps is defining a new level of service for governments to businesses and the public. It is making collaboration between government agencies possible in new and powerful ways (ESRI, n.d.). In the last few years there has been an extensive use of GIS in different applications. Odendaal (2003) highlights its support for intergovernment integration through the increasing use of Web-based GIS applications. Maguire and Longley (2005) explain that the use of GIS is based on the underlying spatial data infrastructure (SDI), which was coined in 1993 by the U.S. National Research Council (Mapping Sciences Committee, 1993) to describe, among other things, the provision of standardized GIS access. This introduces some of the challenges of integration and technology adoption and thus some efforts towards establishing a coordinator have been implemented (FGDC, 1994). Some of these integration challenges and efforts, which seem to be getting more complex, have been discussed by FGDC (2004); Masser (1999); Longley, Goodchild, Maguire, and Rhind (2001); Ryan, DeMulder, DeLoatch, Garie, and Sideralis (2004); Maguire and Longley (2005); and Tait (2005).

Millard (n.d.) presents another e-government trend, which has also been mentioned by Burgelman et al. (2004). On the demand side, much talk revolves around "joined-up" and "borderless" government, that is, different agencies combining to offer improved services, or at least working symbiotically together, and providing user access anytime, anywhere, and any service. So-called Me-Government enables citizens or their electronic agents to actively self personalize the e-government service, which can "learn" (e.g., through neural processing) how the citizen uses the service and adapt accordingly.

To conclude, although a few examples of these trends do already exist, such as u-government in Singapore and Germany (silicon-trust, n.d.), at the moment, new trends such as u-government can still be considered a dream for the future. The e-government services now offered are often limited to providing information as reported by UN studies such as United Nations Division for Public Economics and Public Administration DPEPA and The American Society for Public Administration ASPA. (2001) and and World Public Sector Report: E-Government at the Crossroads (2003). Many countries are still a long way from what UN experts call transactional e-government. Transactional e-government means that citizens can pay for services and other transactions online. However, the main issue that we want to highlight here is the importance of interorganizational integration in the context of technology adoption, whether for current or emerging trends. Further, the trends mentioned previously extend the use of e-government technologies within larger geographical areas, which might necessitate the involvement of more organizations in the integration process. The question here are: what are the challenges of interorganizational integration, how can we overcome it, and are e-government technologies still applicable in this case? The answers of these questions are going to be clarified within the following sections describing the case study presenting the foreign financing decision-making process at the country level and its main contributors.

Foreign Financing in Egypt and IDSC

The foreign financing process is critical for Egypt. In the latter part of 1980s, arrears on external payment obligations became relatively frequent, and Egypt's credit worthiness was lost. The debt amount reached $33 billion in the late 1980s (El Sherif & El Sawy, 1988). While economic conditions have since improved, research attention to the foreign financing process is still important, as foreign financing problems can lead to crisis within a very short time (see, for example, Haque, 1998, for relevant discussions on the Asian Crisis). In a crisis, the weak financial status of a country might lead to a vicious circle of problems; the financial reputation of the country might be affected. This could lead to problems in seeking foreign financing to deal with the crisis. This is because a country that looses its credit worthiness might have limited or no creditors. Consequently, investors are going to be cautious and portfolio investment becomes even more risky. Thus, on the one hand, it is very important to monitor and support the foreign financing process, so that a country does not end up in severe crisis situations. On the other hand, although economic conditions have improved, Egypt lags behind other countries on several accounts, including various financial indicators (Galal, 1998). Thus, the need to support the foreign financing process is obvious; in Egypt, the Cabinet Information and Decision Support Center has a key role in providing support for this process.

The role of IDSC is to support the top decision makers in Egypt, namely, ministers and their CEOs, and therefore is a key strategic player. It is also one of the largest organizations providing decision support in Egypt. The IDSC was established as part of national administrative development plan with the mission to support the Cabinet in the area of socioeconomic development. It is specifically targeted at the strategic level and has implemented several information and decision support systems projects since its initiation (El Sherif & El Sawy, 1988). The objectives of the IDSC include developing information and decision support systems for the Cabinet and top policy makers in Egypt. Also, the IDSC aims to support the establishment of decision support systems and centers in different ministries, and to make more efficient and effective use of information resources. Similarly, it aims to initiate and encourage, as well as support, informatics projects that could accelerate managerial and technological development of the Egyptian ministries and governorates. Finally, the IDSC aims to participate in international cooperation activities in the areas of information and decision support.

The area of IDSC activity that we are concerned with in this chapter is the Project Development Sector, which is responsible for the development of the Debt Management and Foreign Financing Project in Egypt (DMSS). The department staff are project management executives, whose role is to develop, implement, and monitor various projects, responding to the needs of the different ministries and governorates. The Debt Management Project (DMSS) aims to support the main contributors in the foreign financing decision-making process, namely, the Ministry of Economy and Foreign Trade, the Central Bank of Egypt (CBE), and the Ministry of Planning and International Co-operation. The next section presents the approach followed to research how these parties perceived the role of the IDSC system in providing decision support for foreign financing.

Research Approach

As mentioned, this research addresses an in-depth investigation of the foreign financing decision making process nature for the purpose of investigating the DMSS contribution and supplementary technology support, if necessary. This support could vary from stand alone to complex integrated systems or e-government supporting technologies. One of the appropriate research strategies that allows in depth investigation is case study research (Yin, 1993). Our research design reflects the unique nature of the foreign financing decision-making process, the IDSC, and its system (the DMSS) and is not limited to a single case study of the IDSC, but it can be regarded as an embedded case study. This is because the target beneficiaries of the system (the Ministry of Economy and Foreign Trade (MOE), the Central Bank of Egypt (CBE), and the Ministry of Planning and International Co-operation (MOIC) have a key role in foreign financing and, importantly, in evaluating the role of the DMSS.

As mentioned in the previous section, the foreign financing problem is a result of the lack domestic resources of the country to fulfill its financial needs. However, in the course of our empirical research, we found that the foreign financing decision-making process is not documented. Its documentation became part of our research agenda and was achieved through several iterations of interviews. Although our main interviewees were the CEOs, they have referred us, whenever necessary, to their subordinates. The interviews were conducted with the IDSC CEO, Ministry of Economy middle management and CEO, and academics from the Faculty of Economics and Policy in Cairo University and the American University in Cairo. This process was subsequently extensively validated by the Central Bank CEO, who was able to discuss the process at a macrolevel. Indeed, one of the challenging points was to have a global, macroview of the process, especially linking the decision-making phases of several contributors, who do not, in many cases, directly communicate with each other. Middle management, who was also interviewed, lacked knowledge of such a strategic (macro) view and talked about very narrow points, without being able to link a particular task to other organizations involved in the process.

It has to be mentioned that the empirical work took a long time because the contributors are overloaded and have to deal with a lot of ad hoc tasks. This made it difficult for respondents to focus on the research agenda, especially as there were constant interruptions, usually for dealing with ad hoc issues. Furthermore, being overloaded made it difficult for them to concentrate on the issue we were discussing. Also, the time gaps between interviews were a barrier, as the interviewees had to be reminded of what was discussed last time. In response to the problems of elite interviewing, we opted for the structured interview technique. This allowed us to focus more on details, and to direct the interviewee to our main research objectives. This was supplemented with fragmented documentation sources that did not help in understanding the global view of the process. In the following section we are going to present how we were able to understand and document the process.

Understanding the Foreign Financing Decision Making Process at Task Level

Due to its vagueness, we had to refine our understanding of the foreign financing decision-making process though interviews and clarify which organization is involved at each phase. As no documentation existed about this issue we had to build our conclusions based on interviews (several iterations) and the most relevant documentation available. During some stages of the empirical work, it seemed impossible to know the global view at a macrolevel as interviewees did not know the relationships to other organizations, talked at different levels of detail, or provided us with a detailed microview. In most of the cases, decision-making seemed to depend on the availability of finance resources, on the economic condition of the country, or other political factors. Some of the financing alternatives depend on marketing, which in turn depends on other issues that depend on other ministries and organizations (e.g., legislation flexibility: Ministry of Legislation; tourism facilities: Ministry of Tourism; services: Ministry of Infrastructure, Ministry of Electricity, and so on). In addition, any unexpected external factors (some of them are uncontrollable) or internal factors might drop the resources of the country (for example, the Luxor Crisis in 1997 dropped main tourism resources). It therefore became obvious that the process is messy and the roles of the involved organizations are not clear (at least to others). In addition, there are lots of tasks; some of them overlap, which makes the process more complex. However, as can be seen from this process, the interrelationship and coordination are highly important, as lots of decisions depend on coordination between organizations (cf. El Samalouty, 1999).

Based on our observations, we also concluded that a big gap sits between middle management and the executives in qualifications. As a result, the executives are overloaded with additional tasks the middle management has originally to perform, which makes their work more ad hoc and complex. Organizational problems seem to contribute to these difficulties. Some of these have also been discussed by El Sherif and Gray (1994). The involvement of different organizations and different departments in each organization makes the process more complex and the communication between organizations more difficult. Focusing on the process at task level allowed us to detect more complexities. Having a combination of ongoing tasks, dependent tasks, as well as parallel tasks increases this complexity as well. This made the process documentation very difficult and we expect the monitoring phase (by the Central Bank of Egypt) of the whole process is complex as well. In addition, the coordination between tasks is very difficult, as some of them are ad hoc.

Table 1 describes examples of the process tasks we were finally able to identify and document, which correspond to three phases of the strategic decision process phases described in the literature (e.g., Noorderhaven, 1995). What we can see from this description is that there are some phases, such as the scanning the environment and SWOT analysis, that are ongoing. This means they are performed during all the phases of the decision-making process and not just a step in the process. Scanning the environment as an ongoing task is critical, in the case of foreign financing in particular. For example, the portfolio investment and the associated reserves, if not monitored, can lead to serious failure like the Asian crisis.

After conducting several interviews with the Central Bank of Egypt CEO, we were able to present the process tasks including the roles of each organization. As we can see from Table 1, there are different organizations involved in each of these tasks. For some of these tasks different organizations present their point of view based on their domain. Other tasks depend on each other (e.g., proposing areas of investment depends on broader financial strategy). The question is: do the CEOs in different organizations cooperate in these phases? As argued by the CEOs during later interviews, although supporting the same process, there is lack of cooperation between different organizations and even duplication of work. For this reason, sometimes the CEOs might not be aware of other organizations' work characteristics, especially in tasks they are not involved with. Moreover, as can be seen in Table 1, there are different departments in the CBE that are involved in different phases. This

Table 1. Examples of some foreign financing process tasks

Process Phase	Tasks	Involved Organization(s)
Strategy Formulation	Broader financial strategies	Top Decision Makers (Economic Committee*)
	Identifying growth strategies/policies	Ministry of Planning & International Co-operation/ Economic Committee
	Determining the policies and broader strategies of indebtedness	Ministry of Planning & International Co-operation/ Economic Committee
	Prioritizing the investments and expenditures according to some rational selection criteria	Ministry of Planning CBE, All Concerned Ministries*
	Proposing favorite areas for investment in correlation with debt service	Ministry of Planning CBE, All Concerned Ministries*
Scanning the Environment & SWOT Analysis	Following up on international interest rates***	CBE (Economic Department, Foreign Relations Debt Department, Banks Control Department)/Ministry of Economy
	Preparing research and studies in economic fields and monitoring the international activities**	Ministry of Economy/CBE (Economic Research Department)
	Monitoring borrowing activities in the major financial markets**	CBE (Economic Research Unit, Foreign Relations Department)
Pre Pproblem Definition	Proposing long-term strategies (five year plan)	Ministry of Planning
	Receiving proposals from different ministries, governorate, organization, etc., regarding long term and comprehensive planning for economic and social development	Ministry of Planning
	Evaluating investment projects	Ministry of Planning, Concerned Ministries, General Authority of Investment (for private sector projects)

Note:

* The Economic Committee (group decision-making sessions) includes The Prime Minister, The Ministry of Economy (MOE), The Ministry of Finance (MOF), The Ministry of Planning & International Cooperation (MIC), and The Central Bank of Egypt (CBE).

** All ministries are contributors to propose their needs, but not as decision makers.

***Ongoing tasks.

shows, first, the complexity of the process and, second, it explains why the CEOs from different organizations described the process characteristics in a different way. As can be seen by Table 1, different (but not always all) organizations are involved in each task of the process. Moreover, for a specific task, each of the involved organizations sometimes performs their duties separately.

Our review of tasks showed that some of the decision-making phases are iterative, and others are not necessarily executed sequentially. Some of the tasks/activities are performed in parallel as they are executed by some organizations (e.g., CBE), whereas other organizations (e.g., MOE) might be performing other tasks. Other tasks depend on each other's results so they have to be performed in a particular sequence. So, the strategic decision-making process overall is very complex and can be regarded as a set of tasks that often includes other decision-making process phases. In the following section we summarize these challenges.

Organizational Challenges

Investigating the foreign financing process, as well as some of its subprocesses, helped in detecting some organizational problems. For example, in addition to being ill-structured, as noted in previous research (e.g., El Sherif & El Sawy, 1988), the strategic processes of a country like Egypt are inherently complex. There are several contributing organizations, where some tasks of the processes are performed by more than one organization. The decision-making process consists of a set of subprocesses or tasks; some of them are overlapping, parallel, or others are dependent on other processes. Furthermore, the strategic decision-making process is not always a step by step process.

Thus, one of the significant challenges facing process support is that the role of some organizations is not clear to other contributors and thus duplication of work as well as isolation occurs. The lack of coordination and other organizational factors, such as the location of the IDSC system supporting different organizations, hierarchy of the system towards those organizations, and the system used through intermediaries, showed to be very important factors in system use. Furthermore, the lack of documentation and the difficulty in documenting the process proved to be a major problem. We also observed a big difference in qualifications between the middle management and the executives. As a result, the executives are overloaded with additional tasks that middle managers were originally expected to perform, which makes the work of executives more ad hoc and complex.

One of the challenges facing the process is that the strategic environment is very dynamic. For example, not only ministers and executives have been changed but also the roles of the ministries. Some ministries have been merged with others too. This issue caused several barriers to system use, as some of the contributors were not well informed about system capabilities.

The identification of organizational problems in the previous section can help in considering and resolving some issues for decision makers in the IDSC. These solutions, presented in Table 2, derive from the lessons learned while we were investigating the decision-making processes for the purpose of technology support. For example, the first stage of interviews showed that the whole process analysis might not be successful. In the second stage of in-

Table 2. Proposed solutions to some IDSC problems

Domain	Problem	Proposed Organizational Solution	Proposed IT Solution
Decision making process	• Change of roles between ministries • Differences in decision makers view of the global decision-making process • Busy decision makers overloaded with ad hoc tasks, so performing analysis about the global decision-making process is difficult • Vagueness and lack of documentation of the process • Lack of coordination between participating ministries	• Task based view of the decision-making process as the unit of analysis • A coordinator should exist	• Start with a task based analysis and design and then link tasks to form the global decision-making process • business process reengineering • eE-business adoption (G2G)
Use of information	• Duplication of sources of information	• Overall task division, as well as link between information sources of organizations	• Pooled information source for organizations in IDSC • Install network between organizations
Use of technology and organizational structure	• Low impact of the system on the process • Users do not sometimes accept or know about the IDSC contribution • Beneficiaries are always busy and appointments are very difficult	• Different ministries should have an information center • These should be linked by a main IT center such as IDSC (or maybe an IT center in the Central Bank) • This information center should be an official contributor to the process	• Analysis of the tasks could be performed more easily as the IT specialists in the ministries could have access to information, do observations, and have better knowledge of the actual use system. Also, they have formal and easier access to decision makers. Task analysis can be carried out when executives have time.

terviews, task analysis was proposed as it is more focused. Our proposed solutions can be related to the decision-making process, the use of information, and the use of technology and organizational structure.

We expect that these will be helpful for the IDSC and the other organizations involved in the foreign financing decision-making process in Egypt, but also to researchers interested in e-government and process integration. Our experience with this research has been that any seemingly technical problems could be attributed to organizational issues or problems in interorganizational coordination among the stakeholders of the process. Conversely, the technology did not act as a facilitator for rich coordination, partly due to the limited use of network technology. E-government in this case is of much greater help from both a techno-logical and an organizational perspective.

Implications of the Case Study on E-Goverment Adoption

Analyzing the foreign financing decision-making process highlighted the high complexity of the decision-making process at the strategic level of the country. The decision-making process crosses the boundaries of one ministry to several ministries. Analyzing the decision-making process in the context of technology adoption in general and e-government in particular is very challenging. However, this analysis shows that it is necessary to adopt the concept of G2G to facilitate the interaction between ministries involved in the same decision-making process. Thus the main challenge for e-government is to describe the decision-making processes and make the appropriate infrastructure for technology adoption. We look at the concept of e-government with a broad perspective involving cross-functional integration. This involves systems that support those decision-making processes.

Thus although challenging yet beneficial, we believe that technology adoption in general and e-government technologies in particular (especially G2G) are recommendable for the foreign financing process of Egypt or any similar strategic process, if required, with the constraint that some major changes happen in the process. We believe that any system support without solving major organizational problems may not be useful. Thus, we propose, that the foreign financing process would be reorganized, documented, and some organiza-tion should be responsible for the coordination between these ministries and the CBE. This should include reducing redundancy of work as well.

What we recommend here is a change in the process itself before it can be supported ef-fectively by technology. The question here is: How can we change the process? This issue is one of the recent research areas in the domain of IS. There are several opinions of how we can change the process. One of these is the contribution of IT in this change. As Turner (1998) discusses, it is generally acknowledged that information technology plays an im-portant role in organisation change. Davenport and Short (1990) describe business process reengineering (BPR) as:

The analysis and design of workflows and processes within and between organisations busi-ness activities should be viewed as more than collection of individual or even functional tasks; they should be broken down into processes that can be broken down into processes that can be designed for maximum effectiveness, in both manufacturing and service envi-ronment. (pp. 11-12)

This definition is very similar to our recommendation to analyze the strategic process by looking at subprocesses and tasks. The question here is: Should we use IT for the foreign financing process or any other process to change it? Hammer (1996) argues that reengineering should use the power of modern technology to radically redesign our business processes in order to achieve dramatic improvements in their performance (with IT used). This is not intended to automate the existing process but to enable a new one. Davenport and Short (1990) suggest that in BPR, IT should be viewed as more than a automating or mechanizing force; it can fundamentally reshape the way business is done. However, as argued by Galliers (1998) and also by Maruca (1994), information and IT are rarely sufficient to bring about process change; most process innovations are enabled by a combination of IT, information, and organisational / human resource changes. Galliers (1998) in particular, emphasizes that the focus should be neither on the process, nor on technology alone. In addition, we should understand the cultural context in which strategy is being formulated and the change to be implemented. Further, he proposes a sociotechnical approach to BPR, which is based on the idea that the key stakeholders need to be favorably disposed to change, for the change strategies to be successful. In the context of stakeholders culture and their acceptance to technology there have been several research efforts such as the TAM and diffusion theories. For example, Marnik, Parker, and Sarvary (2000) have used TAM theory in the context of cross-country technology adoption, while Chen, Gillenson, and Sherrell (2002) examine consumer behavior in the virtual store context.

E-Goverment Trends Challenges

The issue we want to discuss in the context of the e-government trends mentioned previously is: Are these organizational problems experienced in our case studies still an important issue? Are the solutions proposed still valid? For this purpose we are going to focus on interorganizational integration that can be performed by g-government, as an example. In this context Sharifi and Zarei (2004) discuss the issue of intergovernment integration at a macrolevel and argues that the concept of communication between ministries and the cabinet can be extended to communications among all government agencies and staff, and the concept of improving work processes of the cabinet and its office, stretched to the level of government agencies' operations. Up to 2000 the U.K. rural planning system was predominantly sectoral. The paradigm of integrated rural development is therefore relatively new, so until recently there has been no policy requirement to link data from different socioeconomic and biophysical domains. Building a spatial data infrastructure involves organizational as well as technical changes (Williamson, Rajabifard, & Feeney, 2003). This includes variable integration problems including data integration. For example, integration of data between organizations involves other problems prior to the technical stage of agreeing to, and operating on, common data formats and geographic bases. Sang et al. (2005) mention that the transition from sectoral to integrated rural policy has highlighted the fact that data are highly institutionalized resources that are collected to satisfy the specific remit of the collecting organization, often without reference to wider potential uses. This has led to a wide range of different spatial units being used for data collection, analysis, and representation of data for the same location. These different spatial units are a significant barrier in creating a more integrated spatial data infrastructure to support government.

Sang et al. (2005) highlights additional problems based on the British experience. As they discuss, joined-up government is being developed through a number of "national initiatives" while providing opportunities of data integration and run the risk of complicating rather than simplifying the range of spatial referencing methods available. These complications may arise through uncoordinated development in separate N-initiatives and through the sort of access difficulties outlined in relation to the IACS mapping, even with closely coordinated development of new data models. Concerning the American case (Maguire & Longley, 2005), efforts have been directed towards the establishment of a Web-based portal for one-stop access to maps, data, and other geospatial data and services; to institute a collaborative process to develop data content standards ensuring consistency among datasets and allowing governments to share data and integrate multiple sources of information; to create an easy-to-access inventory of currently available data collected by federal agencies; and to cultivate a planned data investment marketplace that will allow federal, state, and local governments to combine resources with one another on future data collection/purchase plans.

Emphasizing on the role of integrator, Maguire and Longley (2005) mention some of the lessons learned from the American experience, especially in its phase of IT, did not relate to other tiers of government or to the private sector, both major participants in the GIS community. Furthermore, the ideas encapsulated in the order were not backed by financial control because there were no budgetary ties. This organization, under the control of the United States Geologic Survey (USGS), did much to germinate and grow the National Spatial Data Infrastructure (NSDI), but in retrospect its dominantly technical focus, and lack of attention to issues of governance and policy, stymied widespread acceptance across the wider constituency of federal, state and local government organizations, as well as those in the private sector. The role of the coordinator has been not only been suggested, but also implemented in the second phase by NSDI, which aims to promote coordination and alignment of geospatial data collection and maintenance among all levels of government.

Concerning reengineering, Burgelman et al. (2004) emphasize that among the most critical issues around implementation and delivery of electronic government today, rather well known and researched, is the need for back office reengineering.

From the examples mentioned previously, we can see that the issue is still interorganizational integration. Some organizational problems remain similar to our case studies, such as the need of a coordinator and the sectoral nature of the government, and variable data sources as a barrier to integration. The need of reengineering the back office has also been highlighted. Some of the previously mentioned solutions, therefore, remain valid. Further, some additional organizational problems arise while implementing the new trends such as g-government, which necessitate the need of a unified strategy for spatial data. Thus the new trend of e-government, although necessary for cross-organizational integration and G2G initiatives, their attempted implementation faces several barriers; For those we need a national plan to tackle these problems prior to technology adoption. The process and the contributors have to be ready.

Finally, we want to highlight that the e-government challenges addressed in this chapter regard decision-making processes. Future research is going to address other challenges, such as technology, security, and stakeholders' acceptance. This will enable developing an integrated framework addressing e-government challenges.

Conclusion

The chapter provided some recommendations to manage the organizational problems affecting decision processes for the purpose of technology adoption. These include, first, analyzing the decision making process at a task level. This implies a contextual analysis that is shaped by the specific characteristics of the decision-making process as it takes place in the particular research context. Second, we argue that technology adoption, such as e-government, may have a limited impact unless the decision-making process is better understood and the related organizational problems are addressed. In the context of our case studies, our empirical investigation suggests that there is scope for a better organization, documentation, and interorganizational coordination between the contributing organizations. This would result in reducing duplication of work as well. Although the importance of such issues has been emphasized in information systems research, some research in the domain of e-government is still concerned solely with technical challenges, or making information available on the Internet focusing on G2C and G2B. Our work therefore makes a significant contribution in broadening the research agenda in the context of organizational barriers and e-business infrastructure in developing countries and exploring the importance of G2G e-government. The issue of e-government is not isolated but tightly related to other information systems topics such as BPR, TAM, and diffusion theories, as presented in this chapter. It is strongly recommended that future quantitative research would investigate the challenges presented in this chapter as potential constructs for investigation, aiming to extend TAM. Further, as mentioned, e-government encompasses the other information systems, stand alone or integrated, yet crosses organization boundaries. The chapter concludes with highlighting some of the emerging e-government challenges, which show that organizational problems are still an important issue that get more complex in some cases, such as in g-government adoption.

References

Atkinson, R., & Ulevich, D. (2000). *Digital government: The next step to reengineering the federal government.* Technology & New Economy Project. Progressive Policy Institute. Retrieved September 30 2005, from http://www.cb-business.com/documents/CB-BUSINESS%20-%20paper%20EGOV%202002.pdf

Bonham, G. M., Seifert, J. M., & Thorson, S. J. (2003). *The transformational potential of e-government: The role of political leader ship.* Retrieved May 9, 2006, from http://www.maxwell.syr.edu/maxpages/faculty/gmbonham/ecpr.htm

Burgelman, J.-C., Centeno, C., & Bogdanowicz, M. (2004). *E-government in EU in 2010: Key policy and research challenges.* Paper presented at the IPTS Workshop, Sevilla, Spain. Retrieved May 9, 2006, from http://fiste.jrc.es/download/2.%20IPTS_Future%20%20challenges%20for%20e-gov1.pdf

Chen, L., Gillenson, M. L., & Sherrell, D. L. (2002). Enticing online consumers: An extended technology acceptance perspective. *Information & Management, 39*(8), 705-719.

Davenport, T., & Short, J. (1999). The new industrial reengineering: Information technology and business process redesign. *Sloan Management Review, 31*(4), 11-27.

El Samalouty, G. (1999, March). *Corporate tax and investment decisions in Egypt* (Tech. Rep. No. WP35). The Egyptian Center for Economic Studies. Retrieved December 30, 2005, from http://www.eces.org.eg/Publications/Index3.asp?l1=4&l2=1&l3=35

El-Sherif, H., & El-Sawy, O. (1988). Issue-based decision support systems for the Cabinet of Egypt. *MIS Quarterly, 12,* 551-570.

El Sherif, O., & Gray, P. (1994). From crisis management to fast response DSS: An international perspective. In P. Gray (Ed.), *Decision support and executive information systems* (pp. 87-97). Englwood Cliffs, NJ: Prentice Hall.

ESRI. (n.d.). *GIS and mapping software.* Retrieved May 9, 2006, from http://www.esri.com/news/arcuser/0101/umbrella13.html

FGDC. (2004). *Geospatial one-stop: Encouraging partnerships to enhance access to geospatial information.* Retrieved May 9, 2006, from http://www.sciencedirect.com/science?_ob=RedirectURL&_method=externObjLink&_locator=url&_cdi=5901&_plusSign=%2B&_targetURL=http%253A%252F%252Fwww.fgdc.gov%252Fpublications%252Fdocuments%252Fgeninfo%252Fgos.pdf

FGDC. (1994). *The 1994 plan for the national spatial data infrastructure: Building the foundation of an information based society.* Retrieved May 9, 2006, from http://www.fgdc.gov/framework/framdev.html

Galal, A. (1998, January). *Priorities for rapid and shared economic growth in Egypt.* Policy View 3. The Egyptian Center for Economic Studies. Retrieved December 30, 2005, from http://www.eces.org.eg/Publications/Print.asp?l1=4&l2=2&l3=3

Galliers, B. (1998). Reflections on BPR, IT and organizational change. In R. D. Galliers & W. R. J. Bates (Eds.), *Information technology and organisational transformation* (pp. 225-243). Chichester: John Wiley & Sons.

Gilbert, A. (2001, April). President Bush backs e-government, digital signatures. *InformationWeek,* p. 24.

Gupta, M. P., & Jana, D. E. (2003). Government evaluation: A framework and case study. *Government Information Quarterly, 20,* 365-387.

Hammer, M. (1996). *Beyond reengineering: How the process-centred organization is changing our work and our lives.* London: Harper Collins Business.

Haque, N. (1998, June). *The Asian crisis* (Tech. Rep. No. WP30). The Egyptian Center for Economic Studies. Retrieved December 12, 2005, from http://www.eces.org.eg/Publications/Index3.asp?l1=4&l2=1&l3=30

Hasson, J. Z. (2001). Treasury CIO promotes expanded fed portal. *Federal Computer Week, 3,* 14.

Hoffman, D. L., Novak, T. P., & Peralta, M. (1999). Building consumer trust online. *Communications of the ACM, 42*(4), 80-85.

Jaeger, P. T. (2003). The endless wire: E-government as global phenomenon. *Government Information Quarterly, 20,* 323-331.

Lallana, E. C. (2004). *eGovernment for development.* Retrieved May 9, 2006, from http://www.egov4dev.org/mgovdefn.htm

Laudon, K., & Laudon, J. (2003). *Management information systems* (8th ed.). Upper Saddle River, NJ: Prentice Hall.

Longley, P. A., Goodchild, M. F., Maguire, D. J., & Rhind, D. W. (2001). *Geographic information systems and science.* Chichester: Wiley.

Maguire, J. D., & Longley, B. A. (2005). The emergence of geoportals and their role in spatial data infrastructures. *Computers, Environment and Urban Systems., 29*(1), 3-14.

Mapping Sciences Committee. (1993). *Towards a coordinated spatial data infrastructure for the nation.* Washington, DC: National Academy Press.

Marnik G. D., Parker, P. M., & Sarvary, M. (2000). Modelling technology adoption timing across countries. *Technological Forecasting and Social Change, 63*(1), 25-42.

Maruka, R. F. (1994). The right way to go global: An interview with Whirlpool CEO David Whitwam. *Harvard Business Review, 72*(2), 135-145.

Masser, I. (1999). All shapes and sizes: The first generation of national spatial data infrastructures. *International Journal of Geographical Information Science, 13*, 67-84.

Matthews, W. (2000). *Setting a course for e-government.* Retrieved May 9, 2006, from http://www.fcw.com/fcw/articles/2000/1211/cov?egov?12?11?00.asp

Millard, J. (n.d.). *(R)e-balancing government.* Retrieved May 9, 2006, from http://www.prisma-eu.net/deliverables/rebalance.pdf

Moon, M. J. (2002). The evolution of e-government among municipalities: Rhetoric or reality? *Public Administration Review, 42*(4), 424-433.

Moon, J. W., & Kim, Y. G. (2001). Extending the TAM for a World-Wide-Web context. *Information & Management, 38*(4), 217-230.

Noorderhaven, N. G. (1995) *Strategic decision making.* Harlow: Addison-Wesley.

O'Brien, J. (2003). *Management information systems: Managing information technology in the e-business enterprise* (6th ed.). New York: McGraw-Hill.

Odendaal, N. (2003). Information and communication technology and local governance: Understanding the difference between cities in developed and emerging economies. *Computers, Environment and Urban Systems, 27*(6), 585-607.

Reddick, C. G. (2004). A two-state model of e-government growth: Theories and empirical evidence for US cities. *Government Information Quarterly, 21*, 51-64.

Relyea, H. C. (2002). E-gov: Introduction and overview. *Government Information Quarterly, 19*(1), 9–35.

Rötter, A. (2003). *Einführung in das Thema EGovernment.* Retrieved May 9, 2006, from http://www.webagency.de/infopool/e-commerce-knowhow/e-govenment.htm

Ryan, B. J., DeMulder, M. L., DeLoatch, I., Garie, H., & Sideralis, K. (2004). A clear vision of the NSDI. *Geospatial Solutions, 4*, 30-31.

Sakowicz, M. (n.d.). *How to evaluate e-government? Different methodologies and methods.* Retrieved May 9, 2006, from unpan1.un.org/intradoc/groups/ public/documents/NISPAcee/UNPAN009486.pdf

Sang, N., Birnie, R. V., Geddes, A., Bayfield, N. G., Midgley, J. L., Shucksmith, D. M., & Elston, D. (2005). Improving the rural data infrastructure: The problem of addressable spatial units in a rural context. *Land Use Policy., 22*(2), 175-186.

Sharifi, H. and Zarei, B. (2004). An adaptive approach for implementing e-government in I.R. Iran. *Journal of Government Information, 30*(5-6), 600-619.

Silicon Trust. (n.d.). *From Electronic Government to Ubiquitous Government?* Retrieved November 6, 2005, from http://www.silicon-trust.com/trends/tr_u_government.asp

Tait, M. G. (2005). Implementing geoportals: Applications of distributed GIS. *Computer, Environment, and Urban Systems, 29*(1), 33-47.

Turner, J. A. (1998). The role of information technology in organizational transformation. In R. D. Galliers & W. R. J. Bates (Eds.), *Information technology and organisational transformation* (pp. 245-261). Chichester: John Wiley & Sons.

United Nations Department of Economic and Social Affairs (2003). *United Nations world public sector report 2003: E-government at the crossroads* (Rep. No. ST/ESA/PAD/SER.E/49). New York: Author. Retrieved May 9, 2006, from http://unpan1.un.org/in-tradoc/groups/public/docu ments/nispacee/unpan009486.pdf

United Nations Division for Public Economics and Public Administration DPEPA and The American Society for Public Administration ASPA. (2001). *Benchmarking e-government: A global perspective: Assessing the UN member states.* Retrieved May 9, 2006, from http://www.unpan.org/e-government/Benchmarking%20E-gov%202001.pdf

Wang, Y. (2003). The adoption of electronic tax filing systems. *Government Information Quarterly, 20*(4), 333-352.

Weiser, M. (1992, October) *Does ubiquitous computing need interface agents? No.* Paper presented at the MIT Media Lab Symposium on User Interface Agents.

Wescott, C. G. (2002). *E-government in the Asia Pacific Region.* Retrieved May 9, 2006, from http://www.adb.org/Documents/Papers/E_Government/default.asp

Williamson, I., Rajabifard, A., & Feeney, M. F. (Eds.). (2003). *Developing spatial data infrastructures: From concept to reality.* London: Taylor & Francis.

World Bank Group. (n.d.). Retrieved May 9, 2006, from http://www1.worldbank.org/publicsector/egov/definition.htm

Yin, R. K. (1993). *Applications of case study research.* London: Sage Publications.

Zobel, R & Filos, E. (2004). *eEurope 2005 and the European Research Area: Policy and Research measures aiming at Europe to become the world's largest knowledge based economy by 2010.* Brussels: European Commission. Retrieved December 30, 2005, from ftp://ftp.cordis.europa.eu/pub/ist/docs/dir_c/rz-ef_to_echallenges-04-final_en.pdf

Chapter XI

Towards Measuring True E-Readiness of a Third-World Country:
A Case Study on Sri Lanka

Reggie Davidrajuh, University of Stavanger, Norway

Abstract

This chapter talks about measuring true e-readiness of a third-world country. As a case study, e-readiness measurement is done on Sri Lanka. First, this chapter assesses e-readiness of Sri Lanka using a measuring tool that utilizes 52 socio-economic indicators. Second, based on the assessment, this chapter reveals that the measurement does not indicate true e-readiness of the country, as the tool does not model or incorporate parameters for measuring the domestic digital divide that exists between communities or groups within the country. Third, this chapter proposes a method for incorporating the domestic digital divide measures in e-readiness calculations.

Introduction

Many governments across the globe have now resorted to employing e-government initiatives to better position themselves in the Information Age. For these governments, it is important to have some understanding of the level of preparedness in comparison with their performances. The level of preparedness to adopt e-government initiatives and activities is referred to as e-readiness (Ifinedo & Davidrajuh, 2005).

Measuring E-Readiness

There are many tools in use for measuring e-readiness. These tools make use of differing parameters that are classified under a number of categories such as infrastructure, access, applications and services, economy, use of the Internet, skills and human resources, e-business climate, pervasiveness (per capita usage), and so forth; the Bridges Organization (2001) provides a comprehensive coverage of many of the tools and their sources. Some of the organizations that have tools or models for measuring e-readiness include the Center for International Development at Harvard University, the Asian Pacific Economic Cooperation (APEC) Electronic Commerce Steering Group, McConnell International, and The World Information Technology and Services Alliance (WITSA). These tools measure a country's level of preparedness, providing the opportunity for evaluating their performances against their own set objectives in national development plans, and benchmark their progress against the best performing countries; thus, one can measure disparities existing in access and use of ICT between countries (the "international digital divide").

True E-Readiness

Though the previously mentioned tools compare a country's e-readiness with the rest of the world, these tools rarely model or incorporate parameters for measuring the domestic digital divide that exists between communities or groups within a country. This chapter proposes a method for incorporating the domestic digital divide measures in e-readiness calculations.

Structure of This Chapter

In the next section, a tool for measuring e-readiness is presented. Using this tool, e-readiness of Sri Lanka is measured. In the second section, the results of the measurement are analyzed in order to identify the problems associated with omitting domestic digital divide measures in e-readiness calculations. In the third section, a set of proposals is presented for incorporating domestic digital divide measures in e-readiness calculations.

Measuring E-Readiness

As there are many tools available for measuring the e-readiness of a country, different countries tend to use differing tools, guides, and measures in their bid to assess their ability to function and compete in an increasingly networked world. For example, the India e-readiness measure utilized a version that it finds appropriate for the task of assessing development in its states (Department of Information Technology, 2005). For measuring e-readiness of Norway, Davidrajuh (2004) used a tool developed by Bui et al. (2003). Two of the most robust e-readiness tools available are those by the World Bank (2002) and the Economist Intelligence Unit (2004) that covers seven building blocks. Suffice to say that some of the e-readiness tools tend to measure the same metrics using different names.

In this work, a tool developed by Bui, Sankaran, and Sebastian (2002) is used. This tool is selected because it is easily extensible, easy to use, and has a large set of indicators.

The Tool

The tool developed by Bui et al. (2002) consists of three basic building blocks. The three basic building blocks are:

1. Demand forces
2. Supply forces
3. Societal infrastructure

The three basic building blocks are divided into eight major factors, and each of these major factors has a set of indicators. The major factors and the number of indicators that come under these factors are:

1. Demand forces
   a. Culture, understanding and effectiveness: 4 indicators
   b. Knowledgeable citizens: 6 indicators
2. Supply forces
   a. Industry competitiveness: 7 indicators
   b. Access to skilled workforce: 6 indicators
   c. Willingness and ability to invest: 4 indicators
3. Societal infrastructure
   a. Cost of living and pricing: 3 indicators
   b. Access to advanced infrastructure: 10 indicators
   c. Macro economic environment: 12 indicators

The tool uses a total of 52 indicators.

All 52 indicators (e_i) are assigned values on a 1-5 scale; 1 is the worst score and 5 is the best score. Then e-readiness of a country is calculated by a simple Figure-of-Merit (FOM) calculation. In this calculation, all the indicator values are multiplied with corresponding weights and summed together.

$$\text{E-readiness} = \frac{\sum_{i=1}^{52} IWeight_i \times e_i}{\sum_{i=1}^{52} IWeight_i} \quad \text{(Bui et al., 2002)}$$

Measuring E-Readiness of Sri Lanka

In this section, all 52 indicators are evaluated on a 1-5 scale (1 – worst score, 5 – best score). The evaluation is presented in Tables 1 to 3, one table for each basic building block. In these tables, the indicators are grouped into major factors. For example, Table 1 presents the e-readiness scores for indicators that come under the basic building block "demand forces." In Table 1, the indicators are grouped in the two major factors.

Measuring the Demand Forces

There are two major factors under this block. Table 1 shows the two major factors, the indicators that come under these major factors, and the awarded scores for these indicators.

Measuring the Supply Forces

There are three major factors under this block. Table 2 summarizes e-readiness scores for this block.

Table 1. E-readiness score for demand forces

Major Factor 1: Culture, understanding and effectiveness		
Indicator	*Score*	*Reference*
e_1: English language usage	1.4	World Factbook (2003)
e_2: Percentage of urban population	2.1	World Bank (2000)
e_3: Percentage of population over 65 years or older	4.9	SIMA (2003)
e_4: National culture open to foreign influence	N/A	
Major Factor 2: Knowledgeable citizens		
Indicator	Score	Reference
e_5: Adult literacy rate	4.8	HDR (2001)
e_6: Secondary enrollment	3.4	World Bank (2001)
e_7: Tertiary enrollment	1.2	World Bank (2001)
e_8: MGMT education available in 1st class business schools	2.8	World Eco For (2001)
e_9: 8th grade achievement in science	2.5	GIS (2002)

Table 2. E-readiness score for supply forces

Major Factor 3: Industry competitiveness		
Indicator	*Score*	*Reference*
e_{11}: Technology achievement index	2.0	UNDP (2005)
e_{12}: Gross tertiary science & engineering enrollment ratio	1.2	World Bank (2002)
e_{13}: Administrative burden for start-ups	3.6	World Eco For (2001)
e_{14}: Private sector spending on R&D	2.4	World Eco For (2001)
e_{15}: High-tech exports as percentage of manufactured exports	1.2	World Bank (2001)
e_{16}: Patent applications granted by USPTO	N/A	
e_{17}: Total expenditure for R&D as percentage of GNI	N/A	
Major Factor 4: Access to skilled workforce		
Indicator	*Score*	*Reference*
e_{18}: Public spending on education as percentage of GDP	2.5	World Bank (2001)
e_{19}: Extend of staff training	3.0	IMD (2001)
e_{20}: Research collaboration between companies & universities	1.9	IMD (2001)
e_{21}: Number of technical papers per million people	1.8	World Bank (2002)
e_{22}: University education meets the needs of economy	2.0	GIS (2002)
e_{23}: Well-educated people do not emigrate abroad	N/A	
Major Factor 5: Willingness and ability to invest		
Indicator	*Score*	*Reference*
e_{24}: Composite ICRG risk rating	3.6	Country Data (2000)
e_{25}: Availability of venture capital	2.4	World Eco For (2001)
e_{26}: Entrepreneurship among managers	2.8	IMD (2001)
e_{27}: Foreign Direct Investment as percentage of GDP	1.5	SIMA (2003)

Measuring the Societal Infrastructure

There are three major factors under this block. Table 3 summarizes e-readiness score for this block.

Summing Up: The Total E-Readiness

Assuming equal weights of 1 to all the indicators, we summarize the e-readiness value for each major factor.

Major factor 1: Culture, understanding and effectiveness: E-readiness value for this major factor is the average value of the three indicators that come under this major factor:

$$e_{mf\_1} = \frac{1}{3}\sum_{i=1}^{3} e_i = 2.8$$

Table 3. E-readiness score for societal infrastructure

Major Factor 6: Cost of living and pricing		
Indicator	*Score*	*Reference*
e_{28}: International cost of living based on US$ 100	4.0	MHRC (2003)
e_{29}: Inflation rate — CPI in percentage	4.7	CWFB (2005)
e_{30}: GDP per capita (PPP) in US$:	1.4	World Bank (2001)
Major Factor -7: Access to advanced infrastructure		
Indicator	*Score*	*Reference*
e_{31}: Telephone per 1000 people	2.6	World Bank (2001)
e_{32}: Mobile phones per 1000 people	2.0	World Bank (2001)
e_{33}: Computers per 1000 people	1.3	World Bank (2001)
e_{34}: Internet hosts per 10000 people	1.0	World Bank (2001)
e_{35}: International telecom, cost of call to U.S.	1.0	Opex Comm (2003)
e_{36}: E-government	1.0	UNDP (2005)
e_{37}: Computer processing power as a % of worldwide MIPS	N/A	
e_{38}: Freedom on the Internet	2.5	Freedom (2003)
e_{39}: Investment in Telecom as a percentage of GDP	N/A	
e_{40}: ICT expenditure as a percentage of GDP	N/A	
Major Factor 8: Macro economic environment		
Indicator	*Score*	*Reference*
e_{41}: Trade as a percentage of GDP	1.8	World Bank (2001)
e_{42}: Protection of property rights	3.1	World Eco For (2001)
e_{43}: Tariff and nontariff barriers	3.4	IMD (2001)
e_{44}: Soundness of banks	3.9	World Eco For (2001)
e_{45}: Local competition	3.7	World Eco For (2001)
e_{46}: Regulatory framework	2.5	World Bank (2002)
e_{47}: Government effectiveness	1.3	World Bank (2001)
e_{48}: Political stability	1.0	World Bank (2002)
e_{49}: Press freedom	3.8	Freedom (2003)
e_{50}: Rule of law	2.3	World Bank (2002)
e_{51}: Control of corruption	2.3	World Bank (2002)
e_{52}: Adequacy of regulation/supervision of financial institutions	N/A	

Major factor 2: Knowledgeable citizens: E-readiness value for this major factor is the average value of the five indicators:

$$e_{mf\_2} = \frac{1}{5}\sum_{i=5}^{9} e_i = 2.9$$

Major factor 3: Industry competitiveness: E-readiness value for this major factor is the average value of the five indicators:

$$e_{mf\_3} = \frac{1}{5}\sum_{i=11}^{15} e_i = 2.1$$

Major factor 4: Access to skilled workforce: E-readiness value for this major factor is the average value of the five indicators:

$$e_{mf\_4} = \frac{1}{5}\sum_{i=18}^{22} e_i = 2.2 = 2.2$$

Major factor 5: Willingness and ability to invest: E-readiness value for this major factor is the average value of the four indicators:

$$e_{mf\_5} = \frac{1}{4}\sum_{i=24}^{27} e_i = 2.6 = 2.6$$

Major factor 6: Cost of living and pricing: E-readiness value for this major factor is the average value of the three indicators:

$$e_{mf\_6} = \frac{1}{3}\sum_{i=28}^{30} e_i = 3.4 = 3.4$$

Major factor 7: Access to advanced infrastructure: E-readiness value for this major factor is the average value of the seven indicators:

$$e_{mf\_7} = \frac{1}{7}\sum_{i=31}^{36,38} e_i = 1.7 = 1.7$$

Major factor 8: Macro economic environment: E-readiness value for this major factor is the average value of the 11 indicators:

$$e_{mf\_8} = \frac{1}{11}\sum_{i=41}^{51} e_i = 2.6 = 2.6$$

E-readiness values for each building block is give next.

Basic building block 1: Demand forces:

$$e_{DF} = \frac{e_{mf\_1} + e_{mf\_2}}{2} = 2.9$$

Basic building block 2: Supply forces:

$$e_{SF} = \frac{e_{mf\_3} + e_{mf\_4} + e_{mf\_5}}{3} = 2.3$$

Basic building block 3: Societal infrastructure:

$$e_{IN} = \frac{e_{mf\_6} + e_{mf\_7} + e_{mf\_8}}{3} = 2.5$$

Summing all these values together:

$$\text{E-Readiness} = \frac{e_{DF} + e_{SF} + e_{IN}}{3} = 2.5$$

Analysis

By simply going through indicator scores, it is easy to find out where Sri Lanka should concentrate to improve its e-readiness. E-readiness values for all the major factors are below average (the average value is 3.0). And hence, the building blocks and the total e-readiness values are all below the average value.

International Digital Divide

Figure 1 plots e-readiness of Sri Lanka against e-readiness of other well-known economies like G7, USA, and Norway; data for Norway is taken from Davidrajuh (2004); data for G7 and USA is taken from Bui et al. (2001).

Figure 2 depicts detailed benchmarking of e-readiness of Sri Lanka based on the eight major factors. For comparison, values for Norway are also shown in the figure. In Sri Lanka, demand forces (capability of the people) are about the average value. However, supply forces and societal infrastructure are poor. In some of the areas (English language usage, tertiary enrollment, high-tech exports, GDP per capita, computers per 1000 people, and telecom costs) Sri Lanka performs poorly.

Some other indicators (political stability = 1.0 and government effectiveness = 1.0) show that there is a serious problem in running the country. In addition, investment in the ICT sector is low. After many technology investment debacles, private investors are not so enthusiastic about telecom ventures. The government also has problems in investing in the technology sector mainly due to ever increasing health care costs.

Figure 1. Comparing e-readiness

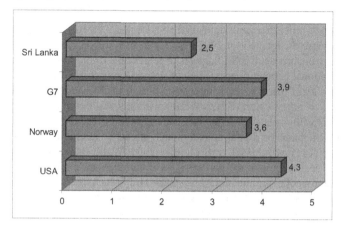

Figure 2. Comparing e-readiness by major factors

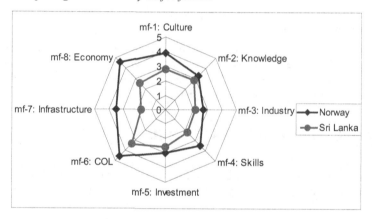

Incorporating Domestic Digital Divide

From the analysis done in the second section, it is clear that e-readiness measures gauge disparities that exist between countries (the "international digital divide"). Thus, improving e-readiness of Sri Lanka means improving its stand on ICT usage compared to the developed countries. However, the analysis in the second section indicates nothing about the "domestic digital divide"; domestic digital divide is the gap between citizens of a country in knowledge, access, usage, and mastery of ICT and the Internet. E-readiness improvements may push a country to a better position in competing with the other countries, but it is not clear whether all the citizens of that country will enjoy the benefits due to the improvements. The following examples are on the effects of e-readiness improvement on domestic digital divide.

Sri Lankan Example

In 2002, the government of Sri Lanka launched e-Sri Lanka — the ICT development roadmap to achieve e-governance by the year 2007 (Sunday Leader, 2003). According to the official document, the main purpose of e-Sri Lanka is to achieve the desired levels of development, by enhancing national competitiveness, reduce or eradicate poverty by realizing enhancements in the quality of life of its citizens (GoSL, 2003); in other terms, the government of Sri Lanka believed in reduction of both the international and domestic digital divides by its e-government initiatives. However, two official reports recently published prove the opposite results on domestic digital divide, though effects on international digital divide is in Sri Lanka's favor (Central Bank of Sri Lanka, 2004; World Bank, 2004). For example, the share of national income of the poorest 10% of the population fell from 1.3% in 1997 (before the induction of e-Sri Lanka) to 1.1% in 2004. For the richest 10%, their share rose from 37.2% to 39.4% over the same period (Central Bank, 2004).

Indian Example

Referring to e-government implementation processes in India, Sharma and Soliman (2003) report similar unintended negative effects on India's domestic digital divide.

There are two problems associated with incorporating indicators into the e-readiness measure in order to determine the domestic digital divide. The first problem is mathematical computation — the way e-readiness is calculated. The second problem is to formulate a set of indicators that will gauge the domestic digital divide correctly.

The Problem in E-Readiness Calculation

Normally, e-readiness measures are based on the Figure-of-Merit (FOM) calculation. A generalized FOM calculation features a series of indicators with corresponding weights (indicator-weights). The indicators are grouped into sectors; the sectors have different weights too (sector-weights). The sectors are further grouped into blocks; each block is assigned a block-weight. Hence, an indicator is multiplied by up to three different weights. The generalized FOM calculation is:

$$\text{Sector score } s_j = \frac{\sum_{Indicator=k}(IndicatorWeight_k \times e_k)}{\sum_{Indicator=k} IndicatorWeight_k}$$

$$\text{Block score } b_i = \frac{\sum_{sector=j}(sectorWeight_j \times s_j)}{\sum_{sector=j} sectorWeight_j}$$

$$\text{E-readiness score} = \frac{\sum_{block=i}(blockWeight_i \times b_i)}{\sum_{block=i} blockWeight_i}$$

In the first equation, e_k represents a score for the indicator k on a scale (e.g., 1-5). In this generalized FOM calculation, cumulative weights assigned to each indicator reflect how important a block, a sector within a block, and an indicator within a sector are. Changing any one or more of the three weights of an indicator relative to the other weights makes that indicator more or less important than the other indicators, depending on whether the product of the weights for the indicator is larger or smaller, respectively. Thus, assigning weights is a planning issue done by the policy makers. During measurement, all the user of the tool has to do is to assign scores for the different indicators.

The fundamental problem with this calculation is that all the indicators are assumed to be homogenous taking scores on a scale (e.g., 1-5). However, in reality, indicators are not homogenous. For example, an indicator may require a Boolean answer (yes or no), or a multivalued answer (within the next 12 months, are you planning to buy a personal computer, mobile phone, Internet access, any of these, or all of these?) or linguistic quantifiers (such as many, most, at least, about, etc.). Obtaining an overall score from a set of scores from unhomogeneous indicators is not feasible with FOM calculation. Hence, the existing tools use only the indicators that are homogeneous.

Instead of FOM, this chapter proposes use of fuzzy ordered waited averaging (OWA) operators for finding overall score from noncomparable (nonhomogenous) indicator scores; see subsection "OWA Operators for E-Readiness Measurement."

Indicators for Gauging Domestic Digital Divide

The sample e-readiness measuring tool given in subsection "The Tool" uses three blocks (Demand forces, Supply forces, and Societal infrastructure) that are divided into eight sectors consisting of 52 indicators. It is clear from subsection "Measuring E-Readiness of Sri Lanka" that the tool totally ignores the domestic digital divide; almost all the tools for measuring e-readiness do not support gauging domestic digital divide in e-readiness calculations.

This chapter proposes the allocation of a separate basic building block for gauging the domestic digital divide. This block is further divided into four sectors: (1) Disparity in Access to ICT; (2) Disparity in Affordability; (3) Disparity in Knowledge; and (4) Disparity in Usage.

The sectors consist of the following indicators:

1. **Disparity in Access to ICT:** (indicator values: richest 20% to poorest 20%); (a) Telephone mainlines, (b) Cellular phone subscription, (c) Personal computers possession, (d) Internet access at home

2. **Disparity in Affordability:** (a) Population below poverty line, (b) Unemployment rate %, (c) inequality measure (richest 20% to poorest 20%), (d) Cost of personal computer as % of monthly income (richest 20% to poorest 20%)

3. **Disparity in Knowledge:** (a) Daily newspapers subscription (richest 20% to poorest 20%), (b) Professional and technical workers as a % of the total workforce

4. **Disparity in Usage:** (a) Share of national consumption (richest 20% to poorest 20%), (b) Population without running water, (c) Homeless population in %, (d) Internet usage (richest 20% to poorest 20%)

OWA Operators for E-Readiness Measurement

Yager (1988, 1995, 1996) provides comprehensive background information on OWA operators. The fuzzy sets based OWA are easy to understand and use. A very concise introduction to OWA is given now.

Definition of Aggregation Operators
Called Ordered Waited Averaging (Yager, 1995)

An aggregation mapping $F: R^n \to R$ is called an ordered weighted averaging (OWA) operator of dimension n if it has associated with it a weighting vector $W = [w_1, w_2, ..., w_n]$ such that:

$$w_i \in [0,1] \text{ and } \sum_{i=1}^{n} w_i = 1$$

$F(A) = \sum_{j=1}^{n} w_j b_j$ where b_j is the jth largest of the a_j; a_i is the input values in the range $[0,1]$, making the input vector $A = [a_1, ..., a_n]$.

A fundamental aspect of the OWA operator is the reordering step, in particular an aggregate a_i is not associated with a particular weight w_i but rather a weight is associated with a particular ordered position of aggregate. When the OWA weights are viewed as a column vector, the weights with the low indices as weights at the top and those with the higher indices with weights at the bottom.

Using OWA to Find the Overall Score
from a Set of Nonhomogenous Indicators

There are basically three sequential processes involved in finding an overall score from a set of nonhomogenous indicators:

1.   Normalization (fuzzification) process
2.   Aggregation process
3.   Defuzzification process

Normalization process. Since the indicators are assumed to be nonhomogenous, the values for the indicators must be mapped into a uniform scale before the aggregation; this process is called the normalization process. Since there could be some indicator values that are linguistic quantifiers or approximate data, the normalization process is sometimes called the fuzzification process.

Aggregation process. After the normalization process, the normalized indicator values are to be aggregated to produce partial sums. For example, the indicator values within a sector are aggregated to produce sector scores, sector scores are then aggregated to produce block scores, and finally the block scores are aggregated to produce the overall score, as described in subsection "The Problem in E-Readiness Calculation."

Defuzzification process. The final step is to transform the aggregate value into an overall score. In other words, in the final step, the fuzzy overall value is mapped into a "crisp" numeric value based on an output scale, say 1 (lowest) and 5 (highest). The overall score can also be produced as a linguistic quantifier; for example, the overall score is "good" on a scale (very good, good, fair, poor).

Due to brevity, the mathematical details behind OWA are not shown here; we refer interested readers to Yager (1995).

Conclusion

The domestic digital divide is the gap between citizens of a country in knowledge, access, usage, and mastery of ICT and the Internet. E-government initiatives and implementations may push a country to a better position in competing with the other countries, but policy makers must make sure that the implementations would not increase the domestic digital divide in that country. Otherwise counterproductive long-term effects are inevitable as the population become more and more polarized as "haves" and "have nots"; this provides enough evidence for this development, and hence puts forward a set of proposals to rectify e-readiness measurements to incorporate the domestic digital divide.

References

Bridges Organization. (2005). *Comparison of e-readiness assessment models.* Retrieved May 9, 2006, from http://www.bridges.org/ereadiness/tools.html

Bui, T. X., Sankaran, S., & Sebastian, I. M. (2003). A framework for measuring national e-readiness. *International journal of Electronic Business, 1*(1), 3 - 22.

Central Bank of Sri Lanka. (2004). *Consumer finance and socioeconomic survey for 2003/2004.* Colombo, Sri Lanka: The Central Bank.

CIAs World Factbook (CWFB). (2005). *The world factbook.* Retrieved May 9, 2006, from http://www.cia.gov/cia/publications/factbook/index.html

Country Data. (2000). *The international country risk guide 2000.* Retrieved May 9, 2006, from http://www.countrydata.com

Davidrajuh, R. (2004, July). *Measuring and improving e-readiness of Norway.* Paper presented at the 2004 International Business Information Management Conference, Amman, Jordan.

Deloitte Research. (2000). *At the dawn of e-government*. New York: Deloitte Research.

Department of Information Technology. (2005). *India: E-readiness assessment report 2004*. Retrieved May 9, 2006, from http://www.mit.gov.in/ereadiness/index.asp

EIU (Economist Intelligence Unit). (2004). *E-readiness rankings 2004*. Retrieved May 9, 2006, from http://graphics.eiu.com/files/ad_pdfs/ERR2004.pdf

Freedomhouse. (2005). *Freedom of the press 2003*. Retrieved May 9, 2006, from http://www. freedomhouse.org/pfs2003/pfs2003.pdf

Government of Sri Lanka. (2003, May). *Policy on e-government*. Columbo, Sri Lanka: Author.

GIS (Greenberg ICT Survey). (2002). *Country ICT survey for Sri Lanka*. Quebec: Author.

HDR (Human Development Report). (2001). *Adult literacy and life skills survey (in Norwegian)*. Retrieved May 9, 2006, from http://www.ssb.no/emner/04/01/notat200306/notat200306.pdf

Ifinedo, P., & Davidrajuh, R. (2005). Digital divide in Europe: Assessing and comparing the e-readiness of a developed and an emerging economy in the Nordic region. *Electronic Government, an International Journal, 2*(2), 111–133.

IMD. (2001). *World competitiveness yearbook 2001*. Retrieved May 9, 2006, from http://www.imd.ch

MHRC (Mercer Human Resource Consulting). (2003). *Global/worldwide 2005 cost of living survey city rankings*. Retrieved May 9, 2006, from http://www.finfacts.ie/costofliving.htm

Opex Communications. (2003). *Direct dialing international calling costs*. Retrieved May 9, 2006, from http://www.opexld.com

Sharma, S. K., & Soliman, K. (2003, June). *Digital divide and e-government implementation*. Paper presented at the Fourth Annual Global Information Technology Management World Conference, Calgary, Canada.

SIMA. (2003). *Quick survey*. Retrieved May 9, 2006, from http://devdata.worldbank.org/query/

Sunday Leader. (2003, May 4). *First ever national e-government conference next week*, p. 7. Colombo, Sri Lanka.

UNDP (United Nations Development Programme). (2005). *Technology achievement index*. Retrieved May 9, 2006, from http://www.undp.org/hdr2001/indicator/indic_267_1_1.html

World Bank. (2000). *Quality of life*. Retrieved May 9, 2006, from http://www.worldbank.org/wdr/2000/pdfs/engtable2.pdf

World Bank. (2001). *World development indicators 2001*. Retrieved May 9, 2006, from http://www.worldbank.org/data/wdi2001/index.htm

World Bank. (2002). *Knowledge assessment matrix*. Retrieved May 9, 2006, from http://www1.worldbank.org/gdlnscripts/programs/kam2002/kamscript.exe/show_page

World Bank. (2004). *Sri Lanka development policy review*. Colombo, Sri Lanka: Author.

World Economic Forum. (2001). *Global competitiveness report 2001*. Retrieved May 9, 2006, from http://www.weforum.org

World Factbook. (2003). *World factbook 2003*. Retrieved May 9, 2006, from http://www.bartleby.com/151/

Yager, R. R. (1988). On ordered weighted averaging aggregation operators in multicriteria decision making. *IEEE Transactions on Systems, Man Cybernet, 18*(1), 183-190.

Yager, R. R. (1995). *Multicriteria decision making using fuzzy quantifiers*. Paper presented at the IEEE/IAFE Conference on Computational Intelligence for Financial Engineering, New York.

Yager, R. R. (1996). Quantifer guided aggregation using OWA operators. *International Journal of Intelligent Systems, 11*, 49–73.

Chapter XII

An Evaluation of Digital Deliberative Democracy in Local Government

Seung-Yong Rho, Seoul Women's University, Korea

Abstract

This chapter evaluates the current status of digital deliberation in the local governments of Seoul Metropolitan area in Korea. In order to do that, this study first reviews literature on digital democracy and develops a Web site evaluation framework of digital deliberative democracy. The four stages of digital deliberative democracy consist of information acquisition, communication and consultation, citizen participation, and public deliberation. Then, after evaluating the current practices in digital deliberative democracy of 25 administrative districts in the City of Seoul based on the four stages of digital deliberative democracy, the results show that a few administrative districts have performed good practices in digital deliberative democracy. Though it could be said that many administrative districts have performed good practices of information acquisition (1ˢᵗ stage of digital deliberative democracy), communication and consultation (2ⁿᵈ stage), and citizen participation (3ʳᵈ stage). Public deliberation (4ᵗʰ stage) is not fully performed in the Web sites of the administrative districts. Based on the results, this research explores some policy recommendations to improve digital deliberative democracy.

Introduction

Two types of government deficit, namely, the "budget deficit" and the "trust deficit," are terms we hear frequently. Of those two types of deficit, citizens' perception of trust in government has decreased in a large number of democratic countries throughout the world (Gore, 1994; Lipset & Schneider, 1983; Miller, 1974; Norris, 1999; Nye, 1997, pp. 1-2). Figure 1 shows the level of trust in the federal government of the United States from 1958 to 2002, indicating a decline of public trust in government since the 1960s. From the early 1960s to the late 1970s, trust in the federal government, in Washington, DC, fell by over 30 points. Even though it improved in the early- and mid-1980s, it declined by about 20 points from the mid-1980s to the mid-1990s.

Most developed democracies are experiencing a collapse of confidence in traditional models of democratic governance. This collapse is manifested in almost every Western country by falling voter turnout, lower levels of public participation in civic life, and public cynicism towards political institutions and parties (Berman, 1997; Erber & Lau, 1990). Traditional structures and cultures of policy formation and decision-making are perceived as being remote from ordinary citizens. Researchers (Baldassare, 2000; Norris, 1999; Rosenthal, 1997) indicate a gap between citizen expectations and the reality of institutional behaviors.

Information and communication technologies (ICTs) have led to the rapid transformation of society and world order (Deibert, 1997), and have had an impact on governance institutions as well. Research concerning the virtual state (Fountain, 2001; Frissen, 1999; Loader, 1997) has become more common in the field of public administration. Researches have pinpointed

Figure 1. Americans' level of trust in the national government, 1958-2002 (Source: American National Election Studies, available at http://www.umich.edu/~nes/)

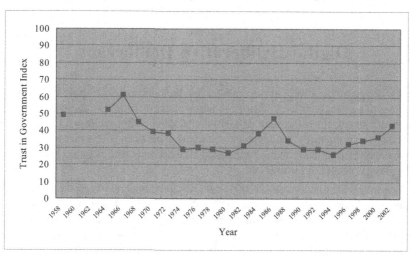

Note: The original questions read, "How much of the time do you think you can trust the government in Washington to do what is right — just about always, most of the time, or only some of the time?"

the issues of ICTs and governance. One of the most important problems in modern public administration is how to embody democratic governance, reflecting citizens' demands and the collective will in the overall process of policy making and public management. Some scholars argue that ICTs can facilitate a more direct interaction between citizens and government and make this interaction a viable next step. Casting one's vote on the Internet, attending Congressional hearings or City Council meetings via the Web, instant public opinion polls, interactive candidate debates, and easy public access to government data are but a few of the potential outcomes.

Despite the historic lack of public involvement in policy making, there is a surprising interest on the part of citizens in exploiting the democratic opportunities for online policy engagement. According to Coleman and Gøtze (n.d.), 23% of respondents had taken part in an online consultation and 73% stated that they would like to take part. 89% favored the creation of an independent space on the Internet where citizens could debate policy issues and 79% thought that the government should be promoting digital democracy. Specifically, when asked which online services they would like to see by 2010 and asked to select their preferred two, "opportunities for the public to contribute to policy making via the Internet" proved to be the most popular, followed by "Internet voting." In addition, when asked to select from a range of policy goals for government, "more public involvement in policy making via the Internet" proved to be the top priority the government should concentrate on achieving.

In this context, this research evaluates the current status of digital deliberation in the local governments of Seoul Metropolitan area in Korea. In order to do that, this study, first, reviews literatures on digital democracy and develops a Web site evaluation framework of digital deliberative democracy. Then, based on the framework, this study evaluates the current practices in digital deliberative democracy of 25 administrative districts in the City of Seoul. Finally, this research explores some policy recommendations to improve digital deliberative democracy.

Digital Deliberative Democracy

Basically, democracy is a form of government in which citizens have some influence over the policies that affect their lives. That is, in terms of democracy, the relationship between government and citizens is the main issue. In digital democracy,[1] therefore, the focus is on the processes and structures that define the relationship between governments and citizens, between the elected officials and the appointed civil servants, and between the legislative and executive branches of government.

According to Hacker and van Dijk (2000, p. 1), digital democracy refers to "a collection of attempts to practice democracy without the limits of time, space, and other physical conditions, using ICTs or computer-mediated communication instead, as an addition, not a replacement, for traditional 'analogue' political practices." In addition, digital democracy refers to "processes carried out online–communicating with fellow citizens and elected representatives about politics" (Nugent, 2001, p. 223). Simply, digital democracy could be defined as all practices to improve democratic values using ICTs. Specifically, digital democracy includes such democratic governance issues as government openness, active citizen participation, and digital voting.

Government should be open to citizens. As a result, citizens' access to government information and knowledge can be improved. If citizens have been well informed, they can play an active role with more responsibility within the sphere of governance. Government openness, therefore, is basic to digital democracy.

Citizens can make their voices heard with well-informed information via active participation in the policy making process. Since citizens should have influence over policies in a democratic system, citizens can make their voices more prominent by sending e-mails to elected officials as well as debating social issues in virtual conference settings.

Finally, digital voting is a more advanced tool to improve digital democracy. In the digital voting experiment of the Arizona Democratic Party in 2000, 86,907 persons voted, as compared to only 36,072 in 1992 and 12,844 in 1996; this indicates that the overall turnout rate improved to 10.56% from 4.3% in 1992 and 1.46% in 1996 (LeBlanc & Wilhelm, 2000). Of course, many problems still need to be solved to implement widespread digital voting.

Digital democracy can be categorized into three perspectives such as plebiscitary model, deliberative model, and pluralist model. According to the plebiscitary model, since ICTs allow citizens to easily access government information and communicate their opinions to public officials (Becker, 2001), ICTs empower citizens to directly make a decision through such mechanisms as digital voting and digital opinion polls (Abrahamson, Arterton & Orren, 1988; van Dijk, 2000) Also, the deliberative model focuses on the role of ICTs in developing deliberations among the public (Behrouzi, 2005; London, 1995), for instance, the electronic Townhall (Abrahamson, Arterton & Orren, 1988), digital forums (Tsagarousianou et al., 1998), and virtual community (Klein, 1999; Rheingold, 2000). In addition, the pluralist model underscores ICT's potential to foster interactive links between citizens and such institutions as political parties, interest groups, and NGOs (Bimber, 2003; Norris, 2001).

Basically, digital democracy gives "ignored" groups throughout the civil society a greater voice. As a result, the democratic deficit, which is the participatory gap in public policy making, can be narrowed. Digital democracy using ICTs has been applied in a number of cities in the United States and Europe (Tsagarousianou et al., 1998).

In order to allow more citizens to participate in a policy discourse of deliberative governance, ICTs can create opportunities both for receiving important information and for participating in discussions. ICTs can improve contact at other political levels between citizens and decision makers. It is important to look for methods for using ICTs in order to publicize views presented by consultative parties and increase the opportunities for citizens to have insight in, and opportunities to influence bases for decisions. As a result, ICTs can offer the means to help educate voters on issues, to facilitate discussion of important decisions, to register instantaneous polls and even to allow people to vote directly on public policy.

As discussed, digital citizen-government interaction leads to well-informed citizens. For instance, based on the quasiexperiment of a deliberative poll, Iyengar, Luskin, and Fishkin (2003) found that participants in digital deliberation became better informed. According to them, participants in digital deliberation became significantly better informed in three of the nine questions, indicating that the average increase in knowledge among participants in digital deliberation was 4%. Also, they showed significant differences between control and

Figure 2. Stages of digital deliberative democracy

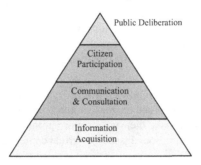

treatment groups after digital deliberation, indicating that participants in digital deliberation became better informed in five of nine questions.

In this context, public space on the Web where people can debate policy issues is needed. Digital deliberation is characterized by (1) access to balanced information, (2) an open agenda, (3) time to consider issues expansively, (4) freedom from manipulation or coercion, (5) a rule-based framework for discussion, (6) participation by an inclusive sample of citizens, (7) scope for free interaction between participants, and (8) recognition of differences between participants, but rejection of status-based prejudice (Coleman & Gøtze, n.d.).

Based on the discussions on digital deliberative democracy, this study identifies four stages of digital deliberative democracy, from the lowest level, (1) information acquisition, (2) communication and consultation, (3) citizen participation, and (4) public deliberation, as can be seen in Figure 2. Based on this development of digital democracy, this study develops the Web site evaluation framework of digital deliberative democracy and evaluates current practices of digital deliberative democracy in administrative districts in the City of Seoul.

Research Design

Based on literature reviews on digital democracy, this study focuses on the evaluation of the current practices in digital deliberative democracy. In order to evaluate the current practices in digital deliberative democracy, this study first develops a Web site evaluation framework of digital deliberative democracy, and evaluates the current practices of digital deliberative democracy in 25 administrative districts in the City of Seoul, Korea.

Based on the four stages of digital deliberative democracy discussed earlier, this study develops a Web site evaluation framework of digital deliberative democracy in Table 1. In order to evaluate the current practice, each stage of digital deliberative democracy includes some measurements.

With regard to the first stage of digital deliberative democracy, information acquisition is closely related with read-only Web sites. In this stage, citizens can get information on poli-

Table 1. Web sites evaluation framework of digital democracy

Stages of Digital Democracy	Measurement
4th Stage: Public Deliberation	• Electronic Town Hall Meeting • Policy Forum • Online Voting with Deliberation • The Number of Participants • Involvement of Public Servants • Background Information on Policy Issues
3rd Stage: Citizen Participation	• Online Poll (Instant Results, Presentation of Previous Polls) • Bulletin Board for Complaints • Bulletin Board for Recommendations
2nd Stage: Communication and Consultation	• E-Mail Communication between Citizens and Officials • Operation of Q & A such as Speed of Answering Questions • E-mail Lists
1st Stage: Information Acquisition	• Information Portal Sites • Various Means of Requesting Information • Information Search Method • Notice of Information Openness • Links to Related Web Sites • Level of Policy Information (White Paper, Publications, etc.) • Quality of Information related with policy issues • FAQ

cies and operations of government. Also, links to other relevant information on the Internet is provided by read-only Web sites.

In terms of the second stage of digital democracy, communication and consultation is two-way communication between citizens and public servants only one time, at best twice. It includes e-mail communication between citizens and public servants through question and answer interaction. In addition, citizens subscribe to free e-mail lists for up-to-the-minute local government news and information.

With respect to the third stage, citizens can participate in the decision-making process. The difference between citizen participation (3rd stage) and public deliberation (4th stage), however, is determined by whether participants are in policy-making positions or not. The stage of citizen participation, therefore, includes online poll and bulletin board for complaints and recommendations.

The final stage of digital deliberative democracy is public deliberation. This stage includes the electronic town hall meeting, policy forums, online voting with deliberation, and background information on policy issues. In this stage, the role of both public servants and professionals is a key element. In addition, while policy deliberation among citizens only is closely related to the cybercommunity, the true meaning of public deliberation includes participation by all, such as citizens, politicians, bureaucrats, interest groups, and media.

An analysis of the Web sites of 25 administrative districts in the City of Seoul, Korea, was performed between July 1 and 5, 2005. Administrative districts in Seoul execute both autonomous administrative functions and those delegated by the city as a self-governing local administrative unit.

Analysis and Results

Table 2 shows the results of Web site evaluation of digital deliberative democracy in 25 administrative districts in the City of Seoul.

With regard to the first stage of digital deliberative democracy, information acquisition, administrative district O is the highest, while K and N are the lowest. Administrative district O has improved almost every element at this stage. It has provided citizens with sufficient information with some links. In addition, administrative districts X, D, A, C, E, and G are followed by O. Administrative districts F, K, and N, however, have not offered documents, reports, or books (publications) online. In addition, they have not used wireless technology such as messages to a mobile phone, a Palm Pilot, or a PDA (Personal Digital Assistance) to update applications and events.

In terms of the second stage of digital deliberative democracy, communication, and consultation, all 25 administrative districts performed relatively well compared to the first stage. Administrative district M, the highest in this second stage, has developed all elements of this stage, for example, allowing citizens to file complaints online. Administrative districts O, W, U, A, and Q are followed by M but there is a gap between the highest and the next group. Administrative districts D, E, G, and R are in the lowest group in this stage. Citizens in these administrative districts have difficulties communicating with public servants through the Internet and getting consultations with public servants through the Internet. In contrast, citizens in administrative districts M, O, W, and U can easily communicate with public servants through the Web and e-mail, and public servants in three administrative districts are likely to try to answer all questions from citizens.

With respect to the third stage of digital deliberative democracy, citizen participation, the results show that administrative districts A and Q have good citizen participation practice on their Web sites, while almost half have never provided the components of this third stage. The results show that 11 administrative districts have conducted and managed online polls including instant results and presentation of previous polls. Although more than half of the administrative districts have poor online poll service during the evaluation period, administrative district A has good practice in managing both online polls and a bulletin board for complaints and recommendations. On the bulletin board at its Web site, there is good interactivity between citizens and public servants.

Finally, all administrative districts except D, B, and G in this study have shown low performance in the final stage of digital deliberative democracy, public deliberation. As discussed earlier, deliberative processes are comprised of discussion and consideration by a group of persons who are for or against a measure. Also, citizens consult with others in a process of reaching a decision. As to the policy deliberation, even though administrative district A has a relatively low score in this stage, citizens in this administrative district have actively

Table 2. Results of Web sites evaluation framework of digital deliberative democracy

Administrative Districts	1st Stage	2nd Stage	3rd Stage	4th Stage	Score	Rank
A	69.23	80.00	22.22	17.65	189.10	3
B	50.00	66.67	11.11	41.18	168.96	7
C	69.23	60.00	16.67	5.88	151.78	11
D	73.08	53.33	16.67	52.94	196.02	2
E	61.54	53.33	0.00	29.41	144.28	12
F	38.46	60.00	11.11	5.88	115.45	23
G	61.54	53.33	0.00	41.18	156.05	10
H	57.69	60.00	11.11	0.00	128.80	17
I	46.15	60.00	11.11	5.88	123.14	20
J	50.00	60.00	11.11	5.88	126.99	18
K	30.77	60.00	0.00	5.88	96.65	25
L	42.31	60.00	11.11	5.88	119.30	21
M	50.00	100	0.00	17.65	167.65	9
N	30.77	73.33	0.00	11.76	115.86	22
O	88.46	86.67	0.00	23.53	198.66	1
P	57.69	66.67	0.00	11.76	136.12	16
Q	57.69	80.00	22.22	23.53	183.44	4
R	50.00	53.33	0.00	5.88	109.21	24
S	57.69	73.33	16.67	35.29	182.98	5
T	53.85	73.33	11.11	5.88	144.17	13
U	46.15	86.67	0.00	5.88	138.70	15
V	46.15	66.67	0.00	11.76	124.58	19
W	53.85	86.67	11.11	23.53	175.16	6
X	73.08	60.00	0.00	35.29	168.37	8
Y	46.15	60.00	11.11	23.53	140.79	14

participated in policy deliberation with online voting. After expressing their thoughts in the discussion, citizens can express whether they support the idea or not.

The results of this study are expressed in graph as shown in Figure 3. As can be seen in Figure 3, with regard to the information acquisition, the average of 25 administrative districts is 54.46 out of 100. In terms of communication and consultation, the results of this study show that the average is 67.73, indicating that most administrative districts have performed well. In addition, with respect to the third stage, citizen participation, the average score is 7.78. The public deliberation average score is 18.12. Though a few administrative districts have performed well, most administrative districts have room for improving both the third and the fourth stages of digital deliberative democracy compared to both the first and the second stages.

Figure 3. Results of Web sites evaluation of digital deliberative democracy in administrative districts

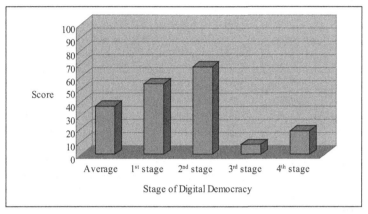

Based on the results, this study calculates the level of digital deliberative democracy of 25 administrative districts in the City of Seoul. Administrative districts *O* and *D* are at the highest level of digital deliberative democracy among 25 administrative districts, while administrative district *K* has poor performance in the practice of digital deliberative democracy. Administrative districts *A*, *Q*, and *S* are in the second group followed by administrative districts *O* and *D*. Administrative districts *A* and *D*, however, have developed and conducted very well balanced practices in digital deliberative democracy based on the evaluation considering all four stages of digital deliberative democracy. Public deliberation on the Web sites of administrative districts *A* and *D* could signal the best practice in digital deliberative democracy and other administrative districts in the City of Seoul can benchmark them as models.

Socioeconomic Factors on Improving Digital Deliberative Democracy

Several factors have an effect on improving digital governance. Some scholars (Heeks, 1999) categorized these factors into 4 groups such as (1) institutional (e.g., political environment and support, business influence, and intergovernment relationships); social (e.g., digital divide and citizen participation); organizational (e.g., leadership, resources, and strategy); and technical factors (e.g., interoperability and privacy and security). These factors are also important in improving digital deliberative democracy. Here, based on the evaluation of digital deliberative democracy in administrative districts in the Seoul Metropolitan Government, the relationship between socioeconomic factors and digital deliberative democracy is analyzed.

Though there is no relationship between the population of an administrative district and the level of digital deliberative democracy, the results show that there is a close relationship between the area of an administrative district and the level of digital deliberative democracy as can be seen in Figure 4. The correlation coefficient between two is 0.440 and it is statistically significant at the level of 0.05.

In addition, as Figure 5 shows, there is a strong relationship between financial independence and the level of digital deliberative democracy. The correlation coefficient between the two is 0.514 and it is statistically significant at the level of 0.05. Moreover, the budget size of an administrative district is related to the level of digital deliberative democracy, even though the correlation coefficient (0.331) is statistically insignificant at the level of 0.05.

Conclusion

Digital deliberation provides citizens with participation in the policy process (Holzer, Melitski, Rho & Schwester, 2004, p. 28). It is useful to citizens and public servants. Personnel can save time, cost, and paperwork. To improve democratic governance, many governments have developed a digital deliberation framework and it is meaningful to evaluate the current status of this practice.

In the Information Age, based on the assumption that ICTs can facilitate digital deliberation beyond direct interactivity between citizens and government, this study seeks to develop the Web site evaluation framework of digital deliberative democracy and conduct the evaluation of current practices of digital deliberative democracy in 25 administrative districts in the Seoul Metropolitan Government.

Figure 4. Relationship between area and level of digital deliberative democracy

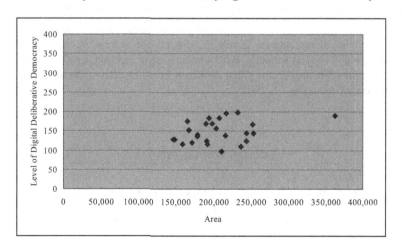

Figure 5. Relationship between financial independence and level of digital deliberative democracy

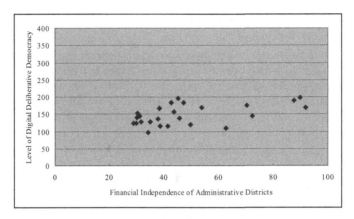

The results of this study show that a few administrative districts have performed good practices in digital deliberative democracy. Though it could be said that many administrative districts have performed good practices of information acquisition (1st stage), communication and consultation (2nd stage), and citizen participation (3rd stage), public deliberation (4th stage) is not fully performed in the Web sites of the administrative districts.

Though the practice of some administrative districts (B, D, and G) could be an example of benchmarking in terms of public deliberation, it also should improve some functions or characteristics of deliberation on their Web sites. One of the basic characteristics of deliberation is consultation. Since citizens sometimes have little awareness of the specific topic, the professional role of consultation is very important for public deliberation. The results of this study show the lack of professional consultation during the deliberative process on the Web sites of administrative districts in the Seoul Metropolitan Government.

Finally, ICTs have an important role in improving digital democracy; however, they are not a panacea. More important factors in developing digital deliberative democracy are the will of citizens as well as public servants. Without changing perceptions and behaviors, fully developed digital deliberative democracy could not be achieved by only information and communication technologies.

Acknowledgment

The author would like to thank Bo-Eun Kim and Yun-Hee Do from Seoul Women's University for help in gathering the data on the activities of digital deliberation in Korea.

References

Abrahamson, J. B., Arterton, F. C., & Orren, G. R. (1988). *The electronic commonwealth: The impact of new media technologies on democratic politics*. New York: Basic Books.

Baldassare, M. (2000). *California in the new millennium: The changing social and political landscape*. Berkeley: University of California Press.

Becker, T. (2001). Rating the impact of new technologies on democracy. *Communication of the ACM, 44*(1), 39-43.

Berman, E. M. (1997). Dealing with cynical citizens. *Public Administration Review, 57*(2), 105-112.

Behrouzi, M. (2005). *Democracy as the political empowerment of the citizen: Direct-deliberative e-democracy*. Lanham: Lexington Books.

Bimber, B. (2003). *Information and American democracy: Technology in the evolution of political power*. Cambridge: Cambridge University Press.

Browning, G. (2002). *Electronic democracy: Using the Internet to transform American politics*. Medford: CyberAge Books.

Christopher, A. (1987). *Teledemocracy: Can technology protect democracy?* Newbury Park: Sage Publications

Coleman, S., & Gotze, J. (n.d.). *Bowling together: Online public engagement in policy deliberation*. Retrieved May 9, 2006, from http://bowlingtogether.net/bowlingtogether.pdf

Coleman and Gøtze. (n.d.). Retrieved November 23, 2002, from http://www.hansard-society.org.uk/bowling.pdf

Cross, B. (1998). Teledemocracy: Canadian political parties listening to their constituents. In C. J. Alexander & L. A. Pal (Eds.), *Digital democracy: Policy and politics in the wired world* (pp. 132-148). Oxford: Oxford University Press.

Deibert, R. J. (1997). *Parchment, printing, and hypermedia: Communication in world order transformation*. New York: Columbia University Press.

van Dijk, J. (2000). Models of democracy and concepts of communication. In K. L. Hacker & J. van Dijk (Eds.), *Digital democracy: Issues of theory and practice* (pp. 30-53). Thousand Oaks, CA: Sage Publications.

Erber, R., & Lau, R. R. (1990). Political cynicism revisited: An information processing reconciliation of policy-based and incumbency-based interpretations of changes in trust in government. *American Journal of Political Science, 34*(1), 236-253.

Fountain, J. E. (2001). *Building the virtual state: Information technology and institutional change*. Washington, DC: Brookings Institution Press.

Frissen, P. H. A. (1999). *Politics, governance, and technology: A postmodern narrative on the virtual state*. Cheltenham, UK: Edward Elgar.

Gore, A. (1994). The new job of the federal executive. *Public Administration Review, 54*(4), 317-321.

Hacker, K. L., & van Dijk, J. (2000). What is digital democracy? In K. L. Hacker & J. van Dijk (Eds.), *Digital democracy: Issues of theory and practice* (pp. 1-9). Thousand Oaks, CA: Sage Publications.

Heeks, R. (1999). *Reinventing government in the Information Age: International practice in IT-enabled public sector reform.* London: Routledge.

Holzer, M., Melitski, J., Rho. S., & Schwester, R. (2004). *Restoring trust in government: The potential of digital citizen participation.* Washington, DC: IBM Center for the Business of Government.

Iyengar, S., Luskin., R. C., & Fishkin, J. S. (2003). *Facilitating informed public opinion: Evidence from face-to-face and online deliberative polls.* Retrieved May 9, 2006, from http://cyberlaw.stanford.edu/events/archives/DeliberativePolling.doc

Jankowski, N. W., & van Selm, M. (2000). The promise and practice of public debate in cyberspace. In K. L. Hacker & J. van Dijk (Eds.), *Digital democracy: Issues of theory and practice* (pp. 149-165). Thousand Oaks, CA: Sage Publications.

Klein, H. K. (1999). Tocqueville in cyberspace: Using the Internet for citizen associations. *The Information Society, 15,* 213-220.

LeBlanc, J., & Wilhelm, A. (2000). Arizona "ahead of its time" in online voting? *The Digital Beat, 2*(27). Retrieved May 9, 2006, from http://www.benton.org/Digital-Beat/db033000.html

Lipset, S. M., & Schneider, W. (1983). *The confidence gap: Business, labor, and government in the public mind.* New York: Free Press.

Loader, B. D. (Ed.). (1997). *The governance of cyberspace.* London: Routledge.

London, S. (1995). Teledemocracy vs. deliberative democracy: A comparative look at two models of public talk. *Journal of Interpersonal Computing and Technology, 3*(2), 33-55.

Miller, A. H. (1974). Political issues and trust in government: 1964-1970. *American Political Science Review, 64*(3), 18-34.

Norris, P. (Ed.). (1999). *Critical citizens: Global support for democratic government.* Cambridge: Oxford University Press.

Norris, P. (2001). *Digital divide: Civic engagement, information poverty, and the Internet worldwide.* Cambridge: Cambridge University Press.

Nugent, J. D. (2001). If e-democracy is the answer, what's the question? *National Civic Review, 90*(3), 221-223.

Nye, J. S., Jr. (1997). Introduction: The decline of confidence in government. In J. S. Nye, Jr., P. D. Zelikow, & D. C. King (Eds.), *Why people don't trust in government.* Cambridge, MA: Harvard University Press.

Ogden, M. R. (1998). Technologies of abstraction: Cyberdemocracy and the changing communications landscape. In C. J. Alexander & L. A. Pal, *Digital democracy: Policy and politics in the wired world* (pp. 63-86). Oxford: Oxford University Press.

Rheingold, H. (2000). *The virtual community: Homesteading in the electronic frontier.* Cambridge, MA: The MIT Press.

Rosenthal, A. (1997). *The decline of representative democracy.* Washington, DC: CQ Press.

Tsagarousianou, R., Tambini, D., & Bryan, C. (1998). *Cyberdemocracy: Technology, cities, and civic networks.* London: Routledge.

Watson, R. T., Akselsen, S., Evjemo, B., & Aarsaether, N. (1999). Teledemocracy in local government. *Communications of the ACM, 42*(12), 58-63.

Endnote

[1]   The term, "digital democracy," is used instead of "electronic democracy" (Browning, 2002), "cyberdemocracy" (Ogden, 1998; Tsagarousianou, Tambini & Bryan, 1998) and "teledemocracy" (Christopher, 1987; Cross, 1998; Watson, Akselsen, Evjemo & Aarsaether. 1999), since digital democracy is more appropriate than others to explain the use of ICTs in the practice of democracy. Jankowski and van Selm (2000) indicated that while teledemocracy is more related with such types of democracy as electronic polling and voting, digital democracy is more generally accepted to include activities related with the democratic process.

Chapter XIII

The Development of Urban E-Government in China

Zi Lu, Hebei Teacher's University, China

Jing Zhang, Hebei Teacher's University, China

Bing Han, Hebei Teacher's University, China

Zhuopeng Deng, Hebei Teacher's University, China

Jie Lu, University of Technology, Sydney (UTS), Australia

Abstract

The chapter assesses and cognizes the development of urban e-government in China from two main aspects: functionality and complexity. To functionality, nine Web sites of urban governments in China at three levels were selected for this assessment. Data needed for the study were tracked and recorded continuously for six weeks from these Web sites. The influence of e-government to urban modality and evolution is explored. Result shows that e-government has a leading role to the gathering and decentralization of urban space, the organization of material (people) flows, and the informal exchange in internal cities.

Introduction

Electronic government (e-government), an Internet based system of information service and information process, deals with internal government bodies, other government bodies, the businesses and the public (Cheng, 2000). E-government, turning grade management structure into network management structure, is fit for the virtual, global, knowledge-based digital economy and the human-based notion of social running. E-government has also broken down the barriers of distance and time, and therefore offers the potential to enhance the quality of government services (OECD, 2001). E-government services not only provide benefits to citizens and businesses but also offer opportunities to reshape public sectors. It has even reorganized relationships between citizens, businesses, and governments (West, 2002). E-government is a symbol, which has been used for demonstrating the development level of a government's informatization for a long time (West, 2001). The construction of e-government involves software development, hardware platform, management and service model, and in particular the construction of government's Web sites (Nian & Yao, 2002). The functionality of an urban government's Web sites reflects the development level of its e-government. This chapter demonstrates the functionality of urban e-government in China by evaluating the construction of Web sites for nine urban governments.

E-government was launched in China in 1999. On January 22, 1999, Government Online Project, initiated by China Telecom, State Economic and Trade Commission and the other 40 departments, committees, offices, bureaus, was formally started (Zhang & Gu, 2002). Then, the main Web site of the Government Online Project (http://www.gov.vninfo.net/) and the guiding Web site (http://www.gov.cn) were formally published. This is the landmark that e-government in China is from planning stage to overall implementation stage. Till now, there are thousands of government and related Web sites with the ending "gov.cn" in their URLs. The whole development process of e-government in China can be divided into three main phases. The first phase is online information presentation and consultation services. Government information and services deliver to citizens and businesses through the Internet at this phase. Furthermore, by adding simple functionalities, such as e-mail and chat rooms, two-way communication is also supported. Most urban e-government Web sites in China are currently in this phase. The second phase is transaction-oriented online services. More and more users use government transaction systems by linking with commercial transaction systems in this stage, such as online taxation and online business registration. The government Web sites of large cities have developed relatively well in this function while small-medium cities are poor. The third phase is integrated online services. The integrated online services refer to functions and services produced by different department governments, which are integrated into a unified government Web site to provide "one-stop service." Most urban government Web sites in China are being developed towards this direction.

"The Evaluation Report of Urban Government Web sites in China," which is released by the research center of PC World, has published evaluation results of local government Web sites in China. The report has also explored the future development of urban government Web sites (Yao, Zhu, & Chen, 2001). However, this report only involves the Web sites of 36 major cities in China. Medium and minor cities such as prefectural cities have not been considered in the report. It will be beneficial to obtain an overall cognition of the functions of urban government Web sites by evaluating urban government Web sites at different levels of cities in China as the majority of the cities in China are medium and small cities. This chapter compares and evaluates the urban government Web sites at three levels: municipalities directly ruled by the central government, provincial capitals, and prefectural cities, and penetrate the functionality of the urban e-government Web sites at the three levels. The research has the following four meanings: (1) urban e-government is a typical part of the whole e-government system, so this research can provide other countries a clear cognition about the development of e-government in China; (2) In "The Evaluation Report of Urban Government Web sites in China," the research object is limited and the selected cities are not systematic, so this study intends to set up a new three-class evaluation system of urban e-government. It will supply a gap of e-government research; (3) Urban e-government of China is influencing society development, economy operation, and space modality through its functionality. So it is necessary to provide an assessment methodology of China urban e-government. This chapter made a valuable attempt, and good results were obtained; (4) This chapter explores the impact of urban e-government development to urban space modality from the angle of spatial economy, which enriches the content of urban economics greatly.

Following the introduction, the next section reviews the relevant research about urban e-government in five aspects. Also, the problems in existing research are pointed out. In the third section, the main body of the chapter, empirical research is conducted pertaining to urban e-government functionality. Furthermore, an explicit analysis is given. Urban e-government plays a promotive role in the transformation of urban function, modality, and public communication. The fourth section introduces an evolution model of urban e-government. In addition, future trends of urban e-government in China are discussed. In last section, conclusions are drawn.

Background

The construction of urban e-government functionality is the process in which urban governments use network and information technologies to deliver government information and to integrate government business. It offers a high-efficient, excellent, standard, and transparent service. The functionality research of urban e-government is to help government enhance management efficiency, realize the reorganization, and optimize organizational structure and procedure. It will explore how to clearly describe the dynamic role of urban e-government in urban development. This section reviews literature from both international researchers and China domestic scholars respectively, and penetrates some existing problems in the research area.

Researchers have made a lot of efforts on urban e-government functionality in recent years. Literature from international researchers shows that the research of urban e-government functionality has become mature in some developed countries. Five main research aspects are listed and analyzed here.

In the area of service function about urban e-government, Bellamy and Taylor (1998) conduct research on how to apply e-government functions to reset the administrative procedure. Wimmer and Tambouris (2002) further point out that the most important connotation of e-government functionality is to break the department partition management system inside administrative organs. Macintosh (2002) clearly puts forward that the service function of urban e-government is linking up the transformation of government function with the rapid development of urban e-government. They all consider e-government as a significant means for government innovation in knowledge-economic society.

In the area of sustainable development of urban e-government, Forman (2002) states that the demand of e-commerce development helps the development of e-government and e-government has also promoted effects on e-commerce development. These strengthened relationships are due to the close relationships of government and enterprise in the Information Age. Westholm (2003) proposes that enhancing the adaptability of e-government is addressed to elevate the vitality and extend the survival cycle of e-government, aiming at government organization reform.

Some researchers have explored the impact of e-government on spatial structure. For example, Moon (2002) discusses the significance of new characteristics of urban spatial evolution is to enlarge the freedom of location choice, to organize people flow with high efficiency, and to change citizens' lifestyles.

In the research on e-government model, Westholm and Aichholzer (2003) analyzes the weakness of the traditional management model and brings forth a careful and attentive e-government management model. This new model can enhance management, reduce cost, and improve management efficiency by advanced network technology.

In the research area of e-government development motivation and key function, West (2003) reveals that the motivation of e-government is to implement all administrative management and daily affairs online by fixed procedure. Desai and Bertucci (2003) impel the research of key functions of urban e-government to a new management system, which transforms the running state of urban government.

With the successful implementation of Government Online Project in China, a lot of research has been conducted by China domestic scholars from the five areas as well.

The Research on Service Function of Urban E-Government

In the field of e-government service function, the development trend is towards the service-dominated type. The development of urban e-government in China keeps pace with this trend. At first, China domestic scholars start with the management functions, pertaining to the functionality research of urban e-government. Yin and Wang (2002) analyze the advantages of e-government in management functions compared with traditional government from the viewpoint of costs. Based on the e-government management solutions in developed countries, a set of urban e-government management solutions in China have been put forward (Xu & Wei, 2004). In the urban e-government function construction in China, the new characteristics in application level and the transformation from administration to service in government function have been taken on. Using the potential of e-government, urban government is realizing the transformation of government function.

The Research on Sustainable
Development of Urban E-Government

The efficiency of e-government function is the base of urban economic competition. Thus, the research of urban e-government functionality combined with urban development is another hot topic. First, the participation of governments and businesses is strengthened. Urban e-government possesses the double identity as suppliers and providers of IST services. Many businesses participate and seek needed services delivered by urban e-government. Second, the traditional industries are reformed. The construction of e-government functionality upgrades traditional industries, develops new urban service industries, and thus enhances comprehensive competency.

The Research on the Impact of
Urban E-Government on Spatial Structure

Urban e-government is a new research area of urban spatial evolution. Some domestic Chinese scholars conduct research on urban spatial modality from the view of urban e-government. A superinfrastructure raised by Bakis and Lu (2001) has been proved to be true. Also, a strategic role should be considered in urban management and thus help to build other urban networks. Lv, Zhou, and Wang (2004) analyze the influences of urban e-government on urban planning, urban construction, urban adjustment, and urban forecast. This study has pointed out that the process of urban spatial transformation would accelerate. Also, urban e-government has also accelerated the process of urban spatial evolution. Urban spatial evolution has new trends and characteristics, as the effect of urban e-government. The evolution changes the external expansion to internal structure extension. The evolution tends to reorganize and adjust the urban internal structure. Deng (2005) finds that urban e-government urges urban regions to span more widely and add potential expansion ability. There are several expansion models such as gradual expansion, jumping expansion, co-adjacent expansion, and vertical expansion.

The Research on Model of Urban E-government

In the research of urban e-government functionality, more and more scholars have studied various models for urban e-government functionality. For example, Wang and Li (2001) put forward a general e-government system model, which aims to establish a basic framework of e-government. The framework elaborates the functional structure of what a perfect government should possess. Liu (2001) proposes a logical model of secure e-government, in which the intelligent credence and authorization is addressed. Business reference model (BRM) and performance reference model (PRM) are analyzed by using the object-oriented analysis. Component reference models (CRM), technical reference model (TRM) and data reference model (DRM) have also been analyzed at the technical layer (Kong & Su, 2003).

The Research on Development Motivation and Key Function of Urban E-Government

Referring to the development motivation of e-government functionality in China, most dominant scholars orient it toward the government-dominated demand. Government is the owner of maximum information resources in China and its e-government functionality has a large demand on government informatization (Zhang, 2004). The key functions of urban e-government are as followings: manage the information resources; refine the information of each government department into unified data; and conduct unified management (Zhang, 2003).

Main Problems in the Research of Urban E-Government in China

The research in urban e-government functionality has obtained good progress in China. However, there are still some problems that need to be solved. First, large cities, like Beijing and Shanghai, have received high attentions and are often selected as samples in the research of urban e-government functionality. However, cities in the middle-west region and small-medium cities have received less attention from researchers. Second, government has three levels of management systems in China and therefore e-government developed with three levels as well. However, there is a lack of research on cross-levels analysis for e-government development in China. The third, comparing with international researchers, much research and many projects conducted in China need to improve in their methodology and research foci. Some researchers still stay in the early stage of urban e-government functionality development and study. They may only focus on static data while not tracking dynamic data. Social issues related to e-government development are less analyzed. This study therefore focuses on the development of e-government in small-medium cities, explores the e-government service delivery across three levels of government agencies, and uses static and dynamic data.

Main Thrust of the Chapter

This section first presents nine Web sites of urban governments selected from three levels: municipalities directly ruled by the central government, provincial capitals, and prefectural cities. It then shows an assessment result about the function degree and complexity degree of urban e-government and the characteristics of content service and function service of urban e-government at different levels. Finally, the influence of e-government on urban evolution and modality is analyzed from two aspects. One is that e-government accelerates the tendency of the coexistence of urban gathering and decentralization, and the other is the effects of e-government on urban spatial evolution and communication behavior.

A Comparison on the Functionality of Urban E-Government at Three Levels

Evaluation Target and Index

Nine cities were selected from three levels in China: Beijing (http://www.beijing.gov.cn/), Shanghai (http://www.sh.gov.cn/), and Guangzhou (http://www.gz.gov.cn/). These three cities scored among 7.0-7.9 (good, outstanding not available). They were selected to represent the most developed cities of urban e-government in China. Hangzhou (http://www.hangzhou.gov.cn/) scored among 6.0-6.9 (pass), is chosen to be the second level as a normal city. Tianjin (http://www.tj.gov.cn/) and Shijiazhuang (http://www.sjz.gov.cn/) scored under 5.9 (fail) as the relatively low level city. In order to have a complete evaluation of the government Web sites, prefectural cities including Nanhai (http://www.nanhai.gov.cn/), Anguo (http://www.anguo.gov.cn/), and Linan (http://www.linan.gov.cn), were also chosen.

Table 1. The evaluation system of urban government Web sites

Grade	Index				
First-class	A Index of Web sites' contents		B Index of Web sites' functions		
Second-class	A.1 government affairs open to public	A.2 city overview	B.1 handle official business online	B.2 online supervision	B.3 public feedback
Third-class	A.1.1 government bulletin		B.1.1 navigation services		B.3.1 government mailbox
	A.1.2 policy and statute		B.1.2 online consultation		B.3.2 online investigate
	A.1.3 government news		B.1.3 online search		B.3.3 communication forum
	A.1.4constitution structure and duty		B.1.4 online declaration		
	A.1.5 daily affair procedure		B.1.5 online examination and approval		
			B.1.6 online government purchasing		
			B.1.7 relevant organization linking		

Table 2. The evaluation criterions of the urban government Web sites of the nine cities with different level

Item	Criterion
1. Government bulletin	Emphasis on integrality and effectiveness. The excellent contains latest information more than half a year. The less and outdated information, the worse.
2. Policy and statute	Emphasis on completeness and practicality. The excellent contains current laws and regulations of state and has links for countries and provinces regulations. The more insufficient and impractical the worse.
3. Administrative news	Emphasis on timing and trends. The excellent reflects the urban development timely. The less and outdated information the worse.
4. Constitution setup and its duty	Emphasis on integrity and service. The excellent have setup introduction, duty descriptions, staffs and contacts. The more impractical the worse.
5. Daily affair procedure	The excellent Contains daily affair process of each department in detailed and it is practical. The more difficult to follow the worse.
6. City overview	The excellent Contains the introduction of local conditions, the content is adequate and the data is precise. The worse is inadequate.
7. Navigation services	The excellent contains websites navigation. The navigation page contains complete links and is categorized properly. The worse are on the contrary.
8. Online consultation	The excellent provides the consultation for social affairs and gives a timely feedback. The slower feedback the worse.
9. Online searching	The excellent provides inquire services of related departments or related affairs. The worse is lack of inquiring services.
10. Online declaration	The excellent Provides online declaration with clear classification. It can be used conveniently and can be handled timely. The worse are on the contrary.
11. Online examination and approval	The excellent Provides examination and approval information clearly and extensively. The results can be accepted online and tracked on schedule.
12. Government online purchasing	The excellent provides the information of products and suppliers clearly and completely.
13. Relevant organization Linking	The excellent provides the links of related constitution with wide range, clear classification. The worse is on the contrary.
14. Online supervision	The excellent contains valid phone number and mailbox for supervision. The worse has not.
15. Government mailbox	The excellent contains available government mailbox, which gives a quick feedback and handled the letters timely. The worse is on the contrary.
16. Online investigation	The excellent investigated the hot social issues and reflects the investigation results. The worse is on the contrary.
17. Communication forum	The excellent has the communication forum with high practical and high visiting rate. The worse is on the contrary.

Table 3. A comparison in contents and functions of nine selected urban government Web sites at different levels

Evaluation criterion			City								
First class	Second class	Third class	A			B			C		
			A1	A2	A3	B1	B2	B3	C1	C2	C3
I	1	Government bulletin	+++	+++	+++	+	++	++	+++	−	−
		Policy and statute	+++	++	++	+	++	+	+	−	− −
		Government news	++	+++	++	+	++	+++	+	−	−
		Constitution setting up and its duty	++	+++	++	++	+++	++	+	+	+
		Rules of handling affairs	++	+++	++	+	++	++	+	−	−
		Local general scanning	+++	+++	+	+	++	++	+	−	− −
II	2	Navigating services	+++	+++	+	+	++	+++	+	− −	+
		Online consulting	− −	+++	+	− −	+++	+	+	− −	− −
		Online searching	+++	+++	+	− −	+	+++	− −	− −	− −
		Online declaring	++	+++	++	+	+	+	− −	− −	− −
		Online examining and approving	+++	+++	++	− −	+	++	− −	−	− −
		Online government purchasing	+++	+++	+++	− −	− −	+++	++	− −	− −
		Relevant organization linking	+++	+++	+++	+++	+++	+++	−	−	−
		Online supervising	+++	+++	+++	− −	+	+	+	− −	− −
	3	Government mailbox	++	+++	+++	− −	+	++	+	− −	−
		Online investigating	++	+++	− −	++	++	++	− −	− −	− −
		Communication forum	++	++	++	+++	+++	+	− −	++	− −

Considering the evaluation index system in "The Evaluation Report of Urban Government Web sites in China," 2 kinds of first-class indexes, 5 kinds of second-class indexes, and 15 kinds of third-class indexes (shown in Table 1) are created as the standard of the evaluation system. According to the given evaluation system, the evaluation group scanned the nine urban government Web sites at different levels layer by layer. 17 evaluation criterion based on contents and functions were set (shown in Table 2).

Table 4. Some explanations about Table 3

I	II	3	A			B			C		
index of Web site content	index of Web site functions		municipality directly under central government			provincial capitals			prefectural city		
1	2		A1	A2	A3	B1	B2	B3	C1	C2	C3
government affairs public	online administration	public feedback	Beijing	Shanghai	Tianjin	Shijiazhuang	Hangzhou	Guangzhou	Nanhai	Anguo	Linan

Table 5. The number of acquiring different evaluation of selected nine urban government Web sites at different levels

	Beijing	Shanghai	Tianjin	Shijiazhuang	Hangzhou	Guangzhou	Nanhai	Anguo	Linan
Excellent	10	15	5	2	4	5	1	0	0
Good	6	2	7	2	7	7	1	1	0
Ordinary	0	0	4	7	5	5	8	1	2
Worse	0	0	0	0	0	0	2	6	5
Vacancy for items	1	0	1	6	1	0	5	8	10

The Results of Evaluation

In order to obtain the data, which reflect the functionality of government Web sites, a research group was set up. The data were recorded between August and November 2003. The research group, as end users, assessed the governments' Web sites. They were asked to mark horizontally from 17 functions and gave comments on the selected questions. In order to get details that have not been referred in the questionnaire, interviews and investigations followed. According to the evaluation criterion mentioned earlier, Table 3 was formed, in which "+++" stands for excellence, "++" stands for fineness, "+" stands for ordinariness, "-" stands for worse, "--" stands for function not available. Table 4 is the explanations of Table 3.

Figure 1. The evaluation of "good" "excellence" of selected nine urban government Web sites at different levels

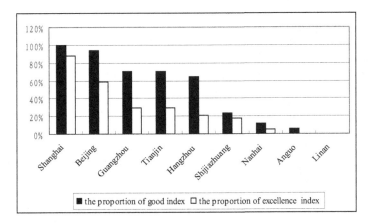

Table 5 shows how many "excellence," "fineness," "ordinariness," "worse," or "not available" scores each city has obtained.

From Table 5, the following results are found:

1.   Fifteen items receive "excellence" in Shanghai, which is 88% in 17 items. In Beijing, the excellence is rated 59%. These two cities are the best; while in Guangzhou and Tianjin, excellence is rated 29%, which stands in the middle. Hangzhou and Shijiazhuang receive less "excellence"; the three other prefectual cities, Nanhai, Anguo, and Linan are with the worst mark.

2.   In the "good" index, Shanghai accounts for 100%; Beijing accounts for 94.1%; Tianjin and Guangzhou account for 70.6%; Hangzhou accounts for 64.7%; Shijiazhuang only accounts for 23.5%; Nanhai accounts for 11.8% in the prefectural cities; and Anguo and Linan are the worst.

3.   In the "ordinariness" index, Shanghai and Guangzhou account for 100%; Beijing, Tianjin, and Hangzhou account for 94.1%; Shijiazhuang accounts for 64.7%; Nanhai accounts for 58.8%; and Anguo and Linan account for 11.8% (as shown in Figure 1).

E-Government Web Site Evaluation Analysis

We have obtained the main findings after analyzing the evaluation results:

1.   A three-dimension diagram will demonstrate the characteristics of the development process of urban e-government in China. In the three-dimension diagram, "the functions of e-government" is characterized by service technology provided

Figure 2. The development mode of e-government

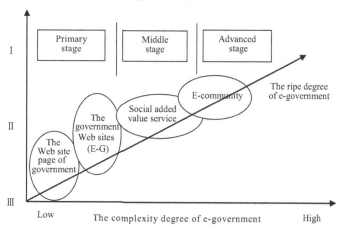

Note: (I) difficult; (II). the function degree of e-government; (III) easy

Figure 3. The categories of Shanghai government Web site

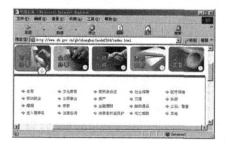

Figure 4. The categories of Guang-zhou government Web site

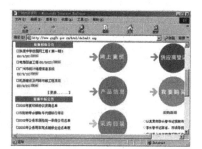

by government; "the complexity of e-government" is characterized by service quality and information interaction provided by government (Yao, Chen, Zhu, & Chen, 2001); "the maturity of e-government" is characterized by how well the e-government is able to satisfy public demand (shown in Figure 2). From the diagram, we can see that the urban e-government construction is moving from a static, one-way information announcement to two-way dynamic, information communication; from citizen passive acceptance of limited information to actively pursue intact, prompt information; from government-centered to public-centered; and from networks as additional means to the development of virtual government. The indexes concerned with Web sites' contents are the sign of one-way information announcement from government to the public, and it gets high evaluation.

While the indexes concerned with Web sites' functions, which indicates the interaction between the public and the government, is not as good as the former. In the second-class indexes, city overview has a better evaluation. While the evaluation for handling official business online, online supervision and public feedback have lower scores. In the third class indexes, daily affairs procedure has a negative evaluation result. Indexes related with the Web sites' functions such as online consultation, online searching, online declaration, online examination and approval, online government purchasing, online investigation and communication forum, got negative evaluation. It indicates that urban e-government in China is still at an earlier development stage. One-way information announcement and lack of interaction is still the current situation of urban e-government in China.

2.   The government Web sites of the three main international metropolises got better evaluation results. They have built many functions of government services. They not only have built the complete functions of government services but also have paid attention to their overall guiding role and the establishment of related indexes. Beijing's index of policies and regulations of its Web site is assessed with the highest positive proportion. The home page is divided into 5 categories and 18 subcategories. Inquiries about policies and regulations can be put into keyword searches. The search results show a local regulation issued in 1963 as the earliest regulation in this page. It is under the column of "polices and regulations" and shows a long-term span of available information. Shanghai is the pioneer city of economic reform and the model city of opening to the outside world, and its index of daily affairs procedure is outstanding compared with the other cities. The column of handling daily affairs procedure is divided into 20 categories (Figure 3). The Web site also lists many different tasks or responsibilities related to what Shanghai citizens might need to fulfill. The Web site publishes clearly which department is taken in charge, office hours, contacts, required documents, and detailed procedures. It is a complete guide. Guangzhou is the pilot city of the advanced management system. The government online purchasing is the most outstanding function. There are 54 items in the purchasing category. It is divided into five main parts: purchasing catalogue, price online, product description, supplier registration, orders, and so forth. Also the announcement for tenders, the announcement of winning a bid, and the competing prices are all published on the Web site (shown in Figure 4).

3.   The scores of provincial capitals are lower than the three metropolises, which indicate that urban e-government in these cities needs to be improved. This result is in accordance with the consequence in "The Evaluation Report of Urban Government Website's in China." In the report, five large cities in the plan list get an average score of 6.3, which is the highest. The average score of municipalities ruled by the central government is 6.15. The lowest is the average score of provincial capitals, 4.54. The main reason why provincial capitals scores are irregular is that they are in different levels, so there is a gap between the development of urban e-government in these cities. The higher level the government, the much more developed the e-government. The results are also in accordance with e-government development in other countries (Yin & Gu, 2002).

4.   All of the prefectural cities lay emphasis on the local characteristics in Web site's contents. The home page of Anguo is a good example. Anguo is famous for its medical tradition, so it is called the "medicine capital." Its Web site has a sign saying, "in ancient times, Herb King temple is here, today, new medicine capital is Anguo." The contents related to the medicine capital are included under the categories of "news of Anguo" and "special news." In the Web site, six local medical enterprises are published under the category "online company lists." There is also a link with "the State Pharmaceutical Inspection and Administration Bureau." The Web site fully represents the characteristics of the "medicine capital" — Anguo. Linan has the characteristics of an "eco-tourism city." Its e-government home page shows the pictures and articles that address the local characteristic of "eco-tourism city." Also, under categories like "announcement and bulletin," there is always space left for an announcement like "the exposition of forest and landscape resources of TianMu Mountain of China," which values the local forest and landscape resources.

5.   Nanhai is one of the first informatization pilot cities in China. The evaluation of the government's Web site contents and functions are relatively high. In the evaluation index of "government purchasing online," there are categories such as "member's system," "announcement for tender," "purchasing process," "purchasing notice," and "purchasing news." There are also categories such as "suppliers' self-recommendation" and "experts' self-recommendation," to provide personalized services to the users. It is a relatively complete and perfect government Web site. It shows the potential for the development of government Web sites in small-medium cities.

Impact of E-Government on Urban Evolution and Modality

E-Government Accelerates the Tendency of the Coexistence of Urban Gathering and Decentralization

Supply gathering. The development of urban e-government depends on the information infrastructure (Liu, 2002). Undoubtedly, the development of information infrastructure is influenced by the foundation and location of the real city. The existing capability and economic status of a city will be taken into consideration when it gets national investments and private capitals. The development of information infrastructure demonstrates an obvious urban-rank-system characteristic. It shows that the higher rank the city, the higher rank the network nodes; the more important location, the better accessibility and guaranty of the networks (Lu & Zhang, 2003). Taking CNC as an example, in the first-phase network construction, Beijing, Shanghai, Guangzhou, and Wuhan all have more than five circuit connections with other cities. Medium cities, like Tianjin, Jinan, Nanjing, Hangzhou, Fuzhou, Xiamen, and Changsha, have double-ways. The network accessibility and the bandwidth of these cities' nodes are much higher than the other nodes. The difference in spatial grade distribution of network infrastructure will make some key information infrastructure cities come into being. The international metropolises or regional large cities will possess the maximum and most perfect information transmission. Thus, they are becoming the advanced nodes in the new urban grade network systems. The cities that have the power to build better information infrastructure will support the development of urban e-government better than others, and in return, the development of e-government promotes a better information infrastructure.

Demand gathering. The "derivational effect" of information technology tells that the movement and development of physical space can be stimulated by the information flow and cyberspace (Lu & Liu, 1998). Therefore, e-government of large cities, which provides more functions, publishes more information, and has better availability and stronger interaction, will attract a large number of people who are seeking information. The demand for government information is increasing. The demand gathering effect in large cities pushes these large cities to be information centers and improves the development of e-government. Also it stimulates the further requirements of e-government's functions. The information gathering effect also attracts global economic activities to metropolises. The government is the "central node" in information flow. The implementation of informatization of a city depends on the participation and support, promotion and enhancement, guidance and adjustment, and construction and cultivation of the government. The government holds 80% of information resources in China. Government's Web sites provide not only a large amount of information, but also convenient and friendly online interaction services. The city is being endowed new glamour because of e-government's information gathering effect. When the city transforms from industry society to information society, both the internal and external aspects of the city change (shown in Table 6). E-government is one of the key compositions of informatization of a city, which has a significant effect on urban transformation.

Service gathering. Government service has become a key function of e-government. It enables government-business and government-public to communicate through e-way (Bovens & Zouridis, 2002). Government information service is greatly strengthened by using the Internet. It helps the government combine information provided by enterprises and social organizations with its own requirements. It also controls and coordinates the process of how the government deals with social activities. A new trend of the international e-government development is the integration and agglomeration of services of government agencies (Guo & Lu, 2002). The portal of government Web site is regarded to be the only Web site offering government services. All the relevant Web sites are integrated into a unified government

Table 6. The exterior and interior evolution of urban from industrial society to information society

Feature	City in industrial society	City in information-intensive society
Main product	Commodity	Knowledge
Labor (regional) division	Regional	International
Social organs	Steelworks, auto-factories	The R&D center/universities
Leading industry of city	Manufacturing industry	Service industry
Tendency of urbanization	Exponentially increase	Decentralized or regressive increase
Configuration of city	Transportation	Multi-nodes
Main means of movement	Vehicle	Footing, vehicle and e-scheduled shift.
Service pattern	Specialization (optimum economy)	Customizing (non-localization)
Position of market	CBD	E-networks

Table 7. The service gathering of e-government compared with traditional government

Feature	Traditional government	E-government
Manifesting feature	The department partition	Virtual gathering based on networks
Space range network-property	regional and hierarchization	Globalization and network-property
Organization and policy-making	Information scattered and policy-making concentrated	Information gathering and policy-making power down decentralized
Management mode	Management with Government entity	Management with systematic Procedure.
Structure of rank order	Vertical layer structure	Radiation structure vertical with horizontal coexisting
Economy running	Slow running in traditional economy	Fast running in knowledge-based digital economy

Web site, which provides integrated government services for different users. The typical examples are the Web sites of first government of the U.S. (www.firstgov.gov) and UK online (www.ukonline.gov.uk). Compared with traditional government, urban e-government has a remarkable service gathering nature (shown in Table 7).

Decentralization under gathering. One of the advantages of e-government is that information can be transmitted remotely. Therefore, e-government will promote population and economies to decentralize. E-government promotes the supply, demand, and service gathering; meanwhile it is creating a kind of dispersed effect on spaces. The point "C" shown in the Figure 5 stands for the government organization in preindustrial society. It shows the lack of traffic networks, hugeness in figure but decentralization of activity centers, narrowness in service scope, shortness distance in average of material (people) flow, and independence between producers and consumers. The point "A" indicates the government organization in industrial society. It shows the constructed traffic networks, the interdependence between producers and consumers, decrease in decentralization degree, and increase in average distance of material (people) flow. The point "B" stands for e-government organizations. It shows e-telecom networks having been constructed, activity space replaced by time element, and the formation of ultimate decentralization. E-purchase and e-conference stand for the social state based on the decentralization of e-information services. No matter the e-government Intranet, which is the application of e-government inside each government's internal departments, or the special network of e-government, which is the application between government departments, or business extranet of e-government, which is the application facing society enterprises or personal application that help overcome time and space obstacles existing in the former human communication (Westholm & Aichholzer, 2003). In addition, they utilize the information transmission to replace or reduce people's movement on scheduled shifts. Citizens, enterprises, and government departments can decentralize or move at any site following every electronic command in the e-government system. The restriction of distance will not exist anymore in people's everyday lives and the economic development. The noncongestion of e-government information is destined to promote policy-making power to be dispersed to each grade, each executive position of

Figure 5. The spatial impact of technological variation

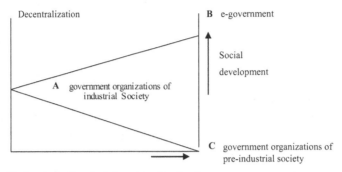

The decentralization of activity and number of center

department, which forms the divided layer power structure of policy making. However, the network of e-government will certainly never replace the way of face-to-face communication (Kearns, Bend & Stern, 2002).

The Effects of E-Government on Urban Spatial Evolution and Communication Behavior

Changing Urban Spatial Modality

The development of e-government also transforms urban spatial modality, which is a new stage in the process of urban evolution. E-government promotes information transmission towards a multiway model. Inside the government network, vertical and horizontal transmission channels coexist, which make information respond immediately in one-many and many-one ways. Traditional government management concerns every step or procedure of the material / people flow while e-government is more flexible and efficient. From a system point of view, e-government balances an overall implementation. It gives feedback to the changes in its eco-environment. The management system is being called a "strengthening effect" which has strengthened the efficiency and capacity of the material network such as road network, electricity network, and water network (Liang, Zhu & Ma, 2002). A good example is traffic-guiding system (TGS), which is an application of urban e-government to control the traffic flow. The system is intellectualized thus improves the road utilization efficiency greatly (Lu & Zhang, 2003). TGS consists of urban geographic information systems (GIS), traffic flow commanding subsystem, traffic flow supervising subsystem, static traffic administration subsystem, road loading flow subsystem, removing obstacles subsystem, security and accident handling subsystem, regulation dissemination and education subsystem. The urban TGS is constructed by the application of regional controlling system software, figure software, controller characteristic software, and geographical information

Figure 6. The hardware system of urban transportation controlling center

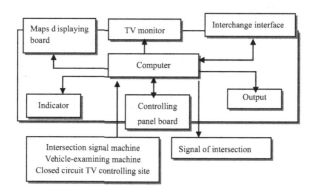

management software (shown in Figure 6). By realization of e-signal controlling to the arterial intersections and the noncloverleaf intersections of outer-ring road, TGS makes the one spot controlling possible and upgrades the multiphase controlling. With another system called ATC system, the gradable management of different types of intersections and channelization design in main blocking intersections are formed. By continuous timing reports of traffic lights and monitoring the excessive accident areas with cameras, the control pattern of "main road + cycle" and "main traffic corridor" of arterial highway in urban areas are formed. The main arterial highways often benefit the public transportation through the enhancement of passing ability. They play an important role in connecting central districts and peripheral areas and impel the development of the secondary centers of peripheral city. Moreover, there are lots of other successful examples of how urban e-government has changed the urban space modality.

Providing Public Communication Platform

Contemporary cities need flexible, initiative, light and free ways to communicate in a loose, democratic environment. E-government provides a unified platform for communication, which is established between governments and their counterparts, between governments and enterprises, between enterprises and their counterparts, and between enterprises and scientific research institutions (Figure 7). Such simplified communication can get the best communication results.

The lifestyles of the citizens are changed to an informal system by e-government. The informal communication provided by e-democracy can take place at anytime and anyplace where the information exists. The informal communication can transit enormous amounts of information, which has the advantage of shortest interval, minimum indirectness losses, fastest spread speed, and strong functions for searching information (Castells, 1996). Large quantities of innovations are excited by large amounts of information and the collision of various thoughts and ideas of informal communication. The informal communication is becoming an important means of information dissemination.

Figure 7. The government structure after the implementation of e-government

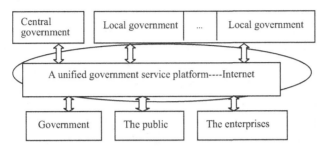

The organizational structure of government is being transformed from a traditionally "pyramid" organizational structure to a thin-and-flat structure by e-democracy in China (Lu, 1998). The urban e-government provides three platforms to e-democracy:

- **Information gathering platform:** The government's Web sites derive information flow by information production, diffusion, sharing, and communication. A users log in government's Web sites search and obtain information, and store or process information for special purposes. This becomes the first step to realize the high efficiency of e-government services. Meanwhile, effective interaction will make the derivative information sent government's Web site again as a feedback. More information flow is derived after the reorganization and reannouncement of feedback information, which makes the information platform more effective.

- **Communication platform:** The platform means a virtual arena, provided by government Web sites, for transmitting thoughts, feelings, and experiences interactively between government officials and online citizens or among citizens. It is obviously different from traditional community established by administrative relations. Lu (2001) considers virtual communication conducted by online relations, which makes citizens fully experience the function of a Web site that can eliminate a lot of barriers in face-to-face communication.

- **Organization platform:** This is a platform launched by a government Web site. It aims to organize citizens to actively participate in the policy-making process online effectively by using several Web site functions. The organization platform links up the demand side (citizens or enterprises) with its supply side (government) practically.

In summary, the implementation of e-democracy has a powerful impact on government in China. The administrative function has moved from administrative-centered to service-centered; the administrative process has changed from obscurity to transparency; the power structure has moved from centralization to decentralization; the government image has been developed from bureaucracy to accountability; and the administrative policy making has improved from autocracy to democratization.

Future Trends of Urban E-Government in China

Urban e-government is a dynamic concept of varying meaning and significance, so it is necessary to research its future trends, which will help in measuring successfully the development of urban e-government (Relyea, 2002). With the transformation of urban e-government and the changes of citizen and business needs, the further evolution of urban e-government would match the future practices. In this section, we explore the future trends of urban e-government in China from the following four aspects, combined with previous practices mentioned earlier.

Service Integration of E-Government

Service integration of urban e-government might be provided by some comprehensive urban e-government Web sites. These services are seamlessly integrated from different urban government departments, different level administration organs, and private sector partners, so that users can carry out multiple transactions during a single instance of service. China urban e-government will first evolve into this integration stage. Through the evaluation of nine urban e-government Web sites, we can see that some international metropolitans have attempted this application, like Beijing, Shanghai, and Guangzhou. Service integration provides different government departments an effective passageway to interchange information, service, and interaction. It makes government departments, that cannot integrate in reality, combined in cyberspace.

Intelligent Service

After completion of integrated e-government online service phases, a higher level of e-government will involve which includes the implementation of intelligent services (Guo & Lu, 2003). Although the full intelligent services have not broadly been realized in China, a few advanced urban government Web sites (like Beijing, Shanghai, Guangzhou) have launched to offer simple intelligent functioning from the following three aspects: (1) Focalized information guidance is provided, which enhances the application effect of information greatly; (2) the users in different locations can consult together at the same time in cyberspace; (3) material flow in reality can be effectively organized, like people flow, information flow, capital flow, and so forth.

Personalized Development

All citizens and businesses have a personalized need when the development of urban e-government spans the early period. Thus, it is one of the main future trends. Personalization is a technique used to generate customized content for each user. Through personalization, government can focus on particular business and individual needs and enhance its overall value. Although the application of personalization services has just started in China, a few government Web sites have provided simple personalization services. As the international metropolitans Beijing, Shanghai and Guangzhou, they provide citizens government mailbox, online investigation, and communication forum to communicate better.

Systematic Globalization

E-government globalization refers to the information sharing and service integration between/across multiple countries; the construction of urban e-government in each country has realized the system joint and transnational administration and service. Many urban e-government Web sites in China have connected with the Internet and realized transnational communication and share of information. There are several problems in further globalization course such as transcultural construction, multilanguage versioning, and regulation and online rules. However, with the development of economy globalization, the international construction of e-government in China affected by politics, government system, management, and culture tradition, would be a long stage.

Conclusion

Since the Chinese government launched the Government Online Project in 1999, the "image display" goal has been fulfilled. It is the primary stage of the Chinese government in building e-government Web sites/systems in China. After a few years' development, various levels of urban e-government in China have been established to delivery services to businesses and citizens with more types and of high quality. Through assessment and analysis of nine Web sites of urban governments in China at three levels, the following conclusions can be drawn.

1. The construction of urban government Web sites in China is still in an early stage. According to the services provided by the government Web sites, many of them only publish one-way, static information without suitable interactive functions, and less integrated information services. Only very few Web sites can provide one-stop-shop services. In addition, there is a big difference among cities of China in the development of urban e-government. Municipalities directly under the central government, especially the international metropolises, grow fast; meanwhile, small cities develop slowly.

2. The urban function and modality are greatly changed by the development of e-government. E-government urges the completed information infrastructure, the gathering of information and capitals to international metropolises and large cities. It strengthens the urban information functions. It also adds the diffusion tendency to an urban region. E-government enhances the control of urban material (people) flow. Also, it intensifies the efficiency and capacities of material networks. E-government provides a public platform for the communication inside internal cities, which enables communication

in a pluralistic and informal way. E-government is not the only factor reshaping urban modality and function, but it is a positive factor in the transition to information society.

References

Bakis, H., & Lu, Z. (2001). The change from the geographical space to geocyber space: Review on the Western scholars on regional effects by telecommunication. *Acta Geography Sinica, 55*(1), 104-111.

Bellamy, C., & Taylor, A. (1998). *Governing in the information age.* Bristol, PA: Open University Press.

Bovens, M., & Zouridis, S. (2002). From street-level to systems-level bureaucracies: How information and communication technology is transforming administrative discretion. *Public Administration Review, 2,* 174–184.

Castells, M. (1996). *The rise of the network society — economy, society and culture.* UK: Oxford University Press.

Cheng, J. C. (2000). Information city and intelligent town-digital city. *Geo-Information Science, 2*(3), 5-7.

Deng, X. P. (2005). The expansion of the digital city. *Journal of Guangdong Institute of Public Administration, 14*(5), 73-76.

Desai, N., & Bertucci, G. (2003). *E-government at the crossroads* (UN World Public Sector Report). Retrieved May 10, 2006, from http://www.unpan.org/dpepa_worldpareport.asp

Forman, M. (2002). *E-government strategy.* Retrieved May 10, 2006, from http://www.insidepolitics.org/egovt02city

Guo, X. T., & Lu, J. (2002, October 19-21). An evaluation for the adoption of government e-services in Australia. In *The 2nd Wuhan International Conference on Electronic Commerce — 21st Century E-commerce: Integration and Innovation* (pp. 393-401). Wuhan: China University of Geosciens.

Guo, X. T., & Lu, J. (2003). *Building intelligent e-government: A strategic development model in context of Australia.* Paper presented at the CollECTeR(LatAm) Conference on Electronic Commerce.

Kearns, I., Bend, J., & Stern, B. (2002). *E-participation in local government.* Institute for Public Policy Research.

Kong, M., & Su, X. N. (2003). *E-government application framework (EGAF).* Retrieved May 10, 2006, from http://www.egovchina.org/zhengwenjx_4.shtml

Liang, H. Q., Zhu, C. G., & Ma, R. H. (2002). Thinking on the innovation in the background of knowledge economics. *Economical Geography, 22*(3), 281-284.

Liu, P. (2001). Electronic political administration and security. *Net Security Technologies and Application, 10,* 45-47.

Liu, W. D. (2002). Development of the Internet in China: Spatial characteristics and implications. *Geographical Research, 21*(3), 347-356.

Lu, Z. (1998). User morphology of communication networks: Individual choice of communication media. *Geographic Science, 18*(2), 63-70.

Lu, J. (2001, July 2-3). Assessing Web-based electronic commerce applications with customer satisfaction: An exploratory study. In *International Telecommunication Society's Asia-Indian Ocean Regional Conference, Telecommunications and E-commerce*, Perth, Australia (pp. 132-144).

Lu, Z., & Liu, Y. (1998). *Geographic study on communication network and telecommunication.* Beijing: Chinese Translation Press.

Lu, Z., & Zhang, H. Q. (2003). The active impact of traffic guide system to urban space distribution in Shijiazhuang. *Economic Geography, 23*(2), 242-246.

Lv, X. B., Zhou, J. Q., & Wang, C. (2004). The influences of digital city on urban development. *Modern urban Research, 19*(1), 61-64.

Macintosh, A. (2002). *Using information and communication technologies to enhance citizen engagement in the policy process.* Paris: OECD PUMA Group.

Moon, M. (2002). The evolution of e-government among municipalities: Rhetoric or reality. *Public Administration Review, 4*, 424–433.

Nian, F. H., & Yao, S. M. (2002). Informatization and development trend of the urban space. *World Regional Studies, 11*(1), 72-76.

OECD. (2001). *Engaging citizens in policy-making: Information, consultation and public participation* (PUMA Policy Brief 10). Retrieved May 10, 2006, from http://www.oecd.org/pdf/M00007000/M00007815.pdf

Relyea, H. C. (2002). E-gov: Introduction and overview. *Government Information Quarterly, 19*, 9-35.

Wang, W., & Li, S. P. (2001). Studies of general systematic structure of electronic governments. *Policy-making Reference, 14*(6), 42-44.

West, D. (2001). *Urban e-government: An assessment of city government Websites.* Retrieved May 10, 2006, from http://www.insidepolitics.org/egovt01us.html

West, D. (2002). *Assessing e-government: The Internet, democracy, and service delivery by state and federal government.* Retrieved May 10, 2006, from http://www.Insidepolitics.org/egovtreportoo

West, D. (2003). *Global e-government 2003.* Center for Public Policy. Retrieved May 10, 2006, from http://www.InsidePolitics.org

Westholm, H. (2003). "Adaptability" in online democratic engagement: A multi-channel strategy to enhance deliberative policies. *The European Journal of Communication Research, 28*, 205-227.

Westholm, H., & Aichholzer, G. (2003). *Prisma strategic guideline 1: E-administration.* Retrieved May 10, 2006, from http://www.prisma-eu.net

Wimmer, M., & Tambouris, E. (2002, August 26-30). Online one-stop government: A working framework and requirements. In *Proceedings of the IFIP World Computer Congress*, Montreal.

Xu, Z. B., & Wei, G. (2004). Constructing Chinese democracy and the effect of state audit: On restricting and supervising the power. *Journal of SunYatSen University (Social Science Edition), 44*(3), 87-92.

Yao, S. M., Chen, S., Zhu, Z. G., & Chen, Z. G. (2001). From the development of information network to the construction of digital-city in urban agglomeration. *Human Geography, 16*(5), 20-23.

Yao, S. M., Zhu, Y. M., & Chen, Z. G. (2001). The development of urban group in the information society. *City Planning Review, 25*(8), 16-18.

Yin, F., & Gu, C. L. (2002). New perspectives on spatial structure research in the Information Era. *Geographical Research, 21*(2), 257-266.

Yin, X., & Wang, H. C. (2002). Analysis on the advantage of electronic governments cost. *Science & Technology Progress and Policy, 11*, 143-147.

Zhang, H. Q. (2003). *Study of the electro-government and the function of modern city: In the case of the Shijiazhuang.* Retrieved May 10, 2006, from http://202.206.108.200/cdmd/mainframe.asp?

Zhang, J. (2004). *The evaluation of the function of e-government of Chinese cities and the effects of e-government to city.* Retrieved May 10, 2006, from http://202.206.108.200/cdmd/mainframe.asp?

Zhang, N. N., & Gu, C. L. (2002). From geographical space to composite space: The urban space under the influence of information networks. *Human Geography, 17*(4), 20-24.

Chapter XIV

Web Services in Government Policy:
Case Study from UK National Health Service

Matthew W. Guah, University of Warwick, UK

Abstract

The public sector accounts for a greater proportion of United Kingdom's information technology (IT) spending, but cutting edge success stories in government IT have suddenly been reported in the popular press. As a result of the electronic delivery of government services (i.e., the National Health Service, Defence and Criminal Justice systems) becomes more commonplace, the public sector is becoming increasingly dependent on technology. This chapter reports on three years of research, which looks at the application of Web services into United Kingdom healthcare as a fulfilment of numerous semi and unsuccessful IT projects, that fell short of delivering any tangible benefits. The author looks at the National Health Service's current IS strategy — fully dependent on Web services application – with the criteria of successful implementation, return on investment, increased productivity, innovation, and user benefits.

Introduction

Information technology (IT) strategies play an increasingly pivotal role in the overall strategies of a national healthcare organization, which has moved them in the focus of recent healthcare management research (Wilson & Lankton, 2004). Web services introduce a different business environment with respect to the institutional framework and the resource endowment of healthcare organizations. The institutions supporting the traditional mechanism for healthcare provision are less sophisticated or effective, and the health services are less well endowed with resources, especially in terms of maintaining valuable resources such as skilled labour in management — particularly IT staff.

Consequently, an understanding of emerging technology strategies in the health sector requires adoption and development of the theories currently applied in the management field, including transaction costs/agents theory and resource based theory and institutional theory. Such theories must account for how contextual influences moderate the strategic decisions taken by healthcare organizations. Recent empirical studies on healthcare organizations have begun to incorporate the specificity of the emerging technology context in their theoretical reasoning. In this chapter, the author takes this line of research further by applying the resource-based view (RBV) (Barney, 1991; Wernerfeld, 1984) to healthcare organizations to explain how Web services technologies are being implemented. The RBV has been found particularly suitable for analyzing organizations in high volatility environments (Eisenhardt & Martin, 2003), and has recently been applied to strategies in the health sector (Scott, Ruef, Mendel, & Caronna, 2004).

In recent years, e-government has received much attention by academics and practitioners as a wide-ranging initiative to use the latest IT to automate government services. One important area that has received large financial investment is healthcare services (Devaraj & Kohli, 2000; Majeed, 2003; Wilson & Lankton, 2004). Traditionally, government run healthcare services have not received large funding for IT, and this has led to a situation where disparate IT systems have produced pockets of efficiency alongside serious shortcomings in organizational processes and services.

Using Web-enabled IT systems as a way of empowering e-government within healthcare, the UK government has embarked upon the largest civil IT programme in the world to re-engineer organizational processes and services to enhance patient care. The current wave of Web-enabled IT systems is expected to play a large role in how the UK government fulfils its agenda for public reform in healthcare. Other examples of public sector reform include, e-democracy (voting and referenda by means of the Internet); Web-enabled delivery of products and services to citizens (healthcare, social services, tax payment, etc.); inter and intragovernmental communication and decision making (immigration and homeland security) enhanced by network applications and the digital integration of front and back office operations (Vriens & Achterbergh, 2004). These examples demonstrate that national governments are keen to adopt Web-enabled IT systems to improve public services.

The chapter is based upon a three-year research project that examined the UK's National Health Service (NHS) information systems strategy, where the National Programme for IT (NPfIT) is being implemented at a cost of $10 billion over 10 ten years. This research involved interviewing over 200 stakeholders in the NpfIT, including healthcare professionals (doctors, consultants, nurses, etc.), healthcare administrators (managers, administrators, secretaries and support staff), IT professionals (managers and technicians, IT vendor firms), government agencies (civil servants), and some patients. The cross-section of respondents enabled the researchers to derive a rich picture of how the NPfIT was perceived at all levels and spectrums within and outside the NHS. About 80% of the interviews were tape recorded and transcribed, with the results sent to the respondents for clarification. A qualitative approach to data collection and analysis using semistructured and open-ended questions was essential as a single, survey-based questionnaire was unsuitable given the variety and diversity of the stakeholders interviewed.

This chapter is divided into four parts. First we give an overview of the UK healthcare service and outline some of the political, economic, and social factors that influence IT expenditure. Second, we discuss the IT platform, which will enable large-scale change within the UK health sector. The technology we examine is Web services. Third, we present the case study, which discusses the current progress of the NPfIT. Next, we include a section that examines the key challenges of the NPfIT in the broader sociopolitical and economic context. Finally, we discuss the findings from our research and offer some guidelines to stakeholders in managing a large-scale, IT-enabled change programme.

What is Web Service?

Web services can be defined as "self-contained modular applications that provide a computation upon request" (Guah & Currie, 2005a, p. 14). These services can be published, located, or invoked over a network, usually the Internet, intranets, or LAN. The popularity of the World Wide Web over the last decade has generated more demand for the request of these services, partly because Web services are independent of the underlying systems providing the computation (Guah & Currie, 2005a). Considering that Web services architecture can provide universal interoperability of software applications, nearly any application in the world could interact with another software application regardless of geographical location, system hardware, operating systems, or programming languages. Thus, permitting a de facto standard for any particular type of computation permitting an organization the capacity to develop an information system for its use based entirely on the computational services is provided by the Web service paradigm.

On the other hand, the service provider is responsible for the process of service provision and therefore required to maintain of the system quality. The characteristics ensure the method of development also impacts the cost of maintaining the information.

In the simplest form, the foundation of Web services is the request/response paradigm. This paradigm involves a client in the Web services environment who requests a service via a specific protocol from a service provider. In response, the service provider, using a specific protocol, sends the service to the client — or a notification of why it cannot provide that service. Such a concept is used to implement the service-oriented architecture (SOA) which implements Web services, containing three entities and three operations.

However, benefiting from the advantages of Web services require an organization to place complete trust in the security of the service. The total relinquishing of an organizational information asset exposes that organization to malicious hackers, industrial espionage, and fraud. Therefore the service provider must equivocally assure the security of confidential data within Web services to win willingness of organizations to adopt this new technology as core parts of their IS strategies (Guah & Currie, 2005a).

The UK National Health Service

The UK National Health Service (NHS) is responsible for healthcare and services, serving around 60 million citizens and free at the point of delivery. The institution was created in 1948 by a parliamentary act initiated by the Labour government following a national health-care review after World War II. Within the past six decades, the NHS has experienced both stability and change. Successive governments have introduced numerous policy documents designed to regulate, reengineer, and monitor all aspects of NHS care and service provision. In contrast, the NHS has, over the years, evolved many institutionalized mechanisms that make change difficult and often highly controversial.

One significant change from the late 1980s to early 1990s was the advent of compulsory competitive tendering (CCT), which fuelled an increase in the number of managers and administrators across the NHS (Scott et al., 2000). The rationale for creating an internal market through a new procurement strategy stemmed from political pressure to reduce costs by introducing the methods and practices more commonly found in the private sector. By the mid-1990s, decisions about organizationwide IT projects remained centralized at the level of government and the NHS Executive, although the NHS governance structure for IT was highly decentralized or division-based. IT divisions were spread across several regional authorities, with medical functions centrally controlled. This precluded many small IT service firms from gaining a foothold in the NHS, as their larger counterparts had the political, organizational, and technical capacity to deliver large-scale IT work.

In the late 1990s, the government increasingly recognized the opportunity to use IT to improve the delivery of service within the NHS. After a series of reviews of NHS IT service delivery, a more integrated and seamless IT method was recommended (DoH, 2000; Wanless, 2002). The NHS Information Authority (NHSIA) embarked on the Integrated Care Report Service (ICRS) project to provide, among other services, a nationwide electronic patient database. The result was a document called "Information for Health" that specified the need for the complete automation and integration of various patient information databases in the country (DoH, 2000). Such a system would be commissioned to selected IT service providers at a combined price of £6.3 billion (US $10 billion).

A DoH document published in 2002 stressed:

It is widely accepted that the NHS Plan to improve care and services in the NHS depends on a number of transformations in quality, speed and capacity of the organization. Information technology and the electronically stored information it handles are key enablers of some of this transformation. With modern IT, information can be captured once and used many times, working practices can be modernized and communications speeded up. (DoH, 2002, p. 3)

In spite of this vision for IT transformation in the NHS, the history of introducing large-scale IT development projects in the government sector have not been successful overall, with some suggesting a failure rate of 80% and others around 60% (Brown, 2001). The UK public sector spends around £2.3 billion per annum on IT, yet the government recognizes that "there is a history of failure of major IT-enabled projects, characterized by delay, overspend, poor performance and abandonment" (NAO, 2004, p. 3). The repercussions from these failures can reflect unfavourably upon government in general (Currie, 1997).

Yet against this backdrop of disappointing results from historical IT investments, the UK NHS is now embarking upon the largest civil IT programme in the world. This initiative has been enabled by the development of the Web services architecture, which will provide an IT platform to facilitate inter and intraorganizational data networks.

Web Service Architecture

Since around 2000, Web services have emerged as a new "silver bullet" technology to transform organizational processes (Guah & Currie, 2005b). This form of emerging technology is expected to transfer IT from an internal to an external (outsourced) activity. Web services are defined as "self-contained modular applications that provide a computation upon request" (Boncella, 2004). These services can be published, located, or invoked over a network, usually the Internet, intranets, local area network, or wide area network. The growth in popularity of the World Wide Web within the last decade has generated more demand for the request of these services, partly because Web services are independent of the underlying systems providing the computation. Considering that Web services architecture can provide universal interoperability of software applications, nearly any application in the world could interact with another software application regardless of geographical location, system hardware, operating systems, or programming languages, thus resulting in a de facto standard that allows an organization to develop an information system based entirely on computational services provided by the Web service paradigm.

The service provider is responsible for the continuous availability of service as well as maintaining the system quality. These characteristics ensure that the method of development also impacts the cost of maintaining the information. In the simplest form, the foundation of Web services is the request / response paradigm: a client in the Web services environment requests a service via a specific protocol from a service provider. In response the service provider, using a specific protocol, sends the service to the client — or a notification of why it cannot provide that service.

Figure 1 shows that a more holistic approach to technology typically works better than a piece-meal approach to information systems solutions. Web services, as it is currently being implemented in most organizations, looks like a two-legged table. The three-legged table represents a version of Web services being sold by some vendors after the dotcom crash; this depiction incorporates people, where cultural changes are imperative if Web services are to be successful. The four-legged table depicts a mature model of Web services where workflow is further added; this model suggests that synergies exist between technology, people, and processes. The analogy here is that a two-legged table is less stable than a three-

Figure 1. Evolution of Web services

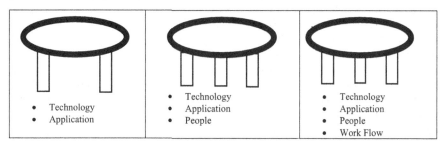

legged table, while a four-legged table is even firmer. At the present time, Web services remain an immature technology.

Further, benefiting from the advantages of Web services requires organizations to trust the security of the service. The service provider must therefore ensure the security of confidential data if Web services are to become a trusted technology. Boncella (2004) has outlined some requirements for Web services security measures:

- **Confidentiality:** a requirement that demands the assurances from a service provider the privacy of users and the prevention of information theft both in transit and data storage. Most Web services environments use symmetric and asymmetric encryptions to create cipher text for transmitting data between the client PC and server as well as data held in storage.

- **Integrity:** a requirement that demands the assurances that information would not be modified (intentionally or unintentionally) either during transit or in storage. An encrypted message digest — or digital signatures — can deal with integrity issues satisfactorily.

- **Nonrepudiation:** a requirement that demands the sender of a message to legitimately claim they intentionally sent a particular message. Digital certificates and public key infrastructure are frequently used for this assurance.

- **Authentication:** a requirement that demands the certifications of both sender and receiver of a particular message. Public key infrastructure and smart cards in combination with user name/password authentication methods are usually used to guarantee this authentication.

- **Authorization:** a requirement that demands the authentication entity can access only those information resources they must have either to request or provide a service. Once authenticated an entity authorization will be determined. Generally an authenticated entity has an associated access control list.

- **Availability:** a requirement that demands the provision of uninterrupted service to authenticated and authorized users. This is in addition to avoidance of the interruptions of services due to denial-of-service attacks.

Boncella (2004) demonstrates how Secure Sockets Layer and Public Key Infrastructure are being used in combination with firewalls to satisfy these requirements for conventional Web traffic using Internet protocol. Yet fears persist that these protections are not adequate to assure these requirements within a Web services environment (Guah & Currie, 2004). For e-government services to be successful, security will increasingly be a major issue. The key question about the use of Web-enabled technologies for the transfer of confidential data is: How can IT service providers ensure that inter and intraorganizational data flows across the Internet are safe and secure? This is especially important within the healthcare sector, where the use of Web services architecture will expose patient data to external networks on an unprecedented scale.

National Programme: Information Technology

The National Programme for IT is an essential element in delivering the NHS Plan for reform over a period of 10 years. It is creating a multibillion pound information infrastructure, which should improve patient care by increasing the efficiency and effectiveness of clinicians and other NHS staff. The NPfIT is procuring, developing, and implementing a modern, integrated IT infrastructure and systems for all organizations in England up through 2010. These are being done by:

- Creating an NHS Care Records Service to improve the sharing of consenting patients' records across the NHS

- Making it easier and faster for GPs and other primary care staff to book hospital appointments for patients

- Providing a system for electronic transmission of prescriptions

- Creating a new National Network for the NHS (N3), ensuring that the IT infrastructure can meet NHS needs now and in the future

- Establishing reliable Picture Archiving and Communications Systems (PACSs) to capture, store, and distribute static and moving digital medical images

- Establishing a reliable Quality Management and Analysis System (QMAS) giving GP practices and primary care trusts objective evidence and feedback on the care delivered to patients

- Establishing a reliable contact systems including a central e-mail and directory service for the NHS

The competitive advantage of a service provider operating in the health sector is determined by its *ability to adapt its competencies* to the needs and capabilities of the specific technology and to utilize available local resources in the best possible combination with its own core competencies. Therefore, the service provider's choice of a service provision model is crucial for developing a resource mix that enables it to compete in the healthcare organizational context. Zhang, Chen, and Zhou (2005) refer to this as "information personalization," which

Table 1. Short-list of companies chosen to be service providers from a reduced long-list

Southern	Eastern	Northwest / West Midlands	London	Northeast / East Midlands	National Provider
Short - List					
Fujitsu	Accenture	CSC	BT Syntegra	Accenture	BT Syntegra
Southern Allianc e	CaP Gemini Ernst & Young	BT Syntegra	IBM C	erner	Lockheed Martin
PlexusCare C	erner	Fujitsu			IBM
P	lexusCare	IBM			
Long - List					
Fujitsu	Accenture	CSC	BT Syntegra	Accenture	BT Sytegra
Southern Alliance	Cap Gemini Ernst & Young	BT Syntegra	IBM C	erner	Lo ckheed Martin
Plexuscare C	erner	Fujitsu	SAIC P	atient First Alliance	IBM
CTG Inc	Plexuscare I	BM X	ansa S	erco F	ujitsu
Lockheed Martin	Torex	McKesson/Capita P	atni Computer Systems	Logica N	orthrup Grumman
Wipro Tech.	S	iemens C	ompuware		McKesson/Capita
				S	AIC

continues to be the most difficult task in dealing with public sector information overload resulting from e-government initiatives.

Given the wide number of potential service providers (see Table 1), the NPfIT team had to take the preferences of the NHS service customers into consideration, which is an essential process of dynamic service composition planning (Zhang et al., 2005). Getting this stage of the project right significantly contributes to GP satisfaction with the service quality.

The national programme is being implemented via two means (see Table 2):

- National application service providers (NASP) are responsible for purchasing and integrating IT systems common to all NHS users at the national level.
- Local service providers (LSP) are responsible for delivering IT systems and services at the local level.

To facilitate this model, the nation has been divided into five regional clusters of strategic health authorities (London, North West, and West Midlands, North East, Southern, and Eastern). These regional clusters were created after consultation with Strategic Health Authorities (SHAs) on how best to deliver local IT solutions as part of the NPfIT. After much discussion, it was decided to split England into the five geographic regions in Figure 2 — with each cluster comprising five, six, or seven SHAs who agreed to work together on the procurement and implementation of NPfIT services at local levels. Applications delivered at the local level are the responsibility of five selected Local Service Providers (LSPs) (see

Table 2. Contracts with service providers for national or regional services

Primary Service Provision Model			
•NASP purchasing & integrating nationally •LSP delivering IT systems & services locally			
CONTRACTS (DEC-2004)	SERVICE PROVISION	PROVIDER	LENGTH
Care Records Service – NASP	National B	ritish Telecom 1	0 years
Care Records Service – LSP N	orth East A	ccenture	10 years
Care Re cords Service – LSP	Eastern	Accenture	10 years
Care Records Service – LSP L	ondon	Capital Care Alliance (BT)	10 years
Care Records Service – LSP N	orth West & West Midlands	CSC	10 years
Care Records Service – LSP S	outhern	Fujitsu Alliance	10 years
National Network for the NHS (N3)	National B	ritish Telecom 7	years
Choose and Book	National A	tos Origin 5	years
Contact (email) N	ational	Cable & Wireless	10 years

Figure 2. Five English regional clusters with approximate population

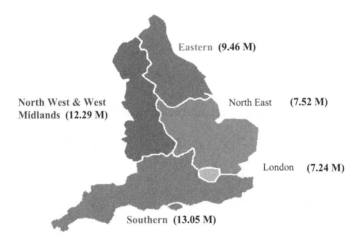

Eastern (9.46 M)

North West & West Midlands (12.29 M)

North East (7.52 M)

London (7.24 M)

Southern (13.05 M)

Table 2). The LSPs work closely with local NHS IT professionals and are overseen by a regional implementation director (RID) from the NPfIT. The LSPs will ensure that existing local systems are compliant with national standards and that data are able to flow between local and national systems. To do this, the NPfIT will deliver upgrades or replacements to hardware and software as appropriate and implement core local training for NHS staff.

The regional implementation directors (RIDs) led the LSP negotiations and are leading the implementation process across their individual areas. An RID manages a NPfIT support team and the relationship with the LSP, as well as coordinates deployment. An RID is part of the NPfIT management team and reports to the National Programme implementation director, but is also responsible to the regional cluster's board for delivery.

Current Achievements

Certain parts of the national programme have been achieved to date:

- **Autumn 2004:** Choose and Book was distributed at several hospitals implementing the first electronic booking of hospital appointments from GPs. The GP will make the appointment in negotiation with the patient.

- **Spring 2004:** The 1st phase of Care Record Service has been developed with basic health record including patient demographic information, birth and death notification, recording of allergies.

- **Winter 2005:** 1st phase roll-out of electronic transfer prescription service.

- **Summer 2004:** 1st phase roll-out of PACS (picture archiving communication system).

- **Autumn 2004:** Launch of Contact — a new service including E-mail and Directory Services (now available to all staff)

- **Autumn 2005:** Roll-out of QMAS — a system to provide timely feedback for GPs on the quality of care delivered to their patients

- **Summer 2004:** Establishment of National Service Desk (running from Leeds offices) for interim help desk purposes — temporarily operated in-house (since NPfIT did not initially contract for the provision of cohesive front line services)

Future Project Phases

Other services planned for future phases of the national programme include:

- The 2nd phase of Care Record Service — planed for Summer 2005 to Summer 2006 — will see health record grow to cover orders and results for diagnostic images and pathology, to support care pathways and notify GPs of emergencies and other out of hours encounters.

- The 3rd phase of Care Record Service — planned for 2006 to 2008 — will provide support for all doctors and nurses to help with decisions. It will also include systems to support care at home using remote links to healthcare professionals anywhere in the community. This would provide better healthcare planning and enable access to facts and figures held on the NHS Care Record Service.

- The final phases of Electronic Transmission of Prescription and Picture Archiving and Communications Systems will be implementation by 2008.

- The final features incorporated to complete full integration between health and social care systems in England should be achieved by 2010.

The future phases demonstrate the difficulty of evaluating the two most important project variables — cost and value — as pointed out in Wanless' (2002) evaluation of management and operation in the NHS. However, the DoH has initiated a strong campaign to inform and engage the GPs and public about patient choice through the final months in 2005. In response to these delays, The Health Minister claimed:

This is the biggest civil IT project under way anywhere in the world today. Not everything is going to go smoothly all of the time, and we're not going to pretend to the public that it is. But one of the biggest challenges facing the NHS is the quality of its technology. If we don't get the technology we need, we won't get the service we want to see. (NHS Modernisation Agency, 2004)

While these delays are explained as technology problems, our research found that much of the delay could loosely be described as cultural issues. These included differences in political objectives between politicians, healthcare professionals, and workers; poor communication between the centre, regions, and individual hospitals; the problem of implementing new IT in conjunction with doing the day-to-day work within hospitals and GP surgeries; issues of security and confidentiality; the time lag between technology implementation and user training and uptake of the new system; and many other factors. These issues are discussed in the next section.

Criticisms of the NPfIT

There have been further objections to the NPfIT plans related to the protection of personal information, with opponents even suggesting that NHS patients' records would be connected to a more controversial e-government initiative — the national identity register requiring all citizens to carry ID cards on their person. However, the NHS has insisted that access to the system would be limited according to the requirements of the individual member of staff.

Many medical practitioners and hospital administrators also challenge the one-size-fits-all approach. NPfIT is intended largely to deliver healthcare data locally on a nationwide basis, but some IT directors in the NHS local trusts resent being pressured to run and manage a technology bought by London-based officials.

NPfIT receives its funding from the DoH, not from the businesses it is serving — which are run by GPs and NHS trusts. A common complaint about NPfIT in the NHS is that some medical practitioners and local trust IT directors believe they are being dictated to by the centre rather than receiving a service. Several regional trust boards have expressed concern about the local costs of introducing national systems. Some may be unable or unwilling to drop other work to spend large sums on a national scheme for which they feel no ownership. Some critics have argued that the NPfIT is led by a centralist approach, unlike the norm in the NHS of adopting systems of GPs' choice, built to standard specifications that followed a "data-centric" approach.

These concerns also show systemic cracks that have appeared in the structures of accountability within NPfIT. Different organizations are in partial control of delivery, including the DoH,

Connecting for Health, clusters, suppliers, PCTs, hospital trusts, and GP organizations.

Further, the director of NHS IT, commenting on the delivery of a system to enable patients and doctors to book hospital appointments electronically, stated:

It is unfortunate we delivered it to schedule because if we had delivered it a year or two late, I think the user input would have caught up with the system being delivered. It is going to be interesting to see, over the next few months, whether the potential of that working technology platform with very high levels of availability is taken up locally in the NHS. (NHS Modernisation Agency, 2004)

The UK government's chief information officer, has rightly argued that governments cannot abandon schemes that should improve how citizens and the public sector interact simply because previous government IT projects have failed, and he recognizes that investment alone is not enough. Having seen the need for experienced professionals and best-of-breed solutions, Mr. Watmore has undertaken to increase levels of professionalism in government IT. However, there is also a need to recognize that IT problems are usually the result of bigger business challenges, and these business challenges of the IT-related government project should be the focus, not only IT itself.

The Challenges of Implementing IT-Enabled Healthcare Service

The complexities of maintaining accurate and up-to-date information are well known to major corporations with large numbers of customers (Baskerville, 1993; Davies, 1989). The task being taken on by the UK government in regard to the NPfIT is massive in comparison with many large-scale private sector IT projects. This complexity is commensurate with increased risk as the NPfIT is both politically contentious and culturally and technologically diverse in scale and scope.

At the heart of many e-government initiatives is the focus on technology at the cost of what the citizen requires by way of improved services. This has led to widespread criticism that public money is being wasted on IT-enabled projects, which achieve little in terms of improving the quality of life of those it is intended to serve. Failure to identify and delineate between the perceived and actual benefits from e-government initiatives is often at the heart of many failures. In addition, the application of stringent performance targets may mean that "all the targets are being met" without considering whether "we are measuring the right targets." According to the UK government's chief information officer:

Not many private sector projects have to deal with the numbers of requests and people that government schemes do, and those that do often suffer the same problems when it comes to whether the system works and end users can actually use it. (NHS Modernisation Agency, 2004)

While it is understandable that government agencies focus upon a narrow range of performance targets to measure success and failure factors of IT projects, this is unlikely to pacify the critics of the NPfIT, many of whom resent any change to their working practices. In meeting the challenge of implementing the NPfIT, government will therefore need to work hard in convincing potential users of the various IT systems that their working lives will be improved and that patients will ultimately receive a better service. The failure to implement a large-scale management change programme in conjunction with the technical changes imposed upon the workforce will only exacerbate the problems of implementation.

Indeed, lessons from past IS research have shown that there is no such thing as an "IT failure," as all technology failures are more appropriately described as "management failures" (Currie, 1995). Using the label *IT failure* to describe an unsuccessful programme or project creates a perception that if only the technology had worked, then the result would have been successful. Such a perception tends to absolve management from any responsibility that the so-called IT failure was a result of their decision making and lack of proper project management.

The need to dispel some of the current perceptions in the media that the NPfIT is the next major "IT disaster-in-waiting" is therefore a critical task for senior politicians, healthcare executives, and IT service providers. Part of this task will involve "managing perceptions," not only to those who will use the various IT systems, but also to the media. One observation from our research is that the media recognize the public interest in stories about healthcare, particularly those that aim to "expose" poor practice. The vast amount of financial investment in the NPfIT offers a soft target for those wishing to publish an *expose* on the mismatch between the objectives and achievements of the programme to date. As a nationwide programme with several thousand users, all of whom will require different levels of access and need to share different databases and receive different levels of training, it is likely that media attention to any shortcomings of the programme will continue for several years to come. Further complications will arise with legislation such as the Freedom of Information Act or Data Protection Act.

Our research suggests that e-government projects should embrace these wider challenges rather than focus solely upon technology imperatives. If this is not done before technologies are identified and installed, the people affected by them are likely to develop attitudes and behavioural patterns that will circumvent their implementation. This scenario suggests the government needs to clearly identify strategies, methods, and techniques for winning the approval of those affected, rather than simply pursuing centrist (top-down) policies by imposing IT-enabled change upon people. This would require public sector officials to closely monitor the various IT projects from end-to-end and not just the IT implementation. Every large programme, like NPfIT, notably has problems and things that will go wrong. Identifying issues and risks early and reacting positively to problems within IT and across other project areas where any changes will have an impact is therefore critical.

While there is a need for highly skilled professional IT suppliers and consultants, the technology should not be the primary focus of such a massive project — a higher chance of ending up with another failed e-government initiative. Government IT strategists need to address the wider culture imperatives in the extent to which the organizational climate and people are predisposed to adopting new IT-enabled working practices. While this may seem self evident, our research shows that the top-down approach for IT adoption and diffusion is likely to engender feelings of resentment and frustration among healthcare workers, rather than a willingness to adopt and adapt to these changes. External service providers also have a role to play in this which extends beyond one of merely implementing new IT systems.

The Critical Role of External Service Providers

As part of the government agent for reforming public services, external IT providers are guaranteed a large role in the NPfIT with many large, long-term contracts being negotiated. The NPfIT seeks to develop applications in the NHS for the design of health service delivery processes across a range of clinical and nonclinical activities. Part of this agenda is to improve the internal and external supply chain of information flows across the NHS to enable healthcare professionals, managers and administrators, and patients to take more informed and better decisions on various aspects of health-related matters, from being able to electronically transfer patient information to allowing patients to choose and book convenient hospital appointments.

By attempting to emulate the methods and practices of private sector firms, in areas such as supply chain, procurement, cost effectiveness, workflow, and so forth, government and healthcare executives hope to transform the UK NHS from a less efficient and effective institution to a lean and agile one. However, the institutional structure, processes, and practices make this an enormous, if not impossible, task particularly in the short to medium term.

In selecting external service providers, our research suggests that one of the key challenges for government and healthcare executives is assessing the capabilities and skills of these firms. Many IT service providers do not have an extensive knowledge of healthcare products and services and, more importantly, the cultural values, attitudes, and beliefs that govern the behaviour of healthcare workers. For example, the cost imperatives that have been introduced by government force many NHS hospitals to evaluate whether or not they can offer a particular medical treatment (i.e., operations and drugs). This has resulted in concerns that patients are likely to receive specific treatments depending upon where they live or which hospital they use, rather than receiving a blanket service which is offered to all, irrespective of geographical region, postal code, or hospital.

As a result of the NPfIT, large IT service providers recognize that lucrative public sector contracts will be offered over a long period of time. Such contracts come at a time when many IT service providers have been damaged by the fall-out of the dotcom crash, where IT contracts were often delayed or even cancelled. But while the NPfIT offers IT service providers new business development opportunities, the healthcare sector is extremely complex and multifaceted, where rudimentary business decisions about cost-cutting and rationalization must be taken in the context of other, more immediate considerations (i.e., which may involve matters of life or death). IT service providers must therefore be sensitive to these issues as healthcare continues to be seen in the UK as a matter of right, and not merely one which is reducible to cost-cutting measures.

The DoH agenda for the NPfIT involves a number of different stages, starting with static applications used solely for providing information and ending with fully interactive databases over a complex WAN that are capable of handling a multitude of transactions that occur in the lifelong relationship between the NHS and its patients and partners. The NPfIT can take lessons from smaller e-government projects, the online tax return system, which demonstrates that transferring money online plays an important role in an e-government initiative to include financial transactions such as paying taxes, fees, or fines.

Trust, both in a functional use of the system and in e-healthcare security, can be seen as an important antecedent for the adoption of the NPfIT on the part of medical practitioners and patients alike. From the government's point of view, the potential for exerting influence seems to be somewhat limited. While national institutions in most Western countries are usually perceived as trustworthy, users' attitudes about having their medical records available online may be more skeptical. *IT service providers will therefore have to ensure that security of their systems are a top priority*, particularly when the media is eager to publish stories about lack of patient confidentiality and other negative aspects about IT-enabled change in the NHS.

Potential Impacts on Healthcare Processes

A recent report of what works in terms of service improvement methodology within the NHS (NHS Modernisation Agency, 2004) points out 10 high impact changes. It illustrates what is possible when clinical teams equipped with the right tools and support networks are given the authority to review and streamline years of accredited processes.

Major changes in healthcare process are required for organizations in UK health and social care to adopt and to make significant and measurable improvements as a result of e-government initiatives. Though evidence based, these changes draw on the lessons learned from earlier work, build on the success already achieved (Atkinson & Peel, 1998), and illustrate the day-to-day experience and achievements of thousands of frontline clinical teams across the NHS.

If these changes were adopted systematically throughout the entire health sector:

- The experience of patients would be greatly enhanced by more appropriate and timely care
- Clinician hours, hospital bed days, and appointments in primary and secondary care would be saved by several hundred thousands
- Clinical quality and clinical outcomes would be tangibly improved
- It would be easier to attract and retain more good quality staff

The following quote, from a senior member of the NHS Modernisation Team, encapsulates this thinking:

We frequently see radiology and endoscopy departments where there are more than 100 separate patient queues within a single schedule. Many sites (hospitals) have been able to reduce the number of queues by between 50% and 80% and with no extra resources to reduce average waiting times by at least 50%. They have also been able to reduce Did Not Attends (DNAs) and cancellations as a by-product of shorter waits for patients. ... One by-product of the MA's work has been the definition of the data that is really required to successfully manage capacity, demand and utilisation. (anonymous interview)

The NPfIT is beginning to show signs of enhancing patient care in the few hospitals that have gone live with certain aspects of the phase implementation. At one NHS hospital, the new way of storing and sharing information is allowing patients to access information more easily when making decisions about their health and care. Patients have faster access to their medical records by using a secure Internet connection than is possible by requesting a paper copy. Once this is implemented across the NHS, this will allow diagnosis and treatment to be safer and speedier, as carers will have the right information available to them at the right time, including X-rays and other medical images. All these images will be stored electronically allowing them to be easily made available at different locations and forwarded to specialists for their advice. The emerging technologies are therefore bringing advantages over paper records and X-ray films that are still used in many parts of the NHS. Nondigital images, however, are frequently lost and sometimes difficult to read, and may lose their quality, as they are stored in a filing cabinet for long periods. One advantage of the new system is the facility to record details of everyone who has accessed an individual's NHS care record, which is not possible with paper records.

The stakeholders who are likely to benefit from the NPfIT programme are as follows:

Patients:

- Will eventually have access to their health record through a secure NHS gateway on the Internet, making patients more informed and involved in decisions about their own care and treatment.

- Provision of safer care with the availability of vital information for diagnosis and treatment (i.e., current medication, details of previous operations, test results, or allergies) regardless of geographical location and time of the day.

- Faster, easier, and a more convenient means of booking hospital appointments (at GP surgery or via telephone call, or over the Internet) allowing patients the luxury of discussing it with family, carers, or colleagues first.

Clinicians:

- Will have ready access to more comprehensive, up-to-date information to support diagnosis.

- Will be able to make more efficient referrals, gain alerts to contraindicated therapies, and significantly achieve early detection of disease outbreaks

- Will significantly reduce administrative burden dealing with chasing up referrals or missing notes.

The NHS management:

• Will provide better intelligence on how the NHS works and health of citizens by collecting anonymous information nationally.

• Will make it easier to observe and control the spreading of infectious diseases.

• Provide real number, in real time, not just a sample from spotter practices

• Will benefit from negotiating power. The first two years of NPfIT has saved the NHS over £430 million through the process of direct negotiation with suppliers and subcontractors.

Knowledge Management and Healthcare Delivery

Significant cost savings for better NHS intelligence for negotiating with suppliers and subcontractors have already been realized. In addition, however, better NHS intelligence can yield other benefits to the healthcare community, including the ability to more effectively respond to potential infectious disease crises.

To classify the KM elements of healthcare delivery, we consider a simple model in which we take the Modernisation Agency's integrated care pathways (NHS Modernisation Agency, 2004) as a descriptor of a generic process in care delivery. Clearly care pathways are no single process, but they reflect the emerging patient centred paradigm in healthcare (see Figure 3). Haines (2002) shows that KM must be targeted at providing the best support for each care pathway. Such a paradigm is followed by an analysis that asks where healthcare knowledge is stored. For the purposes of this analysis, we assume there are four types of knowledge repositories in a healthcare system:

1. **People:** This is perhaps the most obvious place to seek knowledge, particularly in medicine. One key element that distinguishes a medical consultation, for instance, from a counselling session, a tutorial, or a friendly conversation, is the knowledge possessed by the consultant. However, a great deal of healthcare knowledge is possessed and managed by people other than doctors — nurses and other professionals, as well, increasingly, as patients themselves. Finally, well people (those looking to remain well, and those operating as carers) are increasingly knowledgeable.

2. **Information sources:** This category includes paper-based and Web sites and other electronic information. Typical formats include journals, reference material, bulletins, and updates. With an increasing emphasis on process, this will also address strategic specifications for care delivery processes, details of local procedures, or to redesign those procedures (Guah & Currie, 2004).

3. **Data sources:** Here there is clearly scope for overlap with the previous category and, in some cases, with the next. However, data are meant to signify information that has not been processed. In this, we might typically place patient records, images, test results, perhaps even some statistics. The boundary with the previous category is not clean, but between them they define a spectrum of information, from raw digits to content.

Figure 3. Connecting sources of healthcare knowledge for data transfer

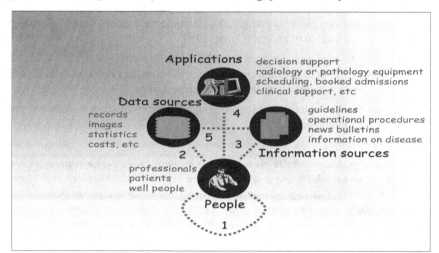

4. **Applications:** Increasingly information about the system is contained in software applications and other equipment. For instance, while an MR machine might generate an image, the workflow system by which it picks up information about the patient, together with the PACS infrastructure may embody a great deal of information about the healthcare delivery system in which it operates. The same can be said about direct booking systems or decision support systems, particularly if they contain an element of drill-down description based on operational procedures.

Figure 3 shows the need for Web services to maintain continuously live repositories of knowledge as opposed to large repositories. For instance, many processes cannot be considered, even theoretically, because the referring clinician (GP) is unable to communicate with an appropriate specialist in real time. Thus, the patient (often using postal and telephone contacts) becomes part of knowledge transfer pathway that can take many weeks to return to the GP.

Future IT Challenges for the NPfIT

With new emphasis now on e-government driving efficiency in the 21st century, IT has become more important than ever. Healthcare is a critical service to citizens where government needs to identify opportunities for increasing efficiency and cost control.

Public sector IT projects in UK — some may argue continental Europe — have not always led to successful outcomes (NAO, 2004). In an attempt to avoid these failures, the government has now introduced Gateway Reviews to evaluate IT projects at various points in their life cycles. There are six key goals for this review process. While this approach is formulaic and procedural, it is a step closer to recognizing the consequences of IT-enabled projects becoming overscoped and out of control (Currie, 1997).

Yet political imperatives of e-government are critical factors that affect public sector procurement for IT. Our research identified competing views about the IT procurement process with some defending the process and others highly critical of it.

According to the MD of a telecommunications and contact centre services company that sells heavily into the public sector:

One of the reasons public sectors IT projects fail is because public sector culture leads to the abdication of responsibility, especially with large projects. With these mega-projects, no one wants to get too close to them in case something bad sticks to them, so they create a structure where decision making responsibility is difficult to locate ... everyone and no-one is responsible! The larger the project, the more likely this will happen. The private sector usually has more stringent roles identified for managers, so this is what we need to do in the public sector.

An interviewee who heads project management software stated:

Government IT project failure isn't all down to individual cowardice or unwillingness to make a decision. The procurement cycles for many public sector projects are simply too long, leading to projects that can often fail to meet changing conditions. What this tends to do is shift focus away from what the organisation is trying to achieve and the outcome it wants to get. All of the brave creative thought that may have been there is stripped out. If the procurement phase of a project takes up too much time, the benefits can be eroded.

According to a member of the NPfIT team:

One reason IT procurement can take so long is that public sector bodies are bound to follow certain rules if the project meets selected criteria. For example, if the project value falls above a certain level, it must be put out to tender through the Official Journal of the European Commission (OJEC). The NHS had to advertize to the whole European Community, going through various rounds of responses. After a lengthy period of consulting with potential suppliers through this process, the service providers finally get to negotiate contracts. Many companies will bid low to get the business but will then define the project requirements so strictly that any minor change requires more investment by the public sector customer. Because projects almost always change, this can introduce extra costs and complexity into the project as it develops.

A CEO for an IT consultancy contributed his verdict:

Even when the contract negotiation phases reached, mistakes are made. Government ne-gotiators were always forced to take the cheapest price in the past, and although this has changed slightly (the emphasis is now on "best value"), a culture of cheapness still exists within the public sector.

And according to a former member of the NPfIT team:

None of this is helped by the fact that many public sector IT projects are driven by politics. Public sector projects are driven by political cycles and so artificial deadlines are often set. They are driven by politicians, which creates a framework that isn't helpful. If politi-cians are driving the project, sometimes for overtly political reasons, it becomes difficult to set the projected benefits and deadlines of the project to benefit the real-world users at the sharp end.

These quotes demonstrate that one of the important differences between the public and private sector is that the political agenda can be a major driver of IT projects. Politicians played a key role in identifying and determining what needed to be changed in the NHS. Yet the follow-through of politicians was generally short-term, and this created a situation where it was difficult to impose a long-term agenda when the individuals taking these deci-sions were unlikely to be around, or indeed, accountable, for the results in the future. This scenario was highly criticized by many healthcare workers, who had become cynical about government policy making for the NHS.

Another key criticism about the IT procurement process was the highly bureaucratic pro-cedures involved in selecting IT service providers. In the European Union, all Requests for Proposals (RFPs) had to be advertized across the EU. This meant that any IT service provider who was part of the EU could apply. Such a system was highly cumbersome and did not always lead to the best outcome. Thus:

The cultural and procedural elements of IT procurement within the EU are not conducive to getting the best deal. The *OJEC (Official Journal of the European Community)* system is the biggest single inefficiency that I can think of. It seems to rely on benchmarking of specific performance indicators rather than generating competitive tension among those who are interested in the tender. Once a contract is signed, then a lot of inertia creeps into it, and the project scope often loses its way. In terms of IT projects, it is better to take on bite-sized chunks, rather than trying to build the whole thing at once. This also makes your project more flexible because you can adapt future requirements as political conditions change. Us-ing pilot projects can also help you to fly at least part of the project under the OJEC radar, keeping you within spending limits that do not require a huge European Commission-wide tender. Our experience is that many people run service lines as ad hoc items. You don't just want to know whether the application is alive and running or not. Identifying things like service levels and response times for your deployed IT service is also important. This will require a structured budget in advance.

Delineating IT projects into their component parts is a lesson that is often put forward as a key driver for success, yet one that is usually ignored. Scale and scope creep of IT projects is often depicted as a critical failure factor. Yet the IT projects that are part of the whole of the NPfIT are large scale and involve numerous stages. IT service providers will therefore need to work closely with all stakeholders if they are to avoid the common pitfalls of many large-scale IT projects.

Conclusion

While there is a great deal of academic literature on e-payment and e-government issues, this chapter combines both topics and proposes a framework and a measurement model that depicts important factors influencing patients' and medical practitioners' online behaviour. A structural equation modelling approach has been used to assess the relative importance and the strength of the relationships among different constructs, including users' previous experience, their trust in the availability of health information electronically, and their perceived convenience of the data access process.

The research results indicate that regional NHS trust (both in a frictionless use of the system and in e-healthcare security) can be seen as an important antecedent for the adoption of NPfIT on the part of the medical practitioners and patients alike. From the government's point of view, the potential for exerting influence seems to be somewhat limited. While national institutions in most Western countries are usually perceived as trustworthy, users' attitudes toward the medical data online may be more skeptical. This widely depends on users' previous experience with the automated systems, sadly through the interaction with businesses in the private sector.

This chapter has presented preliminary research findings about the NPfIT, which is the largest civil IT-enabled change programme in the world with the aim of automating various elements of healthcare service delivery. As a politically controversial, financially large, and technologically complex initiative, the NPfIT continues to attract positive and negative stories within the media. Our research findings confirm many of these negative reports. Yet, we also suggest that all large-scale IT-enabled programmes face similar challenges, and those relating to healthcare carry the addition burden of complex issues about how hospitals can control health costs while at the same time addressing other issues, such as meeting patient demands, ensuring the ability of service providers to deliver IT systems in line with national requirements, and the extent to which health workers are willing to change their working practices.

At the NPfIT, initiatives to control IT-enabled projects offer a potential solution to some of these issues, yet an increasingly bureaucratic approach is no substitute for winning the hearts and minds of the people who are affected by changes to working practices. While the NPfIT offers a unique and timely approach to standardizing the delivery of healthcare across the nation, we suggest that better communication channels are required to convince healthcare stakeholders that such changes are necessary and worthwhile. Finally, we suggest that, in meeting the challenges of a 21st century healthcare system, the NPfIT needs to be understood more as a large-scale programme to transform the culture of healthcare service delivery, rather than narrowly defined as an IT-enabled project evaluated on a narrow set of quantitative key performance indicators.

Analysis of data on the NPfIT to date indicated that there has to be an increase in the connection between service providers and medical practitioners to raise the efficiency of resulting applications. The implementation team also needs to increase the momentum actively in developing collaboration with users and strengthening user education to raise the utilization of the resulting information systems.

Handled properly, the public sector could work toward a more efficient, cost effective way of providing services with the aid of Web services applications. At this stage, any broader conclusion cannot be considered, given that the NPfIT is a 10-year project, part of a long-term modernization process for the future health service of the British people, still in its third year.

References

Atkinson, C. J., & Peel, V. J. (1998). Transforming a hospital through growing, not building, an electronic patient record system. *Methods of Information in Medicine, 37*, 285-293.

Barney, J. (1991). Firm resources and sustained competitive advantages. *Journal of Management, 17*, 99-120.

Baskerville, R. (1993). Information system security design methods: Implications for information systems development. *ACM Computing Surveys, 25*(4).

Boncella, R. J. (2004). Web services and Web services security. *Communications of the Association for Information Systems, 14*, 344-363.

Brown, T. (2001). Modernization or failure? IT development projects in the UK public sector. *Financial Accountability & Management, 17*(4), 363-381.

Currie, W. L. (1995). *Management strategy for IT*. London: Pitman.

Currie, W. L. (1997). Computerising the stock exchange: A comparison of two information systems. *New Technology, Work and Employment, 12*(2), 75-83.

Davis, F. D. (1989). Perceived usefulness, perceived ease of use and of user acceptance of information technology. *MIS Quarterly, 13*(4), 982-1003.

Department of Health (UK). (2000). *NHS plan: An information strategy for the modern NHS*. London: Author.

Department of Health (UK). (2002). *Learning from Bristol*. Oxford: Capstone.

Devaraj, S., & Kohli, R. (2000). Information technology payoff in the health-care industry: A longitudinal study. *Journal of Management Information Systems, 16*(4), 41-68.

Eisenhardt, K. M., & Martin, J. A. (2003). Dynamic capabilities: What are they? *Strategic Management Journal, 21*, 1105-1121.

Guah, M. W., & Currie, W. L. (2004). NHS information quality and integrity: Issues arising from primary service provision. *International Journal of Healthcare Technology and Management, 6*(2), 173-188.

Guah, M. W., & Currie, W. L. (Eds.). (2005a). *Internet strategy: The road to Web services solution.* Hershey, PA: Idea Group.

Guah, M. W., & Currie, W. L. (2005b). Web services in national healthcare: The impact of public and private collaboration. *International Journal of Technology and Human Interaction, 1*(2), 48-61.

Haines, M. (2002). Knowledge management in the NHS: Platform for change. Retrieved May 9, 2006, from http://www.healthknowledge.org.uk

Majeed, A. (2003). Ten ways to improve information technology in the NHS. *British Medical Journal, 326*, 202-206.

National Audit Office. (2004). *Improving IT procurement.* London: The Stationary Office.

NHS Modernisation Agency. (2004). Review of waiting and booking information (ROWBI). Retrieved May 9, 2006, from http://www.content.modern.nhs.uk/NR/

Scott, W. R., Ruef, M., Mendel, P. J., & Caronna, C. A. (2000). *Institutional change and healthcare organizations: From professional dominance to managed care.* Chicago: University of Chicago Press.

Vriens, D., & Achterbergh, J. (2004). Planning local e-government. *Information Systems Management, 21*(1), 45-58.

Wanless, D. (2002). *Securing our future health: Taking a long-term view* (Final Report of an Independent Review of the Long-Term Resource Requirement for the NHS). London.

Wernerfeld, B. (1984, April-June). A resource-based view of the firm. *Strategic Management Journal, 5*, 171-180.

Wilson, E. V., & Lankton, N. K. (2004). Interdisciplinary research and publication opportunities in information systems and healthcare. *Communications of the Association for Information Systems, 14*, 332-343.

Zhang, D., Chen, M., & Zhou, L. (2005). Dynamic and personalized Web services composition in e-business. *Information Systems Management, 22*(3), 50-66.

Chapter XV

Empirical Study of the Municipalities' Motivations for Adopting Online Presence

Susana de Juana-Espinosa, University of Alicante, Spain

Abstract

Nowadays, many public organisations rely on e-government policies to seek modernisation and efficiency, although they might not follow a true strategic purpose. This is particularly common on the subject of Web site development policies. The objective of this chapter is to reveal the motivations for creating a Web page in local administrations, and thus determine the real nature of their Web sites. A personal survey was addressed to the CIOs (chief information officers) of 65 city councils out of the 69 with Web sites of the province of Alicante (Spain), regarding their perceptions about the purpose of their Web pages. The results show that, although most councils confer a strategic orientation to their Web pages, communication goals are more popular than internal efficiency concerns. Consequently, a general lack of commitment is found with local e-government strategies. Understanding the implications of this duality may help other public organisations develop their modernisation strategies.

New Requirements for Public Administrations

It is a major understanding that, in the information economy of the 21st century, organisations must compete by exploiting new sources of advantages and capabilities. This new economy is organised around the technology of Internet, and it has given rise to a dramatic modification of the basic parameters of time and space (Castells, 2001). As Porter (2001) and Carr (2003) affirm, a leading business today must be on the Internet to have a solid entity in the new economy; however, strategy cannot be based only in cyberpresence.

These arguments do not only apply to private sector firms. Those organisations, public or private, which ignore the potential value of and use of new information and communication technologies (NICT) may suffer essential competitive disadvantages. Indeed, public sector organisations also face the constraints of getting the approval of their "shareholders" (the citizens), to whom they must render accounts about how they manage their tax investments. Likewise, public organisations must consider citizens as customers, and thus provide them with best price and quality services (Cortés Carreres, 2001; Osborne & Gabler, 1992).

Therefore, it seems that the public sector is forcibly drawn to follow the same patterns that private firms do; this is, to evolve from efficacy to efficiency, and to use NICT on old structures to improve internal process management (Stamoulis, Gouscos, Georgiadis, & Martakos, 2001) as a result of the technological determinism that pervades this new economy. This is the phenomenon known as e-government, and its success will depend largely on the benefits and level of usefulness of the services it offers to citizens (Holden, Norris, & Fletcher, 2003). The benefits it is expected to deliver are a greater efficiency of the institutions concerned, improvements in public services, and political participation and transparency.

The urge to implement e-government policies has resulted in the adoption of many visions and strategic agendas (Accenture, 2004). However, each vision is driven by its own unique set of social, political, and economic factors and requirements. Consequently, the mission and objectives that emanate from such strategies vary enormously, according to the different views and conceptualisations of each government administration. These visions will be reflected in the applications and mechanisms that governments employ to implement their concept of e-government.

A government's Web page is the most significant application of the presence and dynamics of e-government because, although almost every public organism has e-mail, not all of them have a Web site, so that only a certain percentage have consciously put a step forward to their integration into the new economy, being thus the sole instrument that provides for electronic relationships between both parties (Criado & Ramilo, 2001). This is propped up by the fact that the Web page is the ultimate channel of implantation and support of the e-government policies, in addition to being the basic instrument to develop a minimum level of maturity, according to some authors (Eyob, 2004; Layne & Lee, 2001).

It is especially interesting to study the case of city councils' Web sites adoption. These particular public administrations play an increasingly important role as promoters of e-government plans financed by higher institutions. Moreover, their closeness to citizenship and local businesses contribute to greatly influence their lives (Holden et al., 2003), especially after the administrative decentralisation processes that have been happening lately in countries like Spain (MCYT, 2002).

The fundamental purpose of this chapter is to explore whether the local administrations that have created their Web pages as a means for modernisation have actually done so motivated by strategic purposes. It is also observed if there is any relationship between whoever had the initiative for the Web site and the given motivations. These two objectives will be achieved by directly asking the IT managers of the city councils themselves, specifically those of the Spanish province of Alicante. The chapter begins with a brief introduction to the state of the art, followed by a description of the empirical methodology used in our study. The third section presents and discusses the results, finalising with the main conclusions and implications of the research.

Developing Local E-Government Strategic Initiatives: The State of the Art

Firms must create added value for customers if they want to survive. New, intangible sources for competitive advantage are required in this chaotic environment, that of the Information Era. As a consequence, new strategies will be required to compete, which will depend on several interrelated resources. This evidence affects any kind of organisation, private or public, with or without profit motive, since what really matters for achieving success is the firm's strategic intent and how to comply with it (Prahalad & Hamel, 1990). Among these resources, notwithstanding their organisational relevance, NICT render a necessary service to strategy. Nevertheless, the Internet is no panacea, and therefore the former cannot be subjugated to technology.

Actually, NICT can only support true competitive advantages in combination with human resources management and trust relationships between firms (Kearns & Lederer, 2000). Mata, Fuerst, and Barney (1995) are of the same opinion, because, after applying the VRIN[1] model to NICT, they affirm that NICT management skills and IT managers' contact grids are more important to firms than technology endowments. Still, firms need to keep a close look when designing and implementing their NICT, since these give rise to strategic changes and lead the firm to strategic adaptation, by developing a proactive role in the firm's future (Benson, Bugnitz, & Walton, 2004; Tapscott & Agnew, 1999). This way, NICT is a necessary but not sufficient resource, because of its tangibility, due to technological assets' easiness of imitation and mobility (this is, firms can buy technology easily). As a result, and according to Carr (2003), every firm must treat its technological endowment as a required and pervasive commodity.

The same thing happens regarding online presence, a specific form of deploying NICT. It is common knowledge between the leading firms of the new economy that one must be on the Internet to have a solid entity in the new economy, but, as it has been argued, strategy cannot be based only in cyberpresence. Going online for the sake of it is not recommendable; as a matter of fact, it might be considered a lost investment. Definitely, success does not arise from possessing the right technologies, in the right place, at the right time, if they are not considered from the point of view of the strategic intent of the firm (Porter, 2001). This is a lesson well learned by the enterprises that cracked under the e-bubble burst.

Even though the e-business fashion has started to slow down since then, it seems that interest in e-government has been growing despite its limited success in many areas. Likewise, e-government is a relatively young field, so the concept itself is still at stake among scholars, as Al-Sebie and Irani (2003) have pointed out. Understanding what is meant by e-government becomes complicated because the construct means different things to different people (Grant & Chau, 2005). In addition, there are few cross-national comparisons of e-government practices (Lee, Tan & Trimi, 2005). This lack of consensus indicates that there is significant amount of work for scholars to do, from both theoretical and empirical perspectives. Although its potential benefits have been largely recognised, several studies prove that it has a long way to progress (Accenture, 2002; European Commission, 2002).

Among its many definitions, the Gartner Group (2000) refer to "electronic government" as the continuous optimisation of public services supplying, and of governance and participation by citizens by means of the transformation of internal and external relationships of public administrations through technology and communication channels deployment, specifically the Internet. It encloses, as well, the importance of institutional change and reshaping. The main concept here is that of "added value" of e-business (Amit & Zott, 2001) to be applied on public services, following the strategic objective of supporting and simplifying governance for a community comprised of citizens, civil society organisations, private companies, government lawmakers, and regulators on networks (Tapscott & Agnew, 1999).

From another point of view, Becker, Algermissen, and Niehaves (2003) suggest that e-government also comprehends the simplification and implementation of the information, communication, and transaction processes between and within governmental bodies, and, equally, between government and private business and persons. The development of lean business processes along the public sector value chain is a critical factor for the adoption, diffusion, and acceptance of e-government initiatives, taking into account that the political and managerial demeanours of public organisations add an extra level of complexity to the "e" dimension (Bannister, 2001). Following this thought, the idea that technologies are merely tools for improvement and modernisation must be eradicated. NICT adoption should begin with the deployment of their capacity for making substantial modifications to internal public workflows, as well as for increasing transparency and accessibility to public services, according to citizen demands (McIvor, McHugh, & Cadden, 2002).

On the other hand, Subirats (2001) is of the opinion that e-government's main concern is to improve communication between the government and the citizens, in order to make the latter become faithful consumers of public services. Neither the suitability of such policies nor the effectiveness of the organisations and processes affected are questioned, nor are the present working dynamics, so that traditional power distribution remains. This discrepancy may arise due to the behaviour of politicians who do not fully compromise with e-government policies (MCYT, 2003). The final result is that large scale government NICT projects often fall short on alignment with overall strategy, and few cementing NICT project changes into daily workflow will lead to successful NICT projects (Andersen, 2004).

Whatever the case may be, to create and improve electronic public services may result in a higher pressure on the overexploited technological and human resources (Holden et al., 2003). The magnitude of the costs in which public administrations incur behave then as friend and foe. Positive investment returns will only happen if the e-services provided with that money are widely known, and if citizens and public employees do actually use those applications (Strejcek & Theil, 2002). Other benefits may also be expected to show up, likely in terms of political reputation. This is especially remarkable at local levels because small administrations do not usually have an overall view of the public structure.

Focusing on a local point of view, e-government involves managing all municipal processes, in and outside administrative premises, and deploying intranet and extranet applications. To do so, both managers and managed must be endowed with the proper software to achieve such integration, besides developing whatever changes in the internal workflow may be necessary to make the city council's administration run smoothly (Waisanen, 2002). As a consequence of trying to lessen e-government's risk as much as possible, local governments tend to imitate "successful" initiatives, as long as their costs do not overcome the savings generated by its implementation. Anyhow, to ensure the effectiveness of a local e-government project, it seems crucial that city council members question themselves about how to comply with these budgetary and acceptance issues. This is, local organisations must clarify beforehand the strategic intent (if there is any) of their e-government policies to ensure that public money is properly invested.

The implementation of e-government implies different objectives and levels of transformation in public services in different geographical environments (Weerakkody & Choudrie, 2004). Particularly, Criado and Ramilo (2001) show in their research on Spanish municipalities that size and level of interaction are related, which has been also proved by the empirical work of Eyob (2004), confirming that having less resources has led municipalities to lower levels of e-government maturity.

Actually, Spain ranks 34 in the e-government readiness index among all UN (United Nations) member states,[2] lagging behind most of its fellow members of the EU (European Union).[3] It does not show in the high positions of the latest Accenture reports, neither as "Visionary Follower" nor as "Steady Achiever," nor as "Innovative Leader" (Lee et al., 2005). This means that the degree of sophistication of Spanish e-government is not very high, and that is probably due to the lack of information about this topic between governments (which leads to insufficient integration and collaboration), and between citizens.

E-government's maturity must continue to change and evolve in keeping with stakeholder requirements, despite the current applications and e-services provided. Without discussing this topic in detail, a basic model of Web page adoption is that of Koh and Balthazard (1997), in terms of the organisational use of the Internet:

- **Informative Web:** The Web page only disseminates one-way information. Some feedback can be obtained by means of e-mail. Every organisation is able to get to this level, as long as they have a static Web page. Most e-government programs emphasise this information provision component (Accenture, 2004; Grant & Chau, 2005).

- **Transactional Web:** It allows transactions (monetary or not) of products and services, directly or indirectly. It is a two-way communication Web, where service offering and delivery are the key developments.

- **Operational Web:** The Web page is designed to connect, vertically and/or horizontally, the systems of the implicated agents, to share online information inside and outside the organisation. This underlying transformation ranges from more effective services delivery to greater participation through relationship building with stakeholders, embracing many aspects of the so-called "new public management" (Grant & Chau, 2005).

As said before, most of the Web pages of Spanish city councils can be categorised as informative or transactional. Although many organisations own the means and resources to receive online orders, what lacks is integration between their back-end and front-end activities, which has a lot to do with strategic intent of the technological endowment of the council.

NICT strategies are, following the proposed objective of modernisation of the city councils, a good opportunity to involve citizens in the definition of their municipality's future model. Nevertheless, a lack of strategy and information can also impact the effectiveness and usefulness of the electronic tool itself (Weerakkody & Choudrie, 2004). As von Haldenwang (2004) has put it, fast results can only be expected where a sound institutional base and good technical and infrastructural facilities exist. Therefore, instead of adopting a *Weberian* approach[4] (Mower, 2001), public administrations should change their perspective toward client demands by means of the NICT to get to know and satisfy their needs.

Therefore, the strongest barrier faced by e-government is having it supported on a Web site with no strategic intent. This is, if a public organisation does not consider strategic reasons when deciding to construct a Web site, but of another kind such as communication or imitation. In other words, it seems necessary that city councils should think twice about how and why they are going electronic, so that they develop their own e-government strategy through an analytic and integrated plan.

Given its importance, it is necessary to comprehend the true reasons why a local government chooses to construct its own Web page, whether there is a true strategic intent for modernisation, or if it is only a matter of isomorphism, or if it stands for a communication purpose without further considerations. In any case, investment returns on the Web page creation and maintenance will be affected, in the long and the short term. Empirically studying the reasons for constructing a Web page will reveal whether city councils do actually start off strategic intent in the adoption of municipal Web sites.

Empirical Study of the Motivations for Developing Local Web Pages in Alicante (Spain)

Data and Methodology

Although there is a growing body of e-government literature, little of it comes from empirical research. In addition, current research on e-government, particularly if it regards local administrations, consists mostly in the exposition of individual, limited initiatives, which avoid theoretical frameworks that may provide them with a solid foundation (Becker et al., 2003). While these studies advance the knowledge of e-government, they are limited in nature and scope. Consequently, practical applications of electronic local administration have fully profited neither from a suitable body of knowledge, nor from a conceptualisation of its key elements that may improve its performance, since these practices keep evolving at a fast pace (Norris & Moon, 2005). This has brought up a growing interest for introducing academic perspectives that, from a qualitative and quantitative point of view, may lead to an integrated view of local e-government.

The results shown here are part of a wider study carried on those city councils of the province of Alicante, located on the southeast coast of Spain, that had published a municipal Web page. The province of Alicante was chosen because it has a large number of municipalities, 141, of which almost 50% had created Web pages.[5] Moreover, these municipalities are very diverse in terms of population, economic resources, and richness (as local budget), so it would offer a wide scope for research.

In the outset of the research, 69 city councils had their own municipal Web pages. 65 of them agreed to collaborate, answering to a structured questionnaire regarding their e-government policies. The astonishingly high rate of response, 92%, could be explained because of the use of personal interviews to gather information and the eagerness these professionals showed when asked for their opinion.

This quantitative survey was carried out between February and April of 2004, by means of a personal interview to the CIOs of these city councils (when possible), or to the person in charge of managing IT resources, but nevertheless a civil servant instead of a politician. These subjects have been chosen because they seem to have a professional, objective view of what is the past, present, and likely future of e-government in local administrations. This has been taken after other research in the field such as Fundación Auna (2004), ICMA (2002), and Norris et al. (2001). Since our goal is not to investigate public policies, but organisational efficiency matters, it seems best to get information out of a qualified professional who knows the internal strategic IT process, to provide homogeneity and validity to the given answers.

In order to present a realistic list of motivations for establishing a local online presence, qualitative data were taken into account: six interviews were conducted to chosen local e-government professionals, known by their involvement in e-government best practices. Their information also led to a more interesting and accurate interpretation of the statistical results. This combination of techniques for retrieving information will allow for a comprehensive analysis of the subject, providing the researchers with a more realistic view of what councils do and think. Also, this use of complementary sources is recommended when approaching areas in development such as e-government (Mingers, 2004; Zweig & Dawes, 2000).

Main Qualitative Results

A final list of motivations for the adoption of a local Web page has been designed from the literature review, specifically the questionnaires of Hart and Teeter (2000), and ICMA (2002), as well as from the interviews to e-government experts before mentioned. It comprises the following items.

Being on the Internet

Many councils, as many private organisations, have the belief that having online presence is a reason by itself, specially when there are not many resources to spend on e-government. It is true that having a Web page is a solid indicator of technological modernisation, but, being necessary, it is not sufficient. Still, the experts abide for this better than nothing, since more complex Web pages are a waste of resources because citizens are not prepared to make the most of them.[6] This is a characteristic particular of isomorphic councils.

Creating a New Communication Channel Between the Council and Its Customers, Whether External (Citizens) or Internal (Employees)

This reason is related to a change in the council's orientation towards citizens and employees, fulfilling the need to communicate with them fast and directly. The connectivity of Internet provides an ideal communication channel between the administration and its citizens, permitting instant feedback and information exchange regardless of time and space constraints. The configuration of a very simple Web page allows to the organisation of the city council's information and of organising itself to the eyes of the citizen, who do not have to know the administrative process in order to interact with its local administration.

Improving the Internal Efficiency of the Council's Management

The Web page can be considered a means for improving internal efficiency, since it allows the start of expediency online, as it has been argued before in this chapter. While establishing this new information system, incoherencies and inefficiencies should show up, tasks and processes should be simplified, and bad habits should be eradicated, which calls for the reinvention of government appraised by the "new public management" philosophy. The experts believe, on the other hand, that many councils do not have this consideration because they are not prepared yet (and will not be in the near future) for the necessary internal changes that are implied. It is expected, then, a divergence between literature and practice at this point.

Increasing Public Services Quality by Offering Them Online, or Simply Providing More Information About Them

The public sector must adapt its working procedures to the several communication channels that the citizens may use (telephone, Internet, and physical presence), without duplicating the workflows. The administrative act passes to a second place, being the priority to understand what customers want and how they want it. The trouble is that this approach implies market research, which is an activity that councils do not usually engage in, except in terms of political desires. Nevertheless, informational Web pages can show a list of the public services provided and their responsible person, and that may be very well a reason for adopting an online presence.

Leveraging the Municipality's Degree of Development in Various Accords (Economy, Sociology, Etc.)

This reason is somehow related to reason c, because it implies a deep conception of e-government, but in a less specific manner. This should be particularly important for those local administrations that pretend to deal effectively with multiple stakeholders from social, political, and economic domains. It could be said, according to the interviewees, that this is the political view, and ultimate objective, of the establishment of an official Web page. In spite of this, those councils that act under isomorphic or promotional premises may not have this global perspective.

Making G2B (Government-to-Business) Relationships Easier

Another type of stakeholder that local councils must take into account is the network of businesses of the municipality, as customers of public services themselves. This reason reveals a need for transformation of the local administration towards leveraging market forces to enhance public sector and private sector relationships. What the interviewed experts have to say here is that businesses do not vote, and many of them do not interact directly with the council because, for this kind of administrative work, they hire a consultant.[7] Therefore, no special treatment is expected, regardless of their potential for the municipality's welfare.

Modernising Local Administration by Integrating It into the New Economy

This is the epitomic strategic reason. It is related to creating a holistic commitment of all stakeholders to the overall effort. It can be mistaken, say the experts, with establishing a static online presence, if that is what politicians may understand with integration into the new economy. Enhancing local administrations is more than that, as it has been shown, and it needs a strong political root in strategy; yet it does not necessarily use the Internet.

Promoting the Municipality and Its Resources (Advertising)

This is, for sure, the most important reason for many city councils. Internet is seen as a worldwide window by which to attract tourism and sell themselves as a municipality and as a political force. The kind of services offered in such a Web page are the most required by citizens, believe the interviewed experts. Even more, this objective is cheap and easy to achieve, given that an informational Web is the only requisite. Consequently, experts affirm that it will be the top one.

Reducing the Operating and Overhead Costs of the Public Organism

Even if money should not be the driving force of e-government policies, it is a benefit that has to be kept in mind by politicians and civil servants. Fully deployed e-government applications will bring in gains in productivity because of a smaller stream of paperwork. Breaking the bureaucratic black box should rationalise internal processes, standardise new procedures, and provide them with enhanced transparency.

Ranking of Reasons According to Quantitative Measures

These nine reasons have been presented to the CIOs as a set of 5-point Likert scales in which the interviewees had to position their degree of agreement or disagreement with the several reasons presented (1: None; 5: Total).

Figure 1 illustrates the most valued motivations are "creating a new communication channel" and "promoting the municipality and its resources." It can be inferred that these local organisations have built their Web pages more as an external means of corporative communication (this is, advertising and publicity) than as a tool for the improvement of the public organisation. That means that the organisational side of NICT resources has not been really taken into account, only its role as intermediary between the local administration and society.

Also, Figure 1 shows that the reasons of organisational nature are the least appreciated. Cutting down costs, improving the relationships between administration and local businesses, or improving internal process management do not appear among their main objectives. This stands against the high value granted to public service quality, and, oddly enough, against the theoretical concept of efficiency in public organisations introduced by Weber (1979). Yet it agrees with the negative expectations of the interviewees.

There is, in fact, a disruption in the mean value of the reasons related to modernisation and service quality, and those regarding internal processes and management. It could be said then that NICT have an external orientation towards citizens and service management. This is, NICT are considered as one more resource among many others when complying with local modernisation, as a means of support for other strategies. Nevertheless, regardless of whether politicians bet for e-services or not, most councils see their Web pages as instruments to become known and penetrate the first layers of the new economy. What varies is the degree of importance given to its ability to improve efficiency and competitiveness.

Figure 1. Perceptions on the motivations for local Web pages

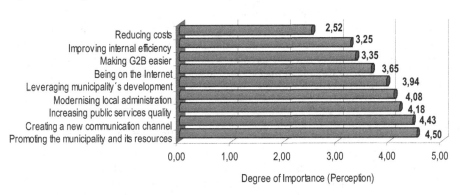

Sources of Initiative for the Web Page

As a secondary objective, it was considered interesting to analyse who had the initiative of creating the page. The aim was to realise whether the research subjects were self-conscious about the importance of public modernisation activities, or if the idea of establishing a Web presence has arisen from an external organisation.

Regarding this issue, the experts affirm that, generally, city councils do not stand out for their organisational skills, since it is difficult for local politicians to understand the relevance of "organisational planning." It is too much of a long-term view, and therefore those local governments that outline strategic plans are a minority. From here, the experts believe that city council Web pages come from a "me too" behaviour: if other councils have it, why not them? These initiatives may even come from third parties, generally a higher organism that may have identified, or believed, a need for e-government in a certain municipality.

Figure 2 shows that, on the one hand, in 55% of the councils the idea came up from a politician. On the other, the 29% of the Web pages were initiatives from the local civil servants. These figures indicate that the city council's workers, either politicians or staff, have a great interest in their environment towards the modernisation of their municipality.

It must not be forgotten, however, that most civil servants do not possess any decision-making power, and thus they will not come up with these types of suggestions to the city council unless they had a strong certainty that it would be well received by the political levels. Consequently, these results corroborate the experts' opinion that the initiative does not belong only to politicians or to public servants, even if the former are the ones that finally approve the project.

Only 16% of the interviewed councils did not create their Web page out of their own initiative. The Web site adoption source was either a higher level public organism (province or regional level), or an association for the promotion of the information society. These organisations have no responsibility for how the council is run, or what strategy is followed, but they are supposed to help out those municipalities with fewer resources. By encouraging the councils to adopt online presence, they intend to break up the digital divide that may arise between differently endowed municipalities.

Figure 2. Web page construction initiative

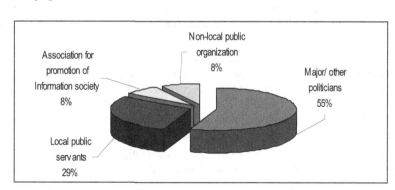

Figure 3. Initiative vs. reasons (χ2 tests)

Web Page Initiative	Chi-Squared	Sign.
Creating a new communication channel	31,790*	0,000
Being on the Internet	11,104	
Modernising local administration	5,204	
Making G2B easier	10,238	
Leveraging municipality's development	16,442	
Reducing costs	10,515	
Improving internal efficiency	7,945	
Promoting the municipality and its resources	37,182*	0,000
Increasing public services quality	29,393*	0,003

*Note: * Significant for p<0,005*

In order to know more about these perceptions, Figure 2 results have been cross-compared with who was responsible for the idea of adopting Web presence, indicating where there was a significant relationship between both variables by means of χ^2 tests, as shown in Figure 3. This figure demonstrates that the only significant relationships affect the following three motivations: creating a new communication channel, promoting the municipality and its resources, and increasing public services quality. Unfortunately, the small number of cases does not allow for establishing a full relationship, and thus the data has not been disclosed in this chapter, but it is suggested that NGOs and nonlocal public administrations give less importance to communication- related initiatives.

Thoughts for Present and Future Practices

Discussion of Results

The city councils studied here regard their Web pages as a double purpose instrument: to make themselves known to their end users and to make a way into, even so slightly, the information society environment. These two objectives can be achieved without having to develop a proper strategy, despite the maintenance and opportunity costs that this behaviour will bring on.

As predicted, communication targets stand out as being the main reasons for local politicians and public servants, as statistics confirm. They are the only goals, apart from increasing public services' quality, that appear to have been thought of in purpose, which is illustrated by the significant χ2 tests, as can be seen in Figure 3. From here it can be assumed, once more, that there is no real strategic intent, at least for the population studied.

Reasons such as improving municipal development or modernising the local administration achieve secondary places with high values, which means that, although this kind of motivation is a true concern for the city councils of Alicante, they are not given top priority, at least from a technological point of view. This goes along the same lines as the eEurope indicators of benchmarking, that focus only on government Web sites such as government-to-citizens (G2C) and government-to-business (G2B) portals, for which significant progress has been made in the last few years (Lee et al., 2005). This is, technology is regarded as a means of support for municipal development strategies when complying with the organisational goals of modernisation. It seems, in the end, that Web pages are generally taken for granted, despite their importance as the basis for the rest of e-government policies.

Nevertheless, the presence of quality objectives between the highest valued reasons provides a door, albeit indirectly, for local councils modernisation and efficiency. Likewise, the results of Eyob (2004) and Norris et al. (2001) go along the same lines, since they have also detected that the external dimension of Web pages, that is, communication and advertising roles, are more important to local councils than modernisation strategies or internal efficiency issues.

In sum, quantitative results concurred with what was declared by the interviewed experts, who thought that local administrations follow the path open by regional or national public organisations, and are frequently a step behind society's needs. Local administrations, say the interviewees, follow the lead of national and regional administrations; some only respond to society's pushing demands. There is no general plan, but a set of limited political actions. They do not suppose that local governments draw general strategies; instead they live on political short-term activities for specific areas.

Another important finding from this research is that Web page adoption initiatives may not even belong to the city council, but from a higher institution or a nongovernmental organisation that sees or provokes an electronic government need in the municipality. Despite this institutional origin, differences in the implementation process shall affect the Web's appearance, contents, and subsequently, success.

It is necessary to explain the role of these types of organisms. The financial sources for Spanish local e-government project are the municipal budgets for the most part. No private funding is usually accepted, so that politicians are not compromised. Other resources come from higher public organisms, but seldom of the monetary kind, save for the European Union programs. Instead, they provide with training courses, qualified personnel, and Web page hosting and assistance, among others. This way they help the smallest and less developed municipalities to achieve at least the informational stage.

We strongly believe that it is a must for these organisations to go back one step before investing more money in their Web pages and other technologies if they really want them to be worthy. This lack of strategic intent may lead to e-administration failure as much as any of the other barriers faced by public administrations. Benefits will arise, though in the middle term, which is one of the main handicaps observed: local councils move along four-year terms (an electoral period), and so it might happen that the present government will not see the effects. Since the initiative, as it has been shown, comes in most cases from a politician, it looks like it will seldom occur.

Some specific policy recommendations that can be suggested to improve the maturity level of municipalities' NICT adoption strategies could be:

- City councils should be aware of the possibility of technological outsourcing as a means for developing more complex Web pages without incurring high costs and personnel training.

- The person responsible for the Web page should be someone from the council, so as to not lose control over its contents and security of the transactions.

- Every municipality is different, and their Web pages should be, too. Canned solutions from isomorphic purposes will not be as efficient as thoroughly studied Web pages that attempt to satisfy the municipalities' stakeholders. A contingent perspective is needed, without incurring a lack of balanced development.

- Incentives should be provided for content development, which means that city councils must learn what citizens, as major stakeholders, want from their public administration, and show them what they have done. Citizens will not use e-services if they do not know of their existence and how they work.

- National coordinating mechanisms for separate local initiatives, as well as universal Internet access, must be two of the pillars of a sound e-government strategy that complement the Web page adoption initiatives.

- And, above all, these governments should promote integrated schemes to planning and implementation public sector reforms and technology adoption. Successful e-government requires a thorough strategic approach from bottom (workflow reengineering) to top (informational Web pages).

Less developed countries can take a leaf of this book, since many of them are starting to implement their Web pages at present, and therefore they can benefit from this experience and try not to repeat the same errors while applying benchmarking policies. For the majority of the world, telephones are a technology beyond reach; food, sanitation, and literacy are more urgent needs (Unesco, 1998). Technology does not in itself solve social and economic discrepancies within societies, and can often exacerbate them: it can be an enabler and peril in itself. Their governments, for those reasons, must not be infatuated with the power of technology, but keep their heads on their shoulders before investing resources that may be more useful in other areas.

Governments should provide a conducive environment to encourage the participation of all stakeholders, rather than letting individual, disparate initiatives sprout as untasty mushrooms.[8] Accordingly, human resource development and universality access policies are compulsory to ensure efficient and adequate NICT adoption strategies at local levels. The digital divide must be broken with quality rather than with quantity, one step at the time.

Conclusion and Final Thoughts

Literature claims that the Internet is a cost-effective means for public information and services management and supply, as demonstrated by the numerous successful e-business experiences of private firms. The new added value of the public sector comes from the transformation of the old impersonal bureaucratic organisation to an interactive model that values two-way communication and service customisation.

Our findings show that there is a wide acceptance of Web pages in Spain's city councils as a means of improving their external communication flows and image, with various degrees of maturity and complexity. In addition, it has been proved that these Web pages are not only political or promotion instruments, even if their main purposes are such. Instead, the strategic nature of these applications has somehow permeated the mentality of city councils, especially those of their public workers.

Spain's NICT potential remains largely unexploited, even though. The empirical results disclose that the general tendency is that of not considering beforehand the strategic applications of their Web pages, showing discrepancies between academic theory and practice. Local councils seem to think that these tools are implemented for improving the relationships between local councils and citizens, but they do not go further into seizing the opportunity for rebuilding their organisations at the same time as they create the Web page, despite the long-term benefits that confer a proper e-government strategy for local councils. A likely reason is that they believe there is no need for such technological deployment, because citizens will not use them, and so they believe that the investment will not be returned. Or maybe it is just a matter of unawareness of the real benefits that well-designed technology may earn.

If public administrations, whether local or not, not fully conscious of the advantages that these new economic strategies bring them to help in achieving their organisational success, they will not be able to transmit the message that is expected from them. This means that they do not understand the business value from efficient online strategies and, as a consequence, their end users will not be properly adapted to the changes that the new environment brings pressure upon. E-government needs to be taken beyond immediate benefits of the NICT; or else, the public sector will not fulfil its role as catalyst of the development of the society they serve and support.

It is time, then, to take a step back and reflect on what has been done and how it has been done, before investing in technological applications which potential will not be fulfilled unless the council reconsiders its strategic purposes. That is to say, local government must reformulate their internal processes and their public service attendance, so that they jump from task automatisation to true e-government. In the middle term, social and monetary profits will override all adaptation and financial costs.

To conclude, we would like to say that technology, indeed, allows instant access to relevant information for public decision-making processes, but, at the same time, it requires a careful daily updating to provide useful information. This feature is not likely to be part of a static Web page, which is the consequence of a static purpose underneath its establishment. It will also incur in dependency on external resources, especially if the initiative for the Web page adoption has not even come from somebody within the council, because a nonstrategic purpose implies a lack of provisions for other resources, specifically know-how, qualified staff or both. That is why is so important to recognise which are the true reasons: whether publicity, strategy, or isomorphism.

Limitations and Future Research Trends

Our conclusions have to be interpreted under the light of our research limitations, being the most relevant of them, we believe, the fact that interviews were done to the CIOs instead of the politicians. This decision had its gains, due mainly to their objectiveness, but also its drawbacks, such as the evidence that CIOs, as public employees, do not often participate in the council decisions. Therefore, these results are built upon their feelings toward these projects, as they have been instructed to perform. Still, we believe that the fact that public servants, as permanent staff, are less influenced by political goals make up for this flaw.

Finally, it must be acknowledged that this research has been carried on a limited geographical space, and in a limited time span. Local e-government's evolution will be greatly benefited from continuing research, particularly comparisons with data from other geographical areas and longitudinal studies, in order to monitor if these communication purposes pervade and persist among local governments, or if they are simply a response to the current "e" fashion and a lack of social pressure for top priority strategies.

References

Accenture. (2002). *eGovernment: Realising the vision*. Retrieved May 9, 2006, from http://www.accenture.com

Accenture. (2004). *eGovernment leadership: High performance, maximum value* (E- Government Executive Series). Retrieved May 10, 2006, from http://www.accenture.com

Al-Sebie, M., & Irani, Z. (2003, July 3-4). E-government: Defining boundaries and lifecycle maturity. In *Proceedings of the 3rd European Conference on e-Government*, Trinity College of Dublin, Ireland (pp. 19-30).

Amit, R., & Zott, C. (2001). Value creation in e-business. *Strategic Management Journal, 22*, 493-520.

Andersen, K. V. (2004). *E-government and public sector process rebuilding (PPR): Dilettantes, wheelbarrows, and diamonds*. Boston: Kluwer Academic Publishers.

Bannister, F. (2001). Dismantling the silos: Extracting new value from IT investments in public administration. *Information Systems Journal, 11*(1), 65-84.

Barney, J. (1991). Firm resources and competitive advantage. *Journal of Management, 17*(1), 99-120.

Becker, J., Algermissen, L., & Niehaves, B. (2003, December 16-18). Implementing e-government strategies. A procedural model for process oriented e-government projects. In *Proceedings of the 2003 International Business Information Management Conference (IBIMA)* [CD publication], El Cairo, Egypt.

Benson, R. J., Bugnitz, T. L., & Walton, W. B. (Eds.). (2004). *From business strategy to IT action*. Hoboken, NJ: John Wiley & Sons.

Carr, N. (2003). IT doesn't matter. *Harvard Business Review, 81*(5), 41-50.

Castells, M. (2001). *The Internet galaxy: Reflections on the Internet, business and society.* London: Oxford University Press.

Cortés Carreres, J. V. (Ed.). (2001). *Manual práctico de gestión de RRHH en la administración local.* Madrid: Dickinson SL.

Criado, J. I., & Ramilo, M. C. (2001). E-government in practice. An analysis of Web site orientation to the citizens in Spanish municipalities. *The International Journal of Public Sector Management, 126*(3), 191-218.

European Commission. (2002). *Web-based survey of electronic public services.* Retrieved May 9, 2006, from http://europa.eu.int/information_society/eeurope/benchmarking/list/2002

Eyob, E. (2004). E-government: Breaking the frontiers of inefficiencies in the public sector. *Electronic Government, 1*(1), 107-114.

Fundación Auna. (2004). *IV Informe anual sobre el desarrollo de la Sociedad de la Información en España eEspaña 2004.* Retrieved May 9, 2006, from http://www.fundacionauna.org

Gartner Group. (2000). *Singapore's e-government initiative.* Stamford, CT: Gartner First Take.

Grant, G., & Chau, D. (2005). Developing a generic framework for e-government. *Journal of Global Information Management, 13*(1), 1-30.

Hart, P., & Teeter, R. (2000). *E-government: The next American revolution.* The Council for Excellence in Government. Retrieved May 9, 2006, from http://www.excelgov/egovpoll/report/report/contents.htm

Holden, S. H., Norris, D. F., & Fletcher, P. D. (2003). Electronic government at the local level. *Public Performance & Management Review, 26*(4), 325-344.

ICMA (International City/County Management Association). (2002). *E-government survey.* Retrieved May 9, 2006, from http://www.icma.org

Kearns, G. S., & Lederer, A. L. (2000). The effect of strategic alignment on the use of IS resources for competitive advantage. *The Journal of Strategic Information Systems, 9*(4), 265-293.

Koh, C. E., & Balthazard, P. (1997). *Business use of the World Wide Web: A model of business usage.* Paper presented at the 1997 Americas Conference on Information Systems, Association for Information Systems, Indianapolis, Indiana. Retrieved May 9, 2006, from http://hsb.baylor.edu/ramsower/ais.ac.97/papers/koh.htm

Layne, K., & Lee, J. (2001). Developing fully functional e-government: A four stage model. *Government Information Quarterly, 18*(2), 122-136.

Lee, S. M., Tan, X., & Trimi, S. (2005). Current practices of leading e-governmet countries. *Communications of the ACM, 48*(10), 99-104.

Mata, F. J., Fuerst, W. L., & Barney, J. B. (1995). Information technology and sustained competitive advantage: A resource based analysis. *MIS Quarterly, 19*(4), 487-506.

McIvor, R., McHugh, M., & Cadden, C. (2002). Internet technologies. Supporting transparency in the public sector. *The International Journal of Public Sector Management, 15*(3), 170-187.

MCYT (Spanish Ministry of Science and Technology). (2003). *Aprovechar la oportunidad de la sociedad de la información en España*. Retrieved May 9, 2006, from http://www.red.es

Mingers, J. (2004). Paradigm wars: Ceasefire announced who will set up the new administration? *Journal of Information Technology, 19*, 165-171.

Mower, M. (2001). Cybercitizens: The electronic evolution in local government. *Management Services, 45*(4), 18-19.

Mutula, S. (2004). Making Botswana an information society: Current developments. *The Electronic Library, 22*(2), 144-153.

Norris, D. F., Fletcher, P. D., & Holden, S. H. (2001). *Is your local government plugged in? Highlights of the 2000 electronic government survey*. Baltimore: International City/County Management Association (ICMA) and Public Technology, Inc. (PTI).

Norris, D. F., & Moon, M. J. (2005). Advancing e-government at the grass roots: Tortoise or hare? *Public Administration Review, 65*(1), 64-75.

Osborne, D., & Gaebler, T. (1992). *Reinventing government: How the entrepreneurial spirit is transforming the public sector*. New York: Plume.

Porter, M. E. (2001, March). Strategy and the Internet. *Harvard Business Review*, 63-78.

Prahalad, C. K., & Hamel, G. (1990). The core competence of the corporation. *Harvard Business Review, 68*, 79-91.

Stamoulis, D., Gouscos, D., Georgiadis, P., & Martakos, D. (2001). Revisiting public information management for effective e-government services. *Information Management & Computer Security, 9*(4), 146-153.

Strejcek, G., & Theil, M. (2002). Technology push, legislation pull? E-government in the European Union. *Decision Support Systems, 34*, 305-313.

Subirats, J. (2001). *Los dilemas de una relación inevitable. Innovación democrática y TIC*. Retrieved May 9, 2006, from http://www.democraciaweb.organización/subirats.pdf

Tapscott, D., & Agnew, D. (1999). Governance in the digital economy. *Finance & Development, 36*(4), 34-37.

von Haldenwang, C. (2004). Electronic government (e-government) and development. *The European Journal of Development Research, 16*(2), 417-432.

Waisanen, B. (2002). The future of e-government: Technology fuelled management tolls. *Public Management, 84*(5), 6-9.

Weber, M. (1979). *Economy and society*. Berkeley: University of California Press.

Weerakkody, V., & Choudrie, J. (2004, July 25-27). Exploring e-government: Challenges, issues and complexities. In *Proceedings of the 2004 European and Mediterranean Conference on Information Systems (EMCIS)* [CD publication], Tunis, Tunisia.

Zweig, M., & Dawes, W. (2000). Qualitative and quantitative methods: A new design for introductory economics. *The American Economist, 44*(2), 30-35.

Endnotes

[1] VRIN: Valuable, rare, imperfectly imitable and nonsubstitutable (Barney, 1991).

[2] United Nations World Public Sector Report 2003: E-Government at the Crossroads. Retrieved May 9, 2006, from http://unpan1.un.org/intradoc/groups/public/documents/un/unpan012733.pdf

[3] We do not consider here the new acquisitions from Eastern Europe.

[4] As in Weber's (1979) bureaucracy model.

[5] By March 31, 2004.

[6] According to the 2005 Report of Fundación BBVA (*Internet as leisure space*), almost 50% of the citizens actually prefer going to the public premises than utilising their online facilities. This fact stands for the opinion mentioned. Retrieved May 9, 2006, from http://www.bbva.es

[7] Indeed, the BBVA report indicates that only 37.2% of the firms employs Internet channels to communicate with public administrations, and that includes the Tax Office.

[8] As planned, for example, by the government of Botswana (Mutula, 2004).

Chapter XVI

User Involvement in E-Government Development Projects

Asbjørn Følstad, SINTEF Research Institute, Norway

John Krogstie, SINTEF Research Institute, Norway

Lars Risan, University of Oslo, Norway

Ingunn Moser, University of Oslo, Norway

Abstract

User involvement in e-government projects is presented and discussed. Different methods and practices are analyzed in relation to a differentiation between traditional government participatory practices and human-computer interaction (HCI). Some of the user involvement practices are exemplified through two Norwegian case studies: (1) An electronic patient journal for hospital based health care and (2) an electronic mail journal, where the Norwegian public (via the Norwegian press) is provided insight in public sector correspondence. User involvement methods and practices are in particular discussed with regard to the challenges of the wide range of users and stakeholders, legal limitations, and evolving goal hierarchies of e-government projects. Future trends and research opportunities within the field of user involvement in e-government development are identified.

Introduction

The development of e-government systems and services is highly prioritized in governments all over the world. Electronic service provision shall enable the governments to reach a number of ambitious goals, typically including citizen-centric service provision, increased service quality, increased efficiency of government service provision, lowered cost of government service provision, and improved democratic processes through improved dialogue between the government and its citizens, for example, European Commission's i2010 (2005) and eNorge2009 of the Norwegian Department of Modernization (Moderniseringsdepartementet, 2005).

Successful implementation of e-government depends on the ability to develop services that match the goals and requirements of users and stakeholders. Also, the democratic involvement of the end users and stakeholders in the decision-making process is important due to the nature of the services provided through e-government. User involvement throughout the development process is a major vehicle to ensure both democratic participation and adequate consideration to user and stakeholder goals and requirements.

In the present chapter, different user involvement practices will be discussed with regard to the degree which makes it possible to meet core challenges of user involvement in the e-government development project. Some of the practices will be exemplified by two case studies from Norwegian e-government development. One of the case studies is from the health sector. The other is related to public insight in government administration. The cases will serve to exemplify different aspects of the general results and discussions presented in the chapter, as well as providing interesting insights in their own right.

Background

Definitions

In order to present and discuss methods and practices of user involvement in e-government service development, broad definitions of users, user involvement, and e-government services are provided.

Users are understood as comprising end users (primary users), secondary users, and stakeholders (Maguire, 1998). End users include internal and external users of a service or system. External users typically include citizens, private enterprises, and organizations as well as other government bodies. Internal end users include employees of the government bodies owning or in other ways responsible for the service or system in question. Secondary users include personnel responsible for installation and maintenance of the system. Stakeholders include persons or bodies directly or indirectly responsible or affected by the system or service. Examples of e-government stakeholders may include different levels of management in the government bodies owning the system, interest organizations, and political actors.

User involvement is understood as activities in information system development processes where information about users and stakeholders is collected, or users and stakeholders are actively involved in the requirements engineering, construction, or deployment phases of the project. This definition of user involvement includes the methods for user involvement traditionally advocated within the framework of Human-Computer Interaction (HCI), as well as practices for user involvement firmly established as part of government development projects.

E-government development will be understood as an IT-based service and system development in the public sector, where the end users may be internal users employed by the government or external users including citizens or private enterprises and businesses. The definition is based on an understanding of *e-government* in line with the Information Society of the European Commission, who defines e-government as "the use of information and communication technology in public administrations combined with organizational change and new skills in order to improve public services and democratic processes and strengthen support to public policies" (European Commission, 2004). Similarly, at eGov, the official Web site of the U.S. president's e-government initiatives, e-government is described as "the use by government agencies of information technologies that have the ability to transform relations with citizens, businesses, and other arms of government" (U.S. Government, 2004).

Practices and Methods of User Involvement

Practices and methods of user involvement include a multitude of different traditions and approaches. One useful way to analyze this multitude is to differentiate between (1) methods and practices designed to fit software engineering processes and (2) government participation practices.

The field of HCI is an example of an approach developed to conduct user involvement in software development projects. This field covers methods and practices suited for the development phases of analyses, requirement specification, design, and evaluation. HCI methods for analyses include analyses of users and stakeholders, user tasks, and context of use; methods for requirements elicitation and description include workshops, interviews, field studies, personas, and use cases; methods for design include rapid prototyping, design patterns, card sorting, and storyboarding; and methods for evaluation include analytical methods like cognitive walkthroughs and heuristic evaluation as well as empirical methods like user tests and field evaluations (Maguire, 2001; Usabilitynet, 2005).

Within the government sector a different form of user involvement has evolved. Government user involvement practices typically include user reference groups following the development project for a substantial period of time, inclusion of user representatives in the project team, inclusion of user and stakeholder representatives in project steering committees, formal and semiformal audits of project plans and system specifications, workshops with user and stakeholder representatives, involvement of user interest organizations, public meetings, and public information activities.

Previous Studies

The importance of user involvement in e-government development projects is accentuated through different studies. Other investigations of government software development projects include the Organization for Economic Cooperation and Development (OECD) document, "The Hidden Threat to E-Government" (Puma, 2001), and the British Government report, "Government IT Projects" (Pearce, 2003). Both of these investigations conclude that e-government development suffers from, among other things, nonoptimal procurement processes and lack of end-user involvement. The British government report also concluded that there is a need for improved requirements specifications in e-government projects.

At the same time it may be argued that public sector software projects have relatively high levels of user involvement, most likely higher than the average private sector software project. One Norwegian study, conducted as an interview study of e-government project leaders, showed that user involvement in the public sector is rife — and surprisingly so, compared to the conclusions in the documents from OECD and the British Government referred to previously. However, the same study reported that the user involvement conducted in ongoing e-government development projects typically are aligned with the approach of government participatory practices rather than the approach of, for example, HCI (Følstad, Jørgensen, & Krogstie, 2004).

There may be several reasons for the amount of user involvement in government projects. Often there exists an obligation to openness to the public, where development projects with sufficient impact on the public will be accompanied with public audits. Further, the government has an obligation to provide an equal public service level to all citizens; thus projects that are critical with regard to accessibility for the public should involve interactions with interest organizations. Finally, the tradition of democratic participation (Emery & Emery, 1976; Emery & Thorsrud, 1976), where the empowerment of employees through participation is often regarded as a goal in itself (Elden, 1986; Wilpert, 1994), is historically more solidly established within the government bodies than within the private sector.

Følstad (2005) points out that user involvement may be conducted to reach two goals:

1. Enable user participation, thereby building a foundation for user ownership, increasing the users accept for new solutions and minimizing resistance in change processes.

2. Provide input in the system development process to facilitate the development of usable or user-friendly systems or services, in line with the needs and requirements of all relevant user groups.

Følstad (2005) argues that government participatory practices may be particularly suited to meet Goal 1, whereas methods and practices of, for example, HCI, are particularly suited to achieve Goal 2. An imbalance between the methods and practices used in a particular project may result in the achievement of only one of the goals of user involvement; the end result is that either the system is not optimally usable and user-friendly, or the implementation process is hampered by lack of ownership or resistance to change.

Challenges of User Involvement in E-Government Development Projects

The tradition for user involvement in e-government development is clearly an asset in past and future public sector software development projects. At the same time it is important to secure that user involvement of public sector software projects is fully utilized with regard to establishing an efficient development process towards a successful result. In order to reap the harvest of user involvement efforts in e-government projects, it is of paramount importance to understand and meet some basic challenges with regard to successful user involvement.

Basic challenges of user involvement particular to e-government development projects include:

1. **Wide range of users and stakeholders:** E-government projects may involve a tremendous range of users and stakeholders. Further, the development process may be the subject of political attention and control, and important stakeholders may be found in several different governmental units.

2. **Legal limitations:** The goals and requirements of several stakeholders and user groups may be at odds with the juridical obligations of system components — for example, with regard to personal privacy. There are also severe legal limitations with regard to the procurement process of public purchases. Most national and transnational regulations concerning bid processes and government contracts are developed with large purchases in mind, which often results in fixed requirements and may make it difficult to specify iterative software development processes in the bids and contracts.

3. **Unclear goal hierarchies:** E-government development may aim to serve several, not necessarily coherent, goals. This is partly due to the multiplicity of stakeholders and to the noncommercial nature of the services, challenging — often by democratic necessity — the development or explication of unified goal hierarchies.

These challenges of successful user involvement in e-government development will be illustrated through two case studies. The case studies are both from the Norwegian public sector.

Case Study 1: Electronic Patient Records in Hospital Based Health Care Practice

This study investigates the strategies for user involvement in the process of implementing an electronic patient record in one of Norway's largest hospitals from 1997 to the present. It shows how the approach has moved from a concern with democratic rights and participatory system development through a "narrowing down" to the mobilization of HCI oriented methods, to the current iterative philosophy in information infrastructure development. In the latter, participatory practices and HCI methods are combined in what is now seen as a continual, ongoing iterative development process.

Case Study 2: The Political Controversy Around the Electronic Mail Journal (EMJ)

This e-government service was initiated by the Norwegian Department of Administration in 1994, when a limited EMJ was implemented on a trial basis providing the Norwegian press with electronic access to the post journals of the central state administration. In 2003 the requirements specification for a permanent EMJ, intended to serve a broader range of end users, was developed, only to be politically discarded. The case study shows that the long trial period was due to a political conflict involving internal and external users, and clearly illustrates how a wide variety of stakeholders, users, and goals may interact to shape an e-government project. The study also provides insight on how an e-government project may be situated between politically important goals such as governmental openness and personal privacy, advocated by a variety of actors at different points in time (Risan, 2004).

In the following two sections the case studies will be presented. In the next two sections the same case studies will be used to actualize the three identified challenges to user involvement, and how the challenges were handled in each of the cases will be presented. In the two final sections future trends of user involvement in e-government projects are identified and a final conclusion is drawn.

Case Study 1: An Electronic Patient Record (EPR) at the Rikshospitalet University Hospital

Rikshospitalet and EPR Background

The Rikshospitalet University Hospital is one of Norway's largest and most specialized hospitals. It has a longstanding history as a university and research hospital and as a national hospital attributed responsibility for competence in rare and complex conditions. Today it functions as a regional hospital for southern Norway but is also still attributed national responsibility for special competence in a range of conditions. This means, first, that many patients with rare, complex, or chronic conditions have a long history with the Rikshospitalet because they are followed up on a long-term basis. Secondly, it means that many cases also require extensive coordination and cooperation involving many different actors and units within the hospital and across large distances in the Norwegian health care system.

The potential advantages in electronic information and communication in planning and administration as well as clinical practice may therefore seem obvious. The challenges identified in public plans and programs for IT in health care, including availability of and access to patient information; improved planning and coordination and cooperation between clinical as well as administrative units; integrated care provision and patient trajectories; and sharing of competence between medical staff and specialties, all seem to apply here.

The Rikshospitalet was an early actor in this field. When the plans to introduce IT into health care first emerged in the mid-1990s (Samferdselsdepartementet, 1996), the Rikshospitalet went into negotiations with the four other regional hospitals in the country about the development of one common electronic patient record system. The first public programs for IT were experienced as top-down and administratively motivated, concerned with patient-administration, planning, resource allocation, and health care management, rather than clinical needs and interests. Recognizing their common interests in future electronic systems for handling patient information, the regional hospitals therefore decided to meet the pressures "from above" with joint and proactive engagement.

Early "Deep" Implementation and Broad User Involvement

In 1996 the Medakis project was born. It was going to be based on one of the existing, locally developed EPR systems and wide user involvement in the process of its redesign and implementation. A bid was advertised and three tenders were submitted. Siemens with its DocuLive EPR was chosen as the platform and contractor, and a deadline for when the EPR was going to be fully implemented was set to 1999. Working close to and involving users was seen to be of paramount importance in order to develop a system that would meet clinical needs and interests in addition to administrative ones. And, crucially, meeting clinical needs and interests was seen as a necessary condition for mobilizing clinical staff as active users. The strategy adopted included:

- "Deep implementation" in a few selected departments at a time
- A participatory design approach with user representation based on different professional interests with regard to the uses of patient related information
- Deployment of existing structures of representation and participation, such as standardization committees
- Workshops with actual users as well as their "political" representatives

The process turned out to be slow, long-lasting, and painstaking. Despite a wide mobilization of representatives of different user groups in diverse working groups, reference groups, and a series of workshops, between 1997 and 2001, DocuLive had been implemented in no more than six clinical departments in the Rikshospitalet. The uptake rate was extremely slow: by the end of 2001 it had only 400 out of 3,500 potential users (among the hospital's 4,000 employees). Deliveries were late and still due. Workshops repeatedly had to be postponed, and it became difficult to get resources, that is, users for participation in the design process out of clinical departments. The actual and practical output from user involvement activities also turned out to be limited. Involving users served other functions like participation and legitimacy, but not feedback for design. A new strategy with much more limited user representation, based partly on testing in usability laboratories and involvement of a small group of (super) users only, was therefore adopted. But Siemens had moved on to new products and left DocuLive EPR behind. By 2003 the Medakis project was formally closed even though its goals had not been met. Although electronic production and exchange of patient related information had been pursued for several years, it was still only partial.

Reorienting towards a Flexible Development Strategy

In 2002-2003 a new national health policy reorganized health care in "health regions" and health organizations based on New Public Management (NPM) principles. Along with this came a new governmental program for the implementation of IT technology in public services, which again pointed out health care as a service particularly ripe for the introduction of IT. Last but not least, Rikshospitalet was about to move into new facilities and become colocated for the first time. All of this radically changed the conditions of possibility for the work on the EPR. The management of the hospital became interested in the potential of IT, not in the least due to an explosive growth of patient records, an acute lack of archive space, and increasing problems with availability of and access to patient information. Financial and structural resources were allocated. The Department for Health Administration also became involved, and altogether a new strategy was laid down.

The new strategy was based on a notion of introduction of IT in large organizations, such as highly specialized hospitals, as an incremental and ongoing process. The idea was that instead of "deep" or "full" implementation of a complete system in one department at a time, one should roll out DocuLive, or at least the documentary part of it, on a grand scale in order to get started with a critical mass of users. Further, one was to start out with a thin layer of functionality, postpone the departmental adaptations and reorganizations as well as the integration of systems, and invest heavily in infrastructure for user support. Within the next six months DocuLive had 1,700 users, and by the end of 2003, 3,400 out of the 3,500 potential users had been mobilized.

As of today, the picture is still one of limited functionality, hybrid solutions (paper records plus digital records), as well as a portfolio of specialized IT systems, for example, for laboratory test results and radiological images. This situation is however not peculiar to our case, but fits with what has been shown and argued in other contexts, too, especially for larger hospitals: The deployment of EPR systems has been slower than expected, and an EPR system is still not found in a completed state (i.e., as a central repository) (Nilson, Grisot, & Aanestad, 2002). Even so, the Rikshospitalet now pursues a strategy proceeding from the infrastructure already in place, viewing information systems as process rather than product, and aiming to integrate existing systems and components (including DocuLive EPR) within an architecture of a flexible portal solution, rather than hoping to construct the ultimate information system from scratch.

Case Study 2: *Electronic Mail Journal (EMJ)*: An Experiment in Openness

Case study 2 is a trial project to let the Norwegian press have Web access to the post (mail) journals of the central Norwegian state administration, called the *Electronic Mail Journal (EMJ)*. EMJ has been a trial project for more than 10 years and the establishment of a permanent service has been postponed several times. At the same time it has become an indispensable part of Norwegian political journalism. There are courses in how to use the system at journalism schools. Political journalists — the end users — have nothing wrong to say about the system. The current — and somewhat strange — situation is that the trial project is still on trial and it has become an institution.

In the following we will use the EMJ case to show how e-government takes place in a heterogeneous space of actors and stakes. This is a contested space, a space where power relations are played out, and where the strategies applied may be open and juridically founded or tacit and informal. We will see that in this contested space and, in this particular case, the experience of the end users is systematically overlooked, whereas the same users also have great powers, as they, as journalists, control the major newspaper and broadcasting offices in Norway.

The Story of EMJ

In 1990 a temporary Norwegian governmental body — the "information committee" of the government in office — took an initiative to develop the *Electronic Mail Journal*. This journal was to provide its users with online access to short descriptions of all mail correspondence sent from or received by a government body. Based on searches in the online mail descriptions, the user could order paper copies of mail thought to be of interest from central archives. Two years earlier similar post journals had been made available in paper format, from an office in the central administration, with access limited to registered journalists.

The first small version of EMJ was launched in 1993, with five ministries/departments delivering their post (mail) journals to the system, and with five newspaper offices as end users. A governmental body with responsibility for developing the computer based infrastructure in the state administration got the responsibility for the system. This office, the Central Information Service (SI), had little political power, but neither was it under close political control. It had fairly free hands to develop new computer systems.

The first version of EMJ was a failure, seen from the perspective of the end users. This was due to — in hindsight — to obvious reasons: At the newspaper offices the systems was technically implemented on a stand alone PC, separated from the daily life of the journalists. This initial trial project tells us one thing, namely that the EMJ was initiated as a small, specialized trial project at a time when no one had the slightest idea of what the Web would become.

SI and the Ministry of Administration nevertheless decided to continue the project. One possible improvement was obvious, due mostly to a new technology: the World Wide Web. The next version was to become Web-based, and from 1995 and onwards it was found on the desktops of the end users. The use of it is now greatly accelerated. SI started a quite considerable expansion of the number of users and content providers. The rumor of its usefulness spread in the press, as well as among the archive personnel in the administration. SI helped the rumor to spread, often in bilateral discussions with the archive personnel of the ministries and departments. By the end of the decade the system had become an established institution, and the number of users has continued to rise ever since, now to include most editorial offices and most of the central governmental bodies.

In 1999 the Ministry of Administration decided to evaluate the further development of the system. One major concern was the fact that there seemed to be no legal basis in keeping such a system of openness running only for a limited segment of the public. A law firm was appointed to evaluate the further legality of the system, together with a consulting company. The layers concluded, on a normative basis, that a continuation was possible, and that the EMJ should be open to the public (Advokatfirmaet Føyen & Andersen Consulting, 1999). The consultants concluded that such a continuation was technically unproblematic, given that fairly standard technical security measures were followed.

However, one of the evaluation report's conclusions was to become problematic; the layers saw a danger in the possibility of using the database to build what they called "person profiles." That is, they feared that systematic searches on person names could result in systematic "profiles" of how people had dealt with the state administration through their own mail correspondence, or through mail correspondence between government bodies or between other persons and the government. Could, for example, political loyalties be extracted from such a systematic search — later to be sold to political interest groups? The lawyers feared such a possibility and suggested that person names should be electronically tagged and made unsearchable if they appeared in post journal records more than one year old. (The person names would still be visible in the result of a search, but it would not be possible to search on them, using a possible search engine.)

The press interest organizations (notably the Norwegian Press Association) reacted very negatively to this proposal, feeling that such a limitation on the search possibility would severely hinder journalism, as it would make it difficult to search named politicians and other official persons of interest. In letters to the Ministry they argued that the actual possibility of building "person profiles" was nonexistent, and that they had a large body of users who could testify to the actual difficulty of such an endeavor. During the next years they made several attempts to make their position heard, but consequently felt neglected. In 2003 a governmental working group presented a report with recommendations on how to further develop the EMJ into a permanent service (Arbeids-og administrasjonsdepartementet, 2003). They referred to the position of the press, but followed the proposal made by the external layers four years earlier. There was to be a 12-month limitation on the searchability on person names, to avoid the possibility of building historically deep person profiles. The press association and leading journalists continued to protest this decision, and continuously felt overlooked in the decision process.

In our research on the EMJ process we have read most of the correspondence and reports on EMJ, and we have interviewed several of the central actors in the politics of the development process. It has given us a picture of how the arguments and stakeholders are situated. In the following we will present two main arguments in the EMJ case: the argument of openness and the argument of personal privacy.

Positions in the Case of EMJ

The Argument of Openness

All the involved parts of the EMJ process agree on an open state administration, where the press as well as the public in general have access to as much as possible of the inner workings of the administration; this is seen as a democratic good. No one questions this explicitly. Furthermore, no one questions that EMJ is a truly helpful tool in achieving a more open state. This gives the EMJ project an unquestionably strong position, used for what it is worth by its supporters and acknowledged by its critics. In line with this argument, it is also argued with authority that a future EMJ must be open to the general public, not only to the press. The "information privilege" of the press in the current institutionalized "trial version" cannot be upheld.

The Argument of Personal Privacy

Since the 1999 report, this has been the most controversial theme, at least the argument most explicitly discussed. Personal privacy has a strong position in Norway, much due to the work of the Data Inspectorate ("Datatilsynet"), a public office with quite broad authorities in cases concerning personal privacy. When the 1999 report introduced this possible problem, they did so by reference to an earlier decision by the Data Inspectorate. The inspectorate had argued that the risk of abuse of post journals warranted a cautious practice.

Ideologically, all actors in the EMJ process recognize the value of a strong protection of personal privacy. In practice most of the actors also support the Data Inspectorate in their cautious line of reasoning. Notably, the departmental 2003 committee followed this line, repeating the conclusions made in the 1999 report, made by the external layers. The press organizations, as we have seen, strongly rejected this cautiousness. Their position, however, was registered but not taken into account. In the context of our investigation of how to involve users in the development of e-government projects, we found this situation interesting: EMJ is an extraordinary deep and wide trial project. It has been running for many years and has many end users. These users are very satisfied. They claim to have relevant experience of how the database may be used. They are not listened to, or so they claim. We looked closely into this situation. Is it really the case that the departmental committee and the Ministry of Administration ignore the argument of the press? And is the press right when they claim that the Ministry and the Data Inspectorate have no empirical support for their cautiousness?

The first thing we noticed when doing our documentary study was that the cautious attitude towards electronic mail journals was first stated by the Data Inspectorate in 1998 (then concerning the journals of a county administration). It was later believed and used as a source of authority and never questioned or in any way tested empirically (except by the press). In this space of opposing claims we did a qualitative survey in order to see if some empirical trends could be found. We tested the presence in the EMJ base of 1,768 random persons and got some strong indications. Only 41 persons had one entry or more in the base, and we interpreted our findings to include only 4 persons with entries that possibly could be used to build person profiles. It does seem very unlikely that these few occurrences (0.23%) will legitimate any systematic attempts to build person profiles.

The Near Future of the EMJ

There are more stories to be told about the strategic moves around the EMJ project. These stories could broaden the picture of the "power game" of this project, and they would further exemplify the points we have made previously. EMJ is not a top-down, politically driven, and politically correct celebration of openness and democracy, like the e-mail address president@whitehouse.gov, just to take a small but well known example. It is not a project that any politician has ever used in order to win votes or promote himself/herself as a promoter of democracy. However, EMJ really works for openness. That is, it shifts power and changes power relations. There is little doubt that this has become possible because the project has been driven "bottom up," by less powerful institutions and through a series of small steps.

The EMJ is also about to get its top-down legitimacy. In June 2005 the Minister of Justice proposed a new Freedom of Information Act. The six-year defenders of EMJ have worked in the committee that has written the proposal (notably the leader of the Norwegian Editorial Association that works closely with the Norwegian Press Association). In the proposal, EMJ is legally authorized, and the law is likely to be approved by the Parliament.

Challenges to User Involvement Actualized in the EPR and EMJ Projects

The two cases presented here provide different, but hopefully complementing, insights with regard to the nature of user involvement in e-government projects.

Both projects have been running for almost a decade. However, in the EPR project of Case 1, the project has been run as a classic large IT project, with clear top-down management, involvement of a large number of users, and gradual transition from a waterfall-like project organization to a more iterative approach. The subsequent approach to user involvement in Case 1 has been to move from the involvement of a large number and broad range of users to the involvement of a smaller number of users and more HCI-like methods.

In the EMJ project of Case 2, on the other hand, has evolved from the bottom up. The nature of the project as a trial project has allowed for a series of smaller developments, rather than a large-scale effort. As a result, the EMJ project of Case 2 has been more iterative in nature, and one has been able to discard dysfunctional solutions like that of the stand-alone system of the first version of the EMJ. User involvement in the project has been small scale and somewhat arbitrary. This has resulted in a system highly suited for the needs of a relatively small number of end users, but not accessible for the vast majority of the population.

The challenges of user involvement is actualized in different manners in the two cases, and in the following three sections the three basic challenges outlined previously will be presented for each of the two cases.

Challenge 1: Wide Range of Users and Stakeholders

In both cases there are a wide range of users and stakeholders. Further, both cases have been subject to political control, and important stakeholders may be found across several government bodies.

In Case 1 there are numerous occupational groups involved as end users of clinical information systems, within as well as beyond the actual hospital, and also beyond the different groups of health care professionals. The management of health care organizations as well as public authorities are, for instance, also users of information from the EPR. Indeed, information in this context serves multiple administrative, legal, and clinical purposes. And, crucially, due to the character of modern health care practice and medical knowledge, the actual information uses, users, and use contexts are also continuously changing (Moser, 2005; Moser & Law, 2006; Star & Ruhleder, 1996).

The number of occupational groups involved as end users of the EMJ in Case 2 is somewhat smaller than in Case 1. However there exist important differences between major user groups such as journalists as external users and archive personnel as internal users. Further, the range of stakeholders in Case 2 may be just as, or even more, overwhelming than in Case 1.

Both in Case 1 and 2, the users, uses, and use contexts of information and information systems are multiple and continuously changing and evolving. This means that contrary to what is assumed in traditional information systems design, they cannot be known beforehand, become represented through user involvement techniques, and laid down once and for all (Bratteteig, 2003, 2004; Nilson, 2002)

Challenge 2: Legal Limitations

The organizational environment of the EPR in Case 1 has been heavily regulated through professional standards as well as through legislation. The case has been subject to fluctuating conditions due to shifting political priorities, strategies, and decisions — in a number of different settings. IT development projects are, for instance, subject to the yearly budget negotiations and allotment in Parliament. So even if the project is given high priority by hospital management, continued investments are dependent upon allotments by Parliament as well as the Regional Health Enterprise. Further, subprojects on user involvement will often be regarded as "extras," coming on top of the "real thing," and consequently be especially exposed to budget cuts — even when they are required by law, as in the Working Environment Act and the Data Agreements (emphasizing the right of all to influence the conditions for their work, including introduction of new technologies) (Bratteteig, 2004). It also means that IT projects are subject to reforms and reorganizations of the health care system, with mergers between hospitals and redrawing of boundaries between health organizations, and the consequences for IT and other infrastructure entailed in such processes. The uses of patient related information is regulated by acts on health registers and data protection, and on patient treatment and delivery of health services. These acts are not necessarily in accordance, and the introduction of electronic systems for storing, retrieving, and communicating patient data makes these conflicts acute and requires resolve.

Case 2 also involves important legal and ethical considerations, in particular with regard to public openness and personal privacy. It is interesting to note that the considerations conducted by the government body of the Data Inspectorate are in direct opposition to the considerations of public openness conducted by the press as an external user. It gives food for thought that the objectivity of relevant juridical and ethical considerations may easily be questioned, thus running the risk of reducing such considerations to little more than the opinions of the parties to the case.

Challenge 3: Unclear and Changing Goal Hierarchies

In the EPR project of Case 1, the fact that information and information systems in health care serve multiple purposes and users goes together with the fact that the introduction of electronic information systems aims to serve many, not necessarily coherent, goals. These include not only improved cost-effectiveness but increased quality of health care services — for instance, through improved availability of and access to patient information; improved planning and coordination and cooperation between clinical as well as administrative units; integrated care provision and patient trajectories; and sharing of competence between medical staff and specialties. The relations between these different purposes, goals, and users are rarely addressed, but the legitimacy of the projects and investments — not in the least due to the character of the services as public services very much relies upon the fact that the different goals go together.

In Case 2 the goal hierarchies related to the EMJ have been evolving slowly throughout the decade-long trial period. In the early phases of the EMJ trial project, none of the involved parties seemed to be able to understand neither the potential impact nor the possibilities of the EMJ. Then the goals for the service have developed bottom-up, resulting in a quite incoherent goal structure across the involved actors. This lack of coherence seems to represent no real problem as long as the service keeps running as a service for the press as is the case today. However, if the grander ambition of the EMJ with a larger number of end users is to be realized, one is clearly in for a challenge with regard to untangle the goals established at the different stakeholders and users.

Handling the Challenges of
User Involvement in Practice

So how can we think about the situations in the EPR and EMJ case studies, the processes that led to them, and what lessons may be learned? Which critical points and challenges have to be taken into account in public service development projects?

Handling the Challenges in Case 1

With regard to the EPR of Case 1, the immediate response is that just as the potential benefits of electronic information and communication in health care may seem immediately obvious, so do the potential difficulties and pitfalls. The lesson learned here, 10 years later, is that a strategy of user involvement does not work as a panacea. User involvement is crucial but very difficult. Leaving aside the four other regional hospitals involved, only trying to make one common electronic patient record for such a huge and diverse organization as the Rikshospitalet, with a history and culture of relatively autonomous departments, equally heterogeneous work practices (including information, communication and documentation practices), and a portfolio of specialized clinical information systems grown out of years of experience and experimentation in refining work practices is truly a difficult task.

The Rikshospitalet and its IT department changed to a strategy of iterative design. In these information systems and the organizational transformations they are involved in, they are treated as ongoing processes rather than as products that are first designed and constructed, then implemented and used (Orlikowski, 1996). Such a reframing of the practice of systems design, use, and real life use is understood as part of a prolonged if not continuous design and development process (Bratteteig, 2003). This move is based on the fact that many organizations, including health care organizations, no longer fit with the image of traditional work organizations for which information systems design was developed. Instead, the organizations into which new technologies are implemented today, including many public service organizations, have less clear and stable boundaries; they have multiple and heterogeneous users; they depend on and interact with numerous other information systems; and both uses and users are evolving rather than stable and fixed (Hanseth & Aanestad, 2003). In such situations, users, user needs, and use situations cannot be known and laid down once and for all in the construction of a system. Instead they have to be flexible and adaptable in order to be usable and useful. Accordingly it has been proposed that system development move from metaphors of system building and construction work to metaphors of cultivation and evolution (Brooks, 1986; Hanseth, 2005; Nilson, 2002).

What does this change in strategy for Case 1 mean for the role of user involvement? Far from having made the identification of user requirements an impossible task, the iterative approach turns it into an ongoing pursuit. It makes the role of use and the analysis and configuring of uses and users more important, not less important. This may however require different approaches and techniques for different purposes, including democratic legitimacy, representation of affected users and interests, as well as usability. In the Rikshospitalet the transition to limited user involvement in the early rounds of design and testing of new products, versions, or components is today supplemented by a structure for the systematic and continued collection and analysis of feedback from use. This is built up of a wide variety of arenas and channels for user involvement which combine components of participatory and usability philosophies. This includes established institutional arenas and ad-hoc forums; buy-out of critical personnel to the IT department for a limited period and specially designed workshops in the clinical departments; lab testing with users and IT department people sitting in and observing clinical practice; formal and informal networks; electronic channels and face-to-face meetings. It is an explicit aim to build up as wide and varied a structure for collecting feedback from use as possible.

The challenge of handling multiple, not necessarily coherent, goals is in Case 1 was tackled as an "art of balancing." The challenge to IT design and user involvement in this view is to be able to include, realize, demonstrate, and balance a wide range of gains, and so possible manifestations of the goal of the change are to open up and make possibilities, and keep the possibilities open rather than closing them down by forcing goal hierarchies or choices to be made. The legitimacy of IT projects and investments in public services very much depends on this multiplicity and coexistence of different goals. Cost-efficiency and cost-saving cannot be the only measures.

Handling the Challenges in Case 2

With regard to Case 2, we see the development of an e-government service in a contested space of various stakeholders and interests that has succeeded so far. This success may be due to the following reasons:

- The system has been developed "bottom up", by small and politically insignificant actors.
- The system was initially developed with very few users (end users as well as internal users). This limited the numbers of stakeholders, and made the system less danger-ous.
- The numbers of users (internal as well as external) have gradually increased, through a series of small and "insignificant" steps.

The EMJ system of Case 2 has scaled gradually, beyond what anybody initially had in mind. The present challenge then is to legitimate and found the project politically. The lack of "top down" political foundation gave birth to the EMJ service. However, in 2005, the lack of political foundation is probably the main reason why the project is hovering in an ambivalent space between a trial project and an institution. Also we have seen that the consolidation or further development of the EMJ may include a range of difficulties with regard to differences in goals between the involved users and stakeholders. Also the ongoing discussion with regard to juridical and ethical considerations needs to be concluded.

Future Trends of User Involvement in E-Government Projects

The future trends of user involvement in e-government projects needs to reflect the tendency to move towards smaller projects with a shorter timeframe and focus on cost-effective ef-fective development. This trend is clearly reflected in the change in Case 1, where there was a transition from large-scale user involvement in a sequential development project to smaller scale user involvement activities in a iterative project structure.

Due to increased focus on cost-efficiency of e-government projects, it is important that the goals of the user involvement activities are clearly established. Furthermore, these goals should be reflected in the choice of methods for user involvement. If the goal of the user involvement is user and stakeholder ownership and acceptance, then the traditional government participation practices of audits, user representatives in project groups, involvement of interest organizations and so forth may be sufficient. However, if the goal is to systematically collect user requirements and conduct user-oriented evaluations according to methods tailored to software development processes, the methods of, for example, the field of HCI, should be utilized.

Users and stakeholders, as well as their goals and requirements need to be viewed as continually evolving. This means that user involvement activities in the system development need to be distributed across the life cycle of the system. At the same time, the user involvement of subprojects included in the life cycle of the system will need to be conducted so that users and stakeholders are sufficiently involved in the analysis and requirements phases of these smaller projects.

Important future work of user involvement of e-government project will be to introduce and gain experience with resource-effective methods of handling the challenge of the multitude of user groups and stakeholders relevant in the development of e-government systems and services. Similarly it will be necessary to have a continued aim to manage evolving goal structures for e-government services, where the goals of different users are reflected. An evolving structure of goals, rather than early explication of a fixed goal hierarchy, seems to be a necessity for sound democratic development of public services. The process of managing a structure of evolving goals will require some central management and involvement of a number of actors. At the same time it is important that this process of continued updating of goal structures should help to facilitate the development process, rather than become a resource consuming activity hampering the development process. Solving the challenge of multiple users and conflicting goals by limiting the number of users, as in Case 2, may prove temporarily successful, but may involve future difficulties when the system is to expand and some of the user groups may be forced to give up some of their privileges.

Handling the legal constraints on e-government development is a challenge related to user involvement that is still not sufficiently solved. This is partly related to the case of cumbersome procurement processes, making it difficult to split a large systems development effort into smaller projects. Change in the government procurement practices will make it easier to conduct effective user involvement activities in the projects. Further, it is important to develop processes to avoid legal and ethical deliberations stalling the development process as in Case 2. In particular it seems to be important that the identification of users' needs and goals is kept separate from legal and ethical discussions, to avoid prolonged discussions where legal considerations are mixed with subjective goals.

Conclusion

User involvement in e-government development projects has been presented, as belonging to two different traditions and as conducted in two different cases. The two traditions of user involvement serve to exemplify two important goals with user involvement, namely participation and usability. The two case studies exemplify two different overall approaches to user involvement. Case 1 of the EPR shows an ambitious large-scale user involvement effort according to a sequential process structure, gradually changing to an iterative and pragmatic cost-effective focus on user involvement. Case 2 shows the bottom-up approach to service development with a strong delimitation of the number of users and stakeholders involved in the process.

The reliability and validity of the results presented from the studies needs to be commented on, given that general conclusions are drawn on the basis of the empirical input of two case studies from Norwegian e-government development. It is important to remember that the two cases are provided as examples of issues and trends identified by the authors through existing literature and documentation. Hopefully, the reported cases will help the reader better understand the challenges of user involvement in e-government projects, and may also facilitate an integration of the points made in the present chapter into the readers' existing experience.

The chapter also presents some future trends and research opportunities for user involvement in e-government projects. The research opportunities are particularly focused on meeting the challenges discussed on basis of the two cases. Often, the path to adequate user involvement may lie between the extremes of the two cases — with a top-down anchoring, planning of user involvement activities, and management of an evolving goal structure, and a bottom-up identification of user goals, needs, and requirements. Both cases indicate that smaller projects with a limited timeframe are more effective than large-scale projects, and that user involvement activities should be planned and managed accordingly.

Acknowledgments

This chapter was written as part of the research project EFFIN — Efficiency through user involvement (see www.effin.org). A main goal of the project is to adapt methods of user-centered design to the context of e-government development. EFFIN runs from 2003-2006 and is financed by the Norwegian Research Council through the FIFOS program.

References

Advokatfirmaet Føyen and Andersen Consulting. (1999). *Konsekvensutredning av prosjekt Elektronisk postjournal* (Public document of the Norwegian Ministry of Work and Administration No. 1999/02858 doc nr: 019). Oslo, Norway.

Arbeids- og administrasjonsdepartementet. (2003). *Elektronisk Postjournal Prinsipper for etablering av en ny elektronisk postjournaltjeneste i en åpen og brukerrettet forvaltning* (Public document of the Norwegian Ministry of Work and Administration No. 1999/02858, doc nr. 082). Oslo, Norway.

Bratteteig, T. (2003). *Making change. Dealing with relations between design and use.* Unpublished doctoral dissertation, University of Oslo, Unipub, Faculty of Mathematics and Natural Sciences.

Bratteteig, T. (2004, March 18). *Participatory design in present society.* Lecture for the doctoral degree, University of Oslo, Department of Informatics.

Brooks, F. P. (1986). No silver bullet. Essence and accidents of software engineering. In H. J. Kugler (Ed.), *Information processing '86* (pp. 1069-1076). Amsterdam, The Netherlands: Elsevier Science Publishers B.V. (North-Holland).

Elden, M. (1986). Sociotechnocal systems ideas as public policy in Norway: Empowering participation through worker-managed change. *The Journal of Applied Behavioral Science, 22*(3), 239-255.

Emery, M., & Emery, F. (1976). *A choice of futures. International series on the quality of working life.* Leiden: Martinus Nijhoff Social Sciences Division.

Emery, F., & Thorsrud, E. (1976). *Democracy at work: The report of the Norwegian industrial democracy program.* Leiden: Martinus Nijhoff Social Sciences Division.

European Commission. (2004). *About e-government.* Retrieved May 11, 2006, from http://europa.eu.int/information_society/programmes/egov_rd/about_us/text_en.htm

European Commission. (2005). *i2010: A European Information Society for growth and employment.* Brussels: Author.

Følstad, A. (2005, September 12). Why do we involve users? The role of the HCI practitioner in e-government projects. In *Proceedings of the Interact 2005 Workshop on User Involvement in E-Government Development Projects*, Rome (pp. 23-28).

Følstad, A., Jørgensen, H. D., & Krogstie, J. (2004, October 23-27). User involvement in e-government development projects. In *Proceedings of NordiCHI 2004*, Tampere, Finland (pp. 217-224).

Hanseth, O. (2005). *From systems and tools to networks and infrastructures — from design to cultivation. Towards a theory of ICT solutions and its design methodology implications.* Retrieved May 11, 2006, from http://heim.ifi.uio.no/~oleha/Publications/ib_ISR_3rd_resubm2.html

Hanseth, O., & Aanestad, M. (2003). Bootstrapping networks, infrastructures and communities. *Methods of Information in Medicine, 42*(4), 385-391.

Maguire, M. (1998). *User-centred requirements handbook.* EC Telematics Applications Programme, Project TE 2010 RESPECT (Requirements Engineering and Specification in Telematics), WP5 Deliverable D5.3, version 3.3.

Maguire, M. (2001). Methods to support human-centred design. *International Journal of Human-Computer Studies, 55*(4), 587-634.

Moderniseringsdepartementet. (2005). *eNorge 2009: Det digitale spranget.* Oslo, Norway: Department of Modernization.

Moser, I. (2005). Does information flow? Managing information flow and fluidity in medical practice. *International Journal of Action Research, 1*(3), 339-372.

Moser, I., & Law, J. (2006). Fluids or flows? Information and the possibility of qualculation in medical practice. *Information Technology and People, 19*(1), 55-73.

Nilson, A., Grisot, M., & Aanestad, M. (2002). *Electronic patient records: An information infrastructure for health care.* Master's thesis, University of Oslo, Department of Informatics. Retrieved May 11, 2006, from http://heim.ifi.uio.no/~margunn/2002/IRIS25.pdf

Orlikowski, W. (1996). Improvising organisational transformation over time: A situated change perspective. *Information Systems Research, 7*(1), 63-92.

Pearce, S. (2003). *Government IT projects.* London: Parliamentary Office of Science and Technology.

Puma. (2001). *The hidden threat to e-government.* Organization for Economic Cooperation and Development (OECD). Retrieved from http://www.oecd.org/dataoecd/46/6/35064033.pdf

Risan, L. (2004). *Prøveprosjektet Elektronisk postjournal: Statlige manøvrer mellom åpenhet og personvern* (Report No. 33/2004). Oslo, Norway: Centre for Technology, Innovation and Culture. Retrieved May 11, 2006, from http://www.effin.org/Dokumenter/EPJ_statlige_manovrer.pdf

Samferdselsdepartementet. (1996). *Den norske IT-veien: Bit for bit.* Oslo, Norway: Ministry of Transport and Communication.

Star, S., & Ruhleder, K. (1996). Steps towards an ecology of infrastructure: Design and access for large information spaces. *Information Systems Research, 7*(1), 111-134.

U.S. Government. (2004). *eGov: The official Web site of the president's e-government initiatives.* Retrieved May 11, 2006, from http://www.whitehouse.gov/omb/egov/index2.html

UsabilityNet. (2005). Retrieved May 11, 2006, from http://www.usabilitynet.org

Wilpert, B. E. (1994). Participatory research in organizational psychology. In G. d'Ydewalle, P. Eelen, & P. N. Bertelson (Eds.), *International perspectives on psychological science: Vol 2. The state of the art* (pp. 293-310). Hillsdale, NJ: Lawrence Erlbaum Associates.

Chapter XVII

Local E-Governments in Japan:
IT Utilization Status and Directions

Sadaya Kubo, Setsunan University, Japan

Tatsumi Shimada, Setsunan University, Japan

Abstract

This chapter explains the actual state of digital readiness of the local governments in Japan, and describes the stages of achievement in digitalization and the direction of digitalization. The items being analyzed are the digitalization of governmental administration, services to residents, and information security. Further, in order to clarify the direction of digitalization, we propose stages of progress of the digitalization of the local governments.

Introduction

In November 2000, the Basic Law on the Formation of an Advanced Information and Tele-communications Network Society was passed in accordance with the "Basic IT Strategy." Since then, there has been an increase in the emphasis placed on digitalization, under the guidance of the government, with the aim of establishing Japan as an IT nation. An IT nation comprises the construction of an e-government (Ministry of Public Management, Home Affairs, Posts and Telecommunication, 2005).

After self-evaluation, Japan came to the realization that it had not kept pace with the other developed nations with respect to its development into an IT nation. Therefore, the formulation of the concept of an e-government merits praise, considering that it was formulated as a national strategy and overcame the lack of a comprehensive IT approach by the government until that time. However, there are still several issues concerning e-government. In Japan, the government formulated a strategy to set up local e-governments, as well as to develop IT and communication infrastructure. The regional administrative bodies are making progress in the establishment of local e-governments through their own refinements within the IT strategy and communication infrastructure framework, while collaborating with the national government.

This chapter explains the actual state of digital readiness of the local governments in Japan, and describes the stages of achievement in digitalization and the direction of digitalization. The items being analyzed are the digitalization of governmental administration, services to residents, and information security.

In this chapter, we address the following three issues. First, digitalization can be classified into digitalization of organizations in order to improve their internal efficiency, and digitalization to improve services to residents. What is the current state of progress on each? Second, what is the current state of progress on information disclosure for the purpose of improving resident democracy and facilitating resident participation? Third, what is the current state of progress on information security for the purpose of satisfying residents' requirements?

Further, in order to clarify the direction of digitalization, we propose stages of progress of the digitalization of the local governments.

Framework of the Analysis and Recognition of Issues

Several studies have examined the digitalization of local governments. They analyzed the effects of the digitalization of local governments on information and cost, the changing nature of public-private partnership, and the improvement of efficiency (Chen & Perry, 2003; Stamoulis, Gouscos, Georgiadis, & Martakos, 2001). Further, these studies also analyzed the increase in the provision of information services to the residents (Siau & Long, 2005), the increase in the autonomy of the residents as well as the improvement in the service provided to them (Marchionini, Samet, & Brandt, 2003). In many cases, the effects were studied only after the digitalization of local governments. However, since information technology (IT) is constantly developing, the effects and the process of digitalization should be studied simultaneously.

The digitalization of the local governments does not only imply the purchase of a personal computer, server, and network facility (Shimada & Ushida, 2003). Some examples of additional requirements are organized activity to increase the efficiency of the business process, development of the service model through information communication technology, and improvement of information security for the safety and relief of residents.

We consider that the digitalization of local e-government is carried out in three stages: computerization in offices, services to residents, and information security. Computerization in offices refers to the infrastructure of the e-government. Services to residents are put out by the e-government. Information security is important for the operation of the e-government.

Previous studies have measured digitalization through the types of technology used, the level of the information system, and the services provided by the system (Chen & Perry, 2003; Thompson & Rust, 2005). However, as far as other measurements, such as the measurement of the equipment, its practical use, and so on, that are essential for the efficient introduction of new technology are concerned, they are related to the improvement of services and cost reduction (Thompson & Rust, 2005). The improvement of services relate to the purpose of the organization and its information system (Brown & Brudney, 2004). These activities are related to the organization's approach toward its residents. In addition to these activities, the safety of the system and information security are also important. With regard to the Internet society, personal information and privacy are important considerations. Therefore, the digitalization of local governments must emphasize developing strong protocols and procedures to ensure information security. In this study, we analyze the digitalization from an integrated viewpoint that comprises the computerization of offices, services to residents, and information security.

As shown in Figure 1, these elements are interrelated and we believe they are associated with the realization of a local e-government. Moreover, the development of each element is thought to exist at several stages. They are considered to form a fundamental part of and play an important role in application and interaction.

These elements are often undertaken and estimated separately. However, the contribution of digitalization cannot be measured merely by considering the amount of investment. We must focus on answering certain fundamental questions, such as "Is a system applied efficiently?" or "Does a system yield the desired results?" (Marchionini et al., 2003; Stamoulis et al., 2001). Therefore, we analyze the contribution of digitalization by considering the activities right from the investments in digitalization to its impacts. Our views on the progress of

Figure 1. Elements of e-government

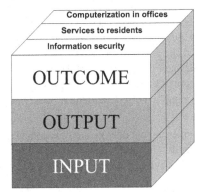

computerization are as follows. When measuring whether digitalization is "progressing" or "lagging behind," let us assume the following three levels:

- **Level 1:** The input (budget) level, as measured by the extent of the development of or investment in information and telecommunications infrastructure, for example, the number of people per PC, the speed of connection of a PC to the LANs (local area networks) and Internet connection speed, the extent of implementation of security policies and counter measures, and the extent of IT utilization in front and back office work.

- **Level 2:** The output (work) level, as measured by the number of employees who are capable of using a PC, e-mail, and so forth for work and the speed at which they work, the extent of the promotion of computerization or operating regimes, the extent of freedom of information and publicity activities for residents, the amount of support for services to residents, the extent of the framework for the participation of residents in administrative services.

- **Level 3:** The outcome (results) level, as measured by the extent of an increase in residents' satisfaction toward services rendered to them, the extent of investment outcomes such as greater energy efficiency through increased productivity, and so forth, the extent of any increase in workforce morale as a result of the workforce being freed from simplistic tasks, the extent to which infiltration by viruses or leakage of personal information is prevented or reduced through security countermeasures.

In general, from the above three levels described, a significant number of people are of the opinion that digitalization progresses due to level 1. However, level 1 only reflects the investment resources. To put this in the extreme, we can state that in order to achieve an increase in level 1, all that is required is to increase the capital directed toward this level. Moreover, level 2 being high does not necessarily mean that results have been achieved. This is because a high output does not necessarily correlate with a high outcome.

What is important is level 3. The question of whether digitalization is "progressing" or "lagging behind" should be evaluated at this level. However, in order to measure level 3, local governments should have the necessary skills and knowledge in system appraisals and administrative appraisal methods; if not, they will be unable to conduct effective appraisals. In the long run, even if one is able to understand this through a cost-benefit analysis, it may still be difficult for local governments that do not use digitalization on a daily basis and where it is yet to become second nature. There has recently been rapid progress in the introduction of public sector evaluation approaches in local governments. If this becomes common, there is no doubt that the ability to measure computerization at level 3 will improve.

In addition, it is necessary to achieve levels 1 and 2, since it is a fact that these levels are prerequisites to the realization of level 3. In short, the municipalities that do not give due consideration to level 3 and only aim at level 1 are likely to face difficulties. Moreover, it is difficult to increase outcomes solely with technology. Rather, this should be accomplished with technology coupled with work reforms and agile and flexible decision making and implementation. It is also vitally important to review any laws and ordinances, regulations, regimes, and procedures that restrict such decision making and implementation.

If the development of information and telecommunications infrastructure and the investment in computerization are carried out without the realization that IT should be utilized in order to raise outcomes, it will not contribute to administrative and financial reforms. Such investments in computerization cannot be said to be financially insignificant in comparison with empty box public works. It is important to remember that such investments will lead to financial pressure in the same manner that public works do.

The stages of progress are proposed for each category — computerization in offices, services to residents, and information security — along the same lines of thinking as earlier in this chapter.

Research Design

We conducted a questionnaire survey on approximately 765 local governments; of these, approximately 500 responded to the questionnaire. Even in the past, the local governments in Japan have undergone several public investigations, and they have always actively cooperated with such research. Moreover, based on the response rate obtained in our study, it is clear that a high response rate is a feature of the local governments in Japan. The methods of the survey are:

- **Period of survey:** May-June 2004
- **Targets:** 765 local governments in Japan (prefectures, government-designated cities, special wards, and cities)
- **Total number of respondents:** 496 local governments (percentage of respondents: 64.8%)

The questions in the survey could be categorized as computerization in offices, services to residents, and information security.

Computerization in offices refers to the infrastructure of the e-government. The questions in this part of the survey were related to client and server machines, training provided to government employees, the use of integrated applications, and the appointment of a chief information officer (CIO).

Services to residents are put out by the e-government. The questions in this part of the survey included information services provided by the government's Web site, information interchange with the residents, the development of original services, and service estimation.

Information security is important for the operation of an e-government. The questions in this section focus on the framing of the security policy, management of client machines and the server room, checking of access logs, and education regarding information ethics.

We calculate the deviations in each part as well as in the total, which comprises all the deviations.

In this chapter, we propose five stages of progress for the three categories. The conceptualization of the stages of progress was based on the following perspectives (Kubo, Higashigawa, & Shimada, 2005): invested resources as the input, produced result as the output, and the effect of the input on the output as the outcome. These stages are based on our previous work. However, other studies have described several other stages and models. Kim's model (Kim & Kim, 2003) focused on organizational learning, digital democracy, information security, and cost efficiency. Reddick, on the other hand, used a two-stage model. Stage I involves the cataloguing of information online, while Stage II involves the completion of transactions online (Reddick, 2004). Another study developed a three-stage process of e-government. The first implies actually going online, that is, digitizing the government; the second refers to delivering interactive services to the citizens; and the third stage is increasingly interactive as it allows governments to use IT tools to engage citizens in the development of policies, programs, and services. These stages are similar to those that we consider for our analysis. Siau and Long (2005) proposed a five-stage model that entails Web presence, interaction, transaction, transformation, and e-democracy.

Although the direction of this model is appropriate, the range of its stages is far too broad. These activities are different during each stage. However, since the development of IT continues in relation to these activities, we believe that each stage of these activities should be examined in detail.

In order to analyze the development of an e-government, we focus on the stages of progress with regard to the services that are provided to the citizens. These stages will contribute to our understanding of the status and nature of digitalization. Thus, we propose our stages of progress for e-government.

Outline of the Results of the Survey

The results of our survey are listed in Table 1. In comparison with cities, prefectures, government-designated cities, and special wards had high scores in the total. Prefectures had a high score in the category of computerization in offices. Government-designated cities had a high score in the category of services to residents, and special wards had a high score in the category of information security.

A typical result is now provided for each category.

Computerization in Government Offices

Table 2 summarizes the results of the survey in the category of computerization in government offices. The introduction rate for LANs (99.6%) is high. The PC diffusion rate (the number of PCs per employee) is 71.5%. High tendencies are shown in these questions. The rate of establishment of a CIO is 61.6%. In the establishment of a CIO, cities and special wards had higher scores than prefectures and government-designated cities.

Table 1. The deviation of average

	Prefecture	Government-designated cities	Special wards	Cities
Computerization in offices	58.3%	55.7%	57.2%	48.9%
Services to residents	57.9%	59.8%	55.7%	48.9%
Information security	51.7%	50.6%	58.7%	49.5%
Total	56.0%	55.4%	57.2%	49.1%

Note: *$p<0.05$; **$p<0.01$

Table 2. Computerization in government offices

	Prefectures	Government-designated cities	Special wards	Cities	Average
Installation of LAN in offices	100.0%	100.0%	100.0%	99.5%	99.6%
PC diffusion	86.5%	50.0%	77.8%	70.4%	71.5%
Appointment and job role of the CIO*	43.2%	40.0%	61.1%	63.7%	61.6%
Introduction and type of GIS*	83.8%	90.0%	66.7%	61.4%	63.8%
Introduction of electronic decision**	56.8%	30.0%	50.0%	15.6%	20.2%
Introduction of electronic bidding**	27.0%	10.0%	5.6%	2.8%	4.8%
Introduction of electronic document management**	61.1%	50.0%	50.0%	30.8%	34.1%
Execution of BPR**	67.6%	87.5%	94.4%	31.2%	37.0%
Reorganization*	55.9%	50.0%	50.0%	32.0%	34.6%
Increase in front office efficiency	52.9%	100.0%	77.8%	74.2%	73.3%
Increase in back office efficiency	88.2%	100.0%	88.2%	90.2%	90.2%
Improvement in staff morale by the release of routine work	46.9%	62.5%	55.6%	40.3%	41.7%
System evaluation prior to digitalization**	78.8%	100.0%	94.4%	48.9%	53.6%
System evaluation after digitalization	41.2%	44.4%	38.9%	28.1%	29.8%

Note: *$p<0.05$; **$p<0.01$

More than half the number of prefectures, government-designated cities, special wards, and cities (63.8%) had introduced geographic information systems (GIS). In the introduction of GIS, prefectures and government-designated cities have higher scores than cities and special wards. The rate of the introduction of electronics is 20.2 %. Here, prefectures and special wards accounted for more than 50 %, and the difference is large, while that of cities is low (15.6 %). The rate of introduction of electronic bidding is low (4.8 %). However, there was a large difference among prefectures. The rate of introduction of electronic document management is 34.1 %. Excluding cities (30.8 %), this rate exceeds 50 %. As for the applications, cities are delayed as mentioned above.

The rate of execution of BPR (business process re-engineering) is 37.0 %. Government-designated cities and special wards had high scores, and the difference was large. The execution of BPR is all the more necessary in order that it can contribute to an increase in efficiency through information technology.

The rate of execution of reorganization is 34.6 %. However, prefectures, government-designated cities, and special wards accounted for more than 50 %. From these results, it can be considered that a reorganization of the organization should be more important for governments whose scale is large.

The rate of improvement of front office efficiency through investments in information technology is 73.3 %. However prefectures accounted for approximately 50 %, displaying an overall high tendency. The rate of improvement of back office efficiency through by investments in information technology is 90.2 %.

The rate of improvement of staff morale by release of routine work is 41.7 %. The rate of execution of system evaluation prior to digitalization is 53.6 %. Prefectures, government-designated cities, and special wards had high scores. The rate of execution of system evaluation after digitalization is 29.8 %. A low tendency can be seen pertaining to improvement of staff morale. However, system evaluation after digitalization is necessary to decide the aim of future digitalization.

Services to Residents

Table 3 summarizes the survey results in the category of services to residents. The rate of enactment of the information disclosure ordinance is 98.8 %. A high tendency can be seen in this question. The rate of execution of Web accessibility is 35.6 %. In Web accessibility, prefectures had a high score and the difference among prefectures was large. Prefectures which have few direct relations with residents had high scores and the difference was large.

The rate of disclosure of regulations on a Web site is 83.6 %. The rate of publication of the governments' main policies, such as the city master plan, is 67.8 %. Excluding the cities, this is high.

Publications and the type of mail magazines for residents is 20.6 %. Prefectures scored the highest (94.6 %), followed by government-designated cities (40.0 %).

Special wards (27.8 %) and cities (13.5 %) had low scores. The rate of enabling a public comments facility on the Web site was 42.8 %. Excluding the cities, this is high, and the difference is large.

Table 3. Services to residents

	Prefectures	Government-designated cities	Special wards	Cities	Average
Enactment of the information disclosure ordinance	100.0%	100.0%	100.0%	98.6%	98.8%
Provision of Web accessibility, taking into consideration the physical condition of the user and the environment of use**	81.1%	55.6%	44.4%	30.8%	35.6%
Disclosure of regulations on the Web site	89.2%	100.0%	88.9%	82.6%	83.6%
Disclosure of serial set on the Web site**	100.0%	100.0%	88.9%	63.5%	67.8%
Publication of the government's main policies such as the city master plan**	100.0%	100.0%	100.0%	78.3%	81.2%
Publication and type of mail magazines for residents**	94.6%	40.0%	27.8%	13.5%	20.6%
Enabling a public comments facility on the Web site**	94.4%	90.0%	88.9%	35.4%	42.8%
Improvement of services to residents through digitalization**	94.1%	100.0%	100.0%	89.8%	90.7%

*Note: *p < 0.05; **p < 0.01*

The rate of improvement of services to residents through digitalization is 90.7%. A high tendency is displayed in this question. However, there is a difference among cities. There are issues regarding the accuracy of the method of measuring this difference, because the answers are self-evaluated.

Information Security

Table 4 summarizes the survey results in the category of information security. In general, the scores for the rate of control (94.2%) of the server room, the use limitation (79.0%), and the security policy (86.2%) are high. The various fundamental components of information security are established.

The rate of the correspondence of each level exceeds 50%, except for government-designated cities. The rate of the special wards was 83.3%, and correspondence proceeds through it.

Table 4. Information security

	Prefecture	Government-designated cities	Special wards	Cities	Average
Access control in server rooms	100.0%	100.0%	100.0%	93.4%	94.2%
Implementation of restriction of and management method for client PCs	71.4%	80.0%	100.0%	78.7%	79.0%
Enactment of security policy	97.3%	90.0%	88.9%	85.0%	86.2%
Establishment of security as a countermeasure at every level*	57.1%	33.3%	83.3%	53.4%	54.4%
Information security training for the entire staff	27.8%	22.2%	61.1%	35.1%	35.3%
Enactment of ordinance or rules for the protection of personal information	100.0%	100.0%	100.0%	91.9%	92.9%
Enactment of information ethics rules such as netiquette and prevention of abuse**	61.1%	60.0%	72.2%	38.0%	41.4%
Checking access logs and notification	82.4%	87.5%	72.2%	66.4%	68.0%

*Note: *p < 0.05; **p < 0.01*

With regard to security education, while the average score was 35.3%, special wards also excelled with 61.1%. Since there was relative enforcement of the law, individual information protection displayed a high score (92.9%). Information ethics (41.4%) exceeded 50%, except in the case of cities. The cities have many contacts to residents. Therefore cities are required to the information ethics. An access log was acquired by 68.0%.

Stages of Progress of Local E-Government

We propose the stages of progress for each category on the basis of the following assumptions. We assume that the fundamental stage — input — is represented by the infrastructure and the configuration of the rules for an information system. The next stage — output — is represented by activities that enable the effective use and planning for the expansion of and compliance to the new situation. The final stage — outcome — involves the estimation and verification of the effects through information technology and information systems. Although the Japanese administrative system aims at decentralization, the system still remains centralized. In Japan, the central government manages 40% of the all the work, while the remaining work is managed by the local governments. However, with regard to budget allocation, the central government enjoys 60% of the budget, while the local governments are only entitled to 40%. Thus, there is a 20% gap between the work and budget allocation. Therefore, most local governments seek financial assistance from the central government. Moreover, most local governments improve the input of digitalization through a block grant.

However, in order to improve the outcome of digitalization, it is necessary that these governments seek the participation and assistance of local residents. The estimation and verification of digitalization are important stages, and therefore, these are placed at a higher stage.

The Stages of Progress

Table 5, 6, and 7 list the stages of progress in the categories of computerization in offices, services to residents, and information security, respectively. These stages correspond to those conceptualized in the previous section. Progress in the category of computerization in offices comprises five stages: Stage 1: preparation of IT infrastructure; Stage 2: support of effective use; Stage 3: improvement of staff efficiency; Stage 4: expansion of applications with IT; and Stage 5: verification of the effects of computerization.

Progress in the category of services to residents comprises the following five stages: stage 1: disclosure of basic information; stage 2: improvement of basic services; stage 3: Internet use; stage 4: expansion of IT effectiveness; and stage 5: verification of services.

Table 5. The stage of progress for computerization in offices

Stage	Title	Content of question
5	Verification of the effects of computerization	Appointment and job role of the CIO Execution of BPR (business process reengineering) Reorganization System evaluation after digitalization
4	Expansion of applications with IT	Introduction and type of GIS Introduction of electronic decision Introduction of electronic bidding Introduction of electronic document management
3	Improvement of staff efficiency	Increase in back office efficiency Realization of a labor-saving method Periodical training of staff for effective IT use Improvement of staff morale by release of routine work Use of a lesser amount of paper
2	Support of effective use	Establishment of an IT help desk for staff use Systematic use of the mailing list Appointment of an IT leader and promotion of EUC Emphasis on labor saving as an objective and aim System evaluation prior to digitalization
1	Preparation of IT infrastructure	Installation of LAN in office PC diffusion Internet connection rate Distribution range of e-mail addresses

Table 6. The stages of progress for services to residents

Stage	Title	Content of question
5	Verification of services	Improvement of services to residents through digitalization
		Increase in front office efficiency
		Promotion of the relationship between local governments and residents or local enterprises
4	Expansion of IT effectiveness	Provision of Web accessibility, taking into consideration the physical condition of the user and the environment of use
		Setting up of an IT school for residents using the Web site
		Provision of individual services by residents IC card
		Methods of opinion collection
		Rebroadcast of the assembly by CATV
3	Internet use	Publication and type of mail magazine for residents
		Provision of system services such as reservation of facilities
		Enabling a public comments facility on the Web site
		Setting up a teleconference room and electronic bulletin board
		Emphasis on improved services for residents as the objective and aim of digitalization
2	Improvement of basic services	Delivery of certificates for extra time
		Placement of information terminal outside offices, such as for the reservation of various facilities
1	Disclosure of basic information	Enactment of the information disclosure ordinance
		Disclosure of regulations on Web site
		Disclosure of serial set on Web site
		Publication of the governments' main policies such as city master plan

Progress in the category of information security comprises five stages: stage 1: enactment of the rules and clarification of the purpose; stage 2: technical correspondence; stage 3: independent correspondence; stage 4: integrated correspondence; and stage 5: improvement of staff consciousness.

We now verify the relationship between these stages of progress and the results of our survey. First, we consider the relationship between the increase in stage and degree of achievement. The degree of achievement is calculated by dividing the mean point by the full point in each stage.

We now describe the relationship among the stages and the changes in the degree of achievement for each category. All the governments that responded were categorized into 10 groups, each of which comprised approximately 50 governments in order of ranking. We then proceed to draw the graphs showing the change in the degree of achievement for the 10 groups. Based on the scores, we segment the local governments into 10 groups. Then, we compare the groups that scored higher with those that scored low. Moreover, we analyze the relationship between the increase in the score and the increase in the degree of achievement at each stage.

Table 7. The stages of progress for information security

Stage	Title	Content of question
5	Improvement of staff consciousness	Checking access logs and notification Enactment of information ethics rules such as netiquette and prevention of abuse
4	Integrated correspondence	Establishment of security as a countermeasure for every level Penal regulations for outside trust dealers Checking access logs for e-mail and the Internet
3	Independent correspondence	Setup of access limitation to files and applications by job role and job grade Information security training for the entire staff (training to be held more than once every year) The rules pertaining to the information erasure process in the event of scrapping of machines Prohibition against sending e-mails to the private outside and Internet access
2	Technical correspondence	Implementation of restriction of and management method for client PC Access control in server rooms
1	Enactment of the rules and clarification of the purpose	Enactment of security policy Enactment of ordinance or rules for the protection of personal information

The Degree of Achievement

Table 8 shows the degree of achievement at each stage. In all the cases, it is evident that the first stage shows the highest degree of achievement. Therefore, if the degree of achievement at a higher stage is greater than that at a lower stage, then, based on the proposed stages, digitalization will be difficult. However, for the categories of computerization in offices and services to residents, the degrees of achievement at stage 5 are higher than those at stage 2.

The degrees of achievement in the proposed stages follow an appropriate pattern. Accordingly, the attainment of a high degree of achievement at a higher stage is difficult. For example, integrated activities in each category are located in the fourth stage and their score was low. On the other hand, the lower stages contained independent correspondences, such as the enactment of rules. However, there were some cases wherein the numerical value of the evaluation and the verification deviated from the pattern (stages 2 and 5). However, it is likely that this was due to the manner in which the question was posed. Therefore, the proposed stages are fairly reflective of the actual situation.

Figures 2 to 4 show the degrees of achievement in each category. The line at the center of each of the figures indicates a 50% degree of achievement.

Table 8. The degree of achievement at each stage

Category	Stages				
	1	2	3	4	5
Computerization in offices	0.78	0.46	0.44	0.31	0.50
Services to residents	0.82	0.51	0.48	0.27	0.67
Information security	0.89	0.77	0.58	0.53	0.40

Figure 2. Computerization in the offices

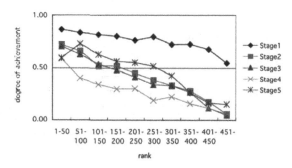

Figure 3. Services to residents

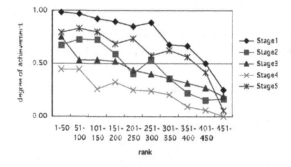

Computerization in Offices

Table 9 shows the relationship of the stages for computerization in offices. Figure 2 depicts the change in the degree of achievement in this category.

The existence of a relationship in this category could imply the preliminary stages and the applied stages of digitalization. If this is not the case, it appears that the contents of these questions can be simultaneously used for all the stages. Block grants are useful in the contingent progress because this content is treated in a parallel manner.

Figure 4. Information security

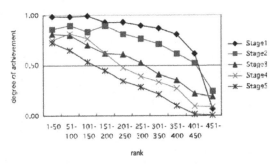

Table 9. Correlation of computerization in the offices

Stage	1	2	3	4	5
1	1				
2	0.14	1			
3	0.07	0.33	1		
4	0.17	0.34	0.28	1	
5	0.00	0.25	0.21	0.10	1

There are low correlations in stages 2, 3, and 4 in this category. Stages 1 and 5 appear to be independent of the other stages. Since the degree of achievement in stage 1 is extremely high, it is important to carry out stages 2 to 4 in an integrative manner.

The change in the degree of achievement displays the following characteristics:

• Stage 1 represents the fundamental stage, and there is a high degree of achievement.

• Stages 2 and 4 display the same trend in score for the order. It appears that these stages are carried out in an integrative manner.

• In stage 4, which has a type of GIS, electronic bidding has a low score and yields the difference in computerization.

Services to Residents

Table 10 shows the relationship among the stages for services to residents. Figure 3 shows the change in the degree of achievement in this category.

There is a comparatively high correlation between improvement of basic services (stage 2) and Internet use (stage 3). It appears that local governments dealing with Internet facili-

Table 10. Correlation of services to residents

Stage	1	2	3	4	5
1	1				
2	0.25	1			
3	0.27	0.42	1		
4	0.21	0.17	0.22	1	
5	0.18	0.12	0.14	0.11	1

Table 11. Correlation of information security

Stage	1	2	3	4	5
1	1				
2	0.14	1			
3	0.28	0.35	1		
4	0.35	0.25	0.45	1	
5	0.22	0.19	0.35	0.49	1

ties have already worked towards an improvement in these services. The effective use of IT relates not only to the technical characteristics of IT but also to the local government's vision or attitude toward this issue to date.

In this category, a relationship exists a tendency between degree of the stages and achievement as difficulties. However, the top 50 ranked local governments are strongly influenced by Internet use (stage 3). Further, the degree of achievement at stage 4 (expansion of IT effectiveness) has an influence on the top 100 ranked local governments.

Information Security

Table 11 shows the relationship among to the stages for information security. Figure 4 shows the change in the degree of achievement in this category.

The correlation of information security is stronger than that of the other two categories. Stages 1 to 4, 2 to 3, 3 to 4 and 5, and 4 to 5 display correlations above 0.3. These correlations become stronger with an increase in the stage. Therefore, it seems that activities in stage 2 are acceleration for higher stages.

Despite the low rank, the degree of achievement of enactment of the rule and clarification of the purpose (stage 1) and technical correspondence (stage 2) are over 0.5. On the other hand, the degree of achievement of improvement of staff consciousness (stage 5) increases linearly from the lower to higher ranks. Therefore, the development of information security can be gauged from the behavior and posture of the staff.

Conclusion

Digitalization of local governments progresses under the e-Japan strategy. This strategy attempts to increase the efficiency of administrative and financial services through the propagation of computerization and the improving of services to residents. Further, residents also demand the establishment of information security.

Regarding the actual situation of local governments, the computerization of the fundamental parts, such as the introduction of PCs and LANs, continues. However, use of the application for issues such as electronic decision making and electronic bidding, BPR, and the reorganization are not in progress. As a result, system evaluation becomes an issue.

Regarding the services to residents, static services by IT are satisfactory in such cases as the regulations and disclosure of serial set on the Web site. However, dynamic services such as mail magazines and public comments are all issues for the future. With regard to information security, the part of the systematic correspondence proceeds through the access control of the server room, the security policy, and so on.

From now, personal activities such as information ethics and security education will be a necessity. The proposed stages of progress have displayed the above characteristics. The examination of the roadmap of digitalization corresponding to each local government is necessary to output it from the input and then to proceed with the digitalization of local government to outcome.

When the proposed stages are applied to other countries, it is important to consider the following.

The State of IT Infrastructure

Japan has a strong background for the maintenance of IT infrastructure that is also supported by a national policy. Therefore, the computerization of local governments in other countries may be an extremely different process as compared with Japan.

The Range of the Official Services

In some countries, the private sector is the primary service provider for the citizens. However, since Japan delayed the use of the private sector in terms of being a service provider, it is possible that some of the proposed stages may not be applicable in these cases. Nevertheless, the stages that refer to the rules, correspondence, and evaluation will be valid and applicable. Therefore, we can use the stages proposed by us albeit with some adjustments according to the specific situations of different countries.

The Management of Personal Information

In Japan, the enactment of a law that protects personal information is a recent phenomenon. In the past, there was limited focus on the development of laws to protect personal information; moreover, the national consciousness toward such laws was not extremely high. However, other countries could have stricter regulations regarding information security, and their corresponding indexes may be higher.

Therefore, the analysis of the progress stages based on the actual condition of other countries is a subject for future study.

References

Brown, M. M., & Brudney, J. L. (2004). Achieving advanced electronic government services: Opposing environmental constraints. *Public Performance & Management Review, 28*(1), 96-113.

Chen, Y. C., & Perry, J. (2003). Outsourcing for e-government: Managing for success. *Public Performance & Management Review, 26*(4), 404-421.

Kim, S., & Kim, D. (2003). South Korean public officials' perceptions of values, failure and consequences of failure in e-government leadership. *Public Performance & Management Review, 26*(4), 360-375.

Kubo, S., Higashigawa, T., & Shimada, T. (2005, May 15). The consideration of progress stages for computerization in local government. In *Proceedings of the 34ᵗʰ Conference on Japan Association for Management System* (In Japanese), Reitaku University, Chiba, Japan (pp. 138-141).

Marchionini, G., Samet, H., & Brandt, L. (2003). Digital government. *Communications of the ACM, 46*(1), 25-27.

Ministry of Public Management, Home Affairs, Posts and Telecommunication, Japan. (2005). *Information and communication in Japan.* Retrieved May 11, 2006, from http://www.johotsusintokei.soumu.go.jp/ whitepaper/eng/WP2004/2004-index.html

Reddick, C. G. (2004). Empirical models of e-government growth in local governments. *e-Service Journal, 3*(2), 59-84.

Shimada, T., & Ushida, K. (2003). Electronic government in Japan: IT utilization status of local governments. In G. Gingrich (Ed.), *Managing IT in government, business & communities* (pp. 111-126). Hershey, PA: IRM Press.

Siau, K., & Long, Y. (2005). Synthesizing e-government stage models: A meta-synthesis based on meta-ethnography approach. *Industrial Management & Data Systems, 105*(4), 443-458.

Stamoulis, D., Gouscos, D., Georgiadis, P., & Martakos, D. (2001). Revisiting public information management for effective e-government services. *Information Management & Computer Security, 9*(4), 146-153.

Thompson, D. V., Rust, R. T., & Rhoda, J. (2005). The business value of e-government for small firms. *International Journal of Service Industry Management, 16*(4), 385-407.

Section III:
E-Government
Benchmarking

Chapter XVIII

E-Government, Democratic Governance and Integrative Prospects for Developing Countries:
The Case for a Globally Federated Architecture

Jeffrey Roy, Dalhousie University, Canada

Abstract

The objectives of this chapter are threefold: first, to provide a conceptual framework for understanding e-government as a set of four interrelated dimensions of public sector change; second, to consider the relevance and applicability of this framework for both developed and developing nations; and third, to explore the interface between domestic and transnational governance reforms in an increasingly digital era. The world in the twenty-first century needs a globally federated governance architecture, the design of which must include social, economic, political, and technological considerations. This strengthened focus on transnational governance systems must also be joined by the recognition of the dysfunctional nature of the present system of bilateral international assistance programs among countries. With improved governance conditions of transparency and trust transnationally — facili-

tated in part by a much more politically creative and aggressive use of new technologies, the resources allocated by each country across their various recipients would serve both developing nations and the world as a whole if they were pooled and coordinated through new transnational mechanisms.

Introduction

The objectives of this chapter are threefold: first, to provide a conceptual framework for understanding e-government as a set of four interrelated dimensions of public sector change; second, to consider the relevance and applicability of this framework for both developed and developing nations; and third, to explore the interface between domestic and transnational governance reforms in an increasingly digital era. As developing countries represent our primary interest in this chapter, efforts to meet this latter objective are sought through the prism of developing countries generally and the African continent specifically.

There is much debate within the literature on e-government as to whether digital technologies and the Internet are new tools to be deployed mainly within current public sector structures and traditions, or whether they are inherently more transformational in driving the need for more holistic changes to our systems of democratic governance. Both views have merit — as futuristic visions shape the actions of governments today that remain nonetheless bound by present processes and structures. As a result, reform is likely to be uneven and contested and it is important to have some appreciation of both levels of change. This interface between the internal and external environments, between current practices and processes and new potentials, represents an increasingly important imperative for all levels of government (as well as transnationally, as will be discussed later).

In order to be more precise on the potential scope of e-government, it is useful to turn to one definition adopted by many governments (such as that of Mexico) as of late, namely: *The continuous innovation in the delivery of services, citizen participation, and governance through the transformation of external and internal relationships by the use of information technology, especially the Internet.*[1] This definition is also a helpful starting point in underscoring the links between government and governance both internally within the public sector and externally across all stakeholders, including the public (as customers and citizens). The application and relevance of this definition, however, differs significantly across developed and developing countries for many reasons, including the characteristics of the broader infrastructure of information and communication technologies (ICTs) across society as a whole, as well as the specific shapes and persistence of varying forms of digital divides.

Within this context the next section of this chapter presents e-government's four main dimensions, considering their relevance across developed and developing countries. Drawing upon this framework, the recent evolution of globalization is then explored in terms of the implications for both e-government and public sector reform nationally as well as for transnational governance systems. The specific case of Africa is then examined — with the aim of underscoring some key directions worthy of exploration in order to build stronger forms of governance both domestically and transnationally through e-government-inspired reforms.

Four Dimensions of Public Sector Change

In order to understand e-governments impacts and potential, a framework of four main dimensions of change includes service, security, transparency, and trust (Roy 2006). All of these dimensions are related — directly or indirectly — to the widening presence and rapidly expanding importance of a digital infrastructure encompassing information and communication technologies and online connectivity.

The first two of these dimensions are primarily focused on changes to the internal decision-making architecture of government, in response to pressures and opportunities associated with the Internet. Indeed, delivering services online became the hallmark of e-government during the 1990s, as more and more citizens conduct their personal and professional affairs online, these "customers" of government look to do the same in dealing with state, whether it is paying their taxes or renewing permits and licenses of one sort or another (Curtin, Sommer, & Vis-Sommer, 2003). Although the initial impetus for utilizing online channels to deliver information and services was often financial savings through improved automation and efficiency, many such forecasts proved excessively optimistic due to investment costs and governance complexities (Allen, Paquet, Juillet, & Roy, 2005; Fountain, 2001). Functionality also remains limited, particularly with respect to the processing of financial payments. This is a limitation due in large measure to the concerns about security.

The ability to interact effectively with customers online requires a safe and reliable architecture, particularly for the handling of personal information — such as credit card numbers — that often underpins financial transactions. Yet fostering government-wide capacities for receiving, storing, and sharing secure information is a complex undertaking (Bryant & Colledge, 2002; Holden, 2004). In areas such as health care, the benefits of more efficient and integrated care through networked information systems are dependent on secure and interconnected governance architectures (Batini, Cappadozzi, Mecella, & Talamo, 2002).

Security issues have clearly risen to the top of political agendas as of late, and governments have become conscious that more citizen-centric manners may not always be consistent with a philosophy of friendly and efficient customer service. Security can mean surveillance as well as service. It may entail extracting and sharing information not only in response to requests by citizens, but also as a way to better forecast potential actions and choices. The trade-offs between privacy, freedom, and convenience have therefore become more politicized, particularly in a post-911 context which has seen the security dimension of e-government expand from a largely technical precursor to better service to a more overarching paradigm of public sector action (Brown, 2003; Denning 2003; Hart-Teeter, 2003, 2004; O'Harrow, 2004; Roy, 2005b).

In terms of the relevance of service and security to both developed and developing nations, there is much common ground. There are many examples from the latter group — including Singapore, Hong Kong, and India — where the pursuit of online service channels has been both vigorous and innovative. In some limited instances, the case for online channels may actually be stronger in developing nations where traditional channels — notably face to face interaction — present numerous hurdles to the citizen including corruption and a lack of geographic proximity (Bhatnagar, 2001; Heeks, 1999, 2002). Yet at the same time, much of the developing world remains hampered by resource, organizational, and political requirements — not unlike but often more pronounced than those present in the most developed countries (Basu, 2004; Ndou, 2004).

The first two challenges shape the way governments organize internally to address opportunities and threats in the external environment. Transparency and trust speak to changes rooted less in the internal structures of government and more in the evolving democratic environment within which governments operate — as the Internet has facilitated the creation of new channels of political mobilization and interaction between citizens and their governments. A fundamental challenge is a clash of cultures between the expectations of an increasingly open and online society and the traditions of secrecy that permeate governments — in both developed and developing world contexts (Geiselhart, 2004). While this level of secrecy varies considerably across different governing regimes; even in democratic countries representational politics coupled with intensifying levels of media and public scrutiny are reinforcing an insular mindset of information control (Reid, 2004). While the emergence of e-government and online connectivity has created a growing recognition of the need for broader democratic reform, difficulties and resistance persist (Coleman & Norris, 2005; Kossick, 2004). A major issue is the notion of trust as a basis for democratic legitimacy — increasingly viewed as eroding in many developed countries while paradoxically, democratization is promoted by these same countries to the developing world (a theme returned to later).

In short, whereas service and security focus primarily on retooling the public sector to better deliver information and services within existing political structures, transparency and trust reflect widening pressures to rethink the structures themselves — particularly from the perspective of public participation. These four dimensions of e-government change are axed on how the public sector makes use of new technologies to better reform both its internal governance and the set of external relationships with all stakeholders. At the same time, however, it is important to acknowledge the other side of the coin, namely the necessity of not only a digital infrastructure across the jurisdiction in question for these stakeholders (notably the citizenry), but also the socioeconomic capacities for making use of this infrastructure to engage with government in either a customer-service-oriented or political-democratic role. This latter challenge is, of course, the Achilles heal for many developing nations, the source of the digital divide globally between the richest and poorest countries (Chen & Wellman, 2003).

Dissecting the "Developing World": Sectoral Balance and Good Governance

In the previous century, the categorization of nations stemmed mainly from political ideology and industrialization. Fukuyama (2004) and others now underscore that today distinctions between countries have more to do with good governance as a more holistic capacity to both facilitate and shape development within national borders in a manner that manages the challenges and opportunities of a globalizing world. There is also broad agreement that the invocation of governance as a national system reflects the existence and relative "co-evolution" of three distinct spheres of personal, organizational, and institutional activities:

the market (private sector), the state (public sector or government), and civil society (or community) (Paquet, 1997).

Across such fluid terminology the usage of the terms *e-government* and *e-governance* can be distinguished — with the former in reference to state mechanisms and the latter denoting the fuller set of sectoral processes and institutional arrangements encompassing the three sectors within a jurisdiction as a whole (even as governance will have other meanings and applications within each sector as well). Much of the preceding discussion has focused on e-government and four dimensions of change that carry at least the potential for a state transformation, but this potential is very much intertwined with how a jurisdiction (most often a country) both views and pursues e-governance as a national strategy and the manner by which the three sectors interact and exert influence on one another.

The most obvious example of this relationship is developed countries with failed states unable or unwilling to provide even a basic level of sustenance for their population: in such circumstances, e-government will be a less pressing matter than other more crisis-driven priorities. The role of the state in facilitating a marketplace generally and specifically for ICT production and adoption is also critical to the emergence of e-governance across all sectors, since developing nations that have effectively deregulated state monopolies in favour of competitive environments have enjoyed faster ICT adoption than others (Waverman, Meschi, & Fuss, 2005).

With respect to the private sector and the existence of a clearly established and well functioning marketplace, such conditions also directly shape e-government's purpose and evolution. First, not only is there more likely to be a strong pool of technology providers from the private sector to facilitate public sector adoption and reformation, but e-government will morel likely be viewed as a national development project designed to both benefit from and underpin economic competitiveness for companies as well as the jurisdiction as a whole (Chou & Hsu, 2004). In the most technologically advanced, newly industrialized countries, governments are pressured by maturing industries adopting new technologies into their own production and customer service strategies, thereby shaping public expectations in the realm of state activity. In contrast, in those least developed nations without strong market actors, e-government may be viewed as a process to facilitate private sector development but there is little evidence to suggest that public sector ICT adoption is instrumental in spurring the creation of domestic market activity and demand.

The existence and relative strength of civil society is an equally important variable. Strong community and civic ties have been shown to be powerful enablers of both economic innovation and democratic development and the capacity to create such ties is a central component of an e-governance system that is strengthened by collective learning and adaptation (Coe, Paquet, & Roy, 2001; Goodman, 2005). The degree to which civil society is aligned with the state — or rather opposing it with the aim of political change — varies considerably across jurisdictions (undoubtedly in both developing and developed world contexts), dependent on, for example, the level of online connectivity and the freedom and ability to use it. Conversely, state efforts to monitor and control such usage and generally deploy technology as a means to social containment and the preservation of power existing structures may reflect the view that digital technology is most likely to be used by those in positions of authority to solidify their positions, at least until the pressure of change is overwhelming (Kraemer & King, 2003).

This latter point speaks to the manner by which democracy has become simultaneously strengthened and weakened by globalization and this somewhat new governance-driven perspective on national development. The strengthening lies in the fact that democratic governance within the state sector is an ideal shared by a widening segment of countries and cultures: conversely, the weakening of the concept comes in its dilution as many different forms of democracy emerge across different sorts of developing countries (while in many developed countries, questions are also raised about the appropriateness of existing institutions). China and India are illustrative as emerging technological powerhouses with important implications for e-government, while the latter functions as the world's largest democracy and the former largely rejects democratic aspirations in favour of a more state-centric development trajectory that has forced the world's largest Western-based technology companies to curtail freedoms and adapt their practices to a uniquely Chinese context.[2]

In sum, the relative strength of a developing country's governance in terms of its state, market, and societal sectors both situates and shapes e-government purpose and prospects for success. At the same time, however, national variables are insufficient in this regard since the actions of developed nations — both in their own domestic environments and transnationally, are also highly consequential (Brown, 2002; Ferguson & Jones, 2002).

Service, Security, or Democracy?

In the developed world, when speaking of e-government's transformative potential from within the public sector, the agenda is most often less about changing the nature of democracy and more about improving the business of government via better customer relations (Norris, 2005; Roy, 2005a). This customer-centric focus has chronologically shaped e-government's first decade in many parts of the world — at the national level in particular, where governments have raced (often with one another) to develop online platforms for service delivery (Langford & Roy, 2005). The following quote is illustrative of the manner by which such changes are often viewed as outside of the purview of the typical citizen:

To make e-Government happen requires a complete re-design of the internal operations of the government and the operating systems of the broader public sector. Our I&IT Strategy guides these efforts. However, much of this re-design work is, and will remain, invisible to the general public. (Government of Ontario, 2005)

The notion of "invisibility" is consistent with the service mentality of more efficient, convenient, and integrated service offerings — a mentality based on a characterization of the public as uninterested and intolerant of jurisdictional boundaries (either within or between governments) and more concerned about outcomes. Invariably, public sector organizations are compared and benchmarked with the practices of private sector reforms operating in the electronic marketplace (Curtin et al., 2003). It is largely because of this service orientation and chronological evolution that the notions of transparency and trust — notions that frame democratic reforms, have not fit easily into the e-government plans of developed nations

(Mahrer, 2005). Not only is there no obvious organizational apparatus to address such issues from within the government of the day but in many countries, politicians are often uncertain and resistant of e-democratic reforms as a result (Mahrer, 2005).

In contrast, much of the focus on developing countries has been on leveraging e-government as a lever to overcome traditional governance weaknesses, notably an absence of openness, excessive corruption, and weak accountability to citizenries as a result. The following quote is indicative of such an emphasis:

To the extent that increased transparency, accountability and predictability (of rules and procedures) are made priorities, e-government can be a weapon against corruption. (Pacific Council on International Policy, 2002, p. 10)[3]

The reality here is a schism between developed and developing countries in terms of their views of e-democracy for themselves and for one another. While many developing countries are themselves beginning to take the prospects for domestic reforms seriously, linking e-governance, e-government, and stronger democracy (Kossick, 2004), the primarily service orientation of developed countries with respect to their own e-government agendas may, in turn, influence their international assistance efforts aimed to recipient countries in the developing world. The first major e-government initiative in the Philippines undertaken by the Canadian government's development agency underscores this point.[4] Such a danger is compounded by findings stemming from a wider set of e-government initiatives involving project sponsors and knowledge transfers from developed to developed countries: an absence of sufficient cultural sensitivity in crafting e-government within the contours of a localized setting is a common source of failure (Heeks, 2004).

The point here is not to suggest that countries such as Canada are abandoning democratic aims in the developing world, but rather that e-government may well be defined in a very precise way, perhaps more reflective of the service-driven mindset that predominates domestically. While this service orientation alone is unlikely to displace democratic capacity building as a centerpiece of developmental assistance, a combination of service aims with a much stronger emphasis on security may, at the very least, overshadow democratic ideals and improvements in transparency and trust dimensions of e-government. Such a risk is accentuated in the post-911 security orientation of many Western democratic governments — by which the meaning of security has shifted from largely underpinning service capacities to those emphasizing public safety and antiterrorism (Hart-Teeter, 2004; Henrich & Link, 2003; Roy, 2005b). Moreover, while Canada may not be abandoning democratic ideals in this context, one major review of the country's development assistance strategies argues persuasively that efforts to forge a democratic culture in recipient countries are insufficient (Sundstrom, 2005).

The parameters of information management, democratic freedom and technological deployment have shifted considerably due to the 911 terrorist attacks. Many governments have begun exploring bolstered forms of identity management through more technologically sophisticated devices for authentication, such as national identification cards and biometrically enabled passports.[5] The former approach, for example, has been adopted by the British government which plans to introduce such a card by 2008.[6] Hong Kong is currently implementing a new national "smart card" that would serve as an identity link to all public and private transactions conducted electronically. Many other jurisdictions, including Canada and the United States, are presently exploring modified passports that would make use of biometric devices to improve authentication and identity management capacities (Salter, 2004).

This expanded focus on security shifts the bilateral relationships between developed and developing nations, forged through traditional efforts of international assistance in numerous ways. For many Western countries, the exporting of democracy must now compete with the implications of an expanded and more technologically sophisticated security apparatus and agenda, with both domestic and international dimensions (Nugent & Raisinghani, 2002). Accordingly, how governments in the developed world reorganize domestically — to better focus on security and terrorism prevention — carries important implications for their ability to reach out and engage developing countries (Fitz-gerald, 2004).

This shifting focus also reshapes global governance realities. Sensing a need to adjust, security has recently been positioned at the heart of the United Nation's encompassing framework for global development. As a basis for both reforming and strengthening existing global institutions, UN Secretary Annan recently framed the issues in this manner:

We cannot have security without development; we cannot have development without security; and we cannot have either without respect for human rights. The challenges we face are truly interconnected. Action on each of these fronts reinforces progress on the others. Inaction on any one of them threatens progress on the others. (United Nations 2005)[7]

However, to act effectively on a transnational plane through a shared system of governance requires both levels of political legitimacy and a degree of technological interoperability that are neither in place nor agreed upon by all countries and cultures as warranted. Such issues are likely to determine the emerging set of linkages between developed and developing nations and the degree to which e-government evolves, primarily as a project for more open and democratic government and governance beyond national borders, or one focused more on service improvement domestically and security arrangements based on national bargaining, relative power (politically, economically, militarily, and technologically), and a much less formalized and more secretive set of governance arrangements.

Here lies a key determinant of e-government's future orientation and the sorts of relationships likely to evolve between developed and developing countries (and through what sort of relational mechanisms). The pursuit of security via new informational, digital, and online capacities has little to do with democracy, and the richest countries of the world are aggressively pursuing military defence and security-oriented alliances where democratic openness is secondary to stability through either cooperative or coercive alliances (Barber, 2003; Denning, 2003; Meyers, 2003; Roy 2005b). Yet, a more open networked and interdependent world requires governance capacities in kind. The prospects for e-governance transnationally — and the implications for e-government — thus merit closer attention.

E-Governance Transnationally

With respect to transparency and trust, existing international bodies face widening questions pertaining to their performance and legitimacy in a manner not unlike national governments. These questions and pressures are rooted in the emergence of some basic tenants of a globalizing civil society (Norris, 2000, 2005). Moreover, existing institutions, such as of the developing world, viewed as instruments under the dominant influence of western, industrialized countries.

In one sense, e-government alone may not provide much optimism in progress for two reasons since the overarching domestic e-government agendas of developed countries emphasize service and security aims nationally, lessening the prospects for meaningful political innovation and institutional reform beyond national borders. Moreover, the absence of any form of direct global polity means that national governments essentially possess a veto over any meaningful project reform (the strength of which correlates to a country's power internationally).

Despite such blockages, however, reasons are put forth to justify a more hopeful, countervailing movement toward strengthened forms of governance transnationally. First and foremost, the existence and expansion of a global communications infrastructure creates visibility and coverage that provides at least one foundational element of transnational community formation (Ougaard & Higgott, 2002). More than mere awareness, the activism and associational capacities of globally-minded citizens represent an important new dimension of globalization in this new century (Hayden, 2005; McGrew, 2002). Viewed as more credible than either government or industry — and often acting as an interface between developed and developing world, NGO and other associational and nonprofit movements are key stakeholders in this new environment (Aart Scholte, 2002; Edelman, 2005; Selian, 2004).

There may also be the basis for an important alliance between civil society and the private sector in this regard, as the sustainability and stakeholder movements of corporate action have grown in prominence. Much as natural resource companies and industries have adapted their practices to new sustainability frameworks, technology companies have been an important force in addressing the global digital divide (with an eye on potentially expanding markets to the vast majority of the world's population). The values of global openness, responsiveness, and democratization that drive many (but not all) segments of civil society may also serve as the basis of a partnership with multinational corporations prepared to embrace wider stakeholder commitments to global development (Brown, 2002).

While such stakeholder considerations may include philanthropy among them, there is also an important market imperative for such corporate leadership. The rise of e-commerce has brought about a major step forward toward broader global interconnectedness, at least in terms of market structure, organization, and behaviour (Ronchi, 2003). Given that the scope of online commerce is inherently transnational (open to all with Internet access at least), there is a corresponding need to ensure that common structural rules and cultural standards are in place to facilitate the effective working of this expanded market place. At least until September 2001, this market-led expansion of online activity underpinned the emergence of a decidedly unpublicized set of governance mechanisms in order to facilitate the growth and reliability of the Internet. Here Drake defines ICT global governance as "the collective rules, procedures and related programs intended to shape social actors' expectations, practises and interactions concerning ICT infrastructure and transactions and content" (W. J. Drake, 2004, Memo #3 for the Social Science Research Council's Research Network on IT and Governance).

ICANN is perhaps the most prominent governance body in this regard: "Neither a government nor a for-profit corporation, ICANN is a hybrid that interacts with both and with individuals as well" (Geiselhart, 2004, p. 334). This entity has even experimented with direct and digital forms of democracy in electing members to the board overseeing its operations, although the "ambiguities of legitimacy and lapses of transparency and accountability that have characterized ICANN are typical of other attempts at global governance" (ibid). Others argue that ICANN's selection also reveals an explicit strategy to bypass traditional intergovernmental bodies (such as the International Telecommunications Union) in favour of a new organizational structure and style (Drezner, 2004). There is much that is American about this new structure and style — a point not lost on those skeptical of ICANN's ability to serve as a global agent of the public interest:

The US government maintains policy control over the "hidden server" root server that sits atop the Internet's hierarchical domain name system. The server, which is operated by VeriSign under contract with the US Department of Commerce, contains the authoritative listing of all generic and country code Top Level Domains called the root zone file. ... The US government's control of the master root server translates into ultimate authority over much of the institutional organization of the Internet's infrastructure.

A great many governments around the world are deeply uncomfortable with this unilateral US control, and some even fear the possibility of politically inspired decisions to manipulate, disrupt or terminate their nation's connections to the Internet. ... For its part, the US government repeatedly has stated that it has no intention of transferring its authority over the master server to any entity, although there is some ambiguity as to whether this will remain the policy. (Drake, 2004, Memo#3 for the Social Science Research Council's Research Network on IT and Governance, p. 18)

Although much new focus on ICANN and other bodies underpinning online connectivity exists, from the perspective of international politics, there is also much that is familiar, in particular the uneven power dynamics between countries of greater wealth and influence and those with less. The U.S.'s most recent pronouncement of its intent to maintain control over the Internet's central infrastructure — in contrast to previous pledges that an eventual transfer of authority to a more neutral, multiparty entity reflects ongoing tensions between unilateralism over multilateralism.[8] Moreover, such a stance is reflective of the security mindset trumping democratic considerations with regard to shaping global governance in the Internet Era.

Africa's Prospects for Reform

It is not difficult to succumb to cynicism or pessimism (or both) when envisioning e-government's prospects in the poorest regions of the world, notably Sub-Saharan Africa. Not only do many countries suffer from an absence or unevenness in the functionality of public, private, and civic institutions, in many areas, more pressing issues than technological connectivity and innovation persist — notably famine, disease, war, and general disorder. As current events in the Sudanese region of Darfur, it is not obvious that the rest of the world is prepared to provide as many resources as rhetoric in addressing such pressing matters.

Conversely, a case for optimism rests in part on the growing presence of e-government and e-governance as key elements of reform agendas. Underpinning this movement is the expansion of a telecommunications infrastructure at impressive, albeit uneven, speeds — most notably the penetration rates of mobile phones to growing segments of the African population. Based on the encouraging experiences of African leaders, such as South Africa and Morocco (the former, leading the world in ICT spending between 1992 and 1999, according to Onyeiwu, 2002), and broader continental awareness and interest in ICT-driven transformation, there is some hope that both the global digital divide may be in decline and that ICT-driven reforms can yield strengthened democracies, improved public sector capacities and more adaptive governance systems (Cunningham, 2004; Gough & Grezo, 2005; Kovacic, 2005).

What is also encouraging for many is the growing awareness and activism of all sectors in recognizing the need for more aggressive global action aimed at the least developed parts of the world. Public sector leaders from G8 countries have begun to champion various African-centric initiatives such as debt relief, the dotcom task force aimed at bridging the digital divide, and trade policy reforms. Industry is increasingly active in addressing Africa's plight, and the Summer 2005 concert initiative, Live 8, reflects the mobilization of at least some elements of civil society in favour of stronger global action (in a manner that sought to reframe developmental assistance away from charity to one of duty and responsibility, an important shift in language that is a precursor to a genuine transnational community). The expansion of digital media coverage both online and through other electronic channels — notably television — suggests that it will become increasingly difficult for citizens of the developed world to not be exposed to the plight of poorer countries, while rising levels of commerce and human mobility mean that this exposure is more than mere imagery, as immigration, security, environmental, and global health systems become more closely intertwined.

Yet, in order to leverage such optimism into concrete progress, three systemic blockages must be recognized and overcome. The first blockage is the now familiar theme of national predominance and interest over transnational governance building. Along with the traditional alignment of the "public sector" to national borders (or jurisdictions within such borders), national economies — and their integration and performance in a broader global marketplace — continue to be viewed as the main prism of wealth creation, and democratic governments are correspondingly accountable to their national citizenries for the results achieved primarily within their own borders.

Secondly and somewhat related to the first point, government actions pertaining to specific international issues such as African development and the digital divide continue to be addressed largely through a set of mechanisms that remain country-centric in terms of their functioning and influence. In other words, the persistence of political sovereignty — despite economic and technological interdependence, continues to dominate transnational political processes generally and international assistance efforts most specifically. This ongoing disconnect is illustrated by the Government of Canada's recent decision to "streamline" its development assistance efforts from an existing set of programs that extends to more than 150 countries to a more "focused" group of 25 (still an unreasonably large number of countries for a country spending just over $3 billion in developmental assistance, an amount encompassing managerial and operational infrastructures as well as actual aid delivered; Canadian developmental assistance in Africa accounts for just 2.2% of total aid flowing into the continent from all donor countries.[9]

The third blockage was dramatically underscored by the July 2005 terrorist bombings in London. The overarching importance of security — domestically and internationally — is clearly intensified by such events, fuelling pressures for international cooperation in ways that do not bode well for more openness and democracy transnationally. The manner by which the London bombings stalled momentum for an Africa agenda (at the G8 summit and even more so in the days and weeks that followed) further underlines the severity of such trends for the developing world.

Continental capacities also matter. In North America, for example, prominent observers have made the point that without sustained and specific commitments by Canada and the U.S., involving financial investments and deeper governance ties, Mexico has little hope of narrowing the development gap between itself and its North American "partners" (Pastor, 2003).[10] Pastor's call for more North American governance — itself partly inspired by the European experience (Jorgensen & Rosamond, 2002) — highlights one important aspects of African governance that is often overlooked, namely, the emergence of a continental dimension to African governance — the African Union.[11] Granted the African Union remains in its infancy, by forging a set of shared governance mechanisms that can leverage the knowledge and leadership of Africa's most successful nations with the struggles of the poorest members, the continent can seek strengthened endogenous capacities for action and a greater voice globally.

Perhaps most importantly, a stronger set of pan-African regional governance capacities can continually facilitate greater transparency within and across countries in terms of how developmental assistance is deployed and the sorts of results that are being achieved. Such openness would help overcome a significant barrier in the developed world, namely, the perception that donor aid does not actually reach the people and communities most in need. Moreover, this openness would also apply to developed countries, often criticized for reannouncing the same funding to multiple projects, placing a variety of conditions on the funding itself, or simply not delivering on public pronouncements. Finally, an agreement by multiple countries to endorse and jointly support a pan-African framework would create some basis for lessening the various national objectives and interests that currently permeate bilateral assistance programs in favour of more collective approaches selected, pursued, and evaluated by agreed-upon mechanisms.

The great leap that is required in terms of governance building involves two interrelated elements transnationally and domestically: first, ensuring greater interoperability between national, regional, and global institutions in order to improve transparency, legitimacy, and trust; and second, abandoning the traditional model of international assistance within Western countries (that at present is more shaped by service and security matters) in favour of larger, more ambitious, and better orchestrated mechanisms to design and deliver aid solutions through such an interoperable governance framework. Whereas scholars such as Sundstrom (2005) argue convincingly for a much stronger emphasis on "democratic partnerships" in bilateral development assistance strategies (an emphasis situated more within the realms of transparency and trust than security and service), what is also required is an elevation of such a mindset to continental, pan-regional, and global dimensions.

In this manner, the nexus between transparency and trust (that at present is discomforting for national governments and transnational institutions) can be leveraged as a basis of a new governance ethos encompassing both developed and developed nations — where openness facilitates an expansion of dialogues and pressures for reform (as well as costs for not doing so) in a manner that creates shared awareness and identities and stronger collective forums and more integrated development processes.

A federated global architecture encompassing an emerging African Union is critical since a more exclusive relationship between a subset of donor countries (i.e., the G8, for instance) and Africa would merely facilitate the expansion of other forms of bilateral ties outside of the purview of what should ideally be a more scrutinized and legitimizing approach to governance the world over (as the case of rising Chinese influence in Africa underscores[12]). Moreover, with respect to support for specific e-government initiatives within countries, this sort of federated architecture would help facilitate more sensitivity in both knowledge transfer and project design, reducing the risk of "contextual collision" between developed and developing world (Heeks, 2004).

As a starting point, what is crucial — and now more feasible than ever with the advent of a global telecommunications infrastructure (including online connectivity in limited parts of the world), is to foster a stronger basis for a globalizing polity based on openness and interdependence (Kamel, 2003). In this respect it is important that an analysis of the multiple digital divides within the African continent, as well as the key explanatory factors, suggests that when a country enjoys a healthy and productive mix of governance conditions its capacity to narrow the digital divide is greatly enhanced: chief among them is openness to globalization (Onyeiwu, 2002).

Such findings suggest that a stronger effort to embrace more segments in the world within a common social, economic, and political framework may be an important precursor to not only reducing the digital divide globally, but leveraging this macroreduction into a set of more country-specific trajectories for accelerated capacities for growth, development, and self-governance.

Conclusion

E-government is only now entering its second decade. Quite aside from digital reforms inside and outside of government, the challenges confronting the world are vast and complex, but they are also becoming more interdependent. Governance building, nationally and transnationally, is therefore a gradual process requiring patience and persistence, but also adaptability, as today's structures and solutions fall short of tomorrow's requirements.

The world in the twenty-first century needs a globally federated governance architecture, the design of which must include social, economic, political, and technological considerations. The emergence of a more digital and interconnected world creates new opportunities for building communities at all levels. In particular, an online infrastructure may well be the most uniquely powerful force for individual freedom and democracy if embraced as such. Without overstating the case as a shift away from democracy, many developed countries appear more intent on deploying new technologies to further service and security capacities. The signal sent to the developing world is, in this regard, worrisome in light of democracy's uneven support and prospects across this large group of countries. Transparency and trust — the pillars of democratic legitimacy, public engagement, and adaptive governance — must be viewed as equally important segments of evolving transnational governance processes, with the former central not only to countering the inherent secrecy of security-driven processes but also to building sound governance capacities within and among countries.

Finally, the strengthened focus on transnational governance systems must also be joined by the recognition of the dysfunctional nature of the present system of bilateral international assistance programs among countries. With improved governance conditions of transparency and trust transnationally — facilitated in part by a much more politically creative and aggressive use of new technologies and online connectivity, the resources allocated by each country across various recipients would serve developing nations and the world as a whole if they were pooled and coordinated through new transnational mechanisms designed to facilitate socioeconomic and political development through a truly globalizing prism.

Acknowledgments

This article was written while on sabbatical at the University of Victoria's School of Public Administration. The author is grateful for the support provided by the School — and in particular, the research assistance of In-In Pujiyono. The helpful comments of the blind reviewers are also graciously acknowledged.

References

Aart Scholte, A. (2002). Civil society and governance. In M. Ougaard & R. Higgott (Eds.), *Towards a global polity*. London: Routledge.

Allen, B. A., Paquet, G., Juillet, L., & Roy, J. (2005). E-government as collaborative governance: Structural, accountability and cultural reform. In M. Khosrow-Pour (Ed.), *Practising e-government: A global perspective* (pp. 1-15). Hershey, PA: Idea Group.

Barber, B. (2003). *Fear's empire: War, terrorism and democracy*. New York: W.W. Norton and Co.

Basu, S. (2004). E-government and developing countries: An overview. *International Review of Law, Computers and Technology, 18*(1), 109-132.

Batini, C., Cappadozzi, E., Mecella, M., & Talamo, M. (2002). Cooperative architectures. In W. J. McIver & A. K. Elmagarmid (Eds.), *Advances in digital government: Technology, human factors and policy*. Boston: Kluwer Academic Publishers.

Bhatnagar, S. (2001). *Enabling e-government in developing countries: From vision to implementation*. Washington, DC: World Bank.

Brown, C. (2002). G-8 collaborative initiatives and the digital divide: Readiness for e-government. In *Proceedings of the 35th Hawaii International Conference on System Sciences.*

Brown, M. (Ed.). (2003). *Grave new world: Security challenges in the 21st century.* Washington, DC: Georgetown University Press.

Bryant, A., & Colledge, B. (2002). Trust in electronic commerce business relationships. *Journal of Electronic Commerce Research, 3*(2), 32-39.

Chen, W., & Wellman, B. (2003). *Charting and bridging digital divides: Comparing socio-economic, gender, life stage, and rural — Urban Internet access in eight countries.* Retrieved May 11, 2006, from the AMD Global Consumer Advisory Board, http://www.amdgcab.org

Chou, T., & Hsu, L. (2004). Managing industry enabled e-government: Lessons learned from the IT industry in Taiwan. *Electronic Government, 1*(3), 335-348.

Coe, A., Paquet, G., & Roy, J. (2001). E-governance and smart communities: A social learning challenge. *Social Science Computer Review, 19*(1), 80-93.

Coleman, S., & Norris, D. (2005). A new agenda for e-democracy. *International Journal of Electronic Government Research, 1*(3), 69-82.

Cunningham, P. (2004). The digital divide and sustainable development in Africa. *International Journal of Technology, Policy and Management, 4*(1), 18-27.

Curtin, G., Sommer, M.H., & Vis-Sommer, V. (Eds.). (2003). *The world of e-government.* New York: Haworth Press.

Denning, D. (2003). Information technology and security. In M. Brown (Ed.). (2003). *Grave new world: Security challenges in the 21st century.* Washington, DC: Georgetown University Press.

Drezner, D. (2004, fall). The Global Governance of the Internet: Bringing the State Back In. *Political Science Quarterly, 119*, 477-498.

Edelman. (2005). *Sixth Annual Edelman Trust Barometer: A global study of opinion leaders.* Retrieved May 11, 2006, from http://www.edelman.com

Ferguson, Y. H., & Jones, B. R. J. (Eds.). (2002). *Political space: Frontiers of change and governance in a globalizing world.* Albany: State University of New York Press.

Fitz-gerald, A. M. (2004). *Addressing the security-development nexus: Implications for joined-up government.* Montreal: Institute for Research on Public Policy.

Fountain, J. E. (2001). *Building the virtual state: Information technology and institutional change.* Washington, DC: Brookings Institution Press.

Fukuyama, F. (2004). State-*building: Governance and world order in the 21st century.* Ithaca: Cornell University Press.

Geiselhart, K. (2004). Digital government and citizen participation internationally. In A. Pavlichev & G. D. Garson (Eds.), *Digital government: Principles and best practises.* Hershey, PA: Idea Group Publishing.

Goodman, J. (2005, March). Linking mobile phone ownership and use to social capital in rural south Africa and Tanzania. In N. Gough & C. Grezo (Eds.). *Africa: The impact of mobile phones* (The Vodafone Policy Series Paper #2).

Gough, N., & Grezo, C. (Eds.). (2005, March). *Africa: The impact of mobile phones* (The Vodafone Policy Series Paper #2.

Government of Ontario. (2005). *E-government*. Retrieved May 11, 2006, from the Office of the Corporate Chief Information Officer, http://www.cio.giv.on.ca

Hart-Teeter. (2003). *The new e-government equation: Ease, engagement, privacy and protection*. Washington, DC: Council for Excellence in Government.

Hart-Teeter. (2004). *From the home front to the front lines: America speaks out about Home and Security*. Washington, DC: Council for Excellence in Government.

Hayden, P. (2005). *Cosmopolitan global politics*. Burlington: Ashgate.

Heeks, R. (Ed.). (1999). *Reinventing government in the Information Age: International practice in IT-enabled public sector reform*. London: Routledge.

Heeks, R. (2002). E-government in Africa: Promise and practise. *Information Polity, 7*, 97-114.

Heeks, R. (2004). *eGovernment as a carrier of context* (iGovernment Working Paper Series #15). Manchester: Institute for Development Policy and Management, University of Manchester.

Henrich, V. C., & Link, A. N. (2003). Deploying Homeland Security technology. *Journal of Technology Transfer, 28*, 363-368.

Holden, S. (2004). *Understanding electronic signatures: The keys to e-government*. Washington, DC: IBM Center for the Business of Government.

Jesdanun, A. (2005, June 30). US won't cede control of Internet computers. *The Globe and Mail*.

Jorgensen, K. E., & Rosamond, B. (2002). Europe: Regional laboratory for a global polity. In M. Ougaard & R. Higgott (Eds.), *Towards a global polity*. London: Routledge.

Kamel, S. (Ed.). (2003). *Managing globally with information technology*. Hershey, PA: IRM Press.

Kossick, R. (2004). *The role of information and communication technology in strengthening citizen participation and shaping democracy: An analysis of Mexico's initial experience and pending challenges*. New York: United Nations Telecommunications Research Program.

Kovacic, Z. J. (2005). A brave new e-world? An exploratory analysis of worldwide e-government readiness, level of democracy, corruption and globalization. *International Journal of Electronic Government Research, 1*(3), 15-32.

Kraemer, K., & King, J. L. (2003). *Information technology and administrative reform: Will the time after e-government be different?* Irvine: Center for Research on Information Technology and Organizations.

Mahrer, J. (2005). Politicians as patrons for e-democracy? Closing the gap between ideals and realities. *International Journal of Electronic Government Research, 1*(3), 1-14.

McGrew, A. (2002). From global governance to good governance: Theories and prospects of democratising the global polity. In M. Ougaard & R. Higgott (Eds.), *Towards a global polity*. London: Routledge.

Meyers, D. W. (2003). Does "smarter" lead to safer? An assessment of the US border accords with Mexico and Canada. *International Migration, 41*(1), 5-44.

Ndou, V. (2004). E-government for developing countries: Opportunities and challenges. *Electronic Journal of Information Systems in Developing Countries, 18*(1), 1-24.

Norris, P. (2000). Global governance and cosmopolitan citizens. In J. S. Nye & J. D. Donahue (Eds.), *Governance in a globalizing world*. Cambridge: Brookings Institution Press.

Norris, D. (2005). Electronic democracy at the American grassroots. *International Journal of Electronic Government Research, 1*(3), 1-14.

Norris, P. (2005). The impact of the Internet on political activism: Evidence from Europe. *International Journal of Electronic Government Research, 1*(1), 20-39.

Nugent, J. H., & Raisinghani, M. S. (2002). The information technology and telecommunications security imperative: Important issues and drivers. *Journal of Electronic Commerce Research, 3*(1), 1-14.

O'Harrow, R. (2004). *No place to hide*. New York: Free Press.

Onyeiwu. (2002). *Inter-country variations in digital technology in Africa: Evidence, determinants and policy implications* (Discussion paper #2002/72). United Nations University, World Institute for Development Economics Research.

Ougaard, M., & Higgott, R. (Eds.). (2002). *Towards a global polity*. London: Routledge.

Pacific Council on International Policy. (2002). *Road-map for e-government in the developing world*. Retrieved May 11, 2006, from http://www.pacificcouncil.org

Paquet, G. (1997). States, communities and markets: The distributed governance scenario. In T. J. Courchene (Ed.), *The nation-state in a global information era: Policy challenges the Bell Canada Papers in Economics and Public Policy* 5 (pp. 25-46). Kingston: John Deutsch Institute for the Study of Economic Policy.

Pastor, R. (2003). *North America's second decade. Foreign affairs*. Retrieved May 11, 2006, from the Council on Foreign Relations, http://www.foreignaffairs.org

Reid, J. (2004). Holding governments accountable by strengthening access to information laws and information management practices. In L. Oliver & L. Sanders (Eds.), *E-government reconsidered: Renewal of governance for the Knowledge Age*. Regina: Canadian Plains Research Center.

Ronchi, S. (2003). *The Internet and the customer-supplier relationship*. Aldershot: Ashgate.

Roy, J. (2005a). Services, security, transparency and trust: Government online or governance renewal in Canada? *International Journal of E-Government Research, 1*(1), 48-58.

Roy, J. (2005b). Security, sovereignty and continental interoperability: Canada's elusive balance. *Social Science Computer Review*.

Roy, J. (2006). *E-government in Canada: Transformation for the Digital Age*. Ottawa: University of Ottawa Press.

Salter, M. (2004). Passports, mobility and security: How smart can the border be? *International Studies Perspective, 5*, 71-91.

Selian, A. (2004). The World Summit on the information society and civil society participation. *The Information Society, 20*(3), 201-215.

Sundstrom, L. M. (2005). Hard choices, good causes: Exploring options for Canada's Overseas Assistance. *IRPP Policy Matters, 6*(4), 1-40. Montreal: IRPP.

United Nations. (2005). *In larger freedom: Towards security, development and human rights for all.* New York: Report of the Secretary General of the United Nations for Decisions by Heads of State and Government.

Waverman, L., Meschi, M., & Fuss, M. (2005, March). The impact of telecoms on economic growth in developing countries. In N. Gough & Grezo (Eds.). *Africa: The impact of mobile phones* (The Vodafone Policy Series Paper #2).

Endnotes

[1]   Among others this definition was deployed by the Government of Mexico in recent years, though its' precise origins are unknown. The author adopted it as the basis for a recent article that developed the framework of the four dimensions discussed in this section (Roy 2005a).

[2]   Many large American-based technology companies — notably Microsoft, Google and Yahoo, have agreed to filter online content according to local laws in China (filtering or blocking discussion forums and sources pertaining to democracy and other politically sensitive concepts and topics), sparking debate about free speech and the role of the Internet. Defenders of the companies point out that they are merely abiding by local laws, and in engage in similar practises to monitor online behaviour in the Western world that pertains to illegal activity of one sort or another.

[3]   As an illustration, "Mexico's federal government established Compranet for government procurement as part of its efforts to curb corruption by automating procurement processes. By facilitating a process of bidding and reverse bidding online, it seeks to make government purchasing more efficient and transparent. The system allows the public to see what services and products the government is spending its resource von and what companies are providing them with these services. There are more than 6,000 public sector tenders logged daily, and more than 20,000 service-providing firms are regular users. Other countries in the region are looking to imitate Mexico's successful Compranet" (ibid.).

[4]   The Electronic Governance for Efficiency and Effectiveness (E3) Project in the Philippines is a five year, $10 million (Cdn) project (including monitoring and evaluation) designed to increase the awareness of the Government of the Philippines about the value and use of (ICTs) in the social services sector through a combination of: (a) increasing the knowledge and skills of the government, (in general), to address the strategic and cross-government issues of e-governance and, (in particular), the capacity for targeted social service agencies to strategically plan and implement e-governance projects; and (b) implementing a number of e-governance ICT pilot projects in selected rural areas of the country, designed to demonstrate the sustainable use of ICTs to sup-

port and improve the provision of social services in rural areas (e.g. credit assistance, employment, health, education, etc.).

5   Because biometrics can be used in such a variety of applications, it is very difficult to establish an all-encompassing definition. The most suitable definition of biometrics is: "The automated use of physiology or behavioural characteristics to determine or verify identity" (http://www.biometricgroup.com).

6   The British Government has introduced legislation to establish a new agency by 2008 that would issue both passports and a national identification card, with the cards being compulsory for all citizens by 2013. The card would feature a biometric chip with an identifier unique for each individual, and its purpose is to facilitate better and more integrated access to government services for citizens, while also enabling authorities to counter identity theft, fraud and domestic security threats. Many European countries already use similar cards and there is general interest and a growing commitment to biometrically enabled forms of identification for both passports and domestic mechanisms in many countries around the world, including the United States and Canada.

7   http://www.unis.unvienna.org/unis/pressrels/2005/sgsm9833.html

8   The U.S. government said Thursday (30/06/05) it would indefinitely retain oversight of the Internet's main traffic-controlling computers, ignoring calls by some countries to turn the function over to an international body. The announcement marked a departure from previously stated U.S. policy. Michael D. Gallagher, assistant secretary for communications and information at the U.S. Commerce Department, shied away from terming the declaration a reversal, calling it instead "the foundation of U.S. policy going forward ... he said other countries should see the move as positive because "uncertainty is not something that we think is in the United States' interest or the world's interest" (Jesdanun 2005).

9   The Government of Canada has promised to double aid directed to Africa by 2008-2009 (from 2003-2004 levels), an increase with an overall doubling of international aid spending by 2010 (from 2001 levels). Such increases (that would translate into annual aid spending in Africa of roughly $3 Billion) do nothing to alter the argumentation put forth here, a problem further compounded by the range of programs and initiatives managed by the Canadian overseas development agency across areas such as health services, education, entrepreneurship and most recently e-governance.

10   Pastor's efforts underpin the trilateral vision endorsed by prominent representatives of Canada, the U.S. and Mexico and released by the Council of Foreign Relations (at a time chosen in part to coincide with the North American Leaders Summit in Waco, Texas in March 2005). The trilateral initiative is bold — albeit incrementally so, in proposing to complement more integrative security measures with a new political dialogue and shared economic investment aimed at the collective prosperity of all parts of the continent.

11   Formerly created in 1999, the African Union (AU) today comprises 53 member nations. Although its institutional composition reflects many aspects of the European Union, many AU bodies and functions remain more intention than reality, an intuitive reflection of the many decades of growth and deepening of the European project. Details on the AU can be found on its' main Web-site: www.african-union.org.

¹²   Many stories of late have circulated in the U.S. media about China's growing activism and economic presence in Africa. A concern raised by some observers, both inside and outside of Africa, is that a form of competitive advantage for Chinese industries exists due to their willingness to ignore issues such as human rights, government corruption, insufficiently rigorous labour standards and other such issues that are predominant in the western world.

Chapter XIX

E-Government
Concepts, Measures,
and Best Practices

Shin Young-Jin, Ministry of Government Administration and Home Affairs,
Republic of Korea

Kim Seang-tae, Sungkyunkwan University, Republic of Korea

Abstract

This chapter introduces e-government theory according to the development of information communication technology (ICT), in which the importance of national informatization has been emphasized and the goal of government has been converted to a new concept: that of e-government. First, we define several national concepts based on the study of those countries and international agencies with the most advanced structures of information society, and from these concepts, we establish the general concept from the viewpoints of supply, demand, and policy. Second, we explain how international agencies (UN, Brown University, Accenture, etc.) measure e-government according to the standards and performance. Third, we explain e-government projects that have been accepted as national policies under the national informatization plans and which have been executed in each country for better public service and efficient administration. Thus we expect that the countries needing a benchmark model while developing their own e-government may adopt the concepts we propose in this chapter and may benefit from our experience to quickly embody e-government and evolve into the new paradigm that is mobile-gov, TV-gov, or ubiquitous-gov.

Introduction

According to the development of information communication technology, the importance of national informatization has been emphasized and the goal of government has been converted to a new concept, which emphasizes the accomplishment of e-government. During the last 10 years, e-government has been constructed on the basis of e-gov through m-gov/t-gov to u-gov.

In particular the scope of public services for citizens has been extended to include the provision of online services with wired telecommunication networks (telephone, Internet, PC, etc.) and mobile and ubiquitous services with wireless telecommunication networks (Mobile, PDA, TV, DMB, etc.). Nevertheless, as the information divide deepens between advanced countries and developing countries, it remains difficult to define useful means to deliver e-government services. Therefore, developing countries need guidelines to establish e-government from the viewpoints of concepts, measures, and best practices.

First, the concepts may not be applied uniformly. Neither theoretical studies nor the interpretation of e-government concepts should be applied uniformly to both advanced and developing countries. Hence, it is necessary to establish a more general concept that is based on supply, demand, and policy, and which has benefited from being benchmarked against the concepts and viewpoints of the best countries.

Second, the information infrastructure is operating quite differently in every country, indicating that e-government needs to be measured by the existing standards and performance, not by laws and organization perspectives. Even though many international agencies (e.g., UN, Brown University, Accenture, etc.) have been developing evaluation schemes, they are not categorized sufficiently to evaluate from different viewpoints on the e-government service such as G2G (government-to-government), G2B (government-to-business), and G2C (government-to-consumer).

Third, countries that have accepted the e-government program as an element of national policy, for example, Government 24, e-Europe, e-Korea, and so forth, are executing their respective national informatization plans to construct and to progress various cooperative projects according to their own standards. In this manner this chapter provides the developing countries with an opportunity to benchmark their own e-gov in order to quickly embody e-gov.

E-government is a form of government that complies with the demands of citizens and businesses by providing high quality ICT service in real time. This chapter is concerned with the following aspects.

First, the chapter suggests the national goal of e-government based on countries that have maximized their synergetic effectiveness with complementary relations. Second, it suggests the direction of e-government toward the "maturity of information technology and demand of advanced public service." E-government service for G2G, G2B, and G2C has to raise the efficiency of public service, to encourage cooperation among organizations, to improve competitiveness, and to instigate rapid change of public service. It offers a foundation for matured standards to improve the national competitiveness for e-government in developing countries. Third, it shows how to benchmark the national infrastructure compared to that of the best countries, such as the U.S., the E.U., Hong Kong, and so forth. Finally, it should be able to progress national public service and policy and reshape the organization and function of government for the benefit of citizens and business by accomplishing the goals of e-government.

The Theoretical Background

The Origin and Viewpoint

The Origin of E-Government

E-government commenced with the administration to "electronic banking" in the story of "reengineering" through the Information Technology Report of the National Performance Review of the U.S. in early 1991. This application increased the convenience in the service sector for the use of banking services by access cards from ATM plastics in the whole country (Chung, 1998). From this inception, it was used to clear and embody the vision and strategy for e-government in the Clinton government that was instigated with the national information infrastructure and public service assessment of 1993. The National Information Infrastructure (NII) Project focused on high life quality, creation of interest groups, health promotion, leisure extension, participation democracy, and so forth. (Choi, 1998). The concept of e-government was established by various main causes, such as the priority of policy, goals, decision-maker intention, and social and economical background of each country (OECD, 2003).

The Viewpoint of E-Government

E-government in the viewpoint of technical determinism is focused on technology. The technical definition of e-government is to support rapid and accurate service for public works by online information technology. The complexity of computer and data communication is based on microelectronics. Finally, the technical definition is limited by the criteria of technical determinism and by the development of information technology to minimize the concept of e-government.

E-government in the viewpoint of social determinism is focused on restructuring the public service by improving the management procedure to support efficiently the introduction of information technology. Because social determinists insist that the relation between information technology and public organization is not one-sided, through a change in the public organizations, new information technology leads to many changes of public organization, such as public works, human resource, organization structure, and so forth. The change of public works from purpose and affairs is needed for proper management of human resources, so that the improvement of organization leads to many changes in the technical system and human resources.

E-government in the viewpoint of the means for economic development is traditionally defined by improved recognition of strategic means. That is, e-government is the concept to recover national competitiveness and economic activation based on developing the pioneering information industry by supporting directly and indirectly the information communication industry with supply distribution and network infrastructures (NCA, 1996, 1997, pp. 19-21).

The Various Definitions

E-Government from Overseas

The concept of e-government is defined as a government that broadly and properly accesses information and services in "Reengineering through Information Technology" in the report of National Performance Review (NPR) in the Department of Administration in the U.S. (National Computerization Agency, 1995). In addition, U.S. Information Infrastructure Task Force (IITF, 1994) defined the means for a government to support each public service based on the information communication infrastructure at anytime, anywhere, anyway, and so forth.

The U.S. defined e-government that provides many opportunities to improve the quality of service provided to citizens. An effective strategy of e-government will significantly improve the federal government, including (Executive Office of the President Office of Management and Budget):

- Simplifying the delivery of services to citizens
- Eliminating layers of government management
- Making it possible for citizens, businesses, other levels of government, and federal employees to easily find information and get service from the federal government
- Simplifying agencies' business process and reducing costs through integrating and eliminating redundant systems
- Streamlining government operations to guarantee rapid response to citizens' needs

The E.U. defined information and communication technology (ICT) as a powerful tool for good governance, with five key principles: openness, participation, accountability, effectiveness, and coherence. The transition to e-government must improve all of these dimensions. ICTs can help strengthen democracy, develop "e-community," and increase awareness, interest, and participation in Europe's democratic process (UNDESA & ASPA, 2002).

Austria defined e-government as information service, information communication service, and e-commerce service. A detailed explanation is presented in Table 1.

In the Republic of Korea (2001), e-government is explained as a form of government to progress public affairs for public agencies or citizens through electronic transmission by law for promoting electronic public service to embody e-government. The Presidential Committee on Government Innovation and Decentralization (PCGID, 2003) defined e-government as a form of government to positively respond to citizens' needs for democracy with efficiency

Table 1. Concept of e-government in Austria (Source: Institute of Technology Assessment, 2003)

Division	Information Service	Information Communication Service	E-Commerce Service
E-Administration	Pubic service list, public procedure guide, etc.	E-Mail for government officer, mailing service, etc.	E-form application, authorization, payment, etc.
E-Democracy	Reference information as law, congress doc, etc.	Discussion board, e-mail for politician, etc.	Voting, application, etc.
E-Assistance	Labor, house, education, etc.	Discussion board related to common life, employment board, etc.	Job link, ticket reservation, lecture registration, etc.

and transparency of public administration related to e-transmission and networks of public services based on the ICT infrastructure. Therefore, its function is to improve the digital environment for public works of government while remaining focused on the support and service. Public operation system is centered on citizens.

E-Government from International Agencies

The UN defined e-government as a permanent commitment by government to improve the relationship between private and public sectors through enhanced, cost-effective and efficient delivery of services, information, and knowledge (UNDESA & ASPA, 2002). The UN analyzed the situation of e-government in the world with "E-Government at the Crossroads" (UNDESA, 2003, p. 8).

The Organization for Economic Cooperation and Development (OECD, 2003) defined e-government as the use of ICT, and particularly the Internet, as simply a tool to achieve a better level of government; that is, e-government is more about government than about "e." It enables better policy outcomes, higher quality services and greater engagement with citizens.

The World Bank defined it as the use by government agencies of information technologies such as wide area networks, the Internet, and mobile computing, having the ability to transform the relation with citizens, businesses, and other arms of government. These technologies can serve a variety of different ends: better delivery of government services to citizens, improved interactions with business and industry, citizen empowerment through access to information, or more efficient government management (www.worldbank.org).

The Association of Southeast Asian Nations (ASEAN, 2004) defined it as the government playing a key role in the digital environment, not only by providing the right regulatory framework, but also by leading the way in using ICT for offering government services, and transforming the internal processes. The following is the description for the e-government initiative in the e-ASEAN Framework:

- To take steps to provide a wide range of government services and transactions online by use of ICT applications to facilitate linkages between public and private sectors and to promote transparency.

- To work towards enhancing intergovernmental cooperation for promoting the use of electronic means in their procurement of goods and services and to facilitate the freer flow of goods, information, and people within ASEAN.

The General Definition of E-Government

The concepts of e-government differ among international agencies, governments, scholars, and so forth. The scope and methods to develop e-government have been limited by the concept definition generally. E-government refers to public sector use with the Internet and other digital devices to delivery services and information. Although personal computers have been around for several decades, recent advances in networking, video imagining, and graphics interfacing have allowed governments to develop Web sites that contain a variety of online materials.

The concept of e-government has fixed viewpoints of technical and economic determinism focused on the effectiveness to embody e-government. The concepts have a limitation to recover in the viewpoint of social determinism, that is, to maximize citizens' needs and satisfaction according to the changing of social environment. The concept is to connect the service quality for citizens and efficiency of public organization based on modification of public services by information technology. Fragmentary concepts are summarized and integrated through e-government in the complete viewpoints.

Thus e-government provides the business and the citizens with high quality service that developing innovation throughout the whole public activity and by transmitting efficient public services with information technology. That is, the aim of e-government is to realize the formation of a small and efficient government that continuously pursues the advance of public service. In a narrow sense, e-government strives to maximize mutual relations by focusing on public service, inner administrative transmission and policy decision, supply, and so forth.

The Comparative Model and Factors

The Model of E-Government

The models of e-government have progressed through four steps: bureaucracy, information management, citizen participation, and governance. Social diversity and maturity are significant factors to improve e-government. E-government is therefore not a product of technology, but rather one of society, culture, and politics. Here are the four models of e-government (Kim, 2003).

First, the *bureaucracy model* has the main policy goal of being focused on efficient administrative functions in government structure and individual sector. The model has not matured in civil society, with a consequence of a very low degree of citizens' participation in policy decision.

Second, the *information management model* is a linkage between government and citizens in terms of electronic public service. However, there remain no significant inputs to the policy decision, because citizens' participation in civil society has been weakened.

Third, the *citizen participation model* has positive and strong citizens' participation in policy decision through two-way interactions. The model tries to emphasize democracy and transparency by using information technology. However, there are many services available through the Internet or information technology applications. In this model, the degree of civil society has matured.

Fourth, the *governance model* explains that various civil groups and citizens actively participate in all policy decision processes and express their opinions through the Internet. All political and administrative activities have a place in the field of e-government. Naturally, strong democratic and transparent processes have been emphasized. Multiple transactions arise through the networking between social entities. No doubt, the degree of civil society has strongly matured. In sum, Figure 1 presents a view of how the models of e-government have evolved. There are two clear criteria of social diversity and civil society representing the development of society.

Based on these four models, the situation of e-government policy initiated by each government can be analyzed. Generally, it is assumed that the bureaucracy model of e-government

Figure 1. Models of e-government

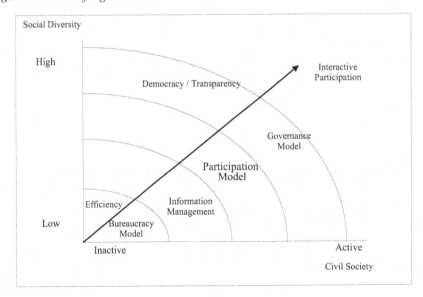

Table 2. The models of e-government

Criteria Model	Area	Ideology	Participation	Degree of Civil Society
Bureaucracy Model	Bureaucratic organization and public servant	Efficiency of inside government	Very low	Very low
Information Management Model	Government to citizen on limited pub-lic service	Efficient linkage between citizen and government	Low	Low
Citizen Participation Model	Public participa-tion to all governmen-tal services on two-interaction	Civil participation and weak democracy and transpar-ency	Middle but two-way interaction	Strong
Governance Model	All partici-pations and democratic participation	Strong de-mocracy and transparency	Strong	Very strong

and the information management model of e-government can be found in less developed and developing countries. In contrast, developed countries have evolved through e-government into the citizen participation model and the governance model. These models and assump-tions need to undergo further examination through international empirical studies. The four models are presented in Table 2.

In the models, it should be understood that the evolution of e-government models is strongly associated with the degree of variety and maturity of civil society. The process of society itself, as a very important environment of the government process, is inevitable. In addition, the degree of civil society has changed the three relationships among government, business, and citizens. It should be recognized that the degree of civil society has played important roles in the development of a more democratic and transparent government system. Natu-rally this applies to the evolution of e-government. It is also associated with administrative ideology ranging from efficiency to democracy, which naturally requires an examination of how the main policy of e-government has responded to the change of society development. The models of e-government have been reflected between three relationships in terms of development society: government-to-government, government-to-business, and govern-ment-to-citizens. Figure 2 demonstrates the three stakeholders in the administrative process: government, business, and citizens (Kim, 2003; UNDESA, 2003).

- **Government-to-government:** As society becomes more varied and complex, the government's role has also changed. Intergovernmental work and policy coordination is emphasized. Sharing information among intergovernment ministries and agencies

Figure 2. Relationship among business, government, and citizens

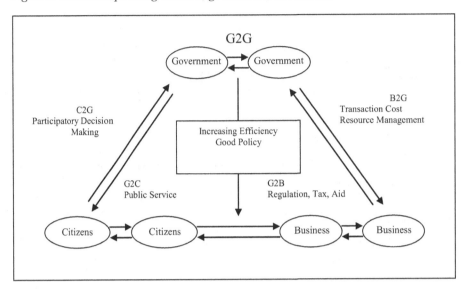

is a very important key to coordinate policy and project. The relationship between governments emphasizes coordination and collaboration rather than the power struggle with other ministries. It also reduces transaction costs and increases the accuracy and efficiency of administrative processes. Therefore, it obviously contributes to increased productivity of administration and better decision making.

- **Government-to-business:** Traditional government has addressed market failures. Governments have been regulating and intervening in the market and business worlds. The focus of the work was on "ruling" rather than on "serving" the market and business companies and industries. However, private sector development has been more important when it relates to citizens' welfare. The relationships between government and business were changed and focused more on issues of deregulation and efficiency of public service rather than on bureaucracy. Now, the role of government is to provide better public services where industry and companies can conduct their business transitions harmoniously and comfortably. By using information technology, government can reduce the transaction costs.

- **Government-to-citizens:** This relationship has constantly been changing as long as society has been developing. In terms of this relationship, democracy and transparency have been prioritized. The public services provided by the government have been varied according to the requests from citizens and the role and scope of government has hence been modified. Based on these trends, the government starts to provide client-oriented services to the public with various choices and customized services. In the meantime, because of higher education and advanced mass media, the capacity of citizens is improved and developed, which increases the degree of citizen's participation in public affairs. In addition, citizens can acquire more access to diverse methods to express their opinions to the government.

The Comparative Factors of E-Government

The ideal goal of e-government is to realize democracy and assure human life. The means for realizing this ideal and purpose of e-government is the class structure model of information policy based on the factors presented in Figure 3. The class structure model to pursue e-government is divided into the following four levels: information transmission, information circulation, information application, and information society. The factors of static relativity are classified to embody e-government according to the details of the following three factors: information demand (information recognition, information literacy, etc.), information supply (transmission infrastructure, circulation infrastructure, application infrastructure, etc.), and information policy (institutional infrastructure, propulsion system). The model can analogize movement and synergy based on the systematical relations of these factors.

Figure 3 clarifies that the factors of e-government complement one another; that is, they propel and embody a successful e-government.

- **Information supply for e-government:** involved in all the elements of the infrastructure such as network infrastructure, hardware, and software, and so forth; the technical factors such as information technology and technical environment; and information experts. The factors play a pivotal role to lead the informatization of an organization.
- **Information demand for e-government:** divided into information application and public service. The information application within an organization is involved in the literacy of servants and the culture of the organization. The public service ensures mutual and universal service for the citizens.
- **Information policy for e-government:** divided into national policy, propulsion system, and so forth. It involves the legal and institutional directions to support resource management strategy, reorganization of business progress, and outsourcing strategy.

Figure 3. Comparison factors to embody e-government

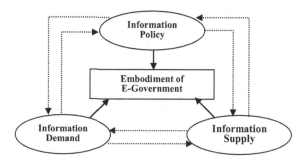

According to the classification of e-government, the first step is start up. Static government information is published on the Web including laws and rules, guidelines, handbooks, organizations, directions, and so forth. E-government is trying to recover each country's situation, economy, culture, environment, and so forth. So the study tries to compare with the cases from several international agencies, and then it suggests best practices from the results.

The Comparison and Best Practices

The Comparison with Cases

United Nations

The draft of e-government readiness assessment methodology by the Division for Public Administration and Development Management (DPADM) of the UN Department of Economic and Social Affairs (UNDESA) offers a menu of complementary surveys measuring various aspects of e-government readiness. Readiness is the degree to which a community is prepared to participate in the networked world to evaluate its opportunities and challenges (Soliman, 2005). The UN approach classifies e-government into the following five categories to measure a country's "e-gov" progress (UNDESA & ASPA, 2005).

- **Emerging presence:** A country may have only a single or a few official national government Web sites that offer static information to the user and serve as public affairs tools.

- **Enhanced presence:** The number of government Web pages increases as information becomes more dynamic with users having more options for accessing information.

- **Interactive presence:** A more formal exchange between users and government service providers takes place such that forms can be downloaded and applications submitted online.

- **Transactional presence:** The users can easily access services prioritized by their needs and conduct formal transactions online such as paying taxes and registration fees.

- **Networked presence:** The complete integration of all online government services through a one-stop portal.

The UN, through its E-Government Readiness Survey 2004, has assessed more than 50,000 features of e-government Web sites of the 191 UN member countries to ascertain how willing and ready the governments around the world are to employ the opportunities offered by ICT to improve the access and quality of basic social services to the people for sustainable human development.

Table 3. Top 15 e-government ready countries (by e-government readiness ranking)

	2005		2004		2003		2002	
	Country	Index	Country	Index	Country	Index	Country	Index
1	The U.S.	0.9062	The U.S.	0.9132	The U.S.	0.927	The U.S.	3.11
2	Denmark	0.9058	Denmark	0.9047	Sweden	0,840	Australia	2.60
3	Sweden	0.8983	UK	0.8852	Australia	0.831	New Zealand	2.59
4	UK	0.8777	Sweden	0.8741	Denmark	0.831	Singapore	2.58
5	R.O.K	0.8727	R.O.K	0.8575	UK	0.814	Norway	2.55
6	Australia	0.8679	Australia	0.8377	Canada	0.806	Canada	2.52
7	Singapore	0.8503	Canada	0.8369	Norway	0.778	UK	2.52
8	Canada	0.8425	Singapore	0.8340	Switzerland	0.764	Netherlands	2.51
9	Finland	0.8231	Finland	0.8239	Germany	0.762	Denmark	2.47
10	Norway	0.8228	Norway	0.8178	Finland	0.761	Germany	2.46
11	Germany	0.8050	The Netherlands	0.8026	The Netherlands	0.746	Sweden	2.45
12	The Netherlands	0.8021	Germany	0.7873	Singapore	0.746	Belgium	2.39
13	New Zealand	0.7987	New Zealand	0.7811	R.O.K	0.744	Finland	2.33
14	Japan	0.7801	Iceland	0.7699	New Zealand	0.718	France	2.33
15	Iceland	0.7794	Switzerland	0.7538	Iceland	0.702	R.O.K	2.30

Employing a statistical model for the measurement of digitized services, this UN survey assessed the public sector e-government initiatives of member countries according to a weighted average composite index of e-readiness based on Web site assessment, telecommunication infrastructure, and human resource endowment. The new imperative of development is to employ ICT applications across the board to create economic opportunities and increase human development.

- **The Web measure index:** based upon a five-stage model, ascending in nature, and building upon the previous level of sophistication, of a country's online presence. For the countries that have established an online presence, the model defines the stages of e-readiness according to a scale of progressively sophisticated citizen services.[1]
- **The telecommunication infrastructure index:** a composite weighted average index of six primary indexes based on basic infrastructure indicators, which define a country's ICT infrastructure capacity.[2]
- **The human capital index:** a composite of the adult literacy rate and the combined primary, secondary, and tertiary gross enrollment ratio with two thirds weight given to adult literacy and one third weight to gross enrollment ratio.

However, all countries of high levels have been maintained in the interactive presence stage (UN, 2002-2005).

Brown University

This global e-government is published by Brown University using a detailed analysis of 1,935 government Web sites in 198 different countries around the world based on a survey conducted from 2001 to 2004. The survey analyzed a range of sites within each country to get a full sense of what is available in particular countries. Among the sites analyzed were those of executive offices (such as president, prime minister, ruler, party leader, or royalty), legislative offices (such as Congress, Parliament, or People's Assemblies), judicial offices (such as major national courts), cabinet offices, and major agencies serving crucial functions of government, such as health, human services, taxation, education, interior, economic development, administration, natural resources, foreign affairs, foreign investment, transportation, military, tourism, and business regulation. Web sites for subnational units, obscure boards and commissions, local government, regional units, and municipal offices were not included in this study.[3]

The factors of the survey were online information (percentage of Web sites offering publications and database: phone contact info, address info, links to other sites, publications, database, audio clips, video clips); electronic services (number of online services, percentage of government sites offering services by region of world); privacy and security (visible policy); disability access; foreign language access; ads; user fees; and premium fees; and public outreach (e-mail, search, comments, e-mail updates, broadcast, Web site personalization, PDA access) (West, 2004). After analyzing the global e-government index, Table 5 shows the high levels of the top 24 of the 198 countries and the change of survey results over the three-year period from 2002 to 2004, inclusive (West, 2002-2004).

Table 4. Top ranking in global e-government (Source: Brown University, 2002-2005)

Rank	Country	Score				Rank	Country	Score			
		2005	2004	2003	2002			2005	2004	2003	2002
1	Taiwan	57.2	44.3	41.3	72.5	11	Great Britain	34.3	33.0	37.7	54.8
2	Singapore	54.5	43.8	46.3	53.5	12	Bahamas	34.0	27.0	32.0	40.0
3	The U.S.	50.5	41.9	45.3	60.1	13	Chile	32.1	29.2	32.0	60.0
4	Hong Kong	46.2	33.7	34.5	51.3	14	Macedonia	32.0	24.0	28.0	45.1
5	China	44.3	37.3	35.9	56.3	14	Chad	32.0	24.0	24.0	36.0
6	Canada	43.3	40.3	42.4	61.1	14	Estonia	32.0	28.5	30.9	48.0
7	Germany	35.3	35.0	34.4	52.6	14	Finland	32.0	29.1	35.5	48.8
8	Australia	35.1	36.7	41.5	58.3	14	Guinea-Bissau	32.0	20.0	29.0	20.0
9	Ireland	34.6	29.9	29.4	48.0	19	TheNetherlands	31.4	31.0	34.3	44.0
10	Vatican	34.5	26.0	36.5	52.0	20	Switzerland	31.2	27.6	35.9	14.0

Accenture

The Web site assessment surveyed 23 countries by 9 main services and 169 public service (welfare service, legal and public security, public finance, national defense, education, traffic & vehicles, legal democracy, government procurement, postal service, etc.).

The standards of survey were divided into 4 levels by service maturity, customer relationship management (CRM), and entire maturity.

- **Innovative leaders:** give full online service. This group of countries has a level over 50 % of the entire maturity.

- **Visionary challengers:** have confirmed service infrastructure. This group of countries has a level about 40~50% of the entire maturity.

- **Emerging performers:** have to maximize the potential by online service, but have low maturity. These countries have a large possibility of improvement by developing the possibility of CRM. This group of countries has a level about 30~40% of the entire maturity.

- **Platform builders:** are located behind the maturity curved line with low online service and poor infrastructure, and so forth. This group of countries has a level entirely under 30% of maturity.

The Web site assessment has 4 levels of service maturity in 23 countries, in detail (2001-2002). The results are as follows.

Table 5. Categories to assess digital governance (Source: Sungkyunkwan University & Rutgers University, 2003)

E-Government Category	Number of Key Concepts	Raw Score	Weight-ed Score	Keywords
Security and privacy	19	28	20	Privacy policies, authentication, encryption, data management, and use of cookies
Usability	20	32	20	User-friendly design, branding, length of homepage, targeted audience link or channels, and site search capabilities
Content	19	47	20	Access to current accurate information, public documents, reports, publications, and multimedia materials
Service	20	57	20	Transactional services involving purchase or register, interaction among business, government, and citizens
Citizen participation	14	39	20	Online civic engagement, Internet based policy deliberation, and citizen based performance measurement
Total	92	203	100	

Table 6. Top cities in digital governance (Source: Sungkyunkwan University & Rutgers University, 2003)

Ranking	City	Country	Score	Privacy	Usability	Content	Service	Participation
1	Seoul	Republic of Korea	73.48	11.07	17.50	13.83	15.44	15.64
2	Hong Kong SAR	Hong Kong SAR	66.57	15.36	19.38	13.19	14.04	4.62
3	Singa-pore	Singapore	62.97	11.79	14.06	14.04	13.33	9.74
4	New York	The U.S.	61.35	11.07	15.63	14.68	12.28	7.6
5	Shang-hai	China	58.00	9.64	17.19	11.28	12.46	7.44
6	Rome	Italy	54.72	6.79	14.69	9.57	13.16	10.51
7	Auck-land	New Zealand	54.61	7.86	16.88	11.06	10.35	8.46
8	Jerusa-lem	Israel	50.34	5.71	18.75	10.85	5.79	9.23
9	Tokyo	Japan	46.52	10.00	15.00	10.00	6.14	5.38
10	Toronto	Canada	46.35	8.57	16.56	9.79	5.79	5.64

- **Innovative Leaders:** Canada, Singapore, and the U.S.
- **Visionary Challengers:** Australia, Denmark, UK, Finland, Hong Kong, Germany, Ireland, The Netherlands, France, and Norway
- **Emerging Performers:** New Zealand, Spain, Belgium, and Japan
- **Platform Builders:** Portugal, Brazil, Malaysia, Italy, South Africa, and Mexico

Sungkyunkwan University and Rutgers University

Sungkyunkwan University and Rutgers, the State University of New Jersey, evaluated the current practice of digital governance in large municipalities worldwide. The assessment is focused on the evaluation of each Web site in terms of digital governance. Digital governance includes both digital government (delivery of public service) and digital democracy (citizen's participation in governance). Specifically, they analyzed security, usability, and content of Web sites; the type of online services currently being offered; and citizen response and participation through Web sites established by city governance. The cities were chosen using the "Internet Indicators" (2002) statistics from the International Telecommunication Union (ITU), an organization affiliated with the UN. ITU's Internet indicators report lists the online population for each of 198 countries. Using the ITU data, 98 UN member countries were identified based on an online population greater than 100,000 people. The research selected 98 countries with the highest percentage of Internet users, and then examined the largest city in each of those countries as a surrogate for all cities in a particular country (Sungkyunkwan Univ. and Rutgers Univ., 2004) The instrument for evaluating city and municipal Web sites consisted of five categories: security and privacy, usability, content, service, and citizen participation.

Table 6 explains the index and each of the following points: security and privacy, usability, content, service, and citizen participation.

The Benchmarking of E-Government

From the assessment of e-government by the UN, Brown University, Accenture, and Sungkyunkwan University and Rutgers University, the results can determine which countries should follow in terms of their development of e-government. According to the results, advanced informatization countries share a common goal to progress public informatization as public productivity and customization to information quality. The best practices of national informatization plans for e-government are UK Online (Office of the e-Envoy, 2001), a blueprint for New Beginnings in the U.S. (United States Department of Health & Human Service, 2001), e-Europe 2005 (Europe's Information Society, 2002), e-Korea (2001), and so forth. It is therefore possible to plot a path for the successful development of e-government.

The U.S. enacted the Government Paperwork Elimination Act of 1999 and accessed an electronic approach to government service and documentation. The U.S. constructed an e-government strategy (2002) and installed an e-government fund. The strategy tried to establish the Office of Management and Budget (OMB, 2002) and expanded into an e-government that was focused on citizens and the performance of e-government. The U.S. constructed 24 e-government projects for simplifying online service procedures and reducing the number of transaction documents among businesses by introducing citizen management technique. The government under Bush suggested establishing e-government funds (2002-2004). The U.S. has served e-government at "firstgov.gov," where one can search more than 51 million Web pages from federal and state governments. This portal is organized around customer groups and topics, rather than agency names. Examples of cross-agency portals include seniors, students, and people with disabilities, workers, and exporters. So the U.S. has progressed the Government without Boundaries projects that are recognized in service connection with federal and regional services (NCA, 2002, p. 126).

The EU focused on online front-end public service. The EU measured a biannual survey of progress in the development of Web-based applications within the framework of the commission's e-Europe initiative and identified the best practices.

Germany published "Internet für alle" as policy projects and maintained an e-government program cooperating with federal and local governments for public service. This program is connected with projects related to the legal and regulative environment of e-government. Germany has opened a portal site of federal government service at "bund.de" which provides various information and services at several levels of government. In addition, the government also planned action programs, such as *Internet for All Innovation and Jobs in the Information Society of the 21ˢᵗ Century* (2001-2005). Bund Online 2005 is one of the projects to modernize the state through the introduction of the e-government. It was started as Bayern Online in the Bavaria state and is focused on services for business and citizens.

Sweden constructed e-Sweden to process digital society, provide a stable economic environment, and encourage overseas investments, and so forth. Sweden passed the "information society for all" act to improve ICT laws and institutions, provide training in information usability, and spread investment of telecommunication infrastructure, and so forth. Sweden began the "Open Sweden Campaign" in 2000 to support "Public Access to Information Principle" and gave all citizens the rights for information to construct the public community. Government e-Link (GeL) treated such problems as individual identity, e-signature, encryption, and so forth as communication security and electronic information transmission policy.

Australia constructed "A Strategic Framework for Information Economy" for developing e-commerce in 1998. It suggested 10 strategies and action guidelines for maximizing the information benefits and constructing a model according to the existing world standard. "Online Australia" was the keyword of basic change to construct innovative communication, improve the competitive power of information industry, create new employment, and so forth. It constructed Government Online and Online Action Plan for integrated e-government. The Australia government cooperated with 150 businesses and related agencies for spreading Internet and networks, and held "AWABA (Online Australia Virtual World)," "Senior Online Day," and over 100 online events. Australia opened australia.gov.au as a portal site to provide extensive government services and minimized duplicate investment through improved online resources such as Education Network Australia Online (www.edna. edu.au). Australian Government Locator Service (AGLS) constructed the Customer Focused Portals Framework to successfully activate metadata in federal government.

Hong Kong constructed the Digital 21 strategy as a master plan to lead the city into the digital 21ˢᵗ century in 1998. To activate IT usability, the government progressed an information policy focused on strengthening the IT usability of teachers and students and on diffusing the spread of PCs and the Internet. In addition, a Community cyberpoint project was installed through PCs for the Internet service. Electronic Service Delivery (ESD) projects of Hong Kong tried to realize lead projects for e-government in 2000. These include the public services of electronic payment, electronic tendering, and Interactive Voice Response System. ESD has been involved in government services such as income tax returns, motor permission renewal, business records, elector registration, job hunting, volunteer registration, travel information, investment information, and so forth. The Hong Kong government has developed an e-government service plan (www.esd.gov.hk) as a complex basis strategy to apply IT infra-architecture and standards in 1988. This e-government service plan involved 70 services provided by 20 governmental departments and related agencies (NCA, 2001, p. 237).

The Republic of Korea enacted an informatization promotion basis law in 1996, and instigated several plans such as the ICT master plan, e-Korea Vision 2006, Cyber Korea 21, and so forth. The Presidential Committee on Government Innovation and Decentralization tried to construct the direction of the next generation of e-government as an e-government plan through the G4C project, local administration complex informatization, national finance information system, national education informatization system, and so forth.

As described, e-governments have progressed to develop the national economy and environment for business and citizens, but continuing developments in information technology must not be overlooked. The information technology caused a change to e-government style through progress in the public service system.

The Direction of Successful E-Government

Strategy for Successful E-Government

E-government must access strategic change to pursue goals rather than merely being temporarily embodied.

- It is possible to simply introduce e-transmission as well as to increase the efficiency of management and usability of information resource within an organization.
- It is possible to improve the competitiveness in the administration and instigate epochal change of public service within a public organization through information collaboration and application that consists of early cooperation and network.
- It is possible to improve the quality of public service based on integrated service for policy information and citizens in line with the increased competitiveness of administration, reconstructing public works, integration system, progressing cooperation, and advancing infrastructure through cooperation and networks connecting to central, local, and other forms of government.
- It is possible to improve national competitive power by activating entire e-business, which connects the public and private sectors to improve informatization levels. This step involves increasing the responsibility of the government for electronic correlation based on the common infrastructure within the public and private sectors.

These steps outline the condition of e-government according to the minimization of the selected steps with policy and strategy.

Principle to Embody E-Government

The principles to successfully embody e-government are as follows.

- Supply public service focused on respective citizens' choice according to citizen intention.
- Secure privacy and human rights by emphasizing e-signature and information security to progress e-government.
- Access convenient and easy public service use for citizens.
- Eliminate the digital divide by increasing the acceptance and access of governmental e-service.

- Pursue efficiency by utilizing the governmental information resources in general.

- Prevent inefficiency from developing during progress in the mid- to long-term by suggesting common standards in the maintenance of mutual operation and system extension.

- Accompany simultaneous changes such as technical infrastructure, public procedure, organization framework, organization members, and values change for e-government.

Table 7. The propulsion strategy for ubiquitous government in main countries (Source: Lee, 2003, August 6)

Division	The U.S.	EU	Japan
Beginning	1991 (High Performance Computing Act of the U.S.)	2001 (Disappearing computing plan of the E.U. RET)	2001 (Ministry of General affairs; The research study community for future perspective of ubiquitous network technology)
Main body	Private sector [university and high-tech IT company by funds of Government agency(DARPA, NIST) and large enterprise]	Special research organization leading by the E.U.	United organization of business, government, academy leading by government
	Xerox, HP, IBM, UC Berkeley, Univ. of Washington, MIT Media Lab.	Switzerland, ETH, Germany Tec, Finland National Technology Research Institution.	NTT, NTT TOCOMO, NTT Telecom, SONY, NEC, Mitsubishi Electronics, MASCIDA Electronics Co.
Direction	Ubiquitous computing technology and application development (especially recognition as main factor to develop HCI technology and standards)	Ubiquitous computing technology and application technology	Development of ubiquitous network technology by Micro technology
	Computing, S/W technology (integration with computing and usual activity	Interface (information artificial objects) (computing environment to support usual activity)	Network, interface (anywhere commuting environment)
Main Projects	Smart Dust, Cool Town, Easy Living, Smart Tag, Oxygen, Things That Think	16 projects as Smart Its, Paper++, Grocer, etc.	Subminiature chip network, MY interface, etc.
Main purpose	Leadership of IT technology in the world; technical vision and application development (practical strategy)	Application and technology in the future; groping response of technology in next generation.	Construction of future new technology; propulsion of policy in the sector of countries (diffusion strategy)

- Promote change of CEO for e-government. That is, new e-governance has to promote e-leadership as leadership of the paradigm to pursue e-policy in the new knowledge information society.

Future Trends

The initial goal of e-government was to increase governmental efficiency. Due to the advancement of information technology and the increased participation by citizens, the new concept of e-government has focused on efficiency as well as democracy. In fact, e-government has witnessed the development of civil society and democratic process with a new trend of political participation using information technology. This trend has placed an emphasis on democracy and participation leading to the development of e-democracy (Fuchs & Kase, 2000; Norris, 2001).

The planning and implementation of e-government, as it continues to develop and grow around the world, will have to focus on finding methods to address various issues. Some of the most important sources of information about meeting the challenges to effective e-government are actual e-government initiatives that are currently operational. The lessons that can be learned from ongoing e-government projects, both in terms of what works and what does not, will provide meaningful guidance in developing and refining e-government.

However, e-government has been changed by new information technology and is pursuing u-government (ubiquitous) to provide public services for government, business, and citizens by wireless terminal, PDA, mobile phone, and so forth. U-government provides services by wired and wireless networks. M-government (mobile) and t-government (television) belong to u-government.

M-government, an integral part of e-government and delivery service by mobile telephone, includes services such as part of transpiration, crime prevention, note issuing, and so forth, in countries in Europe and the U.S., Japan, and so forth. San Carlos in U.S. introduced a new fire fighting system that connects in real time with an equipment server after checking the construction plan when a fire breaks out. A highway management system in Finland provides drivers with highway information and weather situation by using GPS in a car. In other examples, m-government has been incorporated in a guidance system and portable bus location system in Japan, a train travel guidance system in the UK, and a note issuing service in Austria.

T-government incorporates the possibility of offering any public service by TV such as checking and issuing of civil application documents, payment of tax and public charges, and so forth, and the participation in surveys while watching TV. In addition, it is possible to reserve all kinds of facilities and obtain help and service. The UK Online Interactive service has progressed and installed "Thin Portal" for public service from 2002 (DigiTV. org.uk). Over 100 billion people have used the Web site and there are about 600 billion TV users. The site offers public services based on e-government projects for education, jobs and training, heath welfare, regional development, and so forth. Kangnam County in the Republic of Korea offers a two-way network service as t-government.

The purpose of u-government is to realize services such as the 5 Anys (anytime, anywhere, any network, any device, and any service) and the 5 Cs (computing, communication, connectivity, contents, and calm). That is, ubiquitous computing technology is translated as a means of service using all equipment and technology at anytime, anywhere, and any network. In addition, e-Korea Vision 2006 has suggested a plan to realize an advanced information super highway (IPv6, wireless Internet, etc.), home networking infrastructure, wired and wireless integration infrastructures, mobile e-government infrastructure, civil application channel, mobile common service, and so forth. By 2007, a ubiquitous network infrastructure will construct a knowledge-hub country in the world connecting private homes, public places, and civil facilities across the whole country. These days it is possible to provide broad practical technology for u-Korea (2005-2013) through issue documentation by printer, fax, unmanned civil appeal machine, and so forth, if citizens want to apply a civil appeal with wired and wireless sites through mobile phone, personal digital assistant (PDA), advanced record system (ARS), and so forth. The u-Japan (2005-2012) strategy has also played the best role in the construction of informatization.

The drive strategy of u-government is divided into infrastructure, technology, public efficiency, pubic service, and so forth.

- **Infrastructure aspects:** an integrated information communication environment has to be completed on the basis of standardization infrastructure. The spread of a broadband communication network of wired environment is required, along with the technology of wireless infrastructure. Especially, this needs to spread to the use of wireless and mobile technology and the transmission from IPv4 to IPv6. This involves the construction of a mobile environment that enables the connection of universal and ordinary time through the widening of the scope of wired and wireless communication networks such as DTV, telephone, KIOSK, and other electronic home appliances.

- **Technology aspects:** new services and application technology for administrative service (ICTS, medical and distribute fields using minimum chips) need to be developed in terms of the concept of the third space, which is the augmented reality connecting with cyberspace and actuality. The acceptance of P2P technology, or wireless and mobile communication technology, will support this environment.

- **Administrative efficiency aspects:** collaboration between different government ministries, central government and local government, and government and citizens is necessary to secure transparency and raise administrative efficiency. Especially necessary is the preparation of laws and regulations to construct the governance system.

- **Citizen service aspects:** services are offered to citizens anytime and anywhere. To promote services to reduce the digital divide and to extend access to information service, CRM has been extended as two-way communication, e-suggestion activation, and e-voting execution for e-democracy.

Furthermore, an examination of e-government projects from different levels of government and different parts of the world offers a method to share knowledge about e-government. In many ways, the future directions for the development of e-government will be confronting the important policy issues. Studies such as the present study be valuable for the conceptualization and application of current and future e-government projects, regardless of where the projects occur.

Conclusion

As presented here, e-government is different according to the country and international organization, as well as the viewpoint. The definition of e-government is focused on responding to the citizens' demand for information communication technology in real time. The term *e-government* was coined by the U.S. in 1991, after which all countries adopted this representative phrase as their government style. E-government increases the economic development and administrative transmission through the application of new technology. E-government has been explained differently as technical determinism, social determinism, and economic development. Especially, in the viewpoint of economic development it is recognized by strategic means as a way of recovering national competitiveness and economic activation. The concept of e-government is different because it is reflected from government leadership, economy environment, administrative reforms, and so forth. The U.S. defined e-government as providing many opportunities to improve the quality of service presented to citizens. Korea explained e-government as a means to progress public affairs for government agencies and citizens with electronic transmission. The E.U. defined that information and communication technology (ICT) is a powerful tool for good governance, which helps strengthen e-democracy. In this context, what definition of e-government is appropriate in any individual country?

International agencies have also explained e-government in terms of policy and cooperation. The UN defined e-government as a permanent commitment by government to improve the relationship between public and private sectors. The OECD explained that e-government is better government to realize higher quality service and policy outcomes. The World Bank defined information technology as is used for transforming relations with citizens, businesses, and other arms of the government. Therefore, the aim of e-government is to reduce the digital divide in the public sector and to maximize the citizens' needs with high quality and efficient services for citizens and public organizations in the viewpoints of technical and economic determinism.

E-government comprises four models according to the progress of citizens' participation and service transmission: bureaucracy, information management, citizen participation, and governance. With the model, it is easy to assess the informatization levels in a particular government and thereby to answer the question of whether the citizens' opinions are reflected during policy decision making.

These four models are explained by area, ideology, participation, and degree of civil society. Therefore, the governance model features strong democracy and transparency to ensure e-democracy as well as e-government. Consequently, this requires a sufficient level of variety and maturity of the civil society. In addition, the models of e-government reflect the three relationships with the stakeholders in the information society: ggovernment (G2G), government-to-business (G2B), and government-to-citizens (G2C). E-government ensures the realization of factors of static relativity, information demand (information recognition, the information literacy, etc.), information supply (transmission infrastructure, circulation infrastructure, application infrastructure, etc.), and information policy (institutional infrastructure, propulsion system).

E-government has therefore been assessed by various international agencies including the UN, Brown University, Accenture, Sungkyunkwan University and Rutgers State University. The UN assessed e-government Web sites of 191 UN members as "e-gov" progress: emerging Web presence, enhanced Web presence, interactive Web presence, and full integrated Web presence. Brown University also assessed government Web sites in 198 different countries as comparative factors: online information, electronic services, privacy and security, and public outreach. The Accenture assessed public services in 23 countries on 4 levels by service maturity, CRM and entire maturity, innovative leaders, visionary challengers, emerging performers, and platform builders. Rutgers State University assessed the current practice of digital governance in 98 UN countries in five components: security and privacy, usability, content, service and citizen participation. The results of these assessments provide an opportunity for benchmarking with the cases of the U.S., the E.U., Japan, and so forth. However, ubiquitous computing technology has to lead the change of e-government to u-government by offering high quality service by wired and wireless networks. U-government has two styles, m-government and t-government, where the former is an integral part of e-government and delivery service by mobile telephone, and the latter offers any public service by TV. U-government is realized as 5 Anys and 5 Cs. The drive strategy of u-government is divided into infrastructure, technology, public efficiency, pubic service, and so forth.

Finally, e-government has evolved with the new technology, in line with the differences in the social system, culture environment, and the concepts of e-government according to their viewpoints. Therefore, e-government should respond to each proper situation. Even though not all countries have developed information technology, they can greatly improve their poor condition by cooperating with other countries and international agencies. On this basis, it is important to consider what is necessary for the construction of e-government.

References

ASEAN. (2004). *E-readiness assessment guide: ASEAN secretariat.* Retrieved June 25, 2006, from http://unpan1.un.org/intradoc/groups/public/documents/APCITY?UNPAN007633.pdf

Choi, S. M. (1998). *Information society and informatization policy.* Seoul, ROK: Namam Ltd.

Chung. C. S. (1998, June 24). *E-government vision and strategy. International symposium to embody e-Government in 21c.* Seoul, ROK: Ministry of Government Administration and Home Affairs (MOGAHA).

Europe's Information Society. (2002). *E-Europe 2005.* Retrieved from June 29, 2006, from http://www.europa.eu.int/information_society/eeurope/2005/index_en.htm.

Fuchs, D., & Kase, M. (2000, August). *Electronic democracy.* Paper presented at IPSA World Congress (pp. 1-5).

Kim, S. T. (2003). *Global e-government theory.* Seoul, ROK: Bobmoonsa.

Lee, S. K. (2003, January 1). Ubiquitous IT revolution and our response policy. In *Ubiquitous IT Revolution and Our Response Strategy Seminar.* Seoul, ROK: Electronic Telecommunication Research Institute.

National Computerization Agency. (1996). *National informatization master plan manual,* Seoul, ROK: NCA.

National Computerization Agency. (1997). *A study on the public service and public system in informatization society,* Seoul, ROK: NCA.

National Computerization Agency. (2002). *Benchmarking and suggestion of e-government service: Focused on the comparison antecedent study and assessment report of UN member countries.* Seoul, ROK.

Norris, P. (2001). *Digital divide: Civic engagement, information poverty, and the internet worldwide.* Cambridge: Cambridge University Press.

OECD. (2003). *The e-government imperative: Main findings.* Policy brief. OECD Observer. Retrieved May 13, 2006, from http://www.oecd.org/publications/Pol_brief

Office of the e-Envoy. (2001). *UK online annual report.* UK: Author.

Presidential Committee on Government Innovation and Decentralization. (2003). *The vision and principle for e-government in participation government.*

Soliman, N. (2005, Febrary 2-4). *E-readiness assessment for Egypt. World Summit on the information society.* Retrieved June 25, 2006, from http://www.wsisccra2005.gov.gh/conf_updates.htm

West, M. D. (2002). *Global e-government 2002. NJ: Brown University.* Retrieved May 13, 2006, http://www.insidepolitics.org/polls/rel1002.html

West, M. D. (2003). *Global e-government 2003. NJ: Brown University.* Retrieved May 13, 2006, from http://www.insidepolitics.org/polls/QuonsetReport.html

West, M. D. (2004). *Global e-government 2004.* NJ: Brown University. Retrieved May 13, 2006, from http://www.insidepolitics.org/egovt04int.pdf

UN. (2004). *UN global e-government readiness report 2004.* Retrieved May 13, 2006, from http://www.unpan.org/egovernment5.asp

UN. (2005). *UN global e-government readiness report 2005.* Retrieved May 13, 2006, from http://www.unpan.org/egovernment5.asp

UNDESA & ASPA. (2002). *Benchmarking e-government: A global perspective.* New York: Author.

UNDESA & ASPA. (2004). *Global e-government readiness report 2004: Towards access for opportunity. Division for Public Administration and Development Management.* Retrieved June 15, 2005, from http://www.unpan.org/egovernment4.asp

UNDESA & ASPA. (2005). *Global e-government readiness report 2005: From e-government to e-inclusion.* New York: UNDESA. Retrieved December 15, 2005, from http://www.unpan.org/egovernment5.asp

Further Reading

Accenture. (2004). *E-government leadership: High performance, maximum value.* Retrieved from www.accenture.com/Global/Research_and_Insights/By_industry/Government/HighValue.htm

Administrative Management Bureau, Ministry of Internal Affairs and Communications. (n.d.). *The master plan to construct e-Government.* Retrieved November 10, 2005, from http://www.e-gov.go.jp/doc/040614/keikaku.html/

Akgul, M. (2002). *E-government in Turkey: An appraisal from inside.* Paper presented at the Global e-Policy e-Gov Forum (pp. 115-118). Seoul, ROK: Global e-Policy and e-Government Institute.

Altman. D. (2002). *Current situations of e-government and direct democracy in Latin America.* Paper presented at the Global e-Policy e-Gov Forum (pp. 318-328). Seoul, ROK: Global e-Policy and e-Government Institute.

Andersen, D. F., & Sharon, S. D. (1991). *Government information management, a primer and case book.* Upper Saddle River, NJ: Prentice Hall.

Australian Government Informatization Management Office. (2004). *E-government benefits study.* Retrieved May 13, 2006, from http://www.agimo.gov.au/government/benefits_study

Bishop, P. (2002). *E-democracy: Technological challenge to democratic theory.* Paper presented at the Global e-Policy e-Gov Forum (pp. 291-317). Seoul, ROK: Global e-Policy and e-Government Institute.

United States Department of Health & Human Service. (2001, Febrary 28). *Blueprint for new beginnings in the USA.* Retrieved from http://www.whitehouse.gov/news/usbudget/blueprint/budtoc.html

Boddy, D., & Nicky, G. (1996). *Organizations in the network age.* London: Routledge.

Cabinet Office. (2000, April). *E-government: A strategic framework for public services in the information age.* UK: Author.

Cabinet Office. (2000, May). *E-government today.* Retrieved November 10, 2005, from http://archive.cabinetoffice.gov.uk/e-envoy/interm-df/$file/e-gov.htm

Cabinet Office. (2000, May). *Successful IT modernizing government in action.* Retrieved from http://www.citu.gov.uk/itprojectsreview.htm

Chowdary, T. H. (2002). *E-governance in India experienced in AdnhraPradesh.* Paper presented at the Global e-Policy e-Gov Forum (pp. 262-278). Seoul, ROK: Global e-Policy and e-Government Institute.

CITU. (1999). *Intelligent form: A case study of successful electronic government.* Retrieved May 13, 2006, from http://www.citu.gov.uk/iform-close.htm

CITU. (2000). *Information age government: Benchmarking electronic service delivery.* Retrieved May 13, 2006, from http://www.citu.gov.uk/iform-rep.doc

CITU. (2000, May). *Implementing e-government: Guidelines for local government.* UK: Cabinet Office.

Clinton, J. W. (1999, January 30). *Memorandum for the heads of Executive Department and Agencies: Enhancing learning and education through technology.* Washington, DC: Office of the Press Secretary. Retrieved June 25, 2006, from http://www.pub.whitehouse.gov/

Currid, C. & Company (1994). *Computing strategies for reengineering your organization.* Rocklin, CA: Prima Publishing.

Drucker, P. F. (1968). *The age of discontinuity: Guidelines to our changing society.* New York: Harper & Row.

Dunn, C. (2002). *Comparing with Canadian and international approaches to e-government.* Paper presented at the Global e-Policy e-Gov Forum (pp. 385-391). Seoul, ROK: Global e-Policy and e-Government Institute.

Dutton, W. H. (1987). Decision-making in the Information Age. In R. Rinnegan, G. Salaman, & K. Thompson (Eds.), *Information technology: Social issues.* Milton Keynes; Buckingham, UK: Hodder and Stoughton in association with Open University Press.

Dutton, W. H., & Kraemer, K. L. (1985). *Modeling as negotiating: The political dynamics of computer models in the policy process.* Norwood, NJ: Ablex Publishing.

Executive Office of the President. (2004, December). *Expanding e-government partnering for a results-oriented government.* Retrieved May 13, 2006, from http://www.whitehouse.gov/omb/budintegration/expanding_egov12-2004.pdf

Frater, T. (2001, September 26). *E-government in the US federal government, information policy and technology* (pp. 1-10). OMB.

Heeks, R. (1999). *Reinventing government in the Information Age: International practice in IT-enabled public sector reform.* London: Routledge.

Ho, A. (2002). Reinventing local governments and the e-government initiative. *Public Administration Review, 62*(4), 434-444.

Holiday, I., & Kwok, R. C. W. (2002). *Governance in the information age: Building e-government in Hong Kong.* Paper presented at the Global e-Policy e-Gov Forum (pp. 279-287). Seoul, ROK: Global e-Policy and e-Government Institute.

Holmes, D. (2002). *E-Gov: E-business strategies for government.* Paper presented at the Global e-Policy e-Gov Forum (pp. 25-84). Seoul, ROK: Global e-Policy e-Government Institute.

Institute of Technology Assessment. (2003, February). *Public administration 2010.* Australia: Institute of Technology Assessment.

Jaeger, P. T., & Thompson, K. M. (2003). E-government around the world: Lessons, challenges, and future directions. *Government Information Quarterly, 20*, 389-394.

Jamali, D. (2002). *Cooperation for e-government.* Paper presented at the Global e-Policy e-Gov Forum (pp. 134-135). Seoul, ROK: Global e-Policy and e-Government Institute.

Kaylor, C., et al. (2001). Gauging e-government: A report on implementing services among American cities. *Government Information Quarterly, 18*, 293-307.

Keen, P. G. W. (1985). Computer and managerial choice. *Organizational Dynamics, 14*(2), 35-49.

KickStart. I. (1993) *Connecting America's communities to the information superhighway.* Retrieved June 25, 2006, from http://www.benton.org/publibrary/kickstart/kick.home.html

Killian, W., & Wind, M. (1998). Changes in interorganizational coordination and cooperation. In I. T. M. Snellen & W. B. H. J. van de Donk (Eds.), *Public administration in an information age.* Amsterdam, The Netherlands: IOS Press.

Kim, S. T. (1999). *Public information system theory; information policy and e-government.* Seoul, ROK: Bobmoonsa.

Kim, Y. M. (1998). Re-meaning of local informatization policy. *Korea Local Self-Government Review, 10,* 233-249.

Laysa, M. P. D. (2002). *Cooperative actions in implementing e-government.* Paper presented at the Global e-Policy e-Gov Forum (pp. 352-384). Seoul, ROK: Global e-Policy and e-Government Institute.

Lenk, K., Reichard, C., & Brügemeier, M. (2003). *org-e-gov: Organisatorische Gestaltungspotenziale durch E-government.* Germany: Institute of Local Government Studies at the University of Potsdam. Retrieved May 13, 2006, from http://www.orggov.de/contenido/cms/upload/pdf/flyer_englisch.pdf

Lund, G. (2003, December 9). *The Swedish vision of 24-hour public administration and e-government.* Minister for International Economy. Retrieved May 13, 2006, from http://www.regeringen.se/sb/d/1200/a/7656;jsessionid=aevQfzEoupxa

Lyon, D. (1992). *Surveillance societies, privacy and social control: Trends and countertrends.* Artificial Intelligence Society.

Lyon, D. (1994). *The electronic eye.* Oxford, UK: Basil Blackwell Ltd.

Maria Divina Garcia Z. Roldan. (2002). *Public-private partnership in e-government.* Paper presented at the Global e-Policy e-Gov Forum (pp. 91-95). Seoul, ROK: Global e-Policy and e-Government Institute.

McKersie, R. B., & Walton, R. E. (1991). Organizational change. In M. S. S. Morton (Ed.), *The corporation of the 1990s: Information technology and organizational change* (pp. 244-277). New York: Oxford University Press.

Melitski, J. (2003). Capacity and e-government performance: An analysis based on early adopters of Internet technologies in New Jersey. *Public Performance and Management Review, 26*(4), 376-390.

Minoli, D. (1995). *Analyzing outsourcing: Reengineering information and communication systems.* New York: McGraw-Hill.

Moon, J. M. (2002). The evolution of e-government among municipalities: Rhetoric or reality? *Public Administration Review, 62*(4), 424-433.

Moon, J. M., & deLeon, P. (2001). Municipal reinvention: Municipal values and diffusion among municipalities. *Journal of Public Administration Research and Theory, 11*(3), 327-352.

Musso, J., et al. (2000). Designing Web technologies for local governance reform: Good management or good democracy. *Political Communication, 17*(1), 1-19.

Nada, D. H. (2000). Intergovernmental cooperation in the development and use of information systems. In G. D. Garson (Ed.), *Handbook of public information systems* (pp. 165-177). New York: Marcel Dekker Inc.

National Computerization Agency. (1996). *The study to embody e-government after constructing concepts* (Research report). Seoul, ROK: NCA.

National Computerization Agency. (1997, December). *The study on improving public service and public system in informatization society* (pp. 19-21). Seoul, ROK: NCA.

National Computerization Agency. (2000). *An analysis on e-government propel system in main countries.* Seoul, ROK: NCA.

National Computerization Agency. (2001). *The diagnosis of e-government and overseas benchmarking.* Seoul, ROK: NCA

National Computerization Agency. (2002). *National informatization white paper.* Seoul, ROK: NCA.

OECD. (2002). *E-government Flagship Report: The e-government imperative.*

OECD. (2005). *E-government for better government.* Retrieved May 13, 2006, from http://www.agimo.gov.au/media/speeches/2002/e-govt_better_govt

Office of the e-Envoy. (2001). *UK online annual report.* Retrieved May 13, 2006, from http://www.cabinetoffice.gov.uk/e-government/docs/annualreports/2001/annualreportssum.pdf

OGIT. (1997). *Management of government information as a national strategic resource.* Retrieved May 13, 2006, from http://www.nla.gov.au/aglin/documents/submissi/imsc.html

OMB. (2002). *E-government strategy: Simplified delivery of services to citizens.* Retrieved June 25, 2006, from www.e-gov.gov

O'Riordan, P. (1987). The CIO: MIS makes its move into the executive suite. *Journal of Information Systems Management, 4*(3), 54-56.

Park, J. (Ed). (1993). *Information society and politics progress.* Seoul, ROK: BiBong Published Ltd.

Peters, G. (1996). *The future of governing: Four emerging models.* Lawrence, KS: University Press of Kansas.

Presidential Committee on Government Innovation and Decentralization. (2001). *Strategy to embody e-government for leaping top-ranking country in the world.* Seoul, ROK: Author.

Presidential Committee on Government Innovation and Decentralization. (2002). *The progress of e-government Korea: Present and future.* Seoul, ROK: PCGID.

Rhodes, R. (1997). *Understanding governance: Policy networks, governance, reflex and accountability.* Bristol, PA: Open University Press.

Schachter, H. (1995). Reinventing government or reinventing ourselves: Two models for improving government performance. *Public Administration Review, 55*(6), 530-537.

Seliger, B. (2002). *E-government in a federal state as the case of Germany.* Paper presented at the Global e-Policy e-Gov Forum (pp. 241-261). Seoul, ROK: Global e-Policy and e-Government Institute.

Selznick, P. (1957). *Leadership in administration: A sociological interpretation.* Berkeley: University of California Press.

Seo, J. (1998). *Revolution guideline of public works by information technology.* Seoul, ROK: Korea Institute of Public Administration.

Settles, A. (2002). *E-government skills development in the US.* Paper presented at the Global e-Policy e-Gov Forum (pp. 85-90). Seoul, ROK: Global e-Policy e-Government Institute.

Sørgaard, P. (2002, June). *Implementing e-government: Leadership and co-ordination.* Paper presented at the OECD E-government Project Seminar (pp. 20-21). Paris: OECD.

Steins, C. (n.d.). *E-government and planning: APA focuses on e-government.* Retrieved May 13, 2006, from http://www.planning.org/egov/

Strassmann, P. A. (1995). *The politics of information management: Policy guidelines.* New Canaan, CT: The Information Economic Press.

Sungkyunkwan Univ. and Rutgers State Univ. (2003). *Digital governance in municipalities worldwide: An assessment of municipal Web sites throughout the world.* Retrieved May 13, 2006, from http://unpan1.un.org/intradoc/groups/public/documents/aspa/un-pan012905.pdf

Thaens, M., & Zouridis, S. (2002). *E-government towards a public administration approach.* Paper presented at the Global e-Policy e-Gov Forum (pp. 119-134). Seoul, ROK: Global e-Policy and e-Government Institute.

Theodore, T. (2002, April). *E-government and the transitional countries.* Paper presented at 10th NISPAcee, Annual Conference Cracow, UNDESA/ASPA (pp. 25-27).

Toregas. C. (Ed.). (1985). *Managing new technologies: The Information Revolution in local government.* Washington DC: ICMA.

UN. (2003). *UN global e-government readiness report 2004.* Retrieved May 13, 2006, from http://www.unpan.org/egovernment4.asp

UNDESA & ASPA. (2003, January). *E-government readiness survey.* Paper presented at the Fourth Caribbean Regional Consultation and High-Level Workshop on Public Sector management: Strategies for e-government. Retrieved June 15, 2005, from http://www.unpan.org

Walter, et al. (1997). *Managing complex networks strategies for the public sector.* Sage Publications Ltd.

Weare, C., et al. (1999). *Electronic Democracy and the Diffusion of Municipal Web Pages in California. Administration and Society, 31*(1), 3-27.

World Bank. (n.d.). *A definition of e-government.* Retrieved May 13, 2006, from http://www1.worldbank.org/publicsector/egov/definition.htm

Yoo, P. (1996). *Public service of e-government: Case and instruction in USA. Informatization Journal, 3*(3), 85-95.

Yoo, H. L. (1999). *Successful strategy to introduce information technology for public revolution.* Seoul, ROK: Korea Institute of Public Administration.

Yu-Ying, K. (2002). *The research on the policy information systems: A case study of Taiwan's National Health Insurance Policy.* Paper presented at the Global e-Policy e-Gov Forum (pp. 331-351). Seoul, ROK: Global e-Policy and e-Government Institute.

Endnotes

[1]   Stages of e-government evolution is following; Emerging presence (Stage I), Enhanced presence (Stage II), Interactive presence (Stage III), Transactional presence (Stage IV), Networked presence (Stage V) (UNDESA & ASPA, 2004; 17)

[2]   These are: PC's/1000 people; internet users/1000 people; telephone lines/1000 people; online population; mobile phones/1000 people; and TV's/1000 people (UNDESA & ASPA, 2004; 18).

[3]   The regions for the Web sites survey were divided into 20% from Western European countries, followed by 17% from Africa, 14% from Asia, 12% from Eastern Europe, 8% from the Middle East, 7% from South America, 5% from Pacific Ocean countries, 6% from Central America, 6% from North America (which included Canada, the United States, and Mexico), and 5% from Russia and Central Asia (such as the areas of the former Soviet Union).

About the Editor

Latif Al-Hakim is a senior lecturer of supply chain management in the Department of Economics and Resources Management, Faculty of Business at the University of Southern Queensland. His experience spans 35 years in industry, research and development organisations and in universities. Al-Hakim received his first degree in mechanical engineering in 1968. His MSc (1977) in industrial engineering and PhD (1983) in management science were awarded from the University of Wales (UK). Al-Hakim has held various academic appointments and lectured on a wide variety of interdisciplinary management and industrial engineering topics. He has published extensively in facilities planning, information management, and systems modeling. Research papers have appeared in various international journals and have been cited in other research and postgraduate works. Al-Hakim is the editor of the *International Journal of Information Quality* and Aassociate Editor of the *International Journal of Networking and Virtual Organisations*.

About the Authors

Reggie Davidrajuh received an MS in control systems engineering in 1994 and a PhD in industrial engineering in 2000, both from the Norwegian University of Science and Technology (NTNU). He is currently associate professor of computer science at the Department of Electrical and Computer Engineering at the University of Stavanger, Norway. His current research interests include e-commerce, agile virtual enterprises, discrete event systems, and modeling of distributed information systems.

Zhuopeng Deng, a master's student of Hebei Teacher's University, China, has research interests in human geography, e-government, and tourism planning. He has published three papers in these areas in international journals and conferences, and also participated in a Chinese Natural Science Foundation project.

Susana de Juana-Espinosa has been lecturer of business organization at the University of Alicante, Spain, since 2001. She has worked previously at other Spanish research institutions such as CSIC. Her current research interests are e-government and information systems management. Her recent PhD was about e-government strategies in city councils. She has participated in many international conferences on these subjects and has published in several journals like *Quality Assurance in Education*.

Inas Ezz received her PhD in information systems and computing from Brunel University, UK She is currently a lecturer of information systems and computing at the Sadat Academy for Management Sciences (SAMS), Egypt and a visiting research fellow at the Department of Information Systems and Computing (DISC), Brunel University, UK. At SAMS, she is teaching in the Canadian BBA Program of the University of New Brunswick, Canada, several courses such as e-business. At DISC she is a member of the Knowledge Management Center and is also collaborating in founding a Transdisciplinarity Research Center. Her research interests include decision support systems, strategic information systems, business process reengineering, e-business, e-government, information systems adoption challenges, systems integration, geographical information systems, and sustainable development. Her recent publications focus on e-government from different perspectives including integration barriers.

Asbjørn Følstad is currently a researcher at SINTEF ICT, which is part of Scandinavia's largest research institute. He has an MS in psychology with specialization in cognitive psychology and man-machine interaction. His main research areas are user-centered design processes, methods for user requirements specification, and usability evaluation, in particular within the area of mobile applications and services.

Jeffrey Gortmaker is a research assistant at Delft University of Technology, The Netherlands, and a former project manager for Siemens Business Services at the Flemish government in Brussels, Belgium. Currently he is working on his PhD thesis involving designing a reference architecture for governmental cross-agency service-delivery processes.

Matthew Waritay Guah specializes in the organizational issues that surround the use of emerging technologies (i.e., ASP and Web services) in the health care industry. Guah came into academia with a wealth of industrial experience spanning over 10 years within Nuffield Hospitals, Merrill Lynch, CITI Bank, HSBC, British Airways, British Standards Institute, and the United Nations. He is the author of *Internet Strategy: The Road to Web Services.* His recent publications include *Information Systems Management, Journal of Information Technology, International Journal of Service Technology and Management, Information Technology and Interface, International Journal of Knowledge Management, International Journal of Healthcare Technology and Management, International Journal of Technology and Human Interaction*, and others. He is an associate editor of the *Journal of Management Information Systems, International Journal of Electronic Commerce* and a member of AIS, UKAIS, BMiS, BCS, among others. He is currently teaching and working on research at Warwick Business School, UK.

Cory A. Habulin's research interests are focused on environmental sociology, specifically in rural sociology, and native studies. Her recent work has centered on the dissemination of information throughout local and rural communities and the prevalence of religion and philosophy in environmental attitudes. Habulin was actively involved in environmental education for the inaugural Alberta Water Quality Awareness (AWQA) Day program, and she is currently working at the University of Alberta on the databasing of archival Métis scrip application records. Her recent work has motivated an exploration of individual choices for adopting environmental friendly behaviors in rural Canadian locales and within aboriginal communities. She serves on the nominations and selections committee for the Alberta Emerald Awards Foundation for Environmental Excellence.

Bing Han is currently a master's student of Hebei Teacher's University, China. Her research includes e-service and telecommunication geography. She has published three papers in these areas and participated in a Chinese Natural Science Foundation project.

Princely Ifinedo is completing his PhD at the Department of Computer Science (CS) and Information Systems (IS) at the University of Jyväskylä, Finland. He holds an MBA in international management from Royal Holloway, University of London, the U.K., an MSc (Engr.) in informatics from Tallinn University of Technology, Estonia, and a BS in mathematics / computer science from the University of Port-Harcourt, Nigeria. His current research interests include e-government, ERP systems success assessment, and global IT management. He has published in journals such as *Electronic Government: An International Journal (EG), Journal of Information and Knowledge Management (JIKM),* and *International Journal of Education and Development using ICT (IJEDICT),* and various IS conferences.

Marijn Janssen is an assistant professor at Delft University of Technology, The Netherlands, Faculty of Technology, Policy and Management, and a former information and communication technology consultant and architect at the Ministry of Justice. Nowadays his research is focused on designing architectures facilitating cross-agency processes in the public sector (e-government). His research is published in a large number of conference proceedings, book chapters, and journals.

Omar Abou Khaled is a professor in the Information and Communication Department of the University of Applied Sciences of Western Switzerland, Fribourg (EIA-FR). He holds a PhD in computer science from the Perception and Automatic Control Group of HEU-DIASYC Laboratory of University of Technology of Compiegne, and an MS in computer science from University of Technology of Compiegne. Since 1996 he has been working as research assistant in the MEDIA group of the Theoretical Computer Science Laboratory (LITH) of EPFL in the field of educational technologies and Web based training research field on MEDIT and CR2000 projects. His current interests are in the domains of document engineering, mobile infrastructure, ubiquitous computing, and multimodal interfaces.

Ailsa Kolsaker is a lecturer in e-Business, Marketing and Marketing Communications in the post-graduate Management School of the University of Surrey, UK. Before becoming an academian, she worked in the telecommunications industry in Norway and as a manager in the education sector in the UK. Her research interests include e-government, e-business and technology-driven marketing.

John Krogstie has a PhD (1995) and a MSc (1991) in information systems, both from the Norwegian University of Science and Technology (NTNU). He is currently a professor in information systems at IDI, NTNU and a senior advisor at SINTEF. He was employed as a manager in Accenture 1991-2000. Krogstie is the Norwegian representative for IFIP TC8 and a member of IFIP WG 8.1 on information systems design and evaluation, where he is the initiator and leader of the task group for mobile information systems. He has published around 75 refereed papers in journals, books, and archival proceedings since 1991.

Sadaya Kubo is an associate professor at Setsunan University, Faculty of Business Administration and Information in Neyagawa City, Osaka, Japan. He received his PhD in industrial engineering form Osaka Institute of Technology. He is an adviser of information policy at Neyagawa City. His research interests concern industrial engineering, information management, and e-governments. Nowadays his research is especially focused on the interaction between residents and public sector with ICT.

Liz Lee-Kelley is a lecturer in e-business, strategic change and project management in the School of Management, University of Surrey, UK. With over 20 years of senior management and board experience in distribution, engineering and clinical research, she was awarded the Freedom of the City of London in 1992. Her primary research interest is in the sociopsychology of technology and information in society and modern businesses.

Jie Lu is an associate professor and head of the e-Service Research Group in the Faculty of Information Technology, University of Technology, Sydney (UTS), Australia. She received a PhD in information systems in Curtin University of Technology, Perth, Australia. Her research interests include intelligent decision support systems, fuzzy optimization, e-government, and e-service intelligence. She has over 130 publications in international journals, book chapters, and conference proceedings. Most of her research projects are supported by Australian Research Council discovery grants. She has chaired a series of international workshops on e-service intelligence (ESI), and guest edited for a Special Issue on ESI for *International Journal of Intelligent Systems* (2005).

Zi Lu, a professor in geography, is the director of the Institute of Human Geography and Regional Planning, Hebei Teacher's University, China. He has a PhD from University of Technology Sydney, Australia. His research fields include information network, telecommunication geography, human geography, e-government, and urban and regional planning. He is leading several projects mainly funded by Chinese National Science Foundation and Hebei Province Foundation. He has published more than 100 articles in international journals, Chinese journals, and conferences, and two monographs. His monograph "Geography Research of Communication Network and Telecommunication" has been rewarded as the first book of telecommunication in China.

Konstantinos Markellos obtained his BS from the Department of Electrical and Computer Engineering (1999) and his MSc on "Hardware and Software Integrated Systems" (2003) from the Department of Computer Engineering and Informatics, University of Patras, Greece. He is currently working as a researcher (PhD student) at the latter department and also at the Research Academic Computer Technology Institute. He has great experience in design and implementation of Web-based applications and especially e-learning and e-commerce systems and he has worked on many R&D projects, both national and European. His research interests lie in the area of Internet technologies; he has published several research papers in national and international journals and conferences; and he is coauthor of the book "e-Business: From Concept to Action" (in Greek).

Penelope Markellou is a computer engineer and researcher in the Department of Computer Engineering and Informatics at the University of Patras, Greece, as well as in the Research Academic Computer Technology Institute. She obtained her PhD in "Techniques and Systems for Knowledge Management in the Web" (2005) and her MSc in "Usability Models for e-Commerce Systems and Applications" (2000) from the above university. Her current research interests focus on algorithms, techniques and approaches for the design and development of usable e-applications, including e-commerce, e-learning, e-government, and business intelligence. She has worked on many R&D projects, both national and European, has published several research papers in national and international journal and conferences, and is coauthor of six book chapters and four books.

Ingunn Moser has a PhD (2003) in social studies of science and technology from the University of Oslo, Norway. She is currently a postdoctoral researcher in the Centre for Technology, Innovation and Culture in the University of Oslo. Her work focuses on uses of new technologies in medicine, health care, and disability.

Elena Mugellini is a PhD student in the Telematics and Information Society from the University of Florence. Since 2004 she has worked at the University of Applied Sciences of Western Switzerland. In 2002 she received a telecommunication engineering degree form the University of Florence. Her main research interests concern network architecture for e-government seamless service delivery, information system modeling, and grid service for distributed and collaborative resource sharing.

Kyle B. Murray is an assistant professor of marketing at the Richard Ivey School of Business, University of Western Ontario, Canada. Professor Murray's research focuses on consumer judgment and decision making, with an emphasis on how consumers make choices in electronic environments. His work in this area has been published in the *Journal of Consumer Psychology, Communications of the Association for Computing Machinery,* and *Advances in Consumer Research,* as well a number of book chapters and newspaper articles. Murray is a senior research fellow at the Institute for Online.

Angeliki Panayiotaki obtained her BS in computer engineering and informatics from the University of Patras, Greece, (1996) and her MSc in "Advanced Information Systems" from University of Athens (2000). She is currently working as a researcher (PhD student) at the Computer Engineering and Informatics Department of the University of Patras and also at the General Secretariat for Information Systems of the Hellenic Ministry of Economy and Finance. Her research interests focus on personalization, Web mining, and interoperability techniques applied in e-commerce, e-government, and e-health domains. She has published several research papers in international and national conferences.

Maria Chiara Pettenati is currently assistant professor by the Telematics Laboratory of the Electronics and Telecommunications Department of the University of Florence since late 2004. Until 2004 she held a postdoctoral research position in the same laboratory. In

2000 she received the PhD grade in telematics and information society granted from the University of Florence, Italy. From 1997 to 1999, she has been working at the Computer Science Department (DI — LITH Laboratory) of the (Swiss Federal Institute of Technology) EPFL. Her main research interests concern network architectures for trust-enabling and personalized services delivery, e-learning, and e-knowledge applications.

Seung-Yong Rho is a full-time instructor in the Department of Public Administration, Seoul Women's University, Seoul, Korea. Dr. Rho holds the PhD in public administration from Rutgers, the State University of New Jersey, Newark, and received his MPA from the University of Southern California, Los Angeles. His research interests are governance and public management, and information technologies and digital governance. His current research is on the effects of digital deliberative governance on accountability and trust in government.

Lars Risan has a PhD (2003) in social studies of science and technology from the University of Oslo. He is currently a postdoctoral researcher at the Centre for Technology, Innovation and Culture at the University of Oslo, Norway. His work revolves around anthropological studies of engineering and scientific practices, from a study of AI-research (and AI-researchers) to, currently, a study of the social and technical practice of making open source software.

Barbara Roberts is an early career academic in the Faculty of Business at the University of Southern Queensland, Australia, a position held for the last five years. Previous to this, she managed the IT training program available to USQ staff and the local community. Roberts' teaching focus is in information management and processing, particularly in support of the administrative function of organisations. She also acts as an associate supervisor for several research students within her department. Barbara's research focus is in the area of e-business adoption by Australian organisations and includes a study of factors affecting both the nature and extent of the adoption.

Jeffrey Roy is an associate professor in the School of Public Administration at Dalhousie University in Halifax, Nova Scotia, Canada. He specializes in models of democratic and multi-stakeholder governance and electronic government reforms. In 2004-2005, Professor Roy was a visiting faculty member of the School of Public Administration at the University of Victoria. He served as managing director of the Centre on Governance at the University of Ottawa in 2001-2002. He is also a member of the Organization for Economic Cooperation and Development's E-Government Network, associate editor of the *International Journal of E-Government Research*, featured columnist in *CIO Government Review* — a Canadian publication devoted to the nexus between technology and government (www.itworldcanada. com), and author of *E-Government in Canada: Transformation for the Digital Age* (University of Ottawa Press). He may be contacted at jroy44@gmail.com.

Kim Seang-tae is a professor in the Graduate School of Governance, Sungkyunkwan University, Republic of Korea, and is president of the Global e-Policy & e-Government Institute. Kim is a well-known policy advisor to the South Korean government. As a member of the

Presidential Special Commission of E-Government, 2001-2003, he advised the president of the Republic of Korea. He received his MS in political science from the University of Wisconsin, Madison and his PhD of public administration from the University of Georgia.

Tatsumi Shimada is professor of information management in the Department of Business Administration of Information at Setsunan University, Osaka, Japan, where he teaches courses on management information systems and information ethics. He received his PhD in business administration from Osaka City University. His research interests include electronic government, strategic outsourcing, and information ethics. His publications include "The Impacts of Information Technology of Organizations in Japanese Companies" in *Management Impact of Information Technology* (edited by E. Szewczak, C. Snodgrass, & M. Khosrow-Pour, IRM Press, 1991), "IS Outsourcing Practices in the USA, Japan, and Finland: A Comparative Study" in *Journal of Information Technology* (with U. M. Apte, M. G. Sobol, T. Saarinen, T. Salmela, A. P. J. Vepsalainen, & S. Hanaoka, Vol. 12, 1998 and edited by G. Gingrich, IRM Press, 2003), and "Electronic Government in Japan: IT Utilization Status of Local Governments" in *Managing IT in Government, Business & Communities* (with Kiyoshi Ushida, 2003).

Mark Toleman is an associate professor of information systems at the University of Southern Queensland, Australia, where he has supervised postgraduate students and taught undergraduate and postgraduate computing subjects to engineers, scientists, and business students for nearly 20 years. He has a PhD in computer science from the University of Queensland and has published more than 70 articles in books, refereed journals, and refereed conference proceedings. He is director of the Electronic Business Advisory and Research Centre (e-BARC) and deputy chair of the University of Southern Queensland's Academic Board. Toleman is also a member of the Association for Information Systems, Computer-Human Interaction Special Interest of the Human Factors and Ergonomics Society of Australia and the International Federation for Information Processing Working Group.

Athanasios Tsakalidis obtained his BS in mathematics from the University of Thessaloniki, Greece (1973), and his MS in computer science (1981) and his PhD (1983) from the University of Saarland, Saarbuecken, Germany. He is currently a full professor in the Department of Computer Engineering and Informatics, University of Patras, Greece, and the R&D coordinator of the Research Academic Computer Technology Institute (RACTI). His research interests include data structures, graph algorithms, computational geometry, expert systems, medical informatics, databases, multimedia, information retrieval, and bioinformatics. He has published several research papers in national and international journals and conferences and is coauthor of the "Handbook of Theoretical Computer Science" and other book chapters.

Dag von Lubitz serves presently as the chairman and chief scientist at MedSMART, Inc. and an adjunct professor at H&G Dow College of Health Sciences at Central Michigan University, USA. After a very active career in stroke research, the curent work of von Lubitz is devoted to medical simulation, telemedicine, and medical training with the particular emphasis on global dissemination of medical technology and advanced medical education. Much of his work is devoted to the operations at the prehospital and first responder levels. Author of over 100 peer-reviewed publications and holder of prestigious international awards, von Lubitz is a frequent keynote speaker at international scientific conferences and symposia devoted to medical technology and e-health. Working in the U.S. and Europe, von Lubitz also serves as a consultant in the development of distance medical education and telemedicine solutions satisfying the operational needs in remote regions and in the less developed countries.

Nilmini Wickramasinghe researches and teaches in several areas within information systems including knowledge management, e-commerce, and m-commerce and organizational impacts of technology. In addition, Wickramasinghe focuses on the impacts of technologies on the health care industry. She is well published in all these areas and regularly presents her work throughout the U.S. as well as in Europe and Australia. Currently, Wickramasinghe is the U.S. representative of the Health Care Technology Management Association (HCTM), an international organization that focuses on critical health care issues and the role of technology within the domain of health care, and holds an associate professor position at the Stuart Graduate School of Business.

Shin Young-Jin is an expert advisor for the Ministry of Government Administration and Home Affairs, Republic of Korea. Young-Jin is a well-known policy advisor to e-government as well as information policy. She worked as team leader on the Global e-Policy e-Government Institute. She was one of the members in the project work group of indicator development of information security in the Ministry of Information Communication. She received her PhD of public administration from Sungkyunkwan University.

Jing Zhang received her MS from Hebei Teacher's University, China, in 2003. Her research areas include e-government and e-service evaluation models. She has published five papers in these areas. She has participated in a number of projects funded by Chinese Natural Science Foundation and Hebei Province Science Foundation.

Index